BIBLIOGRAPHY ON SCRIPTURE AND CHRISTIAN ETHICS

BIBLIOGRAPHY ON SCRIPTURE AND CHRISTIAN ETHICS

Compiled by

James T. Bretzke, S.J.

Studies in Religion and Society
Volume 39

The Edwin Mellen Press
Lewiston•Queenston•Lampeter

Library of Congress Cataloging-in-Publication Data

Bretzke, James T., 1952-
    Bibliography on scripture and Christian ethics / compiled by James
T. Bretzke.
        p. cm - (Studies in religion and society ; v. 39)
    Includes bibliographical references and index.
    ISBN 0-7734-8460-4 (hardcover)
    1. Ethics in the Bible--Bibliography. 2. Christian ethics-
-Bibliography. I. Title. II. Series: Studies in religion and
society (New York, N.Y.) ; v. 39.
Z7771.5.E84B74   1997
016.241--dc21   97-38505
                                                                     CIP

```
This is volume 39 in the continuing series
Studies in Religion and Society
Volume 39  ISBN  0-7734-8460-4
SRS Series  ISBN  0-88946-863-X
```

A CIP catalog record for this book is available from the British Library.

        The Edwin Mellen Press   The Edwin Mellen Press
                Box 450   Box 67
        Lewiston, New York   Queenston, Ontario
        USA 14092-0450   CANADA L0S 1L0

                        The Edwin Mellen Press, Ltd.
                        Lampeter, Ceredigion, Wales
                        UNITED KINGDOM SA48 8LT

                Printed in the United States of America

To John R. Donahue and William C. Spohn

Two mentors in Scripture and Ethics

TABLE OF CONTENTS

BIBLIOGRAPHY ON SCRIPTURE AND CHRISTIAN ETHICS

LIST OF ABBREVIATIONS AND FOREIGN CONVENTIONS

AA.VV.	Various authors (collective work)
A cura di	Edited by (Italian)
Festschrift	Essays done in honor of an individual, usually by former students and/or professional colleagues. (German, though used in English)
Herausgegeben von	Edited by (German)
Hrsg.	Edited by (German: Herausgegeben von)
Mélanges	French version of a Festschrift
S.T.D.	Doctor of Sacred Theology; terminal degree in theology according to the ecclesiastical academic system. Equivalent to a Ph.D.
Religious order initials:	Initials following an individual's name indicate that person is a member of a Roman Catholic Religious Order of either men or women (i.e., priest, brother, or sister). Some of the more common examples found in this bibliography are *C.Ss.R.* (Congregation of the Most Holy Redeemer--Redemptorist); *O.P.* (Order of Preachers--Dominican); and *S.J.* (Society of Jesus--Jesuit). Often the initials stand for the Latin name of the Religious Order, and so are not always easily identifiable with its English equivalent, e.g. *C.S.C.* refers to the Latin name of the Holy Cross Fathers and Brothers.

INTRODUCTION

Scripture has always played an important role in ethics in the Judeo-Christian tradition, though the ways in which the biblical material has been employed has differed widely throughout history, not to mention the considerable differences found among both individual authors and confessional approaches. Just how one conceives of Scripture and its authority for the life of the believers who hold the text as sacred and revelatory, and therefore as having a sacred claim on their lives will do much to determine how this text is employed in moral and ethical reflection. Similarly, how one conceives of the nature of morality and task of ethics will figure in what sources, the Bible included, will be brought to bear on one's ethical reflection. Obviously a reference bibliography of this sort cannot answer these questions for the individual works listed, but it is important to bear in mind these two organizing questions of what is Scripture and what is ethics as one uses the material contained in the bibliography.

The bibliography itself contains works in English, French, German, Italian and Spanish. English titles are listed according to the University of Chicago (Turabian) manual of style, but the non-English titles are entered according to the most common academic bibliographic conventions of the language of the particular entry. The *List of Abbreviations and Foreign Conventions* contains some commonly used terms in these non-English titles which will aid the unfamiliar reader in understanding terms such as "editor" in non-English titles (e.g., *a cura di* for Italian, and *Hrsg.* or *Herausgegeben* for German).

The bibliography itself is divided into five major sections. The first section, *General Works and /or Methodology* which contains articles and books dealing with methodological issues on the usage of Scripture in ethics, or general works which treat a broad topic related to Scripture and ethics. The second section, *Ethics in the Hebrew Scriptures and/or Jewish Ethics* contains works dealing with what Christians traditionally term the Old Testament. Though the majority of the titles contained in this section are from Christian authors, several entries are from Jewish authors as well, and some titles concern themselves primarily with how Jewish ethics uses biblical material. The third section, *New Testament Ethics*, contains a number of subsections dealing with New Testament ethics, the individual authors of the New Testament books, and two principal New Testament ethical themes, namely, Law and Gospel, and the Love Command. The fourth section, *Special Questions in Scripture and Ethics*, contains a number of sub-sections which list books and articles dealing with a variety of individual ethical issues--ranging from ecology to war and peace. The fifth and final section of the bibliography gathers together *Pre-1962 and/or Historical Works on Scripture and Ethics*. The date for this last section corresponds to the opening of the Second Vatican Ecumenical Council of the Roman Catholic Church (1962-1965). Vatican II, as it is commonly called, proved to be a major watershed for a renaissance of the employment of Scripture in Roman Catholic moral theology, and therefore works written after that time often differ markedly from approaches prior to the Council.

Cross-referencing has been included as far as possible within the bibliography. Thus, if a given title deals, for example, with Paul's use of the theme of Law and Gospel in Galatians the same title will be entered in both the sections of Pauline Ethics and the Love Command in the New Testament. Similarly, a title deal with ecological themes in the Book of Genesis will be listed under Ecology and Ethics in the Hebrew Scriptures. Because of the extensive cross-referencing employed throughout the bibliography the Index is limited almost exclusively to individual authors (and a few texts, such as a papal encyclical like *Veritatis Splendor* (Pope John Paul II's 1993 encyclical on moral theology) which uses Scripture in a major way.

It would be impossible in a work of this size to include an annotation for each and every entry, but a good number of such annotations are included, as well as an indication of the individual's professional background. This latter information is included so that the reader might better know the professional and/or confessional context out of which a given author is writing.

Finally, while it would be impossible to provide a workable list of "key" titles in any given section of the bibliography it might be helpful to indicate a couple of works which have proven especially helpful in dealing with a number of the central methodological issues in approaching Scripture and ethics. To this end I would suggest the following texts: William C. Spohn's *What Are They Saying About Scripture and Ethics?* (Rev. ed., New York: Paulist Press, 1984, 1995), is a very good introduction to the field and discusses five principal models or ways in which Scripture is and has been used in Christian ethics and/or moral theology, with illustrations from well-known Protestant and Roman Catholic theologians, including Divine Command (Karl Barth and Dietrich Bonhoeffer) Moral Reminder (Josef Fuchs, S.J. and Bruno Schüller, S.J.), Liberation (e.g., Gustavo Gutiérrez), Response to Revelation (H. Richard Niebuhr), Call to Discipleship (e.g., Stanley Hauerwas), and Spohn's own model of Responding Love (based partially on Spohn's work on Jonathan Edwards' notion of religious affections. The original 1984 edition contains a discussion of Rudolf Bultmann, Sallie McFague, Letty Russell, Phyllis Trible and John Howard Yoder; treatment of these authors has been largely dropped from the revised edition.

The essays edited by Charles E. Curran and Richard A. McCormick, S.J. in *Readings in Moral Theology No. 4: The Use of Scripture in Moral Theology* (New York: Paulist Press, 1984) contain a good cross-section of representative theologians, both Protestant and Roman Catholic, on the use of Scripture in Christian ethics. Each individual article is listed separately in this bibliography, and I would recommend especially James M. Gustafson's two essays: "The Changing Use of the Bible in Christian Ethics" and "The Place of Scripture in Christian Ethics: A Methodological Study."

For two particularly important works done by biblical exegetes on New Testament ethics see Wolfgang Schrage's *The Ethics of the New Testament*, (Philadelphia: Fortress Press, 1988) and Richard B. Hays' *The Moral Vision of the New Testament* (San Francisco: HarperSanFrancisco, 1996). Schrage's work discusses in detail the "ethical material" contained in the individual books of the New Testament, while Hays proposes three central organizing metaphors from the New Testament, namely, Community, Cross, and New Creation, as a basic methodological approach to utilizing the biblical material in Christian ethics. Hays also names and treats four principal "tasks" of using the Bible in ethics: the descriptive task (what is being said); the synthetic task (how does this or that passage, text, etc., fit within the larger biblical text in a coherent manner); the hermeneutical task of interpreting the biblical texts for ethics, and finally the "pragmatic" task of "living under the Word" (applying the biblical texts to concrete moral issues). Finally Hays treats several such issues in individual chapters: non-violence, divorce and remarriage, homosexuality, anti-Judaism and ethnic conflict, and abortion.

Finally, since so much of the whole task of using Scripture in ethics depends on how one reads, interprets and applies the biblical text in the first place it is important to attend to the whole area of biblical hermeneutics. Numerous works which deal with this area are included in the bibliography, but for a good introduction to the field see Sandra M. Schneiders' *The Revelatory Text: Interpreting the New Testament as Sacred Scripture*, (San Francisco. HarperSanFrancisco, 1991).

This bibliography, while extensive, makes no pretensions to absolute completeness. Moreover, the whole field of Scripture and ethics grows almost daily with the publication of new articles and books. As one way of trying to keep abreast of some of the more important contributions in this field see the annual bibliographies in moral theology published in the periodicals *Moralia* (in Spanish) and *Studia Moralia* (in English and French). Both usually contain sections on biblical ethics. Also helpful are the abstracts contained in *Old Testament Abstracts, New Testament Abstracts,* and *Elenchus Bibliographicus Biblicus.*

GENERAL WORKS AND/OR METHODOLOGY

Articles on General Works and/or Methodology

AA.VV. "Lateinamerikanische Exegese." *Evangelische Theologie* 51 (1991).

German translations of Latin American theological articles on biblical hermeneutics and exegesis in the Latin American context.

AA.VV. "Perspectivas de moral bíblica." *Moralia* 6 (1984), n. 21-22.

Adeney, Bernard T. "The Bible and Culture in Ethics." Chapter 4 in Idem. *Strange Virtues: Ethics in a Multicultural World*, 79-105. Downers Grove IL: InterVarsity Press, 1995.

Discussion of cross-cultural perceptions and how they may inform and misinform a Christian biblical ethics. Adeney grew up in Asia as a child of missionary parents, and currently teaches in Indonesia.

Allsopp, Michael. "The Role of Sacred Scripture in Richard A. McCormick's Ethics." *Chicago Studies* 35 (August 1995): 185-196.

Discusses how noted American Roman Catholic moral theologian Richard McCormick utilizes (and fails to utilize) the Bible in his moral reasoning and methodology.

Alonso Díaz, José. "El nomismo como agente corruptor de la ética bíblica." In *La Etica Bíblica*, 167-192. XXIX Semana Bíblica Española. Madrid: Consejo Superior de Investigaciones Científicas, 1971.

Alvarez-Verdes, Lorenzo, C.Ss.R. "Il nuovo nel messaggio etico della Bibbia." In *Il Problema del nuovo nella teologia morale*, 99-128. A cura di Lorenzo Alvarez-Verdes. Questiones Morales, 2. Roma: Editrice Rogate, e Editrice Accademia Alfonsiana, 1986.

_____. "La Paz Biblica como imperativo de liberacion." En *Perspectivas de moral bíblica*, 41-78. Estudios de Etica Teologica. Edd. Marciano Vidal, Francisco Lage y Alfosno Ruiz-Mateos. Madrid: Instituto Superior de Ciencas Morales, PS Editorial, 1984.

Ashley, Benedict M., O.P. "Scriptural Grounding of Concrete Moral Norms." In *Persona Verità e Morale: Atti del Congresso Internazionale di Teologia Morale (Roma, 7-12 aprile 1986)*, 637-651. Roma: Città Nuova Editrice, 1987.

Also found as "Scriptural Grounds for Concrete Moral Norms." *The Thomist* 52 (1988): 1-22.

Ashley lists eight "difficulties" proposed by various theologians against the use of Scripture in moral theology, and then refutes these. He argues that Jesus Christ is the supreme norm of all Christian morality, and that therefore "we must turn to the Scriptures as authentically interpreted in the living tradition of the Church for an account of Him and his Way" (p. 651).

The Congress was sponsored jointly the John Paul II Pontifical Institute for the Study of Matrimony and the Family of the Lateran University (Msgr. Carlo Caffarra), and the Holy Cross (Santa Croce) Center in Rome of the University of Navarra (Opus Dei).

Ashley is Professor of Moral Theology at the Aquinas Institute of St. Louis University, St. Louis, Missouri.

Balthasar, Hans Urs von. "Nine Theses in Christian Ethics." In Charles E. Curran and Richard A. McCormick, S.J., eds., *Readings in Moral Theology, No. 2: The Distinctiveness of Christian Ethics*, 190-206. New York: Paulist Press, 1980.

Also found under the title, "Nine Propositions on Christian Ethics," in *Principles of Christian Morality*, 77-104. Translated by Graham Harrison. San Francisco: Ignatius Press, 1986.

Originally appeared as "Neuen Sätze zur christlichen Ethik," in Joseph Ratzinger, Hrsg., *Prinzipien Christlicher Moral*, 67-93. Einsiedeln, 1975.

Italian translation in *Prospettive di morale cristiana*. Contributi di teologia, 3. Ed. Joseph Cardinal Ratzinger. Roma: Città Nuova Editrice, 1986.

French translation in Joseph Ratzinger et Philippe Delhaye, ed., *Principes d'éthique chrétienne*. Le Sycomore. Paris: Editions Lethielleux, 1979.

See the four essays under the name of Marc Ouellet, et. al, in *Communio* 17 (3:1990) for a discussion of Balthasar's Christian ethics.

Barnhart, Joe Edward. "The Relativity of Biblical Ethics." In *Biblical and Secular Ethics: The Conflict*, 109-116. Edited by R. Joseph Hoffman and Gerald A. Larue. Buffalo: Prometheus Press, 1988.

Contribution which came out of a meeting of social philosophers, biblical scholars, and ethicians which met at the University of Richmond in the autumn of 1986 under the sponsorship of the Committee for the Scientific Examination of Religion (CSER) and its Biblical Criticism Research Project.

Barr, James. "The Bible as a Political Document." *Bulletin of the John Rylands University Library of Manchester* 62 (1980): 268-298.

Offers certain cautions about the use of the Bible for social ethics.

Barton, John. "The Place of the Bible in Moral Debate." *Theology* 88 (1985): 204-209.

Bastianel, Sergio, S.J. e Di Pinto, Luigi, S.J. "Per una fondazione biblica dell'etica." Parte Prima, Capitolo 3 in *Corso di morale*. Vol. 1. A cura di Tullo Goffi e Giannino Piana. Brescia: Queriniana, 1983.

Contiene anche una bibliografia ampia del tema.

Also contains an ample bibliography on the subject.

Bastianel, Sergio, S.J. "La normatività del testo biblico." In *Morale e coscienza storica: Il dialogo con Josef Fuchs*, 197-203. Collana Saggi n. 26. Ed. Sergio Ferraro, S.J. Roma: Ave, 1988.

The answer to the question, "in che senso intendere la *normatività* del testo biblico per la nostra morale cristiana oggi?" (p. 197) [in what sense does one understand the *normativity* of the biblical text for our contemporary Christian morality?] depends largely on our pre-understanding of what morality and moral theology or ethics are all about. According to Bastianel, "Il testo [biblico] è normativo non in primo luogo per un contenuto specifico isolabile come tale, bensì in primo luogo per il modello etico che vi è presentato. Dire che è normativo significa che vincola in coscienza, non alla maniera della legge, ma al modo della coscienza, nella sua verità, nella sua libertà e responsabilità." p. 201. [The {biblical} text is not normative in the first place for a specific content which can be isolated from the text itself, but rather for the ethical model which is presented. This is to say that the normative significance of the biblical text binds the conscience, not in the manner of a law, but in the mode of conscience which perceives truth in freedom and responsibility.]

Intervento presentato al seminario sul tema "Morale e Coscienza storica," tenuto a Villa San Luigi, 1-2 maggio 1987.

Paper given at a seminar on The Historicity of Morality and Conscience held at Villa San Luigi, Italy on 1-2 May 1987.

Bastianel is professor of moral theology at the Pontifical Gregorian University in Rome.

Benzarath, Martin, C.Ss.R. "Selected Bibliography in Moral Theology: 1984-1988." *Studia Moralia* 27 (1989): 219-772.

For a listing of recent books on Scripture and ethics, see especially Section 6, "Biblical Moral Theology," pp. 277-289.

Bertalot, Renzo. "Fondazione biblico-teologica dell'etica: *Prospettiva protestante*." In *Questione etica e impegno ecumenico delle Chiese. Atti dell 23e sessione di formazione ecumenica del Segretariato Attività Ecumeniche (SAE)*, 57-70. Napoli: Edizioni Dehoniane Napoli, 1986.

Intervento al congresso tenuto a La Mendola (Trento) 27 luglio - 4 agosto 1985.

Paper given at a conference held at La Mendola (Trent, Italy) from 27 July to 4 August 1985.

Birch, Bruce C. "Biblical preaching as moral reflection." *Journal for Preachers* 15 (3/1992): 13-17.

Böckle, Franz. "Moraltheologie und Exegese heute." In *Ethik im Neuen Testament,* 197-210. Herausgegeben von Karl Kertelge. Freiburg: Herder, 1984.

Böckle was professor of moral theology at the University of Bonn, Germany.

Bosetti, Elena. "Morale e Bibbia." *Rivista di teologia morale* 25 (1993): 493-496.

A brief article for the periodical's 25th anniversary, highlighting contributions published in the field. Of little value, however, since the article is neither critical nor comprehensive.

Bosetti is professor of Scripture at the Pontifical Gregorian University in Rome.

Brawley, Robert L. "To Have, to Hold, and--in Time--Let G): Ethics and Interpreting the Bible." *Currents in Theology and Mission* 21 (1994): 113-116.

Bretzke, James T., S.J. "Scripture and Ethics: *Some Methodological Considerations for an Ecumenical Christian Ethics.*"

Considers some aspects of an "ecumenical methodology," which, though cognizant of the traditional differences between Protestant Christian ethics and Roman Catholic moral theology, nevertheless aims to develop an approach of complementarity and mutual enrichment. To this end, greater attention should be given to the "sacred claim" of Scripture in any Christian ethics. In particular, Roman Catholic moral theology will have to take more seriously the mandate given in *Optatam Totius* (Vatican II's 1965 Decree on the Training for Priests) that Scripture be the "soul" for all theology. Suggests a hybrid model of a Four-Sector Grid (Scripture, Tradition, Philosophical Ethics, and Science and Experiential Data), based on the work of James Gustafson, as an approach which both Protestants and Catholics can use which allows them to develop both the biblical aspect of Christian ethics, as well as allowing the voices of the different theological traditions to be heard and taken in account.

12

Paper given during the *Seminar on The Theology of Moral Issues*, sponsored by the Boston Theological Institute in collaboration with The Pontifical Council for the Unity of Christians (Rome, 26 May 1993). At that time Bretzke was professor of moral theology at the Pontifical Gregorian University in Rome. Currently he is a professor of Christian ethics at the Jesuit School of Theology-at-Berkeley, California.

_____. "Scripture: the `Soul' of Moral Theology? -- *The Second Stage.*" *Irish Theological Quarterly* 60 (1994): 259-271.

The initial response of Vatican II's call in *Optatam Totius* (Vatican II's 1965 Decree on the Training for Priests) for greater attention to Scripture in all moral theology, might be termed a "First Stage," in which both ethicians and exegetes tried to highlight better the ethical dimension of Scripture better in their respective disciplines and to allow Scripture as a whole to nourish theology more completely. However, now we need to move beyond this First Stage to a Second and Third Stage. This Second Stage, which is the focus of this article, suggests a reconsideration of some of the relevant documents from Vatican II, especially *Optatam Totius* and *Dei Verbum* (Vatican II's 1965 Dogmatic Constitution on Divine Revelation), in order to ground better our reflections on the integration of Scripture with theology as whole, and moral theology in particular. The article concludes by outlining some of the issues, such as the authority of Scripture and the problematic of hermeneutics, which still need to be addressed if Scripture is truly to nourish our Roman Catholic moral theology. Finally, this Second Stage itself points to the necessity of a Third Stage in which reflection will center on development of a concrete and practical *methodology* for the use of Scripture in Christian ethics.

The author is a professor of Christian ethics at the Jesuit School of Theology-at-Berkeley, California.

Cahill, Lisa Sowle. "The Bible and Christian Moral Practices." In *Christian Ethics: Problems and Prospects*, 3-17. Edited by Lisa Sowle Cahill and James F. Childress. Cleveland: Pilgrim Press, 1996.

Article done for the *Festschrift* for James M. Gustafson made up of contributions from his former students.

Cahill is a Roman Catholic and did her doctoral studies at the University of Chicago under the direction of James M. Gustafson. She is Professor of

Theological Ethics at Boston College, and past President of both the Catholic Theological Society of America (CTSA) and the Society of Christian Ethics (SCE).

_____. "The Bible and Ethics: Hermeneutical Dilemmas." Ch. 2 in Idem. *Between the Sexes: Foundations for a Christian Ethics of Sexuality*, 15-44. New York: Paulist Press; and Philadelphia: Fortress Press, 1985.

_____. "Biblical Sources of Ethics." In Idem. *Women and Sexuality*. New York: Paulist Press, 1992.

Part of the 1992 Madeleva Lecture in Spirituality.

_____. "Is Catholic Ethics Biblical? The Example of Sex and Gender." *Warren Lecture Series in Catholic Studies* 20 (1992).

Using the example of sexual ethics, Cahill gives an overview of the traditional approaches of Roman Catholic moral theology, contrasts these with various Protestant usages of Scripture in ethics, and then concludes by outlining a revised approach to sexuality and gender issues which would be more sensitive to the creative use of the Bible.

Lecture presented at the University of Tulsa on 15 March 1992.

Cartwright, Michael G. "The Practice and Performance of Scripture: Grounding Christian Ethics in a Communal Hermeneutic." *Annual of the Society of Christian Ethics* (1988): 31-53.

Chiavacci, Enrico. "Il Morale nella rivelazione." Cap. 2 in *Teologia morale: Vol. 1 morale generale*, 27-48. Assisi: Cittadella Editrice, 1977.

Chiavacci is a moral theologian.

_____. "Il Sociale nella Scrittura." Cap. 5 in *Teologia morale: Vol. 2 Complementi di morale generale*, 86-108. Assisi: Cittadella Editrice, 1980.

14

Childress, James F. "Scripture and Christian Ethics." In *Readings in Moral Theology No. 4: The Use of Scripture in Moral Theology*, 276-288. Edited by Charles E. Curran and Richard A. McCormick, S.J. New York: Paulist Press, 1984.

Also found as "Scripture and Christian Ethics: Some Reflections on the Role of Scripture in Moral Deliberation and Justification." *Interpretation* 34 (1980): 371-380.

Clark, Michael, O.M.I. "The Major Scriptural Themes in the Moral Theology of Father Bernhard Häring." (Two parts). *Studia Moralia* 30 (1992): 3-16; 277-288.

Two-part article which traces the overall vision and development of Häring's use of Scripture in his writings in moral theology. Häring (born 1912) is a major Roman Catholic moral theologian who sought to incorporate Scripture into his approach to moral theology, and who taught moral theology for a number of years at the Academia Alphonsianum in Rome. Clark did his doctoral dissertation on the same theme at the Pontifical Gregorian University. See his *The Use of Sacred Scripture in the Moral Theology of Father Bernard Häring, C.Ss.R.* Excerpta ex dissertatione ad Doctoratum in Facultate Theologiae Pontificiae Universitatis Gregorianae. Roma, 1979.

Clark is a professor of Scripture at the Oblate College of Mary Immaculate in Washington, D.C.

Clowney, David. "The Use of the Bible in Ethics." In *Inerrancy and Hermeneutic*, 211-236. Edited by H. Conn. 1988.

Collins, Raymond F. "Scripture and Christian Ethics." *Catholic Theological Society of America Proceedings of the Twenty-Ninth Annual Convention.* (1974): 215-53.

Collins taught New Testament for many years at Louvain in Belgium, and is now at Catholic University in Washington, D.C.

Cone, James H. "Biblical Revelation and Social Existence." In *Readings in Moral Theology No. 4: The Use of Scripture in Moral Theology*, 21-44. Edited by Charles E. Curran and Richard A. McCormick, S.J. New York: Paulist Press, 1984.

Crosby, Michael H., O.F.M. "The Biblical Vision of Conversion." In *The Human Experience of Conversion: Persons and Structures in Transformation*, 31-74. Edited by Francis A. Eigo. Proceedings of the Theology Institute of Villanova University, 29. Villanova: Villanova University Press, 1987.

Crotty, Nicholas, C.P. "Biblical Perspectives in Moral Theology." *Theological Studies* 26 (1965): 574-595.

Attempts to present the main lines of a biblical ethic in order to clarify its chief features which would characterize any Christian moral doctrine.

Cuenca, J.F. "De la ley del Sinaí a la ley de Cristo." *Carthaginensia* 3 (1987): 37-55.

Curran, Charles E. "Dialogue with the Scriptures: The Role and Function of the Scriptures in Moral Theology." In *Catholic Moral Theology in Dialogue*, 24-64. Notre Dame: Fides Publishers, 1972.

Originally appeared in *Proceedings of the Catholic Theology Society of America* in 1971.

Also found in Charles E. Curran and Richard A. McCormick, S.J., eds., *Readings in Moral Theology No. 4: The Use of Scripture in Moral Theology*, 178-212. New York: Paulist Press, 1984.

Daly, Robert J., S.J., et. al. "The Bible and Ethics." In *Christian Biblical Ethics: From Biblical Revelation to Contemporary Christian Praxis: Method and Content*, 66-155. New York: Paulist Press, 1984.

_____. "A Methodology for Applying Biblical Texts to Ethical Decisions." In *Christian Biblical Ethics: From Biblical Revelation to Contemporary Christian Praxis: Method and Content*, 289-295. New York: Paulist Press, 1984.

Dayton, Donald W. "The Use of Scripture in the Wesleyan Tradition." In *The Use of the Bible in Theology: Evangelical Options* 121-136. Edited by Robert K. Johnson. Atlanta: John Knox Press, 1985.

16

Delhaye, Philippe. "Le recours à l'Ecriture Sainte dans l'enseignement de la théologie morale." *Bulletin des Facultes Catholiques de Lyon* 77 (1955): 5-19; 78 (1956): 5-25.

_____. "Le recours à l'Ecriture Sainte en théologie morale." *Esprit et Vie* 85 (1975): 33-43; 49-50.

Demmer, Klaus, M.S.C. "Vernunftbegründung und biblische Begründung in der Ethik." *Zeitschrift für Evangelische Ethik* 37 (1993): 10-21.

One of several articles in this issue by Protestant and Catholic German theologians discussing various aspects of ecumenical Christian ethics.

Demmer is Professor of Moral Theology at the Pontifical Gregorian University in Rome.

Di Giovanni, Alberto. "L'«opzione fondamentale» nella Bibbia." In *Fondamenti biblici della teologia morale*, 61-82. Atti della XXII Settimana Biblica. Associazione biblica italiana. Brescia: Paideia, 1973.

Di Marino, A. "Fondamenti biblici della teologia morale. Riflessioni di un moralista." *Rassegna di Teologia* 14 (1973): 10-14.

Di Pinto, Luigi, S.J. "Fondamenti biblici della teologia morale, ricerche recenti, bilancio e prospettive." *Rassegna di Teologia* 14 (1973): 32-61.

A bibliographical essay on various themes connected with the use of Scripture in moral theology, obviously a bit dated, but still valuable for the history of the movement. Emphasis is on European works, though some mention is made of English language contributions.

Dillmann, Rainer. "Aufbruch zu einer neuen Sittlichkeit: Biblisch-narrative Begründung ethischen Handelns." *Theologie und Glaube* 82 (1992): 34-35.

Considers Mk 7: 31-35; Lk 13:10-17, and 1 Kings 21:17-19.

Dohmen, Christoph. "Origins and goals of biblical ethics as illustrated by the first commandment of the Decalogue." *Communio* 29 (1992): 36-57.

In German: "Um unsere Freiheit willen. Ursprung und Ziel biblischer Ethik im «Hauptgebot» des Dekalogs." *Communio* 21 (1992): 7-24

In Italian: "Per amore della nostra libertà. Origine e fine dell'etica biblica nel `comandamento principale' del decalogo." *Communio* 121 (1992): 27-46.

In Portuguese: "Por amor da nossa liberdade. E'tica bíblica e «primeiro mandamento» do Decálogo." *Communio* 9 (1992): 136-152.

Detailed exegetical consideration of the two versions of the Decalogue contained in the Old Testament, considering also their historical context, linguistic formulations, etc. Dohmen stresses the unity of composition of the whole Decalogue as the key for its authentic ethical interpretation: "It follows that the individual commandments of the Decalogue have their meaning only within this unity, a unity that is rooted in God's act of deliverance as described in the prologue. This unity is underscored by the broadly formulated principal commandment, which stipulates that our `image of God' determines our `image of man' to the extent that our relationship with God becomes a mirror of our interhuman relationships. Consequently, every ethical precept derived from the Bible, especially from the Decalogue, needs to orient itself toward the unity and completeness of the Decalogue. Thus, no social commandments may claim their authority from the Decalogue if they stand isolated from the context of its principal commandment and its prologue; neither can there be a `theology of the Decalogue' without a consideration of the social commandments." p. 56.

Dohmen is professor of Old Testament exegesis at the University of Osnabrück, Germany.

Donahue, John R., S.J. "The Challenge of the Biblical Renewal to Moral Theology." In *Riding Time Like a River: The Catholic Moral Tradition Since Vatican II*, 59-80. Edited by William J. O'Brien. Washington, D.C.: Georgetown University Press, 1993.

Donahue studied under Norman Perrin at the University of Chicago is Professor of Biblical Studies (New Testament) at the Jesuit School of Theology and Graduate Theological Union, Berkeley, California.

_____. "What Does the Lord Require? *A Bibliographical Essay on the Bible and Social Justice.*" *Studies in the Spirituality of Jesuits* 25 (March, 1993).

Excellent introductory essay to the major themes of biblical social ethics, plus an annotated bibliography 211 titles thematically arranged, complete with index.

Douma, Jochem. "The Use of Scripture in Ethics." *European Journal of Theology* 1/2 (1992): 105-121.

Dreyfus, François. "Hermeneutique biblique des normes morales." In *Persona Verità e Morale: Atti del Congresso Internazionale di Teologia Morale (Roma, 7-12 aprile 1986)*, 621-626. Roma: Città Nuova Editrice, 1987.

Comment dégager la valeur actuelle des normes morales contenues dans la Bible, en respectant leur historicité, c'est-à-dire en dégageant leurs valeurs permanentes au-delà des circonstances concrètes de mentalité de civilisation, de culture dans lesquelles elles ont été promulguées, et qui ne sont plus les nôtres?

Treats the question of how one extracts the contemporary value of moral norms contained in the Bible while continuing to respect the historicity and cultural formation in which the biblical norms are necessarily formulated.

Dreyfus teaches at the Ecole Biblique et Archeologie Française in Jerusalem.

Espinel, J.L. "Biblia y moral cristiana." *Ciencia Tomística* 113 (1986): 583-595.

Etienne, J. "Théologie morale et renouveau biblique." *Ephemerides Theologicae Lovanienses* 40 (1964): 232-241.

Evans, C. F. "Difficulties in Using the Bible for Christian Ethics." *Modern Churchman* ns 26 (3/1984): 27-34.

Federici, Tommaso. "Aspetti Biblici della Solidarietà." *Per La Filosofia: Filosofia e insegnamento* 7 (1990): 13-25.

Fernández Ramos, F. "Sagrada Escritura y moral cristiana." *Salmanticensis* 24 (1977): 5-47.

Festorazzi, Franco. "La Sacra Scrittura anima del rinnovamento della teologia morale." *La Scuola Cattolica* 94 (1966): 91-115.

____. "Il valore dell'esperienza e la morale sapienziale." In *Fondamenti biblici della teologia morale*, 117-146. Atti della XXII Settimana Biblica. Associazione biblica italiana. Brescia: Paideia, 1973.

Fischer, James A., C.M. "Story and Image." In *Christian Biblical Ethics: From Biblical Revelation to Contemporary Christian Praxis: Method and Content*, 156-169. New York: Paulist Press, 1984.

Includes treatment of "Human Life as Story" and "The Bible as Ethical Story."

Flynn, Eileen P. "Seminar on Moral Theology: How Scripture Influences the Work of Moral Theologians." *Catholic Theological Society of America Proceedings of the Forty-Seventh Annual Convention* 47 (1992): 152-153.

Brief report of the Continuing Seminar in Moral Theology on some of the issues in the use of Scripture in Christian ethics.

Forte, Bruno. "Fondazione biblico-teologica dell'etica: *Prospettiva cattolica*." In *Questione etica e impegno ecumenico delle Chiese. Atti dell 23e sessione di formazione ecumenica del Segretariato Attività Ecumeniche (SAE)*, 40-56. Napoli: Edizioni Dehoniane Napoli, 1986.

Intervento al congresso tenuto a La Mendola (Trento) 27 luglio - 4 agosto 1985.

Paper given at a conference held at La Mendola (Trent, Italy) from 27 July to 4 August 1985.

Fiorenza, Elisabeth Schüssler. "The Ethics of Decentering Biblical Scholarship." *Journal of Biblical Literature* 107 (1988): 3-17.

France, R.T. "Conversion in the Bible." *Evangelical Quarterly* 65 (1993): 291-310.

Overview of the biblical theme of conversion. Originally presented as a paper for a "Consultation on Conversion" held in Hong Kong in January 1988.

France is Principal of Wycliffe Hall, Oxford.

Frey, Christofer. "The function of the Bible in recent Protestant ethics." In *Creative biblical exegesis: Christian and Jewish hermeneutics through the centuries*, 63-70. Edited by Benjamin Uffenheimer and Henning Graf Reventlow. Sheffield: JSOT Press, 1988.

Paper presented at a conference on Creative Biblical Exegesis at Tel-Aviv University, 16-17 December 1985.

Frey is Professor of Christian Ethics on the Evangelisch-Theologische Fakultät of the Ruhr-Universität in Bochum.

Freyne, Seán. "The Bible and Christian Morality." In *Introduction to Christian Ethics: A Reader*, edited by Ronald P. Hamel and Kenneth R. Himes, O.F.M., 9-32. New York: Paulist Press, 1989.

Also in *Morals, Law and Authority*, 1-38. Edited by J.P. Mackey. Dayton: Pflaum, 1969.

Froehlich, Herbert. "Biblische Zeugnisse gewaltloser Befreiung." *Ordensnachrichten* 32 (5/1993): 13-18.

English digest: "Biblical Witnesses to Nonviolent Liberation." *Theology Digest* 41 (1994): 113-116.

Explores examples from both Testaments to indicate that the way of God and Christ does not employ violence. Christians, therefore, may have to suffer violence at times so as not to replace old injustice with new.

Fuchs, Eric. "Faire mémoire du modèle biblique." Dans Ch. 9 de *L'Ethique Protestante: Histoire et enjeux*, 102-112. Le Champ Ethique, 19. Paris: Les Bergers et les Mages; Genève: Editions Labor et Fides, 1990.

Fuchs, Josef, S.J. "Christian Morality: Biblical Orientation and Human Evaluation." *Gregorianum* 67 (1986): 745-763.

German original: "Christliche Moral. Biblische Orientierung und menschliche Wertung." *Stimmen der Zeit* 205 (1987): 37-55.

Italian translation: "Etica cristiana: orientamento biblico e valutazione umana." Cap. 1 in Id. *Il Verbo si fa carne; teologia morale*, 7-30. Casale Monferrato, Piemme, 1989.

Fuchs is professor emeritus of moral theology at the Pontifical Gregorian University in Rome, and one of the leading Roman Catholic moral theologians of the twentieth century.

Gaffney, James. "On Paranesis and Fundamental Moral Theology." *The Journal of Religious Ethics* 11 (1983): 24-34.

Also found as Chapter 10 in Gaffney's *Matters of Faith and Morals*, 134-151, (Kansas City: Sheed and Ward, 1987).

This article is a response to Bruno Schüller, S.J.'s 1976 article, "The Debate on the Specific Character of Christian Ethics: Some Remarks," which first appeared in English in 1980 in *Readings in Moral Theology, No. 2*, 207-233. Edited by Charles E. Curran and Richard A. McCormick, S.J. New York: Paulist Press, 1980.

Galbiati, E. "L'uso della Sacra Scrittura nella teologia morale." *Rivista del Clero Italiano* 61 (1980): 936-943.

Geffré, Claude, O.P. "Autorité des Ecritures et autonomie de la conscience." *Le Supplément* 155 (1985): 65-73.

Giavini, Giovanni. "Le norme etiche della Bibbia e l'uomo d'oggi." *La Scuola Cattolica* 100 (1972): 1-15; 83-97.

La prima parte è dedicata a una presentazione sintetica della legislazione mosaica, mentre la seconda parte è sostanzialmente lo stesso testo pubblicato sul titolo "Il discorso della montagna nella problematica attuale circa il valore delle norme etiche del Nuovo Testamento," negli Atti della Settimana Biblica, in *Fondamenti biblici della teologia morale: Atti della XXII Settimana Biblica*, 253-272. Brescia, 1973.

Part One of the article gives a synthesis of the Mosiac legislation, while Part Two is essentially the same text published as "Il discorso della montagna nella problematica attuale circa il valore delle norme etiche del Nuovo Testamento," (The Sermon on the Mount in light of the contemporary problematic concerning the value of ethical norms of the New Testament), which is found in Atti della Settimana Biblica, in *Fondamenti biblici della teologia morale: Atti della XXII Settimana Biblica*, 253-272. Brescia, 1973

Gilbert, Maurice, S.J. "Rencontre entre moralistes et exégètes." *Revue Théologique de Louvain* 5 (1974): 127-128.

Gilbert is on the faculty and former rector of the Pontifical Biblical Institute in Rome.

Goffi, Tullo. "L'uso della parola di Dio in teologia morale." *Rivista di Teologia Morale* 3 (1971): 13-23.

Grelot, Pierre. "La Parole de Dieu s'addresse-t-elle à l'homme d'aujourd'hui?" *La Maison Dieu* 80 (1964): 151-200.

Guevin, Benedict M. "The Moral Imagination and the Shaping Power of the Parables." *Journal of Religious Ethics* 17 (1989): 63-79.

Discusses how the literary impact of the parable story can affect the shaping of character. Much of Guevin's essay is done in light of the work of Stanley Hauerwas.

Gula, Richard M., S.S. "Scripture in Moral Theology." Chapter 12 in Idem. *Reason Informed by Faith: Foundations of Catholic Morality*, 165-184. New York: Paulist Press, 1989.

Gula was Professor of Moral Theology for many years at St. Patrick's Seminary in Menlo Park, California, and now is Professor of Moral Theology at the Franciscan School of Theology in Berkeley, California. This selection is taken from his widely-used textbook on moral theology.

Guroian, Vigen. "Bible and Ethics: An Ecclesial and Liturgical Interpretation." *Journal of Religious Ethics* 18 (1990): 129-157.

Recent scholarship on the relation between Scripture and ethics has often overlooked the ecclesial and liturgical contexts in which the believing communities interpret and apply the Bible. The author aims to correct this omission through investigation of the uses of the Bible in the ecclesial and liturgical contexts of the Orthodox tradition, analyzing, for example, the uses of the beatitudes in Byzantine liturgy, John Chrysostom's homiletics, use of Pauline texts for ethical instruction in the celebration of baptism, etc.

A revised version of this article appears under the title "The Bible in Orthodox Ethics" as chapter 3 in Guroian's *Ethics after Christendom: Toward an Ecclesial Christian Ethic*, 53-80. Grand Rapids: William B. Eerdmans, 1994.

Guroian teaches theology and ethics at Loyola College in Baltimore.

Gustafson, James M. "The Changing Use of the Bible in Christian Ethics." In *Readings in Moral Theology No. 4: The Use of Scripture in Moral Theology*, 133-150. Edited by Charles E. Curran and Richard A. McCormick, S.J. New York: Paulist Press, 1984.

Gustafson is an ordained minister in the United Church of Christ, and currently Henry R. Luce Professor of Humanities and Comparative Studies at Emory University. Previously he taught at Yale and the University of Chicago. He has studied at the Chicago Theological Seminary, University of Chicago, and his Ph.D. is from Yale (1955), done under H. Richard Niebuhr. He has also taught at Yale and the University of Chicago.

_____. "The Place of Scripture in Christian Ethics: A Methodological Study." Chapter 6 in *Theology and Christian Ethics*, 121-145. Philadelphia: Pilgrim Press, 1974.

Also found in *Readings in Moral Theology No. 4: The Use of Scripture in Moral Theology*, 151-177. Edited by Charles E. Curran and Richard A. McCormick, S.J. New York: Paulist Press, 1984.

This is a very key article for a consideration of many of the methodological issues involved in Scripture and Christian ethics.

Hamel, Edouard, S.J. "Ecriture et théologie morale. Un bilan (1940-1980)." *Studia Moralia* 20 (1982): 177-193.

Cette étude indique les principales étapes du renouveau de la morale par l'Ecriture, entre les années 1940-1980. Une première partie montre comment on est passé du biblicisme des années 1940 à l'attitude plus critique des années 1970-1980. Quelles furent les orientations données par le Magistère sur la question? Pourquoi les Protestants ont connu une crise de la référence biblique en morale? Ces jalons d'histoire sont suivis de quelques réflexions d'ordre méthodologique. Pourquoi et comment retourner à l'Ecriture en morale? Comment l'Eglise primitive a relu ou interprété les textes normatifs de l'Ancien et du Nouveau Testament?

This study discusses the principal developments in the renewal of moral theology in reference to the usage of Scripture in the years 1940-1980, and considers how the Roman Catholic Magisterium addressed the issue, makes reference to Protestant employment of Scripture in Christian ethics, and moves on to methodological questions of why and how Scripture should be used in moral theology. For an English digest of this article see Hamel's "Scripture and Moral Theology: 1940-1980." *Theology Digest* 36 (1989): 203-207.

Hamel was professor of moral theology at the Pontifical Gregorian University until 1986.

_____. "La legge morale e i problemi che pone al biblista." In *Fondamenti biblici della teologia morale*, 23-44. Atti della XXII Settimana Biblica. Associazione biblica italiana. Brescia: Paideia, 1973.

_____. "Le Magnificat et le Renversement des Situations: Réflexion théologico-biblique." *Gregorianum* 60 (1979): 55-84.

Examines the theme of the "overview of situations" in the Old and New Testament, as well as Hellenistic literature, and then proceeds to a hermeneutical consideration of the Magnificat for the contemporary Church, concluding that the prayer should be interpreted as an incentive to the promotion of justice.

_____. "Scripture and Moral Theology: 1940-1980." *Theology Digest* 36 (1989): 203-207.

A digested form of Hamel's original French article published as "Ecriture et théologie morale. Un bilan (1940-1980)," in *Studia Moralia* 20 (1982): 177-193.

Hamel distinguishes three stages of moral renewal in the Roman Catholic Church since 1940: 1) addition of brief scriptural introductions to moral tracts; 2) "renewal" of moral theology in the light of charity and the imitation of Christ; and 3) moralists joining forces with exegetes in using Scripture as a decisive force in theology. Meanwhile in the Protestant community since 1940 Hamel discerns an inverse movement, from Biblical "infallibility" to a divided Protestant view with some holding that now there is "too much" Bible in moral theology.

_____. "Scripture, the Soul of Moral Theology?" In *Readings in Moral Theology No. 4: The Use of Scripture in Moral Theology*, 105-132. Edited by Charles E. Curran and Richard A. McCormick, S.J. New York: Paulist Press, 1984.

French original: "L'Ecriture âme de la Théologie." *Gregorianum* 52 (1971): 511-535.

Unpacks the metaphors of "soul" and "nourishment" used by Vatican II to indicate possible roles and applications of Scripture to moral theology. Concludes with a brief look at Pauline morality to illustrate the relationship between a moral theology rooted in both the faith kerygma and human reason. The text was given as a lecture at the University of Sydney (Australia), and follows upon another study published in *Fondamenti biblici della teologia morale* (Brescia: Paideia, 1973.)

_____. "La théologie morale entre l'Ecriture et la raison." *Gregorianum* 56 (1975): 273-319.

Texte d'un rapport rédigé pour la Commission Théologique Internationale.

Text prepared for a meeting of the International Theological Commission, of which Hamel was a member at the time.

Hamel considers the proper role and relationship of Scripture to moral theology, outlining some of the methodological problems, stressing the need for an ongoing hermeneutical application, and discussing in brief how St. Paul utilized both Scripture and contemporary Greek moral philosophy in his Letters.

_____. "L'usage de l'Ecriture Sainte en théologie morale." *Gregorianum* 47 (1966): 53-85.

Article written shortly after the approval by the Council of *Optatam Totius* (Vatican II's 1965 Decree on the Training for Priests) in October 1965. Perhaps written to allay fears of some moralists as to the both the nature and parameters of the Decree's call for a return to Scripture in moral.

Hauerwas, Stanley. "The Moral Authority of Scripture: The Politics and Ethics of Remembering." *Interpretation* 34 (1980): 356-370.

Also found as Chapter 3 in *A Community of Character: Toward a Constructive Christian Social Ethic*, 53-71. Notre Dame and London: University of Notre Dame Press, 1981.

Also found in *Readings in Moral Theology No. 4: The Use of Scripture in Moral Theology*, 242-275. Edited by Charles E. Curran and Richard A. McCormick, S.J. New York: Paulist Press, 1984.

The moral authority of Scripture depends ultimately about what kind of community the church must be, a life centered on a faithful remembering based on the narratives of Scripture.

Hauerwas (born 1940) is a Methodist who currently is Gilbert T. Rowe Professor of ethics at the Divinity School of Duke University in North Carolina. He studied under James M. Gustafson and for over a dozen years was on the faculty of the University of Notre Dame.

Hendel, Ronald S. "When God acts immorally: is the Bible a good book?" *Bible Review* 7 (June 1991): 34,37,46,48,50.

Himes, Kenneth R., O.F.M. "Scripture and Ethics: A Review Essay." *Biblical Theology Bulletin* 15 (1985): 65-73.

Hütter, Reinhard. "Ecclesial Ethics, the Church's Vocation, and Paraclesis." *Pro Ecclesia* 2/4 (1994): 433-450.

Ibáñez, Arana A. "La S. Escritura en la renovación de la teología moral." *Lumen* 16 (1967): 332-348.

Instituto Superior de Ciencas Morales. See "Vidal, Marciano, et. al."

Kaustermann, A.P. "Biblische Motive als Argumente in Autonomie-Denken der Aufklärung." *Theologische Quartelschrift* 161 (1981): 33-42.

Kerber, Walter. "Grenzen der biblischen Moral." In Klaus Demmer und Bruno Schüller, Hrsg. *Christlich Glauben und Handeln*, 112-123. Dusseldorf, 1977.

Italian translation found in *Fede cristiana e agire morale*. A cura di Klaus Demmer, M.S.C. e Bruno Schüller, S.J. Traduzione italiana di Giuliano Riva. Assisi: Cittadella, 1980. Assisi: Cittadella, 1980.

Lage, Francisco. "Puntos para una introducción al problema de la fundamentacíon bíblica de la moral." *Pentacostés* 12 (1974): 293-331.

Lamau, M.-L. "Ecriture et éthique. Typologies." *Le Supplément* 163 (1987): 105-115.

Larue, Gerald A. "Biblical Ethics and Continuing Interpretation." In *Biblical and Secular Ethics: The Conflict*, 17-28. Edited by R. Joseph Hoffman and Gerald A. Larue. Buffalo: Prometheus Press, 1988.

Contribution which came out of a meeting of social philosophers, biblical scholars, and ethicians which met at the University of Richmond in the autumn of 1986 under the sponsorship of the Committee for the Scientific Examination of Religion (CSER) and its Biblical Criticism Research Project.

Larue is Professor Emeritus of Archaeology and Biblical History at the University of Southern California.

Laurenzi, Maria Cristina. "Perché la Scrittura? La letter biblica come fatto etico." *Rassegna di Teologia* 32 (1991): 233-255.

Lindars, Barnabas. "The Bible and Christian Ethics." In *Duty and Discernment*, 64-75. Edited by G.R. Dunstan. London: SCM Press, 1975.

Long, Edward LeRoy, Jr. "The Use of the Bible in Christian Ethics." *Interpretation* 19 (1965): 149-162.

Exposition of Protestant research in the field.

Lorenzetti, Luigi. "L'etica sociale cristiana nel nuovo orizzonte biblico, teologico, ecclesiale." Capitolo 2 in *Corso di morale*, 23-46. Vol. 4. A cura di Tullo Goffi e Giannino Piana. Brescia: Queriniana, 1985.

MacNamara, Vincent. "The Use of the Bible in Moral Theology." *The Month* 248 (March, 1987): 104-107.

A brief overview of some of the issues of using Scripture in connection to contemporary moral theology, including some recent use of Scripture in magisterial documents such as *Persona humana* (1975 Vatican document on sexual ethics issued by the Congregation for the Doctrine of the Faith document).

Mannucci, Valerio. "Teologia biblica del lavoro. A dieci anni dalla «Laborem Exercens»." *Rassegna di Teologia* 32 (1991): 443-468.

Mannucci riesamina da biblista la teologia sui cui si fonda l'enciclica col suo ripetuto richiamo alla Genesi che disegna l'uomo nelle sue relazioni fondamentali, di cui il lavoro è tratto essenziale.

Mannucci examines from the perspective of a biblical exegete the theology on *Laborem Exercens* (Pope John Paul II's 1981 Encyclical on Work), especially the usage of Genesis which holds that work is foundational to a consideration of the nature of the human person.

Marshall, Christopher. "The Use of Scripture in Ethics." *Evangelical Review of Theology* 18 (1994): 222-233.

First section of an extended paper which was presented at a symposium on "The Church, State and Justice" at Victoria University of Wellington, New

Zealand on 19 November 1993. Marshall outlines five interrelated sources of Christian ethics and discusses why a *sola scriptura* approach is inadequate in dealing with many complex contemporary ethical issues.

Marshall is Head of the Department of the New Testament Studies Bible College of New Zealand in Auckland, New Zealand.

Marshall, I. Howard. "Using the Bible in Ethics." In *Essays in Evangelical Social Ethics*, 39-55. Edited by David F. Wright. Exeter: Paternoster Press, 1973; Wilton CT: Morehouse-Barlow Co., Inc., 1983.

Marshall's essay comes out of the September, 1978 National Evangelical Conference in Hertfordshire, England. He gives a brief overview of the problematic, as well as some traditional approaches to the Bible in ethics. Marshall then concludes with what he terms an "evangelical approach" which is based on a hermeneutical reading of the Bible. To illustrate his approach Marshall employs the Foot-Washing command of John 13:14ff.

McCormick, Richard A., S.J. "Scripture, Liturgy, Character and Morality." In Charles E. Curran and Richard A. McCormick, S.J., eds., *Readings in Moral Theology No. 4: The Use of Scripture in Moral Theology*, 289-302. New York: Paulist Press, 1984.

This article originally appeared in *Theological Studies* in 1981.

Meier, John P. "The Bible as a Source for Theology." *Catholic Theological Society of America Proceedings of the Forty-Third Annual Convention* (1988): 1-15.

Meier is professor of New Testament at the Catholic University of America.

Mieth, Dietmar. "Autonomy of Ethics--Neutrality of the Gospel," *Concilium* 153 (1982): 32-39.

Mieth is a moral theologian.

Moore, Gareth. "Some Remarks on the Use of Scripture in Veritatis Splendor." In *The Splendor of Accuracy: An Examination of the Assertions Made by*

Veritatis Splendor. 71-98. Edited by Joseph A. Selling and Jan Jans. Grand Rapids: William B. Eerdmans Publishing Company, 1994.

Discusses the use of Scripture in Pope John Paul II's 1993 Encyclical *Veritatis Splendor* on fundamental moral theology.

Mouw, Richard J. "Commands for Grown-Ups." In *Readings in Moral Theology No. 4: The Use of Scripture in Moral Theology*, 66-77. Edited by Charles E. Curran and Richard A. McCormick, S.J. New York: Paulist Press, 1984.

Mouw is an ethician and president of Fuller Theological Seminary in California.

Navone, John, S.J. "Scripture for Christian Conversion." *New Blackfriars* 74 (1993): 21-33.

Navone is professor of biblical theology in the Institute of Spirituality of the Pontifical Gregorian University in Rome.

Nelson, Paul. "The Place of Biblical Narrative in Christian Ethics." Chapter 6 in Idem. *Narrative and Morality: A Theological Inquiry*, 85-107. University Park: Pennsylvania State University, 1987.

Brief overview of some principal biblical theologians and Christian ethicians' approaches to Scripture and ethics in the context of narrative.

Revised version of a 1984 doctoral dissertation done at Yale.

O'Connell, Timothy E. "The Moral Law in Scripture." Chapter 12 in *Principles for a Catholic Morality*, 139-148. Minneapolis: The Seabury Press, 1976, 1978. Revised edition, San Francisco: Harper and Row, 1990.

Is a popular textbook in moral theology for seminarians which aims to replace the old moral manuals, yet without falling into the legalistic approach which characterized that genre.

O'Donovan, Oliver. "The Possibility of a Biblical Ethic." *TSF Bulletin* 67 (Autumn, 1973): 15-23.

O'Donovan is an evangelical Anglican ethician.

_____. "Towards an Interpretation of Biblical Ethics." *Tyndale Bulletin* 27 (1976): 54-78.

van Ouwerkerk, C[onrad].A.J. "Biblisches Ethos und menschlicher Kompromiss." *Concilium* 1 (1965): 367-374.

Paul VI, Pope. "Iis qui interfuerunt Coetui vigesimo secundo per hebdomadam Romae habito, biblicis studiis provehendis." *AAS (Acta Apolostolicae Sedis)* 64 (1972): 634-637.

Discourse given in Italian on 29 September 1972 to the Associazione Biblica Italiana on their "Settimana Biblica" (Biblical Week) in which Paul VI speaks of the necessary cooperation between biblical exegetes and moral theologians in the use of Scripture in Christian ethics. The Pope cites *Optatam Totius* #16 in reference to the place of Scripture in moral, and also quotes *Dei Verbum* #1, which speaks of the need of the Church to listen to the Word of God, and of the role of the exegete (*Dei Verbum* #12).

Paul VI was Pope from 1963 to 1978, and presided over the Second Vatican Council (1962-1965) after the death of Pope John XXIII in 1963.

_____. "Membris Pontificiae Commissionis Biblicae Romae plenarium coetum habentibus." *AAS (Acta Apolostolicae Sedis)* 66 (1974): 235-241.

Allocution given in French on 14 March 1974 to members of the Pontifical Biblical Commission in which Pope Paul VI underlined the necessity of cooperation among biblical exegetes and dogmatic and moral theologians in their respective disciplines.

Pinckaers, Servais, O.P. "The Use of Scripture and the Revewal of Moral Theology: The *Catechism* and *Veritatis Splendor*." *The Thomist* 59 (1995): 1-19.

Discusses the use of Scripture in Pope John Paul II's 1993 Encyclical *Veritatis Splendor* on fundamental moral theology.

Pinckaers is a moral theologian who teaches in Switzerland and who is often consulted by the Vatican concerning Roman Catholic moral theology.

Platten, S. "The Biblical Critic and Moral Theologian." *Kings Theological Review* 12 (1989): 11-17.

Polk, Timothy. "In the Image: Aesthetics and Ethics through the Glass of Scripture." *Horizons in Biblical Theology* 8 (1986): 27-59.

Ratzinger, Joseph Cardinal. "Magisterium of the Church, Faith, Morality." In Charles E. Curran and Richard A. McCormick, S.J., eds., *Readings in Moral Theology, No. 2: The Distinctiveness of Christian Ethics*, 174-189. New York: Paulist Press, 1980.

Originally appeared in English in *Problems of the Church Today*, 74-83. Washington, D.C.: U.S. Catholic Conference.

Also found under the title, "The Church's Teaching Authority--Faith--Morals," in *Principles of Christian Morality*, 47-73. Translated by Graham Harrison. San Francisco: Ignatius Press, 1986.

In German: "Kirchliches Lehramt, Glaube, Moral." In Id., Hrsg. *Prinzipien Christlicher Moral*, 41-66. Einsiedeln, 1975.

In French: In Joseph Ratzinger et Philippe Delhaye, ed., *Principes d'éthique chrétienne*. Le Sycomore. Paris: Editions Lethielleux, 1979.

In Italian: in *Prospettive di morale cristiana*. Contributi di teologia, 3. Ed. Joseph Cardinal Ratzinger. Roma: Città Nuova Editrice, 1986.

Ratzinger attended Vatican II as a *peritus* (theological expert) and is head of the Vatican's Congregation for the Doctrine of the Faith (CDF).

Rivkin, Ellis. "Building a Biblical Foundation for Contemporary Ethics." In *Biblical and Secular Ethics: The Conflict*, 99-105. Edited by R. Joseph Hoffman and Gerald A. Larue. Buffalo: Prometheus Press, 1988.

Contribution which came out of a meeting of social philosophers, biblical scholars, and ethicians which met at the University of Richmond in the autumn of 1986 under the sponsorship of the Committee for the Scientific Examination of Religion (CSER) and its Biblical Criticism Research Project.

Rivista di Teologia Morale. "Rassegna Bibliografica: Etica e Bibbia." *Rivista di Teologia Morale* 23 (1991): 393-410.

Una rassegna bibliografica dei libri italiani sul tema dell'etica e la Scrittura.

A bibliographical essay of Italian books on the theme of Scripture and ethics.

Robert, Ch. "Morale et Ecriture." *Seminarium* [N.S.] 11 (1971): 596-622.

Robinson, N.H.G. "How the Bible Speaks to Conscience." In *Conscience: Theological and Psychological Perspectives,* 72-78. Edited by C. Ellis Nelson. New York: Newman Press, 1973.

Also found in Robinson's own book, *Christ and Conscience,* 171-178. London: James Nisbet, 1956.

Robinson develops the thesis that conscience is the area where the individual experiences the Spirit of God, and that the Bible is the means by which God addresses the human person today. This address is not so much a narrative as a confrontation with conscience which results in confession, repentance, restitution and change. Uses the story of David and Nathan, plus makes some remarks about Jesus' use of parables.

Sacchi, Alessandro. "La legge naturale nella bibbia." In AA. VV. *La legge naturale,* 17-59. Studi e ricerche, 4. Bologna: Edizioni Dehoniane Bologna, 1970.

Salguero, José, O.P. "Relazione tra l'Antica e la Nuova Alleanza." *Angelicum* 60 (1983): 165-189.

Schneider, Gerhard. "The Biblical Grounding of Ethical Norms." *Theology Digest* 22 (1974): 117-120.

Schüller, Bruno, S.J. "The Debate on the Specific Character of Christian Ethics: Some Remarks." In Charles E. Curran and Richard A. McCormick, S.J., eds. *Readings in Moral Theology No. 2*, 207-233. New York: Paulist Press, 1980.

Also found as Chapter 1 of Schüller's *Wholly Human: Essays on the Theory and Language of Morality*, 15-42. Translated by Peter Heinegg. Dublin: Gill and Macmillan; Washington, D.C.: Georgetown University Press, 1986.

German original: "Zur Discussion über das Proprium einer christlichen Ethik." *Theologie und Philosophie* 51 (1976): 321-343.

For a good critique of, and response to, Schüller's position, see James Gaffney's "On Paranesis and Fundamental Moral Theology." *The Journal of Religious Ethics* 11 (1983): 24-34. This same article is also found as Chapter 10 in Gaffney's *Matters of Faith and Morals*, 134-151, (Kansas City: Sheed and Ward, 1987).

Schüller did his doctorate in moral theology at the Pontifical Gregorian University in Rome, and was professor of moral theology at the University of Muenster, Germany.

Schürmann, Heinz. "How Normative Are the Values and Precepts of the New Testament?" In *Principles of Christian Morality*, 9-44. Translated by Graham Harrison. San Francisco: Ignatius Press, 1986.

Also found under the title, "Report from the International Theological Commission, «The Actual Impact of Moral Norms in the New Testament: *Text by Hans Schürmann, Introduction and Commentary by Philippe Delhaye,*»" in Charles E. Curran and Richard A. McCormick, S.J., eds., *Readings in Moral Theology No. 4: The Use of Scripture in Moral Theology*, (New York: Paulist Press, 1984): 78-104.

Also found in *International Theological Commission: Texts and Documents (1969-1985)*, 121-128. Edited by Michael Sharkey. San Francisco: Ignatius Press, 1989.

German original: "Die Frage nach der Verbindlichkeit der neutestamentlichen Wertungen und Weisungen." In Joseph Ratzinger, Hrsg. *Prinzipien Christlicher Moral*, 9-39. Einsiedeln, 1975.

French translation: "Du caractère obligatoire des normes et directives morales du Nouveau Testament." In Joseph Ratzinger et Philippe Delhaye, ed.,

Principes d'éthique chrétienne, 37-71. Le Sycomore. Paris: Editions Lethielleux, 1979.

Italian translation: "Sul problema del contenuto e del fondamento dell'ethos cristiano." In *Prospettive di morale cristiana*. Contributi di teologia, 3. Ed. Joseph Cardinal Ratzinger. Roma: Città Nuova Editrice, 1986.

Schweiker, William. "Iconoclasts, builders, and dramatists: the use of scripture in theological ethics." *Annual of the Society of Christian Ethics* (1986): 129-162.

Discusses Stanley Hauerwas and Elisabeth Schüssler Fiorenza.

Segalla, Giuseppe. "L'Ermeneutica biblica femminista di E. Schüssler Fiorenza." *Studia Patavina* 37 (1990): 585-599.

Discussione critica sulla metodologia di Elisabeth Schüssler Fiorenza nel suo libro *In memoria di lei: Una ricostruzione femminista delle origini cristiane*. Edizione italiana a cura di M. Corsani Comba. Torino: Claudiana, 1990.

Critical discussion of Elisabeth Schüssler Fiorenza's methodology employed in her *In Memory of Her: A Feminist Theological Reconstruction of Christian Origins*. New York: Crossroad, 1983.

Segalla is professor of New Testament Exegesis at the Theological Faculty of Milan.

Spohn, William C. "Jesus and Ethics." *Catholic Theological Society of America Proceedings* 49 (1994): 40-57.

Presented as a Plenary Address at the 1994 Catholic Theology Society of America (CTSA) Convention.

Spohn studied under James Gustafson at the University of Chicago, taught moral theology at the Jesuit School of Theology-Berkeley for many years, and currently teaches at the University of Santa Clara.

_____. "Morality on the Way of Discipleship: The Use of Scripture in *Veritatis Splendor*." In *Veritatis Splendor: American Responses*, ed. Michael E.

———. "Morality on the Way of Discipleship: The Use of Scripture in *Veritatis Splendor*." In *Veritatis Splendor: American Responses*, ed. Michael E. Allsopp and John J. O'Keefe, 83-105. Kansas City, M.O.: Sheed & Ward, 1995.

Discusses the use of Scripture in Pope John Paul II's 1993 Encyclical *Veritatis Splendor* on fundamental moral theology.

———. "Parable and Narrative in Christian Ethics." *Theological Studies* 51 (1990): 100-114.

Discusses recent biblical scholarship on parables and the approach of narrative theology in reference to their uses in Christian ethics.

———. "The Use of Scripture in Moral Theology." *Theological Studies* 47 (1986): 88-102.

Brief overview of the exegetical, hermeneutical, methodological and theological tasks involved in the employment of Scripture in the area of moral theology.

Ting, John. "Biblical Ethics in a Fallen World." *Evangelical Review of Theology* 7 (1983): 328-334.

Reprinted from *Asian Challenge*.

Valdman, Traian. "Fondazione biblico-teologica dell'etica: *Prospettiva ortodossa*." *Questione etica e impegno ecumenico delle Chiese. Atti dell 23e sessione di formazione ecumenica del Segretariato Attività Ecumeniche (SAE)*, 71-81. Napoli: Edizioni Dehoniane Napoli, 1986.

Intervento al congresso tenuto a La Mendola (Trento) 27 luglio - 4 agosto 1985.

Paper given at a conference held at La Mendola (Trent), Italy from 27 July to 4 August 1985.

Valeri, Mark, and Wilson, John F. "Scripture and Society: From Reform in the Old World to Revival in the New." In *The Bible in American Law, Politics, and Political Rhetoric*, 13-38. Edited by James Turner Johnson. Philadelphia: Fortress Press; Chico, CA: Scholars Press, 1985.

van den Beld, Antonie. "Eschatology and ethics." *Theology Digest* 27 (1979): 21-24.

Vanoni, Gottfried. "Schalom als zentrale biblische Botschaft." *Theologisch-praktische Quartalschrift* 141 (1993): 3-12.

English digest: "Shalom and the Bible." *Theology Digest* 41 (1994): 171-121.

Shalom means more than peace and its opposite is not merely war, but evil and calamity. Shalom is closely related to biblical righteousness, and is God's gift to humankind. For Christians shalom is also understood as the offering of mutual forgiveness.

Vellanickal, M. "Norm of Morality according to the Scripture." *Bible Bhashyam* 7 (3, 1981): 121-146.

Verhey, Allen. "Scripture and Ethics: Practices, Performances, and Prescriptions." In *Christian Ethics: Problems and Prospects*, 18-44. Edited by Lisa Sowle Cahill and James F. Childress. Cleveland: Pilgrim Press, 1996.

Article done for the *Festschrift* for James M. Gustafson made up of contributions from his former students.

Verhey is the Evert J. and Hattie E. Blekkink Professor of Religion at Hope College.

_____. "The Use of Scripture in Ethics." In *Readings in Moral Theology No. 4: The Use of Scripture in Moral Theology*, 213-241. Edited by Charles E. Curran and Richard A. McCormick, S.J. New York: Paulist Press, 1984.

Also found in *Religious Studies Review* 4 (January, 1978): 28-39.

Wattiaux, Henri. "La référence à l'Ecriture sainte en vue de l'agir moral des chrétiens. Raison d'une option." *Revue Théologique de Louvain* 14 (1983): 53-70.

Review of Louis-Jean Frahier's *Le jugement dernier. Implications éthiques pour le bonheur de l'homme (Mt 25, 31-46).* Recherches morales, Synthèses. Paris: Editions du Cerf, 1992.

Wilch, John R. "The Use and Misuse of Scripture in Ethics." *Consensus* 11 (July 1985): 15-31.

Abstract: Christian ethics is founded upon three major hermeneutical principles: *sola scriptura,* the distinction between law and Gospel, and *solus Christus.* Scripture has been misused, e.g., in respect to: not treating a human fetus as a human being and its father not assuming his parental responsibility, men and women not accepting the roles assigned them by God in this world, the church engaging in politics or denying her principles because of political expediency, and building Christian ethics upon so-called inherent human rights. Providing everything Christians need physically and spiritually, God as Creator and Saviour calls them to responsibility and sacrificial service.

Wolbert, Werner. "Die Goldene Regel und das ius talionis." *Trier Theologische Zeitschrift* 95 (1986): 169-181.

Wright, Christopher J.H. "Bibliography on Biblical Ethics." *Transformation* 10 (3/1993): 27-33.

———. "The Use of the Bible in Social Ethics: Paradigms, Types and Eschatology." *Transformation* 1 (1984): 11-20.

Abstract: This article examines ways in which the Bible can be validly used in applying it to social ethical issues. In order to avoid the common approach of randomly picking texts, it seeks first to adopt a canonical approach, seeing the Bible as fundamentally a story with a beginning (creation), an end (new creation), and a middle (redemption in history), and then allowing each important section of the biblical story to shed its light on any particular issue that one is bringing inductively to the biblical text. When working deductively, outwards from the text to see its relevance to various issues, the article applies a triangular approach, seeing the Bible's fundamental "angles" as God, humans, and the earth, within which the redemptive triangle also operates, i.e., God, Israel, and the land. This redemptive triangle then extends into the NT church and the social and economic dimensions of its fellowship and ultimately becomes eschatological: God, redeemed humanity, and the new creation. The article mentions a number of polarizations in contemporary social thought which this approach helps to reconcile.

Zemek, George J. "Aiming the Mind: A Key to Godly Living." *Grace Theological Journal* 5 (1984): 205-227.

Abstract: The Bible is a persistent witness to the fact that behavior flows from a noetic wellspring. Noetic depravity, expressed by various terms and idiomatic combinations in both testaments, necessitates a redirection of man's faculties. Repentance establishes an initial reorientation; however, the Scriptures stress that the key to a godly life-style is a sustained spiritual mind-set. This is the focal point of biblical ethics.

Books on General Works and/or Methodology

AA.VV. *Fondamenti biblici della teologia morale*. Atti della XXII Settimana Biblica. Associazione biblica italiana. Brescia: Paideia, 1973.

_____. *L'Ecriture âme de la théologie*. Actes du Colloque tenu à Bruxelles du 17 au 19 septembre 1989. Collection IET, 9. Bruxelles: Institut d'Etudes Théologiques, 1990.

Abadamloora, Lucas. *Some Modern Attempts Towards Biblical Renewal in Moral Theology (A Study of Some Recent Catholic Authors)*. Dissertatio ad Doctoratum in Facultate Theologiae Pontificiae Universitatis Gregorianae. Romae, 1975.

STD doctoral dissertation done under Edouard Hamel, S.J. at the Pontifical Gregorian University in Rome.

Adler, L. *La signification morale des fêtes juives*. Genève: Labor et Fides.

40

Allen, Steve. *More Steve Allen on the Bible, Religion and Morality*. Buffalo, NY: Prometheus Books, 1994.

Allen is a well-known American comedian.

Barr, O. Sydney. *The Christian New Morality: A Biblical Study of Situation Ethics*. New York: Oxford University Press, 1969.

Bauckham, Richard. *The Bible in Politics: How to Read the Bible Politically*. Louisville: Westminster/John Knox Press, 1989.

Discusses how to use the Scriptures to bring political and ethical guidance to modern cultures, while still being aware of the distinctive nature of the biblical texts and their own historico-cultural milieu.

Bauckham is lecturer in the History of Christian Thought at the University of Manchester.

Bilheimer, Robert S. *A Spirituality for the Long Haul: Biblical Risk and Moral Stand*. Philadelphia: Fortress Press, 1984.

Birch, Bruce C. and Rasmussen, Larry L. *Bible and Ethics in the Christian Life*. Revised and expanded edition. Minneapolis: Augsburg Publishing House, 1976, 1989.

German translation: *Bibel und christliche Ethik*. Öffentliche Theologie, 1. München: Christian Kaiser Verlag, 1992.

Reviewed by Eric Mount, Jr. in *Theology Today* 46 (1990): 438.

Bonnet, G. *Au nom de la Bible et de l'Evangile, quelle morale?*. Paris, 1978.

Boone, Kathleen C. *The Bible Tells Them So: The Discourse of Protestant Fundamentalism*. Albany: SUNY Press, 1989.

Discusses how fundamentalists perceive the Bible as their only authority, maintaining at the same time that fundamentalism is *not* anti-intellectual as such, but rather an intellectual movement of a very particular type.

Reviewed by James Barr in *Theology Today* 46 (1990): 422.

Brett, P. *Love Your Neighbour: The Bible and Christian Ethics Today.* London: Darton, Longman and Todd, 1993.

Burton-Christie, Douglas. *The Word in the Desert: Scripture and the Quest for Holiness in Early Christian Monasticism.* Oxford: Oxford University Press, 1992.

Burton-Christie teaches at Loyola Marymount University in Los Angeles, California.

Calle, Flavio. *La Sagrada Escritura en la teologia moral: Estudio sobre el pensamiento teologico de Edouard Hamel.* Excerpta ex dissertatione ad Doctoratum in Facultate Theologiae Pontificiae Universitatis Gregorianae. Roma, 1988.

Treats the use of Scripture in moral theology by Edouard Hamel, S.J., who was professor of moral theology at the Pontifical Gregorian University in Rome until 1986.

Carter, Charles W., and Thompson, R. Duane. *The Biblical Ethic of Love.* American University Studies: Series 7, Theology and Religion, 79. Frankfurt-am-Main, Bern, New York, Paris: Peter Lang, 1990.

The authors explore "the relevance of divine love, as revealed in the Judeo-Christian Scripture, to the ethical decisions and moral conduct of mankind." Topic treated include: the inadequacy of humanistic ethics, the Ten Commandments, ethics of the Old Testament Prophets and Wisdom literature, ethics of the New Testament. Attention is also given to the ethics of John Wesley, and Christian ethics in relation to the state, military defense, public education, the family, and other trends in contemporary Christian ethics.

Carter is scholar-in-residence, and Thompson is professor of philosophy and religion at Indiana Wesleyan University.

Clark, Michael, O.M.I. *The Use of Sacred Scripture in the Moral Theology of Father Bernard Häring, C.Ss.R.* Excerpta ex dissertatione ad Doctoratum in Facultate Theologiae Pontificiae Universitatis Gregorianae. Roma, 1979.

> Much of this material can also be found in Clark's "The Major Scriptural Themes in the Moral Theology of Father Bernhard Häring." (Two parts). *Studia Moralia* 30 (1992): 3-16; 277-288. This two-part article which traces the overall vision and development of Häring's use of Scripture in his writings in moral theology. Häring (born 1912) is a major Roman Catholic moral theologian who sought to incorporate Scripture into his approach to moral theology, and who taught moral theology for a number of years at the Academia Alphonsianum in Rome.

> Clark is a professor of Scripture at the Oblate College of Mary Immaculate in Washington, D.C.

Collins, Raymond F. *Christian Morality: Biblical Foundations.* Notre Dame: University of Notre Dame Press, 1986.

> Collins taught New Testament for many years at Louvain in Belgium, and is now at Catholic University in Washington, D.C.

Cranfield, C.E.B. *The Bible and Christian Life.* Edinburgh: T. & T. Clark, 1985.

Curran, Charles E. and McCormick, Richard A., S.J., eds. *Readings in Moral Theology No. 4: The Use of Scripture in Moral Theology.* New York: Paulist Press, 1984.

> Contains a good cross-section of representative theologians, both Protestant and Roman Catholic, on the use of Scripture in Christian ethics. Each individual article is listed separately in this bibliography.

Daly, Robert J., S.J., ed. *Christian Biblical Ethics: From Biblical Revelation to Contemporary Christian Praxis: Method and Content.* New York: Paulist Press, 1984.

Contributions by Robert Daly, James A. Fischer, Terence J. Keegan, Anthony J. Tambasco, L. John Topel, and Frederick E. Schuele. Done in consultation with the Catholic Biblical Association Task Force.

Dewar, Lindsay. *An Outline of New Testament Ethics.* Philadelphia: The Westminster Press, 1949.

Duchrow, Ulrich, and Liedke, Gerhard. *Shalom: Biblical Perspectives on Creation, Justice and Peace.* Geneva: WCC Publications, 1989.

In German: *Schalom: Der Schöpfung Befreiung, den Menschen Gerechtigkeit, den Völkern Frieden.* Stuttgart: Kreuz Verlag, 1987.

Written in part for the 1990 Seoul World Council of Churches (WCC) Conference on Justice, Peace, and the Integrity of Creation.

Reviewed by Newton B. Fowler, Jr. in *Mid-Stream* 29 (1990): 442-444.

Eenigenburg, Elton M. *Biblical Foundations and a Method for Doing Christian Ethics.* Edited by Susan E. Eenigenburg. Lanham: University Press of America, 1993.

Eenigenburg was Professor Christian Ethics and Philosophy of Religion at Western Theological Seminary.

Everding, H. Edward, and Willbanks, Dana W. *Decision-Making and the Bible.* Valley Forge: Judson Press, 1975.

Fabris, Rinaldo. *La virtù del coraggio. La «franchezza» nella Bibbia.* Martyria, 1. Casale Monferrato: Piemme, 1985.

Farley, Benjamin W. *In Praise of Virtue: An Exploration of the Biblical Virtues in a Christian Context.* Grand Rapids, MI: Wm. B. Eerdmans Publishing Company, 1995.

Farley examines both the Old and the New Testament and applies their teachings on moral character to the Christian life today. In the process, Farley

Brings Scripture to bear on ethical decision making.

Forlines, F. Leroy. *Biblical Ethics: Ethics for Happier Living.* Nashville: Randall
House, 1973.

Designed as a basic textbook for either college or church courses.

Fowl, Stephen E., and Jones, L. Gregory. *Reading in Communion: Scripture and
Ethics in Christian Life.* Grand Rapids: William B. Eerdmans, 1991.

The authors, an Anglican and a United Methodist, maintain that recent writing
on the relevance of the Bible to contemporary ethical issues has placed too
much emphasis on an agenda set by professional exegetes and ethicians.
According to the authors, it is the vocation of all Christians to *embody*
Scripture in their lives, and therefore believers need to develop the moral and
theological judgment that will enable them to discern faithfully Scripture's
claims on contemporary life. Fowl and Jones develop their argument in
relation to the friendships and practices of Christian communities, analyzing
"interpretive disputes" among Christians, and also by stressing the importance
of listening to the voices of outsiders. A final chapter considers Dietrich
Bonhoeffer as a model "performer" of Scripture.

Reviewed by James T. Bretzke, S.J. in *Gregorianum* 74 (1993): 375-376; and
by William C. Spohn in *Theological Studies* 53 (1992): 597.

Both authors taught theology at the time at Loyola College, Baltimore.

Furger, Franz, Hrsg. *Biblische Ethik: Fragen und Antworten.* Freiburg Schweiz:
Kanisius Verlag, 1974.

Short booklet, with contributions from Furger, Fredrich Beutter, Eugen
Ruckstuhl and Hermann-Josef Venetz. Topics include: Freiheit, Gebote,
Verschiedene Wertung biblischer Forderungen, Fordert Jesus die Revolution?,
Sklaven, Arme, Ehelosigkeit, Unkeuschheit, Ehebruch, and Onanie.

Gallagher, John, C.S.B. *The Basis for Christian Ethics.* New York: Paulist Press,
1985.

Short booklet, with contributions from Furger, Fredrich Beutter, Eugen Ruckstuhl and Hermann-Josef Venetz. Topics include: Frieheit, Gebote, Verschiedene Wertung biblischer Forderungen, Fordert Jesus die Revolution?, Sklaven, Arme, Ehelosigkeit, Unkeuschheit, Ehebruch, and Onanie.

Gallagher, John, C.S.B. *The Basis for Christian Ethics.* New York: Paulist Press, 1985.

See especially Part II, "The Criteria for Moral Judgment: Sacred Scripture," Chapters 8-13, pp. 65-125. Chapters 8 and 9 discuss the Old Testament, Chapters 10-12 the New Testament, and Chapter 13 is on the relation of Scriptural ethics to non-scriptural ethics.

Gardner, E. Clinton. *Biblical Faith and Social Ethics.* New York: Harper & Row, 1960.

de Gennaro, G., A cura di. *L'antropologia bilbica.* Napoli, 1982.

Gerhardsson, Birger. *The Ethos of the Bible.* Translated by Stephen Westerholm. Philadelphia: Fortress Press; London: Darton, Longman & Todd, 1981.

Grelot, Pierre. *Problèmes de morale fondamentale. Un éclairage biblique.* Recherches Morale, 6. Paris: Editions du Cerf, 1982.

Hagen, Kenneth, Daniel J. Harrington, S.J., Grant Osborne, Joseph A. Burgress. *The Bible in the Churches: How Different Christians Interpret the Scriptures.*

Biblical scholars from the Lutheran, Roman Catholic, and Evangelical Churches discuss how Scripture is viewed in their respective traditions.

Hanson, Paul D. *The People Called: The Growth of Community in the Bible.* Philadelphia: Fortress Press, 1986.

See especially Chapter 15, "The Biblical Notion of Community: Contemporary Implications," 467-518; and the Appendix, "Underlying Presuppositions and Method," 5-19-546.

Reviewed by Walter Harrelson in *Journal of the American Academy of Religion* 58 (1990): 283-285.

Hanson is Bussey Professor of Divinity and of Old Testament at Harvard University.

Harrison, R.K., ed. *Encyclopedia of Biblical and Christian Ethics.* Nashville: Thomas Nelson Publishers, 1987.

Hauerwas, Stanley. *Unleashing the Scripture: Freeing the Bible from Captivity to America.* Nashville : Abingdon Press, 1993.

Includes twelve sermons preached by Hauerwas on various topics.

Hauerwas (born 1940) is a Methodist who currently is Gilbert T. Rowe Professor of ethics at the Divinity School of Duke University in North Carolina. He studied under James M. Gustafson and for over a dozen years was on the faculty of the University of Notre Dame.

Hoffman, R. Joseph, and Larue, Gerald A., eds. *Biblical and Secular Ethics: The Conflict.* Buffalo: Prometheus Press, 1988.

Contributions which came out of a meeting of social philosophers, biblical scholars, and ethicians which met at the University of Richmond in the autumn of 1986 under the sponsorship of the Committee for the Scientific Examination of Religion (CSER) and its Biblical Criticism Research Project.

Hynson, Leon O., and Scott, Lane A., eds. *Christian Ethics: An Inquiry into Christian Ethics from a Biblical Theological Perspective.* Wesleyan Theological Perspectives, 3. Anderson IN: Warner Press, 1983.

This book is divided into two parts: Part I contains essays on Old and New Testament Ethics, as well as a consideration of John Wesley's Ethics and a discussion of Christian perfection as love for God; Part II addresses contemporary issues, such as abortion, homosexuality, economy, etc., though not necessarily from a strictly biblical ethical point of view.

Contents: "Introduction," L. Hynson and L. Scott; "The Ethics of the Old Testament, V. Hamilton; "New Testament Ethics," R. Wall; "Counterforce:

A Review of Wesley's Ethics," J. Mercer; "Christian Perfection as Love for God," W. Johnson; "Abortion," H. Kuhn; "Homosexuality," W. Sailer; "Divorce and the Remarriage of Divorced Persons," L. Scott; "The Economy of God and the Ecology of the Church," H. Snyder; "The Church: Tomorrow's People for Today's World," B. Callen; "The Ordered State and Christian Responsibility; L. Hynson; "A Christian View of the Arts," R. Thompson.

Jordan, Ben. "The Use of Scripture in the Ethics of H. Richard Niebuhr." Ph.D. Dissertation. Atlanta: Emory University, 1974.

Kaye, B.N., and Wenham, G.J. *Law, Morality and the Bible.* Downers Grove IL: Intervaristy Press, 1978.

Keeling, Michael. *The Foundations of Christian Ethics.* Edinburgh: T. & T. Clark, 1990.

Concentrating on three themes: sexuality, property, and political power, Keeling examines the foundations of Christian ethics in the Bible and their embodiment in the Church. Follows a chronological structure and considers the influence of liberation theology on perceptions of social justice.

Kimpel, Benjamin Franklin. *Moral Principles in the Bible: A Study of the Contribution of the Bible to Moral Philosophy.* New York: Philosophical Library, 1956.

Kotva, Joseph J., Jr. *The Christian Case for Virtue Ethics.* Moral Traditions and Moral Arguments Series. Washington, D.C.: Georgetown University Press, 1996.

See especially Ch. 5 "Biblical Connections" (which discusses Paul and the Gospel of Matthew) and Ch. 6 "Theological and Biblical Objections" for a discussion of how the Bible can figure in the development of a Christian approach to virtue ethics.

Revised version of Kotva's doctoral dissertation done at Fordham University.

Kotva is pastor of the First Mennonite Church in Allentown, Pennsylvania.

48

Originally presented as lectures at the Ecumenical Institute IV at the WCC conference center at Château de Bossey, Switzerland.

Lambrecht, Jan, S.J. *Eh bien! Moi Je vous dis.* Lectio Divina, 125. Paris: Editions de Cerf, 1986.

Lambrecht is a New Testament exegete.

La Rondelle, H.K. *Perfection and Perfectionism: A Dogmatic-Ethical Study of Biblical Perfection and Phenomenal Perfectionism.* Andrews Monographs, Studies in Religion, 3. Berrien Springs MI: Andrew University Press, 1984.

Lohfink, Norbert. *Il sapore della speranza. Nella Bibbia e nella teologia.* Casale Monferrato: Piemme, 1989.

Tradotto dal tedesco.

Translated from the German.

Lohfink is professor of Old Testament Exegesis at Sankt Georgen in Frankfurt-am-Main.

Long, Edward LeRoy, Jr. *To Liberate and Redeem: Moral Reflections on the Biblical Narrative.* Foreword by J. Philip Wogaman. Cleveland: Pilgrim Press, 1997.

Takes a contrasting approach to that of Stanley Hauerwas, Long discusses how contemporary moral decisions can be enlightened by considering the biblical stories of persons and groups who confronted similar concerns.

Maston, T.B. (Thomas Buford). *Biblical Ethics: A Survey.* Cleveland: World Publishing Co., 1967.

McKenzie, John L. *Source: What the Bible Says About the Problems of Contemporary Life.* Chicago: Thomas More Press, 1981.

Reviewed by Paul S. Berg in *Theology Today* 42 (1986): 268.

Maston, T.B. (Thomas Buford). *Biblical Ethics: A Survey.* Cleveland: World Publishing Co., 1967.

McKenzie, John L. *Source: What the Bible Says About the Problems of Contemporary Life.* Chicago: Thomas More Press, 1981.

Reviewed by Paul S. Berg in *Theology Today* 42 (1986): 268.

McDonald, James I.H. (James Ian Hamilton). *Biblical Interpretation and Christian Ethics.* New Studies in Christian Ethics. New York: Cambridge University Press, 1993.

McKim, Donald K. *What Christians Believe About the Bible.* Nashville: Thomas Nelson Publishers, 1985.

Treats the theme of how Christians, Roman Catholic and Protestant, interpret the Bible both in its historical dimension, as well as contemporary approaches such as Story Theology, Liberation Theology, Process Theology, etc.

Mott, Stephen Charles. *Biblical Ethics and Social Change.* Oxford University Press, 1982.

Reviewed by Beverly J. Crute in *Theology Today* 39 (1983): 483.

Muilenburg, James. *The Way of Israel: Biblical Faith and Ethics.* New York: Harper, 1961.

Murray, John. *Principles of Conduct: Aspects of Biblical Ethics.* Grand Rapids: Eerdmans, 1957.

Niebuhr, H. Richard. *The Kingdom of God in America.* New York, Evanston, and London: Harper and Row, 1937.

H[elmut] Richard Niebuhr lived from 1894-1962 and was professor of Christian ethics at Yale University.

Oden, Thomas C. *John Wesley's Scriptural Christianity: A Plain Exposition of His Teaching on Christian Doctrine.* Grand Rapids: Zondervan Publishing House, 1994.

Ogletree, Thomas. *The Use of the Bible in Christian Ethics: A Constructive Essay.* Philadelphia: Fortress Press, 1983. Oxford: Basil Blackwell, 1984.

Reviewed by Gary Comstock in *Journal of Religion* 66 (1986): 213-214.

Ogletree was at the time Professor of Theological Ethics at Drew University in Madison, New Jersey.

Patte, Daniel. *Ethics of Biblical Interpretation: a Reevaluation.* Nashville TN: Cokesbury; Louisville, KY: Westminster John Knox Press, 1995.

This highly confessional book chronicles the process by which the author became conscious of the fallacy of detached, disinterested exegesis and plunged into the world of multidimensional readings of biblical texts.

Pausch, Alfons, und Pausch, Jutta. *Steuern in der Bibel.* Köln: Dr. Otto Schmidt Verlag, 1986.

Rogerson, John W., et. al., eds. *The Bible in Ethics: The Second Sheffield Colloquium.* JSOT Supplement Series, 207. Sheffield Academic Press, 1995.

Salm, C. Luke, ed. *Readings in Biblical Morality.* Englewood Cliffs: Prentice Hall, 1967.

Schneiders, Sandra M., I.H.M. *The Revelatory Text: Interpreting the New Testament as Sacred Scripture.* San Francisco: HarperSanFrancisco, 1991.

Excellent work on biblical interpretation and hermeneutical theory, particular that of Hans Georg Gadamer and Paul Ricoeur. While not explicitly dealing with the interplay between Scripture and ethics, the book is nevertheless quite useful in approaching methodological issues of the exegesis and interpretation of biblical texts and their subsequent application to ethical issues.

Excellent work on biblical interpretation and hermeneutical theory, particular that of Hans Georg Gadamer and Paul Ricoeur. While not explicitly dealing with the interplay between Scripture and ethics, the book is nevertheless quite useful in approaching methodological issues of the exegesis and interepretation of biblical texts and their subsequent application to ethical issues.

Schneiders is professor of New Testament and Spirituality at the Jesuit School of Theology in Berkeley, California.

Shin, In Hyun. "A Biblical Study of Specific Texts from the Perspective of Moral Education for Young Adults in the Presbyterian Church of Korea." Thesis (D. Min.)--San Francisco Theological Seminary, 1987.

Siker, Jeffrey S. *Scripture and Ethics: Twentieth-Century Portraits*. New York: Oxford University Press, 1997.

Analyzes eight twentieth-century Protestant and Catholic theologians' use of Scripture in their respective works: Reinhold Niebuhr, H. Richard Niebuhr, Bernhard Häring, Paul Ramsey, Stanley Hauerwas, Gustavo Gutiérrez, James Cone, and Rosemary Radford Ruether. Siker addresses five questions to each author's work: 1) which biblical texts are used; 2) how are the texts used; 3) how does the author envision biblical authority; 4) what kind of hermeneutics are employed; and 5) what does the respective author's approach to the Bible yield in terms of Christian ethics. A concluding chapter focuses on the authors' respective appropriations of the Sermon on the Mount.

Siker is an ordained Presbyterian minister and Associate Professor of Theology at Loyola Marymount University in Los Angeles.

Sire, James W. *Scripture Twisting*. Downers Grove, IL: InterVarsity Press, 1980.

Describes 20 different ways that cults misread the Bible.

Sleeper, C. Freeman. *The Bible and the Moral Life*. Louisville: Westminster/John Knox Press, 1992.

Looks at how various churches use the Bible to address contemporary ethical issues, particularly nuclear war and abortion, and also considers the issue of biblical authority in terms of four major styles of moral reflection, i.e., law, prophecy, apocalypse, and wisdom. The book is designed for adult study groups and contains practical exercises.

Sleeper is Professor of Religion at Roanoke College in Salem, Virginia.

Smith, Adrian B. *Applying Scripture to Life*. Eldoret, Kenya: Gaba Publications, 1978.

Spicq, Ceslas, O.P. *Connaissance et Morale dans la Bible*. Etudes d'Ethique Chrétienne, 13. Fribourg: Editions Universitaires Fribourg Suisse; Paris: Editions du Cerf, 1985.

Spohn, William C. *What Are They Saying About Scripture and Ethics?*. Rev. ed., New York: Paulist Press, 1984, 1995.

Discusses five principal models or ways in which Scripture is and has been used in Christian ethics and/or moral theology, with illustrations from well-known Protestant and Roman Catholic theologians, including Divine Command (Karl Barth and Dietrich Bonhoeffer) Moral Reminder (Josef Fuchs, S.J. and Bruno Schüller, S.J.), Liberation (e.g., Gustavo Gutiérrez), Response to Revelation (H. Richard Niebuhr), Call to Discipleship (e.g., Stanley Hauerwas), and Spohn's model of Responding Love (based partially on Spohn's work on Jonathan Edwards' notion of religious affections). The original 1984 edition contains a discussion of Rudolf Bultmann, Sallie McFague, Letty Russell, Phyllis Trible and John Howard Yoder; treatment of these authors has been largely dropped from the revised edition. Very good introduction to the field.

Spohn studied under James Gustafson at the University of Chicago, taught moral theology at the Jesuit School of Theology-Berkeley for many years, and currently teaches Christian ethics at the University of Santa Clara.

Stöhr, Martin, Hrsg. *Zur biblischen Begründung sozial-ethischen Handelns*. Arnoldshainer Texte, 37. Frankfurt-am-Main: Haag + Herchen Verlag, 1985.

Stuhlmacher, Peter. *Reconciliation, Law and Righteousness: Essays on Biblical Theology*. Philadelphia: Fortress Press, 1986.

Translated from the German.

de Surgy, Paul, ed., *Ecriture et pratique chrétienne*, Congrès de l'ACFEB (Association Catholique Française pour l'Etude de la Bible), Angers 1977. Lectio Divina 96. Paris: Editions du Cerf, 1978.

Avec la participation [with contributions from] de P. de Surgy, B. Renaud, P. Arribard, Ch. Perrot, A. Juabert, A. Dumas, R. Simon, L. Panier, F. Dumortier, P. Valadier, et F. Refoulé.

Targonski, F. *Morale biblica e teologia morale*. Roma, 1982.

Thorsen, Donald A. D. *The Wesleyan Quadrilateral: Scripture, Tradition, Reason, and Experience as a Model of Evangelical Theology*. Grand Rapids: Zondervan, 1990.

Tübinger Theologischen Fachschaftsinitiativen, Hrsg. *Bibel und Befreiung. Beiträge zu einer nichtidealistischen Bibellektüre*. Münster: Edition Liberación; Freiburg, Schw.: Exodus, 1985.

Veijola, T., ed. *The Law in the Bible and in its Environment*. Helsinki: The Finnish Exegetical Society; Göttingen: Vandenhoeck & Ruprecht, 1990.

Vidal, Marciano; Lage, Francisco; y Ruiz-Mateos, Alfonso., edd. *Perspectivas de moral bíblica*. Estudios de Etica Teologica. Madrid: Instituto Superior de Ciencas Morales, PS Editorial, 1984.

Wallis, Jim. *Agenda for Biblical People*. New York: Harper & Row, 1976.

Wallis is a well-known evangelical pastor, justice activist, and founder of the progressive periodical, *Sojourners*.

Reviewed by Paul H. Sherry in *Theology Today* 34 (1978): 199.

_____. *The Call to Conversion*. San Francisco: Harper & Row, 1981.

Addresses two fundamental questions: What is the nature of authentic conversion? and How can we heed the biblical call to conversion today? Wallis presents a new social vision grounded in the gospel, and directions for action in justice issues.

White, R.E.O. *The Changing Continuity of Christian Ethics. Volume 1: Biblical Ethics.* Exeter: Paternoster Press, 1979.

Reviewed by Lewis B. Smedes in *Theology Today* 38 (1982): 400.

Volume 2, "The Insights of History" was published in 1981.

Wilder, Amos N. *Kerygma, Eschatology, and Social Ethics.* Facet Books: Social Ethics Series, no. 12. Philadelphia: Fortress Press, 1966.

Wright, Christopher J.H. *Human Rights: A Study in Biblical Themes.* Grove Booklet on Ethics, 31. Downers Grove Il: Grove Books, 1979.

_____. *Using the Bible in Social Ethics.* Grove Booklet on Ethics, 51. Downers Grove Il: Grove Books, 1983.

****

ETHICS IN THE HEBREW SCRIPTURES AND/OR JEWISH ETHICS

Articles on Ethics in the Hebrew Scriptures and/or Jewish Ethics

Ahituv, Shmuel. "Land and Justice." In *Justice and Righteousness: Biblical Themes and their Influence*, 11-28. Edited by Henning Graf Reventlow and Yair Hoffman. Sheffield: JSOT Press, 1992.

Allen, L.C. "Micah's Social Concern." *Vox Evangelica* 8 (1973): 22-32.

Alvarez, Barredo, M. "Culto y ética: su conexión en el Salmo 15." *Carthaginensia* 5 (1989): 3-17.

Amir, Yehoshua. "Measure for Measure in Talmudic Literature and in the Wisdom of Solomon." In *Justice and Righteousness: Biblical Themes and their Influence*, 29-46. Edited by Henning Graf Reventlow and Yair Hoffman. Sheffield: JSOT Press, 1992.

Amit, Yairah. "The Jubilee Law--An Attempt at Instituting Social Justice." In *Justice and Righteousness: Biblical Themes and their Influence*, 47-59. Edited by Henning Graf Reventlow and Yair Hoffman. Sheffield: JSOT Press, 1992.

Arnaldich, Luis. "Interpretación exegético-teológica del relato de la Torre de Babel (Gen 11, 1-9)." In *La Etica Bíblica*, 245-269. XXIX Semana Bíblica Española. Madrid: Consejo Superior de Investigaciones Científicas, 1971.

Auneau, Joseph. "De la justice d'Amos à la justice de Paul." *La Vie Spirituelle* 72 (1992): 307-322.

Bailey, Kenneth C. "The Decalogue as Morality and Ethics." *Theology Today* 20 (1964): 183-195.

56

Barton, John. "Approaches to Ethics in the Old Testament." In *Beginning Old Testament Study*, 113-130. Edited by John Rogerson. London: SPCK, and Philadelphia: Westminister, 1982.

_____. "The Basics of Ethics in the Hebrew Bible." *Semeia*, no. 66 (1995): 11-22.

One of several articles on Old Testament ethics in this issue.

_____. "Ethics in Isaiah of Jerusalem." *Journal of Theological Studies* 32 (1981): 1-18.

_____. "Natural Law and Poetic Justice in the Old Testament." *Journal of Theological Studies* 39 (1979): 1-14.

_____. "Understanding Old Testament Ethics." *Journal for the Study of the Old Testament* 9 (1978): 44-64.

Berkovits, Eliezer. "The Biblical Meaning of Justice." *Judaism* 18 (1969): 188-209.

Survey of various meanings of the term "justice" in Hebrew Scriptures.

Bianchi, Enzo. "The Status of Those without Dignity in the Old Testament." *Concilium* 130 (1979): 3-11.

One of a series of articles under the general theme, "The Dignity of the Despised of the Earth."

Biesinger, A. "Zur Relevanz des Dekalogs für die ethische Erziehung." *Theologische Quartelschrift* 164 (1984): 281-293.

Bird, Phyliss A. "'Male and Female He Created Them': Gen. 1:27b in the Context of the Priestly Account of Creation." *Harvard Theological Review* 74 (1981): 129-159.

Birch, Bruce C. "Moral Agency, Community, and the Character of God in the Hebrew Bible." *Semeia*, no. 66 (1995): 23-41.

One of several articles on Old Testament ethics in this issue.

Blank, Sheldon H. "The Hebrew Scriptures as a Source for Moral Guidance." In *Scripture in the Jewish and Christian Traditions: Authority, Interpretation, Relevance*, 168-182. Edited by Frederick E. Greenspahn. Nashville: Abingdon, 1982.

Bloom, A. "Human Rights in Israel's Thought." *Interpretation* 8 (1954): 422-432.

Bohlen, Reinhold. "Die Rutrolle--Ein aktuelles Beispiel narrativer Ethik im Alten Testament." *Trier Theologische Zeitschrift* 101 (1992): 1-19.

_____. "Zur Sozialkritik des Propheten Amos." *Trier Theologische Zeitschrift* 95 (1986): 282-301.

Botterweck, Gerhard J. "The Form and Growth of the Decalogue." *Concilium* 5 (1/1965): 33-44.

Bramlik, G. "Das Deuteronomium und die Menschenrechte." *Theologische Quartelschrift* 166 (1986): 8-24.

Briend, Jacques. "Honore ton père et ta mère." *Christus* 31 (122, 1984): 203-216.

Jesus' often paradoxical attitude toward this commandment reflected the conflict between the role of parents in transmitting God's word to their children, and Jesus' call to revelation and discipleship.

"Le paradoxe existe, mais il s'explique si on rapelle que le rôle des parents est, entre autres, de transmettre la parole de Dieu à leurs enfants. Or, face à la révélation qu'apporte Jésus comme envoyé du Père, les liens familiaux peuvent constituer des obstacles, car les parents peuvent s'opposer à ce que leurs enfants puissent devenir disciples de Jésus. Dès lors ils ne remplissent plus le rôle qui était le leur avec l'irruption de la Bonne Nouvelle de Jésus-Christ. En passant de l'ancienne à la nouvelle alliance les parents, compris comme ceux qui sont chargés de transmettre la parole de Dieu, sont confrontés eux-mêmes à celui qui est le Verbe fait chair; en fonction des choix qu'ils font des tensions peuvent naître au sein d'une même famille. La croix de Jésus est un signe de contradiction qui peut bouleverser les rapport entre parents et enfants tels qu'ils étaient définis dans le judaïsme." p. 215.

Brin, Gershon. "The Development of Some Laws in the Book of the Covenant." In *Justice and Righteousness: Biblical Themes and their Influence*, 60-70. Edited by Henning Graf Reventlow and Yair Hoffman. Sheffield: JSOT Press, 1992.

Burrows, Millar. "Old Testament Ethics and the Ethics of Jesus." In *Essays in Old Testament Ethics (J. Philip Hyatt, In Memoriam)*, 215-223. Edited by James L. Crenshaw and John T. Willis. New York: Ktav Publishing House, 1974.

Butler, Sr. M. Pierce, M.S.B.T. "Must We Teach Morality according to the Decalogue?" *Worship* 37 (1963): 293-300.

Cahill, Lisa Sowle. "'Male and Female': Sexual Differentiation in Genesis." Chapter 3 in Idem. *Between the Sexes: Foundations for a Christian Ethics of Sexuality*. New York: Paulist Press; and Philadelphia: Fortress Press, 1985.

Cahill is a Roman Catholic and did her doctoral studies at the University of Chicago under the direction of James M. Gustafson. She is Professor of Theological Ethics at Boston College, and past President of both the Catholic Theological Society of America (CTSA) and the Society of Christian Ethics (SCE).

Cañellas, G. "La preocupación social en el Antiguo Testamento." *Verdad y Vida* 48 (1990): 137-163.

Carny, Pin'has. "Theodicy in the Book of Quohelet." In *Justice and Righteousness: Biblical Themes and their Influence*, 71-81. Edited by Henning Graf Reventlow and Yair Hoffman. Sheffield: JSOT Press, 1992.

Casabó Suqué, J.M. "La justicia en el Antiguo Testamento." *Stromata* 25 (1969): 3-20.

Cavedo, Romeo. "Morale dell'Antico Testamento e del Giudaismo." In *Nuovo Dizionario di Teologia Morale*, 770-786. A cura di Francesco Compagnoni, Giannino Piana, e Salvatore Privitera. Cinisello Balsamo: Edizioni Paoline, 1990.

Chrostowski, Waldemar. "An examination of conscience by God's people as exemplified in Neh 9:6-37." *Biblische Zeitschrift* 34 (1990): 253-261.

Collins, Raymond F. "Obedience, Children and the Fourth Commandment--A New Testament Perspective." *Louvain Studies* 4 (1972): 157-173.

Collins taught New Testament for many years at Louvain in Belgium, and is now at Catholic University in Washington, D.C.

_____. "The Ten Commandments." Part Two, chs. 2-4, in *Christian Morality: Biblical Foundations*, 49-97. Notre Dame: University of Notre Dame Press, 1986.

Chapter 2: "The Ten Commandments in Current Perspective," pp. 49-63. Chapter 3: The Ten Commandments and the Christian Response, pp. 64-81. Chapter 4: The Fourth Commandment--For Children or for Adults?," pp. 82-97.

Cooper, Howard. "Sin in Biblical and Rabbinical Thought." *The Month* 254 (September/October 1993): 348-354.

One of a series of articles on various theological aspects of sin. Cooper looks at the various ways "sin" is presented in the Hebrew Scriptures and rabbinic interpretation.

Cooper is a rabbi and psychotherapist.

Craghan, John F. "Sin, Cleansing and Restoration." *The Bible Today* 31 (1993): 68-72.

Focuses on Psalm 51, and is one of several articles in this issue on the theme of "The Bible on Sin."

Crüsemann, Frank. "Dominion, Guilt, and Reconciliation: The Contribution of the Jacob Narrative in Genesis to Political Ethics." *Semeia*, no. 66 (1995): 67-77.

One of several articles on Old Testament ethics in this issue.

David, Robert. "Prolégomènes à l'étude écologique des récits de Gn 1-11." *Eglise et théologie* 22 (1991): 275-292.

Davidson, R. "Some Aspects of the Old Testament Contribution to the Pattern of Christian Ethics." *Scottish Journal of Theology* 12 (1959): 373-387.

Davies, Eryl W. "Ethics of the Hebrew Bible: The Problem of Methodology." *Semeia*, no. 66 (1995): 43-53.

Outlines some of the methodological problems of the study of Old Testament ethics when the focus is limited to the functions of Israelite law, since ethical values, conduct, and obligations frequently go beyond what is legally prescribed or proscribed. Also considers how a "natural law" type of ethics might be operative in both ancient Israel and some of the biblical texts of the Old Testament.

One of several articles on Old Testament ethics in this issue.

Delhaye, Philippe. "Le recours à l'Ancien Testament dans l'étude de la théologie morale." *Ephemerides Theologicae Lovanienses* 31 (1955): 637-657.

Dempsey, Carol J., O.P. "Economic Injustice in Micah." *The Bible Today* 32 (1994): 272-276.

One of several articles on biblical economic justice in this issue.

Devasahayam, Jebaraj. "Understanding Violence: Learning from the Old Testament." *ATA Journal* 2 (1994): 5-15.

Dillmann, Rainer. "Aufbruch zu einer neuen Sittlichkeit: Biblisch-narrative Begründung ethischen Handelns." *Theologie und Glaube* 82 (1992): 34-35.

Considers Mk 7: 31-35; Lk 13:10-17, and 1 Kings 21:17-19.

Dion, Paul E. "Changements sociaux et législatifs dans le Deutéronome." *Eglise et théologie* 24 (1993): 343-360.

Dohmen, Christoph. "Origins and goals of biblical ethics as illustrated by the first commandment of the Decalogue." *Communio* 29 (1992): 36-57.

German original: "Um unsere Freiheit willen. Ursprung und Ziel biblischer Ethik im «Hauptgebot» des Dekalogs." *Communio* 21 (1992): 7-24

Italian translation: "Per amore della nostra libertà. Origine e fine dell'etica biblica nel `comandamento principale' del decalogo." *Communio* 121 (1992): 27-46.

Spanish translation: "Para neustra libertad. Origen y objeto de la ética bíblica en el primer mandamento del Decálogo." *Communio* 14 (1992): 137-153.

Portuguese translation: "Por amor da nossa liberdade. E'tica bíblica e «primeiro mandamento» do Decálogo." *Communio* 9 (1992): 136-152.

Detailed exegetical consideration of the two versions of the Decalogue contained in the Old Testament, considering also their historical context, linguistic formulations, etc. Dohmen stresses the unity of composition of the whole Decalogue as the key for its authentic ethical interpretation: "It follows that the individual commandments of the Decalogue have their meaning only within this unity, a unity that is rooted in God's act of deliverance as described in the prologue. This unity is underscored by the broadly formulated principal commandment, which stipulates that our `image of God' determines our `image of man' to the extent that our relationship with God becomes a mirror of our interhuman relationships. Consequently, every ethical precept derived from the Bible, especially from the Decalogue, needs to orient itself toward the unity and completeness of the Decalogue. Thus, no social commandments may claim their authority from the Decalogue if they stand isolated from the context of its principal commandment and its prologue; neither can there be a `theology of the Decalogue' without a consideration of the social commandments." p. 56.

Dohmen is professor of Old Testament exegesis at the University of Osnabrück, Germany.

Dreyfus, François. "La valeur existentielle de l'Ancien Testament." *Concilium* 30 (1967): 35-43.

Dreyfus teaches at the Ecole Biblique et Archeologie Française in Jerusalem.

Eichrodt, Walter [Walther]. "The Law and the Gospel: The Meaning of the Ten Commandments in Israel and for Us." *Interpretation* 11 (1957): 23-40.

Elliott, Mark W. "Ethics and Aesthetics in the Song of Songs." *Tyndale Bulletin* 45 (1994): 137-152.

Escobar, Donoso S. "Social Justice in the Book of Amos," *Review and Expositor* 92 (1995): 169-174.

Falk, Ze'ev W. "Law and Ethics in the Hebrew Bible." In *Justice and Righteousness: Biblical Themes and their Influence*, 82-90. Edited by Henning Graf Reventlow and Yair Hoffman. Sheffield: JSOT Press, 1992.

Fensham, F.C. "Widow, Orphan and the Poor in Ancient Near Eastern Legal and Wisdom Literature." *Journal of Near Eastern Studies* 21 (1962): 129-139.

Fiedler, Peter. "La Tora in Gesù e nella tradizione di Gesù." In *Saggi esegetici sulla legge nel Nuovo Testamento*, 65-81. A cura di Karl Kertelge. Cinisello Balsamo: Edizioni Paoline, 1990.

Original version in *Das Gesetz im Neuen Testament*. Herausgegeben von Karl Kertelge. Questiones Disputatae, 108. Freiburg: Herder, 1986.

Fingarette, Herbert. "The Meaning of Law in the Book of Job." In *Revisions: Changing Perspectives in Moral Philosophy*, 249-286. Edited by Stanley M. Hauerwas and Alasdair MacIntyre. Notre Dame: University of Notre Dame Press, 1983.

Originally appeared in the *Hastings Law Journal* 29 (1978): 1581-1617.

Fletcher, V. "The Shape of Old Testament Ethics." *Scottish Journal of Theology* 24 (1959): 47-73.

Fohrer, Georg. "The Righteous Man in Job 31." In *Essays in Old Testament Ethics (J. Philip Hyatt, In Memoriam)*, 23-55. Edited by James L. Crenshaw and John T. Willis. New York: Ktav Publishing House, 1974.

Frey, Christofer. "The Impact of the Biblical Idea of Justice on Present Discussions of Social Justice." In *Justice and Righteousness: Biblical Themes and their Influence*, 91-104. Edited by Henning Graf Reventlow and Yair Hoffman. Sheffield: JSOT Press, 1992.

Fuller, Reginald H. "The Decalogue in the New Testament." *Interpretation* 43 (1989): 243-255.

Gallego, Epifanio, O.S.A. "La sexualidad. Aporte de los relatos de la creación." *Biblia y Fe* 18 (1992): 21-36.

One of several articles under this number's general theme of "La Sexualidad: *Aproximacion Biblica.*"

Gamoran, H. "The Biblical Law against Loans on Interest." *Journal of Near Eastern Studies* 30 (1971): 127-134.

Garcia de la Fuente, Olegario. "El cumplimiento de la ley en la nueva alianza según los profetas." In *La Etica Bíblica*, 145-165. XXIX Semana Bíblica Española. Madrid: Consejo Superior de Investigaciones Científicas, 1971.

García Trapiello, Jesús. "El `Prólogo histórico' como fundamento de las `Estipulaciones' en la Alianza del Sinaí." In *La Etica Bíblica*, 57-73. XXIX Semana Bíblica Española. Madrid: Consejo Superior de Investigaciones Científicas, 1971.

_____. "El rey de Israel, valedor de la justicia social." *Salmanticensis* 28 (1981): 171-192.

Gehman, H.S. "Natural Law and the Old Testament." In *Biblical Studies in Memory of H.C. Alleman*, 109-122. Edited by J.M. Myers, et. al. New York: Augustin, 1960.

Gelin, Albert, and Descamps, Albert. *Sin in the Bible. Old Testament* by Albert Gelin; *New Testament* by Albert Descamps. Translated by Charles Schaldenbrand. New York: Desclée, 1965.

Originally appeared in French as part of *Theologie du péché*.

Gemser, B. "The Importance of the Motive Clause in Old Testament Law." *Supplements to Vetus Testamentum* 1 (1953): 50-66.

George, P.G. "Ecological Agenda in the Book of Psalms." *Bible Bhashyam* 19 (1993): 169-175.

Gilbert, Maurice, S.J. "La procréation: ce qu'en sait le Livre de la Sagesse." *Nouvelle Revue Théologique* (1989): 824-841.

Biblical texts examined from the Book of Wisdom consider the human embryo as a person, especially in view of the relation with God, seen as a vivifying spirit, who gives life to the embryo.

Gilbert is on the faculty and former rector of the Pontifical Biblical Institute in Rome.

_____. "'Une seule chair' (Gn 2,24)." *Nouvelle revue théologique* 100 (1978): 66-89.

Gillingham, Sue. "The Poor in the Psalms." *Expository Times* 100 (1989): 15-19.

González Lamadrid, Antonio. "La Ley el marco de la alianza." In *La Etica Bíblica*, 5-21. XXIX Semana Bíblica Española. Madrid: Consejo Superior de Investigaciones Científicas, 1971.

González Nuñez, Angel. "El consejo del sabio. Una moral de indole humanista." *Moralia* 6 (1984): 103-128.

Tambien [also found in] en *Perspectivas de moral bíblica,* 103-128. Estudios de Etica Teologica. Edd. Marciano Vidal, Francisco Lage y Alfosno Ruiz-Mateos. Madrid: Instituto Superior de Ciencas Morales, PS Editorial, 1984.

_____. "Fundamentación y sentido de la ley en la historia yahvista elohísta." In *La Etica Bíblica,* 23-56. XXIX Semana Bíblica Española. Madrid: Consejo Superior de Investigaciones Científicas, 1971.

Gonzalo Maeso, David. "Proyección del Decálogo sobre todo el pentateuco." In *La Etica Bíblica,* 111-120. XXIX Semana Bíblica Española. Madrid: Consejo Superior de Investigaciones Científicas, 1971.

_____. "Puntualizaciones sobre Gn 2, 20-24: formación de la primera mujer y concepto del matrimonio." In *La Etica Bíblica,* 235-244. XXIX Semana Bíblica Española. Madrid: Consejo Superior de Investigaciones Científicas, 1971.

Gowan, Donald E. "Wealth and Poverty in the Old Testament: The Case of the Widow, the Orphan and the Sojourner." *Interpretation* 41 (1987): 341-353.

Granberg-Michaelson, Wesley. "Covenant and Creation." In *Liberating Life: Contemporary Approaches to Ecological Theology,* 27-36. Edited by Charles Birch, William Eakin and Jay B. McDaniel. Maryknoll: Orbis Press, 1990.

Green, Gene L. "The Use of the Old Testament for Christian Ethics in 1 Peter." *Tyndale Bulletin* 41 (1990): 276-289.

Greene, W. B. "The Ethics of the Old Testament." *Princeton Theological Review* 27 (1929): 153-193; 313-366.

Guillén Torralba, Juan. "Motivación deuteronómica del descanso sabático." In *La Etica Bíblica,* 121-144. XXIX Semana Bíblica Española. Madrid: Consejo Superior de Investigaciones Científicas, 1971.

Guillet, Jacques, S.J. "L'étranger dans la tradition biblique." *Christus* 150 (Avril, 1990): 171-180.

> L'accueil: une loi pour Israël.

> Hospitality is a law for Israel.

Guinan, Michael D., O.F.M. "Instruction for Life." *The Bible Today* 31 (1993): 260-264.

> General overview of moral themes in the Pentateuch.

> Guinan is professor of Old Testament at the Franciscan School of Theology in Berkeley, California.

Haas, Peter, J. "The Quest for Hebrew Bible Ethics: A Jewish Response." *Semeia*, no. 66 (1995): 151-59.

> One of several articles on Old Testament ethics in this issue.

Hamel, Edouard, S.J. "Le Magnificat et le Renversement des Situations: Réflexion théologico-biblique." *Gregorianum* 60 (1979): 55-84.

> Examines the theme of the "overview of situations" in the Old and New Testament, as well as Hellenistic literature, and then proceeds to a hermeneutical consideration of the Magnificat for the contemporary Church, concluding that the prayer should be interpreted as an incentive to the promotion of justice.

> Hamel was professor of moral theology at the Pontifical Gregorian University until 1986.

Hammershaimb, E. "On the Ethics of the Old Testament Prophets." *Supplements to Vetus Testamentum* 7 (1959): 75-101.

Hamilton, Victor P. "The Ethics of the Old Testament." In *Christian Ethics: An Inquiry into Christian Ethics from a Biblical Theological Perspective*, 9-30.

Edited by Leon O. Hynson and Lane A. Scott. Anderson IN: Warner Press, 1983.

Hamilton has a Ph.D from Brandeis University and is professor of religion at Ashbury College.

Harrelson, Walter J. "The Significance of `Last Words' for Intertestamental Ethics." In *Essays in Old Testament Ethics (J. Philip Hyatt, In Memoriam)*, 203-213. Edited by James L. Crenshaw and John T. Willis. New York: Ktav Publishing House, 1974.

Hengel, Martin. "Property and Riches in the Old Testament and Judaism." In Id. *Property and Riches in the Early Church: Aspects of a Social History of Early Christianity*, 12-22. Translated by John Bowden. London: SCM Press; Philadelphia: Fortress Press, 1974.

Shorter version also found in *On Moral Business: Classical and Contemporary Resources for Ethics in Economic Life*, 67-68. Edited by Max L. Stackhouse, et. al. Grand Rapids: Wm. B. Eerdmans Publishing Co., 1995.

Hoffman, Yair. "The Creativity of Theodicy." In *Justice and Righteousness: Biblical Themes and their Influence*, 117-130. Edited by Henning Graf Reventlow and Yair Hoffman. Sheffield: JSOT Press, 1992.

Hoppe, Leslie J., O.F.M. "The Torah Responds to the Poor." *The Bible Today* 32 (1994): 277-282.

One of several articles on biblical economic justice in this issue.

Horst, Friedrich. "Naturrecht und Altes Testament." *Evangelische Theologie* 10 (1950/51): 253-273.

Also found reprinted in *Gottes Recht: Gesammelte Studien zum Recht in Alten Testament*, 235-259. Herausgegeben von Hans Walter Wolff. München: Christian Kaiser Verlag, 1961.

Hübner, Hans. "Zur Ethik der Sapientia Salomonis." In *Studien zum Text und zur Ethik des Neuen Testaments. Festschrift zum 80. Geburtstag von Heinrich Greeven*, 166-187. Herausgegeben von Wolfgang Schrage. Berlin/New York: Walter de Gruyter, 1986.

Ibáñez, Arana A. "Los valores éticos en las narraciones del Génesis." *Lumen* 35 (1986): 361-396; 473-500.

Isser, Stanley. "Two Traditions: The Law of Exodus 21:22-23 Revisited." *Catholic Biblical Quarterly* 52 (1990): 30-45

Jacob, E. "Les bases théologique de l'éthique de l'Ancien Testament." *Supplements to Vetus Testamentum* 7 (1968).

Johnson, L. "Old Testament Morality." *Catholic Biblical Quarterly* 20 (1958): 19-25.

de Jonge, Marinus. "Die Paränese in den Schriften des Neuen Testaments und in den Testamenten der Zwölf Patriarchen. Einege Überlegungen." In *Neues Testament und Ethik. Für Rudolf Schnackenburg*, 538-550. Herausgegeben von Helmut Merklein. Freiburg: Herder, 1989.

Juárez, Miguel A. Martín, O.S.A. "La Sexualidad. Aporte de los escritos sapiensiales." *Biblia y Fe* 18 (1992): 51-66.

One of several articles under this number's general theme of "La Sexualidad: *Aproximacion Biblica.*"

Knight, Douglas A. "Introduction: Ethics, Ancient Israel, and the Hebrew Bible." *Semeia*, no. 66 (1995): 1-8.

One of several articles on Old Testament ethics in this issue.

_____. "Old Testament Ethics." *Christian Century* 20 January 1982, 55-59.

Most of the article focusses on a summary of the principal issues facing the use of Scripture in ethics. The Old Testament is used as a point of reference for Knight's discussion, and the fundamental values of the Old Testament ethos are presented.

Kovacs, Brian W. "Is There a Class-Ethic in Proverbs?" In *Essays in Old Testament Ethics (J. Philip Hyatt, In Memoriam)*, 171-189. Edited by James L. Crenshaw and John T. Willis. New York: Ktav Publishing House, 1974.

Krolzik, M. "«Dominium terrae». Storia di Genesi 1, 28." *Rivista di Teologia Morale* 22 (1990): 257-267.

Krüger, Thomas. "»Du sollst nicht töten!« »Ehrfurht vor dem Lelbe« in Ethik und Recht des Alten Testaments." *Zeitschrift für Evangelische Ethik* 38 (1994): 17-30.

Kurz, William S., S.J. "Genesis and Abortion: An Exegetical Test of a Biblical Warrant in Ethics." *Theological Studies* 47 (1986): 668-680.

Kurz is professor of New Testament at Marquette University in Milwaukee, Wisconsin.

Lage, Francisco. "La crítica del comercio en los profetas de Israel." *Moralia* 8 (1986): 3-28.

_____. "Ley y Alianza. Autonomía de la ética en el pensamiento del Antiguo Testamento." *Moralia* 6 (1984): 9-39.

Tambien en [also found in] *Perspectivas de moral bíblica*, 9-39. Estudios de Etica Teologica. Edd. Marciano Vidal, Francisco Lage y Alfosno Ruiz-Mateos. Madrid: Instituto Superior de Ciencas Morales, PS Editorial, 1984.

____. "Sobre la contribución de los apócrifos del AT a la ética cristiana." *Moralia* 6 (1984): 385-416.

Lamadrid, A.G. "Canaán y América. La biblia y la teología moral ante la conquista de la tierra. *Salmanticensis* 28 (1981): 392-346.

Lance, H. Darell. "The Bible and Homosexuality." *American Baptist Quarterly* 8 (1989): 140-151.

Reviews some of the major changes that have occurred in the understanding of some biblical texts traditionally used in reference to homosexuality, such as Gn 19; Jg 19; Lv 18-20; Dt 23:17-18; 1 Cor 6:9-11; Rm 1:26-27; and Jde 6-7. Raises hermeneutical questions which these texts present, and includes bibliography for further study.

Lang, B. "'Du sollst nicht der Frau eines anderen verlangen'. *Eine neue Deutung des 9. und 10. Gebots.*" *Zeitschrift für die Alttestamentliche Wissenschaft* 93 (1981): 216-224.

_____. "Neues über den Dekalog." *Theologische Quartelschrift* 164 (1984): 58-65.

Lapidus, Rina. "Halakah and Haggadah: Two Opposing Approaches to Fulfilling the Religious Law." *Journal of Jewish Studies* 44 (1993): 100-113.

The sequence of most talmudic discussion on religious law opens with a Mishnah which includes a religious law, followed by a halakhic discussion on the ways in which this law is to be put in practice, and a variety of interpretations and opinions of the Sages on this subject. Then the discussion crystallizes into the application of objective principles which are formal, logical and rational. Then a detailed haggadic story is introduced which shows a person fulfills the law. The story concludes with "justification" in form of a miracle, or admission by the Sages that this individual has furthers the preservation of the Jewish tradition.

LaVerdière, Eugene A. "Covenant Morality." *Worship* 38 (1964): 240-246.

Lavoie, Jean-Jacques. "Création de l'être humain et éthique sapientiale selon le livre des Proverbs." *Eglise et théologie* 24 (1993): 361-390.

Lehmann, Paul L. "The Commandments and the Common Life." *Interpretation* 34 (1980): 341-355.

Leider, H. "Die Zehn Gebote heute." *Theologische Quartelschrift* 160 (1980): 60-63.

Levin, C. "Der Dekalog am Sinai." *Vetus Testamentum* 35 (1985): 165-191.

Limburg, James. "Human Rights in the Old Testament." *Concilium* 124 (1979): 20-26.

One of a series of articles on various aspects of the theological meaning and significance of human rights.

Lindemann, Andreas. "Die biblischen Toragebote und die paulinische Ethik." In *Studien zum Text und zur Ethik des Neuen Testaments. Festschrift zum 80. Geburtstag von Heinrich Greeven*, 242-265. Herausgegeben von Wolfgang Schrage. Berlin/New York: Walter de Gruyter, 1986.

Lochman, Jan Milic. "Die Vorstellung des Namens Gottes im dekalog als Begründung einer Ethik der Freiheit." *Theologische Zeitschrift* 34 (1978): 257-264.

Lochman is a Czechoslovakian Protestant (Reformed) theologian. His work considers not only the Bible, but also the Protestant tradition as well as Marxism.

Lohfink, Norbert. "Altes Testament-Ethos." In *Weltgestaltung und Gewaltlosigkeit. Ethische Aspekte des Alten und Neuen Testaments in Einheit und Gegensatz.* Herausgegeben von Norbert Lohfink und Rudolf Pesch. Düsseldorf: Patmos Verlag, 1978.

Lohfink is professor of Old Testament Exegesis at Sankt Georgen in Frankfurt-am-Main.

_____. "'Holy War' and 'Ban' in the Bible." *Theology Digest* 38 (1991): 109-114.

72

Violence is the central human sin, and this creates a difficult theological problem in evaluating the Old Testaments concepts of the Holy War and the Ban (consecration to destruction). Lohfink argues that this "holy war" ethos might be understood as only an intermediate (i.e., not permanent) phase in Israel's life, and the God's People must ultimately renounce all forms of violence as Jesus offered God's Lordship without violence.

_____. "Poverty in the Laws of the Ancient Near East and of the Bible." *Theological Studies* 52 (1991): 34-50.

Lohfink finds that the law codes of ancient Mesopotamia and Israel evidence a better care for the poor than our modern societies.

Originally given as a paper at the 53rd General Meeting of the Catholic Biblical Association of America on 14 August 1990 at the University of Notre Dame.

Loss, N. "La dottrina antropologica di Genesi I-II." In de *L'antropologia bilbica*. A cura di G. de Gennar. Napoli, 1982.

Malchow, Bruce. "Social Justice in the Israelite Law Codes." *Word and Word* 4 (1984): 293-306.

Overview of this theme.

_____. "Social Justice in the Wisdom Literature." *Biblical Theological Bulletin* 12 (1982): 120-124.

Maraval, P. "Modèles bibliques de l'hospitalité chez les Pères." *Studia Moralia* 28 (1990): 27-41.

Mariani, Bonaventura. "Ritual Sin in the Old Testament." In *Sin: Its Reality and Nature: A Historical Survey*, 41-56. Edited by Pietro Palazzini. Translated by Brendan Devlin. Dublin: Scepter Publishers, 1964.

Martin-Achard, Robert. "Brèves remarques sur la signification théologique de la loi selon l' AT." *Etudes Théologiques et Religieuses* 57 (1982): 343-360.

_____. "Récents travaux sur la loi du talion, selon l'AT." *Revue d'Histoire et de Philosophie Religieuses* 69 (1989): 173-188.

Martin, Thomas. "Marriage in the Old Testament." Chapter 2 in *The Challenge of Christian Marriage: Marriage in Scripture, History and Contemporary Life*, 9-31. New York: Paulist Press, 1990.

Historical study which moves from Scripture through the early Church, the Church Fathers, and the medieval and reformation periods. Modern challenges to Christian marriage are addressed, as well as an attempt to spell out a contemporary theology of marriage. Designed as an undergraduate text, includes study questions and recommendations for further reading after each chapter. See also Chapter 3, "Marriage in the New Testament."

Martin is a professor in the Religious Studies Department of Dayton University.

Mathew, K.V. "Ecological Perspectives in the Book of Psalms." *Bible Bhashyam* 19 (1993): 159-168.

One of several articles in this issue on various theological aspects of ecology.

Mays, James L. "Justice: Perspectives from the Prophetic Tradition." In *Prophecy in Israel*, 144-158. Edited by David L. Petersen. Philadelphia: Fortress Press, 1987.

Originally appeared in *Interpretation* 37 (1983): 5-17.

McFayden, J.E. "Poverty in the Old Testament." *Expository Times* 37 (1925): 184-189.

McKeating, H. "Sanctions against Adultery in Ancient Israelite with some Reflections on Methodology in the Study of Old Testament Ethics." *Journal for the Study of the Old Testament* 11 (1979): 57-72.

74

McKenzie, John L. "The Values of the Old Testament." *Concilium* 10 (1967): 4-17.

Menzes, Ruiz de. "Social Justice in Israel's Law." *Bible Bhashyam* 11 (1985): 10-46.

Survey of social concerns in Israel's legal traditions.

Milgrom, Jacob. "The Biblical Diet Laws as an Ethical System: Food and Faith." *Interpretation* 17 (1963): 288-301.

Milgrom is Professor Emeritus of Bible at the University of California at Berkeley.

Miller, Patrick D., Jr. "The Place of the Decalogue in the Old Testament and Its Law." *Interpretation* 43 (1989): 2292-242.

Molinski, W. "Die Zehn Gebote. *Eine Grundlage für einen ethischen Konsens unter Glaubenden?*" *Stimmen der Zeit* 201 (1983): 53-60.

Mueller, G. "Der Dekalog im NT." *Theologische Zeitschrift* 38 (1982): 79-97.

Mullen, Alyce Miller. "A Study of the Relationship of Sin, Distress, and Health in the Old Testament Psalms: As a Basis for a Biblical Theology of Wholeness in Pastoral Ministry. Thesis (doctoral)--Wesley Theological Seminary, 1985.

Müller, Karlheinz. "Legge e adempimento della legge nel giudaismo antico." In *Saggi esegetici sulla legge nel Nuovo Testamento*, 9-23. A cura di Karl Kertelge. Cinisello Balsamo: Edizioni Paoline, 1990.

German original in *Das Gesetz im Neuen Testament.* Herausgegeben von Karl Kertelge. Questiones Disputatae, 108. Freiburg: Herder, 1986.

Mulroney, Joseph. "Wisdom to Live By." *The Bible Today* 31 (1993): 272-276.

Brief overview of the moral message of the Book of Proverbs.

Mulroney teaches biblical studies at Heythrop College.

Muñoz Iglesias, Salvador. "Old Testament Values superseded by the New." *Concilium* 10 (1967): 50-55.

Murphy, Roland E. "Prophets and Wise Men as Provokers of Dissent." *Concilium* 158 (1982): 61-66.

One of a series of articles on various aspects of this issue.

Mußner, Franz. "La vita secondo la Tora nell'interpretazione ebraica." In *Saggi esegetici sulla legge nel Nuovo Testamento*, 24-40. A cura di Karl Kertelge. Cinisello Balsamo: Edizioni Paoline, 1990.

German original in *Das Gesetz im Neuen Testament*. Herausgegeben von Karl Kertelge. Questiones Disputatae, 108. Freiburg: Herder, 1986.

Nash, Kathleen, S.S.N.D. "'Let Justice Surge'." *The Bible Today* 31 (1993): 265-271.

General overview of the Exodus theme and its moral implications in the Book of Amos.

Nash teaches Religious Studies at LeMoyne College.

Nickelsburg, George W. "Riches, the Rich, and God's Judgment in 1 Enoch 92-105 and the Gospel According to Luke." *New Testament Studies* 25 (1978-79): 324-344.

Nobuko, Morimura. "The Story of Tamar: A Feminist Interpretation of Genesis 38." *The Japan Christian Review* 59 (1993): 55-68.

One of several articles dealing with feminist issues in Japan.

North, Robert, S.J. "The Biblical Jubilee and Social Reform." *Scripture* 4 (1951): 3232-335.

North is Professor Emeritus at the Pontifical Biblical Institute in Rome.

Oates, Wayne E. "A Biblical Perspective on Addiction." *Review and Expositor* 91 (1994): 71-75.

Treats Dt 5:6-7; Mt 22:340-40; and Gal 4:3,8.

O'Connell, Matthew. "Some Aspects of Commandment in the Old Testament." In *Readings in Biblical Morality*, 9-29. Edited by C. Luke Salm. Englewood Cliffs: Prentice Hall, 1967.

Oeming, M. "Ethik in der Spätzeit des Alten Testaments am Beispiel von Hiob 31 und Tobit 4." In *Altes Testament--Forschung und Wirkung. Festschrift für Henning Graf Reventlow*, 159-174. Herausgegeben von P. Mommer und W. Thiel. Frankfurt-am-Main, Bern, New York: Peter Lang, 1994.

Otto, Eckart. "Kultus und Ethos in Jerusalemer Theologie. *Ein Beitrag zur theologischen Begründung der Ethik im Alten Testament.*" *Zeitschrift für die Alttestamentliche Wissenschaft* 98 (1986): 161-179.

_____. "Of Aims and Methods in Hebrew Bible Ethics." *Semeia*, no. 66 (1995): 161-72.

One of several articles on Old Testament ethics in this issue.

Paris, Peter J. "An Ethicist's Concerns about Biblical Ethics." *Semeia*, no. 66 (1995): 173-79.

One of several articles on Old Testament ethics in this issue.

Patterson, R. "The Widow, the Orphan and the Poor in the Old Testament and Extra-Biblical Literature." *Bibliotheca Sacra* 130 (1973): 223-235.

Penna, Angelo. "I diritti umani nel Vecchio Testamento." In *I Diritti Umani: Dottrina e Prassi*, 61-95. A cura di Gino Concetti. Roma: AVE, 1982.

Pfeifer, B. "Bücher um den Zehn Gebote." *Geist und Leben* 54 (1981): 395-397.

Pleins, J. David. "How Ought We Think about Poverty?--Rethinking the Diversity of the Hebrew Bible." *Irish Theological Quarterly* 60 (1994): 280-286.

____. "Poverty in the Social World of the Wise." *Journal for the Study of the Old Testament* 37 (1987): 61-78.

Porteous, N.W. "The Care of the Poor in the Old Testament." In *Living the Mystery*, 143-155. Blackwell, 1967.

Prato, Gian Luigi. "Un'etica teologica dell'Antico Testamento condannata a fallire?" *Rassegna di Teologia* 37 (1996): 63-78.

An extended review of Eckart Otto's *Theologische Ethik des Alten Testaments* (Stuttgart, Berlin, Köln: Kohlhammer, 1994), in which Prato presents a wide-ranging discussion of the problematic, as well as includes much helpful recent bibliography.

Ravasi, Gianfranco. "All'ombra dell'albero della conoscenza del bene e del male. Note ermeneutiche su Genesi 2-3." *Communio* 118 (luglio-agosto, 1991): 25-35.

One of a series of articles on various aspects of this theme.

_____. "«Tra di voi no vi sia nessun bisogno!». Solidarietà nel popolo di Dio dell'Antico Testamento." *Communio* 125 (settembre-ottobre 1992).

One of a series of articles on various aspects of the theme of solidarity.

Raurell, F. "El plaer erotic en el Càntic dels Càntics." *Revista Catalana de Teología* 6 (1981): 257-298.

Rebić, Adalbert."Righteousness in the Old Testament." *Theology Digest* 39 (1992): 139-142.

Digested version of   "Der Gerechtigkeitsbegriff im Alten Testament."
Communio 19 (1990): 390-396.

The Occidental Christian concepts of retributive and punitive justice are
inadequate for understanding the Hebrew concept of righteousness (*zedaqah*).
In the Hebrew Scriptures righteousness refers above all to God's relationship
with God's people. Several Old Testament texts, plus the opinion of many
biblical exegetes are marshalled to support the author's thesis.

Reventlow, Henning Graf. "Righteousness as Order of the World: Some Remarks
    towards a Programme." In *Justice and Righteousness: Biblical Themes and
    their Influence*, 163-172. Edited by Henning Graf Reventlow and Yair
    Hoffman. Sheffield: JSOT Press, 1992.

Robinson, N.H.G. "How the Bible Speaks to Conscience." In *Conscience:
    Theological and Psychological Perspectives*, 72-78. Edited by C. Ellis
    Nelson. New York: Newman Press, 1973.

Also found in Robinson's own book, *Christ and Conscience*, 171-178.
London: James Nisbet, 1956.

Robinson develops the thesis that conscience is the area where the individual
experiences the Spirit of God, and that the Bible is the means by which God
addresses the human person today. This address is not so much a narrative
as a confrontation with conscience which results in confession, repentance,
restitution and change. Uses the story of David and Nathan, plus makes some
remarks about Jesus' use of parables.

Rodd, C.S. "New Occasions Teach New Duties? 1. The Use of the Old Testament
    in Christian Ethics." *Expository Times* 105 (January 1994): 100-106.

Rodd is editor of *Expository Times*.

Ruiz, Gregorio. "La ética profética: frente a la pobreza desde la justicia." *Moralia*
    6 (1984): 79-101.

Tambien en [also found in] *Perspectivas de moral bíblica*, 79-101. Estudios
de Etica Teologica. Edd. Marciano Vidal, Francisco Lage y Alfosno Ruiz-
Mateos. Madrid: Instituto Superior de Ciencas Morales, PS Editorial, 1984.

Sabugal, S. "El concepto de pecado en el Antiguo Testamento." *Estudios Eclesiásticos* 59 (1984): 459-469.

Salguero, José, O.P. "El mandamiento capital y las leyes específicas." In *La Etica Bíblica*, 75-109. XXIX Semana Bíblica Española. Madrid: Consejo Superior de Investigaciones Científicas, 1971.

_____. "Relazione tra l'Antica e la Nuova Alleanza." *Angelicum* 60 (1983): 165-189.

Schenker, A. "Der Monotheismus im ersten Gebot, die Stellung der Frau im Sabbatgebot und zwei andere Sachfragen zum Dekalog." *Freiburger Zeitschrift für Philosophie und Theologie* 32 (1985): 323-341.

Schnackenburg, Rudolf. "Das Ethos des Alten Bundes und die sittliche Botschaft Jesu." In *Der Mensch und sein sittlicher Auftrag.* Hrsg. H. Althaus. Freiburg, 1983.

Schofield, J.N. "Righteousness in the Old Testament." *Bible Translator* 16 (1965): 112-116.

Scholz, F. "Um die Verbindlichkeit des Dekalogs. *Prinzipien oder Faustregeln.*" *Theologie der Gegenwart* 25 (1982): 316-327.

Schreiner, Josef. "Die bleibende Bedeutung der sittlichen Forderung des Alten Testaments." In *Herausforderung und Kritik der Moraltheologie*, ed. Georg Teichtweier and Wilhelm Dreier, 151-71. Würzburg: Echter Verlag, 1971.

Schulte, Hannelis. "The End of the Omride Dynasty: Social-Ethical Observations on the Subject of Power and Violence." *Semeia*, no. 66 (1995): 133-48.

One of several articles on Old Testament ethics in this issue.

Segal, B.Z., ed. *The Ten Commandments in History and Tradition*. Publications of the Perry Foundation for Biblical Research--The Hebrew University of Jerusalem. Jerusalem: The Magnes Press-- The Hebrew University of Jerusalem, 1990.

Seow, Choon-Leong. "A Heterosexual Perspective." In *Homosexuality and Christian Community*, 14-27. Edited by Choon-Leong Seow. Louisville: Westminister/John Knox Press, 1996.

Looks primarily at the Old Testament texts used most frequently in the debate, but suggests the inclusion of other texts as well, such as texts from the Wisdom literature. One of a series of essays in Part I, "What Do the Scriptures Say?". The other two sections are Part II, "How Do the Scriptures Inform Our Theological Reflection?" and Part III, "How Do We Live Faithfully?". All the contributors are members of the Princeton Theological Faculty.

Seow is the Henry Snyder Gehman Professor of Old Testament Language and Literature and Princeton Theological Seminary and an ordained minister of the Presbyterian Church.

Sharp, D.B. "A Biblical Foundation for an Environmental Theology: A New Perspective on Genesis 1: 26-28 and 6: 11-13," *Science et Esprit* 47 (1995): 305-313.

Shepherd, J.J. "Man's Morals and Israel's Religion." *Expository Times* 92 (1981): 171-174.

Sicre, José Luis. "La precoupación por la justicia en el Antiguo Oriente (I y II)." *Proyección* 28 (1981): 3-19; 91-104.

Silberman, Lou H. "The Human Deed in a Time of Despair: The Ethics of Apocalyptic." In *Essays in Old Testament Ethics (J. Philip Hyatt, In Memoriam)*, 191-202. Edited by James L. Crenshaw and John T. Willis. New York: Ktav Publishing House, 1974.

Soggin, A. "Alcuni testi-chiave per l'antropologia dell'Antico Testamento." In de *L'antropologia bilbica.* A cura di G. de Gennar. Napoli, 1982.

Spadafora, Francesco. "Sin in the Old Testament." In *Sin: Its Reality and Nature: A Historical Survey,* 29-40. Edited by Pietro Palazzini. Translated by Brendan Devlin. Dublin: Scepter Publishers, 1964.

Sprinkle, Joe M. "The Interpretation of Exodus 21:22-25 (*lex talionis*) and Abortion." *Westminster Theological Journal* 55 (1993): 233-253.

Stackhouse, Max L. "The Ten Commandments: Economic Implications." In *On Moral Business: Classical and Contemporary Resources for Ethics in Economic Life,* 59-62. Edited by Max L. Stackhouse, et. al. Grand Rapids: Wm. B. Eerdmans Publishing Co., 1995.

Adapted from an address given to the Convocation of the National Council of Churches of Christ held in Cleveland in 1982.

Stein, S. "The Laws on Interest in the Old Testament." *Journal of Theological Studies* 4 (1953): 161-170.

Stek, J.H. "Salvation, Justice and Liberation in the Old Testament." *Calvin Theological Journal* 13 (1978): 133-165.

Stinespring, William F. "A Problem of Theological Ethics in Hosea." In *Essays in Old Testament Ethics (J. Philip Hyatt, In Memoriam),* 131-144. Edited by James L. Crenshaw and John T. Willis. New York: Ktav Publishing House, 1974.

Stone, Lawson G. "Ethical and Apologetic Tendencies in the Redaction of the Book of Joshua." *Catholic Biblical Quarterly* 53 (1991): 25-36.

Stuhlmueller, Carroll, C.P. "Option for the Poor: *Old Testament Directives.*" In *Economic Justice: CTU's Pastoral Commentary on The Bishops' Letter on the Economy*, 19-27. Edited by John Pawlikowski, O.S.M. and Donald Senior, C.P. Washington, D.C.: The Pastoral Press, 1988.

Book includes the text of the Bishops' Letter on the Economy, plus 12 essays organized into three sections: 1) The Biblical Perspective; 2) The Ethical Perspective; and 3) The Pastoral Perspective.

_____. "The Search for Original Sin." *The Bible Today* 31 (1993): 73-78.

Conducts a "biblical search" on the doctrine of original sin. One of several articles in this issue on the theme of "The Bible on Sin."

Tambasco, Anthony J. "Prophetic Teaching on Sin." *The Bible Today* 31 (1993): 79-84.

Considers especially the prophetic teaching of sin in the aspects of idolatry, externalism and injustice. One of several articles in this issue on the theme of "The Bible on Sin."

Trible, Phyllis. "A Tempest in a Text: ecological soundings in the book of Jonah." *Theology Digest* 43 (4/1996): 303-312.

Trible finds in Jonah not entertainment and humor, but rather dissonances of sovereignty and freedom, mercy and caprice, leaving readers with unsettling questions regarding both theology and ecology.

Uffenheimer, Benjamin. "Theodicy and Ethics in the Prophecy of Ezekiel." In *Justice and Righteousness: Biblical Themes and their Influence*, 200-227. Edited by Henning Graf Reventlow and Yair Hoffman. Sheffield: JSOT Press, 1992.

Valle, José Luis del, O.S.A. "La Sexualidad. Simbología matrimonial en los escritos proféticos." *Biblia y Fe* 18 (1992): 37-50.

One of several articles under this number's general theme of "La Sexualidad: *Aproximacion Biblica.*"

Verhey, Allen. "Scripture and Medical Ethics: Psalm 51:10a, the Jarvik VII, and Psalm 50:9." In *Religious Methods and Resources in Bioethics*, 261-288. Edited by Paul F. Camenisch. Dordrecht: Kluwer Academic Publishers, 1994.

    Verhey is the Evert J. and Hattie E. Blekkink Professor of Religion at Hope College.

von Waldow, H. E. "Social Responsibility and Social Structure in Early Israel." *Catholic Biblical Quarterly* 32 (1970): 182-204.

Weinfeld, Moshe. "'Justice and Righteousness'--The Expression and its Meaning." In *Justice and Righteousness: Biblical Themes and their Influence*, 228-246. Edited by Henning Graf Reventlow and Yair Hoffman. Sheffield: JSOT Press, 1992.

Wenham, G.J. "Law and the Legal System in the Old Testament." In *Law, Morality and the Bible*. Edited by B.N. Kaye and G.J. Wenham. Downers Grove IL: Intervaristy Press, 1978.

Wénin, André. "Foi et justice dans l'Ancien Testament." *Lumen Vitae* 46 (1991): 380-392.

    Chercher à articuler sans cesse foi et justice est une constante du message biblique; encore faut-il étudier de près la *manière* dont la Bible s'y prend. A partir d'un texte précis (Dt 26), finement analysé, l'auteur montre comment la Loi de Moïse contient une exigence de justice; puis il en présente les échos dans l'A.T. (Dieu et le prochain; injustice et idôlatrie; les prophètes) et les prolongements dan le N.T. Ainsi est dégagé, non sans clarté, un message central, très éloquent pour notre temps.

    Maintains that faith and justice are constant terms in the biblical message, and that it is necessary to investigate the manner in which the Bible takes up these terms.

_____. "Le décalogue, révélation de Dieu et chemin de l'homme." *Révue Théologique de Louvain* 25 (1994): 148-182.

Wenz, Gunther. "Die Zehn Gebote als Grundlage christlicher Ethik. Zur Auslegung des ersten Hauptstücks in Luthers Katechismen." *Zeitschrift für Theologie und Kirche* 89 (1992): 404-439.

Westbrook, Raymond. "Adultery in Ancient Near Eastern Law." *RB* 97 (1990): 542-580.

Westbrook teaches at Johns Hopkins University.

_____. "Jubilee Laws." *Israel Law Review* 6 (1971): 209-225.

Also found as Chapter Two in his *Property and the Family in Biblical Law*, 36-57. Journal for the Study of the Old Testament Supplement Series, 113. Sheffield: Sheffield Academic Press, 1991.

Whitaker, Richard E. "Creation and Human Sexuality." In *Homosexuality and Christian Community*, 3-13. Edited by Choon-Leong Seow. Louisville: Westminister/John Knox Press, 1996.

Examines the creation narratives in the first three chapters of Genesis. One of a series of essays in Part I, "What Do the Scriptures Say?". The other two sections are Part II, "How Do the Scriptures Inform Our Theological Reflection?" and Part III, "How Do We Live Faithfully?". All the contributors are members of the Princeton Theological Faculty.

Whitaker is Information Research Specialist and Lecturer in Old Testament at Princeton Theological Seminary and an ordained minister in the United Methodist Church.

White, Leland J. "Biblical Texts and Contemporary Gay People: A Response to Boswell and Boughton." *Irish Theological Quarterly* 59 (1993): 286-301.

Argues that neither Boughton nor Boswell uses "sufficiently elaborated models of culture and cultural variation to address the issue of whether the actions proscribed in the Bible are equivalent in meaning (p. 286)."

See Lynne C. Boughton's "Biblical Texts and Homosexuality: A Response to John Boswell." *Irish Theological Quarterly* 58 (1992): 141-153, as well as Chapter 4, "The Scriptures," of John Boswell's *Christianity, Social*

Tolerance, and Homosexuality: Gay People in Western Europe from the Beginning of the Christian Era to the Fourteenth Century, (Chicago: University of Chicago Press, 1980): 91-117 for the treatment discussed in this article, as well as for a listing of other works which deal with Boswell's position.

_____. "Does the Bible Speak about Gays or Same-Sex Orientation? A Test Case in Biblical Ethics: Part I." *Biblical Theological Bulletin* (1995): 14-23.

Examines the biblical texts of Genesis 19, Leviticus 18-20, Romans 1:1, 1 Corinthians 6, and 1 Timothy 1 in light of three traditional core values of Mediterranean culture: honor, reproductivity, and holiness. White's thesis is that these texts frame the ethical issue of "homosexuality" in terms of fulfilling traditional cultural roles, and therefore these texts do not address the contemporary issues of same-sex orientation.

Whybray, R.N. "Poverty, Wealth, and Point of View in Proverbs." *Expository Times* 100 (1988-89): 332-336.

Williamson, David. "Il nuovo nel contesto del «ricordo». Le nuove soluzioni desunte da antichi principi nelle leggi dell'Antico Testamento." In *Il Problema del nuovo nella teologia morale,* 129-150. A cura di Lorenzo Alvarez-Verdes. Questiones Morales, 2. Roma: Editrice Rogate, e Editrice Accademia Alfonsiana, 1986.

Willis, John T. "Ethics in A Cultic Setting." In *Essays in Old Testament Ethics (J. Philip Hyatt, In Memoriam),* 145-169. Edited by James L. Crenshaw and John T. Willis. New York: Ktav Publishing House, 1974.

Treats Psalms 15 and 24.

Wilson, Robert R. "Approaches to Old Testament Ethics." In *Canon, Theology, and Old Testament Interpretation: Essays in Honor of Brevard S. Childs,* 62-74. Edited by Gene M. Tucker, David L. Petersen, and Robert R. Wilson. Philadelphia: Fortress Press, 1988.

_____. "Sources and Methods in the Study of Ancient Israelite Ethics." *Semeia,* no. 66 (1995): 55-63.

One of several articles on Old Testament ethics in this issue.

Yoder, John Howard. "Exodus and Exile: The Two Faces of Liberation." In Charles E. Curran and Richard A. McCormick, S.J., eds., *Readings in Moral Theology No. 4: The Use of Scripture in Moral Theology*, 337-353. New York: Paulist Press, 1984.

This article appeared originally in *Cross Currents* in 1973.

Books on Ethics in the Hebrew Scriptures and/or Jewish Ethics

Albertz, Heinrich, Hrsg. *Du sollst dir kein Bildnis noch irgendein Gleichnis machen.* Die zehn Gebote, 2. Stuttgart: Radius Verlag, 1986.

____. *Du sollst Gott deinen Herrn lieben...und deinen Nächsten wie dich selbst.* Die zehn Gebote, 11. Stuttgart: Radius Verlag, 1989.

____. *Du sollst nicht ehebrechen.* Die zehn Gebote, 7. Stuttgart: Radius Verlag, 1987.

____. *Lass dich nicht gelüsten deines Nächsten Hauses... noch alles, was dein Nächsten hat.* Die zehn Gebote, 10. Stuttgart: Radius Verlag, 1988.

Berger, Klaus. *Die Gesetzesauslegung Jesu. Ihr historischer Hintergrund im Alten Testament. Teil I: Markus und die Parallelen.* WMANT, 40. Neukirchen, 1972.

Birch, Bruce C. *Let Justice Roll Down: The Old Testament, Ethics, and Christian Life.* Louisville: Westminster/John Knox, 1991.

Discusses methodological questions, the importance of the Hebrew narratives as a moral resource, and specific texts and themes which might inform Christian ethics.

Reviewed by Dennis T. Olson in *Theology Today* 50 (1994): 148.

_____. *What Does the Lord Require? The Old Testament Call to Social Witness.* Philadelphia: Westminster Press, 1985.

Bloch, Abraham P. *A Book of Jewish Ethical Concepts: Biblical and Post-Biblical.* New York: KTAV, 1984.

Bloch is a Jewish rabbi and author of several other books.

Boecker, H.J. *Law and the Administration of Justice in the Old Testament and Ancient Near East.* London: SPCK, 1981.

Borowitz, Eugene B. *Exploring Jewish Ethics: Papers on Covenant Responsibility.* Detroit: Wayne State University Press, 1990.

Articles previously published over the last twenty years.

Reviewed by Leslie A. Muray in *Journal of Ecumenical Studies* 28 (1991): 652-653.

Breslauer, S. Daniel. *Contemporary Jewish Ethics: A Bibliographical Survey.* Westport CT: Greenwood Press, 1985.

_____. *Modern Jewish Morality: A Bibliographical Survey.* New York: Greenwood, 1986.

Brin, Gershon. *Studies in Biblical Law: From the Hebrew Bible to the Dead Sea Scrolls.* Translated by Jonathan Chipman. Journal for the Study of the Old Testament Supplement Series 176. Sheffield: JSOT Press, 1994.

The book contains both revised studies originally published in Hebrew or English, as well as several new studies. Part I on "Selected Problems in Biblical Law" deals with the "double laws" in the Bible, namely laws that treat different circumstances of the same essential case, as well as sanctions against those who fail to fulfill legal obligations, the treatment of the poor, and various other issues in Qumran law. Part II on "The Laws of the First Born" deals with the various components of the first born laws.

Brooks, Roger. *The Spirit of the Ten Commandments: Shattering the Myth of Rabbinic Legalism*. San Francisco: Harper & Row, 1990.

Brown, William P. *Character in Crisis: A Fresh Approach to the Wisdom Literature of the Old Testament*. Grand Rapids MI: Wm. B. Eerdmans, 1997.

This book traces the theme of moral identity and conduct throughout the wisdom literature of the Old Testament, with a concluding reflection on the Epistle of James in the New Testament, and explores a range of issues that includes literary characterization, moral discourse, world view, and the theology of the ancient sages. Brown argues that the aim of the biblical wisdom literature is for the formation of moral character, both for individuals and for the community as a whole.

Brueggemann, Walter. *The Land: Place as Gift, Promise, and Challenge in Biblical Faith*. Overtures to Biblical Theology. Philadelphia: Fortress Press, 1977.

Excellent book for understanding the theological function of the Promised Land in the Covenant Theology of the Old Testament, as well as its implications for the New Testament.

Brueggemann is McPheeder Professor of Old Testament at Columbia Theological Seminary in Decatur, Georgia.

_____. *A Social Reading of the Old Testament: Prophetic Approaches to Israel's Communal Life*. Edited by Patrick D. Miller. Minneapolis: Fortress Press, 1994.

A collection of fifteen essays by Professor Brueggemann which appeared from 1977 to 1991. They include: Covenant as a Subversive Paradigm; Israel's Social Criticism and Yahweh's Sexuality; Theodicy in a Social Dimension; The Prophet as a Destablilizing Presence; Rethinking Church Models through Scripture; and Revelation and Violence: a Study in Contexualization.

Carmichael, Calum M. *Law and Narrative in the Bible: The Evidence of the Deuteronomic Laws and the Decalogue*. Ithaca: Cornell University Press, 1985.

Reviewed by Ze'ev W. Falk in *Journal of Religion* 67 (1987): 533.

Carroll, Robert P. *When Prophecy Failed: Cognitive Dissonance in the Prophetic Traditions of the Old Testament.* New York: The Seabury Press, 1979.

Carter, Charles W., and Thompson, R. Duane. *The Biblical Ethic of Love.* American University Studies: Series 7, Theology and Religion, 79. Frankfurt-am-Main, Bern, New York, Paris: Peter Lang, 1990.

The authors explore "the relevance of divine love, as revealed in the Judeo-Christian Scripture, to the ethical decisions and moral conduct of mankind." Topic treated include: the inadequacy of humanistic ethics, the Ten Commandments, ethics of the Old Testament Prophets and Wisdom literature, ethics of the New Testament. Attention is also given to the ethics of John Wesley, and Christian ethics in relation to the state, military defense, public education, the family, and other trends in contemporary Christian ethics.

Carter is scholar-in-residence, and Thompson is professor of philosophy and religion at Indiana Wesleyan University.

Chicchese, M. *Le dieci parole.* Collana di etica biblica, 2. Roma: Edizioni Gruppi Biblici Universitari, 1987.

Reviewed by Elena Bosetti in *Rivista di Teologia Morale* 23 (1991): 409-410.

Craigie, Peter C. *The Problem of War in the Old Testament.* Grand Rapids: William B. Eerdmans, 1978.

Reviewed by Ronald G. Goetz in *Theology Today* 36 (1980): 598.

Crenshaw, James L., and Willis, John T., eds. *Essays in Old Testament Ethics (J. Philip Hyatt, In Memoriam).* New York: Ktav Publishing House, 1974.

Fourteen essays on Old Testament ethical themes by various authors, plus a curriculum vitae and bibliography of J. Philip Hyatt.

Crenshaw, James L., ed. *Theodicy in the Old Testament.* Issues in Religion and Theology, 4. Philadelphia: Fortress Press; London: SPCK, 1983.

An introduction plus 8 articles ranging from A.S. Peake's 1905 essay on Job to Crenshaw's own 1975 treatment on the problem of human bondage in Sirach. Other contributors include Walther Eichrodt, Ronald J. Williams, Klaus Koch, Gerhard von Rad, Martin Buber, and Harmut Gese.

Dakin, David Martin. *Peace and Brotherhood in the Old Testament.* London: Bannisdale Press, 1956.

Davidman, Joy. *Smoke on the Mountain: An Interpretation of the Ten Commandments.* Philadelphia: Westminster Press, 1985.

Davies, Eryl W. *Prophecy and Ethics: Isaiah and the Ethical Traditions of Israel.* Journal for the Study of the Old Testament. Supplement Series, 16. Sheffield: JSOT Press, 1981.

Dearman, John Andrew. *Property Rights in the Eighth-Century Prophets.* Society for Biblical Literature Dissertation Series, 106. Atlanta: Scholars Press, 1988.

Delhaye, Philippe. *Le Décalogue et sa place dans la morale chrétienne.* Bruxelles: La Pensée Catholique, 1963.

Doorly, William J. *Obsession with Justice: The Story of the Deuteronomists.* New York: Paulist Press, 1994.

Written primarily for Bible study groups at the adult level.

Doorly holds a D.Min. degree from Lancaster Seminary.

_____. *Prophet of Justice: Understanding the Book of Amos.* New York: Paulist Press, 1989.

Short introductory book on Amos, with discussion of economic justice, including ten homiletic themes drawn this topic in Amos.

_____. *Prophet of Love: Understanding the Book of Hosea.* New York: Paulist Press, 1991.

Treats the Book of Hosea in its social and political context, and concludes with some contemporary spiritual lessons which can be learned from Hosea.

Epsztein, Léon. *Social Justice in the Ancient Near East and the People of the Bible.* London: SCM Press, 1986.

French original: *La justice sociale dans le Proche-Orient ancien et le peuple de la Bible.* Paris: Editions du Cerf, 1983.

Helpful background study on Israel's social legislation.

Exeler, Adolf. *Vivere nella libertà di Dio: I dieci comandamenti.* Andate e annunciate. Studi e ricerche, 3. Roma: Edizioni Paoline, 1985.

Original in German.

Spanish translation: *Los Diez mandamientos: Vivir en la libertad de Dios.* Santander, 1983.

Fager, Jeffrey A. *Land Tenure and the Biblical Jubilee: Uncovering Hebrew Ethics through the Sociology of Knowledge.* Journal for the Study of the Old Testament; Supplement Series, 155. Sheffield: JSOT, 1993.

This volume addresses the perennial questions concerning the legislation in Leviticus 25 on the Jubilee with the method of the sociology of knowledge, especially as articulated by Berger and Luckmann. An earlier version of this work was the author's dissertation (1987).

Falk, Randall M., and Walter J. Harrelson. *Jews and Christians in Pursuit of Social Justice.* Nashville, TN: Abingdon Press, 1996.

With Scripture and other classic texts as bases readers will explore faith responses to personal and family ethical issues, community and national ethical concerns, and international and interfaith issues.

92

Falk, Ze'ev W. *Hebrew Law in Biblical Times*. Jerusalem: Wahrmann, 1964.

_____. *Religious Law and Ethics: Studies in Biblical and Rabbinical Theonomy*. Jerusalem: Mesharim, 1991.

Farley, Benjamin W. *In Praise of Virtue: An Exploration of the Biblical Virtues in a Christian Context*. Grand Rapids, MI: Wm. B. Eerdmans Publishing Company, 1995.

Farley examines both the Old and the New Testament and applies their teachings on moral character to the Christian life today. In the process, Farley critically reviews the current philosophical and theological interest in virtue, engages the Aristotelian, Thomist, and modern views of virtue, incorporates and responds to feminist concerns, and discusses the importance of the biblical virtues for our pluralistic age.

Feldman, Emanuel. *Biblical and Post-Biblical Defilement and Mourning: Law as Theology*. The Library of Jewish Law and Ethics. New York: Yeshiva University Press, 1977.

Fewell, Danna Nolan, and David M. Gunn. *Gender, Power & Promise*. Nashville, TN: Abingdon Press, 1993.

The authors explore ways in which the Bible's "first story" (Genesis through Kings) presents images of gender, and how this story, with its embedded legal codes, affects our understanding of the theological motifs of power and promise. They contend that reading Scripture is each time an exercise of power: interpretation is always invested in ideology, whether spoken or unspoken. By according special attention to the construction and depiction of character, the authors examine and seek to understand these ideologies. They demonstrate that the reader's choice of a character's perspective as a basis for his or her reading and understanding of the text is a crucial interpretive decision.

Forster, G. *Christian Ethics in the Old Testament*. Grove Booklet on Ethics, 35. Downers Grove IL: Grove Books, 1980.

Gallagher, John, C.S.B. *The Basis for Christian Ethics*. New York: Paulist Press, 1985.

> See especially in Part II, "The Criteria for Moral Judgment: Sacred Scripture," Chapters 8 and 9 which discuss respectively the Old Testament notions of Law and Covenant, and Flesh and Spirit.

García Trapiello, Jesús *El problema de la moral en la Antiguo Testamento*. Barcelona: Herder, 1977.

> Italian translation: *Il problema morale nell'Antico Testamento*. Sorgenti di Vita, 17. Traduzione di Raimondo Sorgia. Milano: Editrice Massimo, 1983.

Gatti, Guido. *Una legge che libera. Il decalogo nella catechesi*. Leumann: Elle Di Ci, 1991.

Gnuse, Robert. *You Shall Not Steal: Community and Property in the Biblical Tradition*. Maryknoll: Orbis Books, 1985.

> Spanish translation: *Comunidad y propiedad en la tradición bíblica*. Col. Buena Noticia, 16. Estella: Ed. Verbo Divino, 1987.

> Traces the biblical attitudes on possessions from the Old Testament through the New Testament.

Gornick, Herbert A., Hrsg. *Du sollst in Freiheit leben. Eine neue Dimension der Zehn Gebote*. Freiburg: Christophorus Verlag; Offenbach: Burckardthaus, Laetare Verlag, 1986.

Gossai, Hemchand. *Justice, Righteousness and the Social Critique of the Eighth-Century Prophets*. American University Studies, Series 7, Theology and Religion, 141. New York: Peter Lang, 1993.

Gottwald, Norman K. *The Tribes of Yahweh: A Sociology of the Religion of Liberated Israel 1250-1050 BCE*. London: SCM Press, 1979.

Controversial account of Israel's entry into the Promised Land. Gottwald uses a certain Marxist analysis in his interpretation.

Gowan, Donald E. *Eschatology in the Old Testament*. Minneapolis: Fortress Press, 1986.

Gradwohl, R. *Hasse nicht in deinen Herzen. Grundgesetz des Judentums*. Stuttgart: Calwer Verlag, 1991.

Grosseteste, Robert. *De decem mandatis*. Auctores Britannici Medii Aevi, 10. New York: British Academy by the Oxford University Press, 1987.

Hamel, Edouard, S.J. *Les dix paroles: Perspectives bibliques*. Essais pour notre temps. Section de théologie, 7. Bruxelles: Desclée de Brouwer, 1969.

In Spanish: *Los diez mandamientos*. Santander, 1972.

Hamel was professor of moral theology at the Pontifical Gregorian University until 1986.

Harrelson, Walter J. *The Ten Commandments and Human Rights*. Macon GA: Mercer University Press, 1997.

Harrelson argues that the ten commandments are important not only for Jews and Christians, but for all who seek to find or to reaffirm a moral foundation for their life and for the life of their children, their religious community, and their society. The fact that the commandments are put negatively means that the community that claims them and builds on them must work out for itself the positive import of not having other gods, not worshiping idols, not profaning the Sabbath, not killing and stealing, and committing adultery. Put negatively, these commitments become the groundwork for a humanly free and responsible search for the will of God for individual, family, and corporate life today and in any day.

Walter Harrelson was University Professor at Wake Forest University and Distinguished Professor emeritus of Hebrew Bible at Vanderbilt University Divinity School.

Reviewed by Edward F. Campbell, Jr. in *Journal of Religion* 64 (1984): 242-244.

Herring, Basil F. *Jewish Ethics and Halakhah for Our Time: Sources and Commentary*. 2 vols. The Library of Jewish Law and Ethics, 16-17. New York: KTAV, 1984.

Volume One contains three major sections on Bioethics, Law and Public Policy, and Psycho-social Ethics, and Volume Two contains four major sections on Bioethics, The Social Contract, Family Law, and Business Ethics.

Hobbs, T.R. *A Time for War: A Study of Warfare in the Old Testament*. Old Testament Studies, 3. Collegeville: The Liturgical Press/Michael Glazier Books, 1989.

Besides discussion of the Old Testament material, Hobbs includes sections devoted to "New Testament Insights." Brief bibliography is also included, pp. 234-242.

Reviewed by Scott Morschauser in *Theology Today* 48 (1992): 154.

Hobbs is Professor of Old Testament Interpretation at McMaster Divinity College in Hamilton, Ontario.

Hugenberger, Gordon P. *Marriage as a Covenant: A Study of Biblical Law and Ethics Governing Marriage Developed from the Perspective of Malachi*. Supplements to Vetus Testamentum, 52. Leiden and New York: Brill, 1994.

Israel, Martin. *The Discipline of Love: The Ten Commandments for Today*. London: SPCK, 1985.

Janzen, Waldemar. *Old Testament Ethics: A Paradigmatic Approach*. Louisville: Westminster/John Knox Press, 1994.

Uses five Old Testament stories to exemplify proper ethical behavior and a way of understanding the ethical message of the Old Testament. The five paradigms used include 1) the priestly paradigm and the holy life; 2) the sapiential paradigm and the wise life; 3) the royal paradigm and the just life;

4) the prophetic paradigm and the suffering servant life; and 5) the familial paradigm, which involves three particular components: human life modeled on the family and genealogy, a specific relationship to the land, and a commitment to others symbolized through hospitality.

Janzen is Professor of Old Testament and German at the Canadian Mennonite Bible College in Winnipeg.

Kaiser, Walter C., Jr. *Toward Old Testament Ethics.* Grand Rapids: Zondervan, 1983.

Considers exegetical principles for the study of Old Testament ethics, as well as examining the "moral" texts of the Old Testament and considers their meaning for contemporary believers.

Kang, Sa-Moon. *Divine War in the Old Testament and in the Ancient Near East.* Beihefte zur Zeitschrift für die alttestamentliche Wissenschaft, 177. Berlin & New York: Walter de Gruyer, 1989.

Kealy, Sean P. *The Vision of the Ten Commandments: Charter of Freedom.* Living Flame Series, 33. Dublin: Carmelite Centre of Spirituality, 1989.

Koch, Robert. *Die Bundesmoral im Alten Testament.* Frankfurt-am-Main and New York: P. Lang, 1994.

Koch, Traugott. *Zehn Gebote fur die Freiheit: Eine kleine Ethik.* Tubingen: J. C. B. Mohr, 1995.

Kraxner, Alois. *Die zehn Gebote als Wegweisung.* Linz: Veritas Verlag, 1988.

Kuhn, Johannes, Hrsg. *Ecksteine. Die zehn gebote.* Stuttgart: Quell Verlag, 1988.

Lehmann, Paul L. *The Decalogue and a Human Future: The Meaning of the commandments for Making and Keeping Human Life Human.* Grand Rapids, MI: W. B. Eerdmans, 1995.

Légasse, Simon. *«Et qui est mon prochain?» Etude sur l'agape dans le Nouveau Testament.* Lectio Divina, 136. Paris Editions du Cerf, 1989.

Italian translation: *E chi è il mio prossimo?*. Roma: Edizioni Dehoniane, 1991.

See especially chapters 2-4 for Old Testament background and material.

Lelyveld, Arthur. *The Steadfast Stream: An Introduction to Jewish Social Values.* Cleveland: The Pilgrim Press, 1995.

Draws on Scripture and rabbinic literature and recounts anecdotes from Jewish lore. Lelyveld reveals which values became normative in the liberal Jewish tradition and how tradition has attempted to resolve conflicts between these values in cases of abortion, warfare, and capital punishment.

Loader, J.A. *A Tale of Two Cities: Sodom and Gomorrah in the Old Testament, Early Jewish and Early Christian Traditions.* Contributions to Biblical Exegesis and Theology, 1. Kampen: J.H. Kok Publishing House, 1990.

Details how the Sodom and Gomorrah account has been used in the Bible as well as in extra-biblical literature and traditions.

Lochman, Jan Milic. *Wegweisung der Freiheit. Abriss der Ethik in der Perspektive des Dekalogs.* Gütersloh: Gütersloher Verlagshaus Gerd Mohn, 1979.

In French: *Faut-il parler encore des commandements?*. Paris: Editions du Cerf, 1981.

Italian translation: *I comandamenti, segnali verso la libertà.* Torino: Elle Di Ci, 1986.

Reviewed, in French, by Jean Desclos in *Studia Moralia* 36 (1989): 309-311.

Lochman is a Czechoslovakian Protestant (Reformed) theologian. His work considers not only the Bible, but also the Protestant tradition as well as Marxism.

Lohfink, Norbert, Hrsg. *Gewalt und Gewaltlosigkeit im Alten Testament.* Questiones disputate, 96. Freiburg: Herder, 1983.

Italian translation: *Il Dio della Bibbia e la violenza. Studi sul Pentateuco.* Brescia: Morcelliana, 1986.

Malchow, Bruce. *Social Justice in the Hebrew Bible: What is New and What is Old.* Collegeville MN: Liturgical Press, 1996.

Malchow demonstrates that Israel did not originate the concept of social justice. Rather, it drew its resources for overcoming justice crises from Near Eastern thought on the subject. By combining its own ideas of social justice with those of its neighbors, Israel's people fought injustice with what was "new" *and* what was "old."

Marthys, Hans-Peter. *Liebe deinen Nächsten wie dich selbst. Untersuchungen zum alttestamentlichen Gebot der Nächstenliebe (Lev 19,18).* Orbis biblicus et orientatalis, 71. Freiburg/Schweiz: Universitäts Verlag; Göttingen: Vandenhoeck & Ruprecht, 1986.

McBride, Alfred, O. Praem. *The Ten Commandments: Sounds of Love From Sinai.* Cincinnati: St. Anthony Messenger Press, 1990.

Examines the positive value of each commandment and places it in the context of contemporary culture. Treats the commandments as "ten liberating values" which can function as "persuasive moral guides" when seen in the context of love.

Mesters, Carlos. *Befreit-gebunden. Die 10 Gebote. Das Bundesbuch.* Erlanger Taschenbücher, 94. Erlangen: Verlag der Evangelisch-Lutherischen Mission, 1989.

_____. *Los Diez Mandamientos.* Buenos Aires: Ediciones Paulinas, 1988.

Miller, Patrick D., Jr. *Sin and Judgment in the Prophets: A Stylistic and Theological Analysis.* Society of Biblical Literature Monograph Series, 27. Chico CA: Scholars Press, 1982.

Treats the question of the correspondence of sin and judgment in the prophetic writings, concentrating on Hosea, Amos, Micah and Isaiah.

Muilenburg, James. *The Way of Israel: Biblical Faith and Ethics.* Religious Perspectives, 5. New York: Harper Torchbooks, 1961.

Nahmani, H.S. *Human Rights in the Old Testament.* Tel Aviv, 1964.

Nakanose, Shigeyuki. *Josiah's Passover: Sociology and the Liberating Bible.* Bible & Liberation Series. Maryknoll: Orbis Press, 1993.

Shigeyuki Nakanose, a Catholic priest born in Japan, now works with base communities in Brazil. He shows how "the so-called Deuteronomic reform spearheaded by King Josiah - including a revamped Passover festival as one of its cardinal features - decisively strengthened the small ruling elite of Judah to the detriment of the economic, social, political, and religious well-being of the majority of Israelites." He then goes on to show "how his understanding of biblical Passover was shared with leaders and lay participants in Brazilian basic ecclesial communities in and around Sâo Paulo, as well as how they responded to it."

Niditch, Susan. *War in the Hebrew Bible: A Study in the Ethics of Violence.* New York: Oxford University Press, 1993.

Using approaches from anthropology, comparative literature, and feminist studies, the author considers a number of war ideologies present in the Hebrew Bible.

Nielsen, E. *The Ten Commandments in New Perspective: A Traditio-historical Approach.* London: SCM Press; Naperville IL: Allenson, 1968.

Otto, Eckart. *Theologische Ethik des Alten Testaments.* Theologische Wissenschaft 3,2. Stuttgart, Berlin, Köln: Kohlhammer, 1994.

Reviewed by Gian Luigi Prato under the title, "Un'etica teologica dell'Antico Testamento condannata a fallire?" *Rassegna di Teologia* 37 (1996): 63-78.

100

van Oyen, Hendrik. *Ethik des Alten Testaments.* Geschichte der Ethik, 2. Gütersloh: Mohn, 1967.

In French: *Ethique de l'Ancien Testament.* Genève: Labor et Fides, 1974.

Palmer, Earl F. *Old Law--New Life: The Ten Commandments and New Testament Faith.* Nashville: Abingdon Press, 1984.

Priest, James E. *Governmental and Judicial Ethics in the Bible and Rabbinic Literature.* Malibu CA: Pepperdine University Press, 1980.

Reviewed by Michael Fishbane in *Journal of Religion* 64 (1984): 107-109.

Rad, Gerhard von. *Holy War in Ancient Israel.* Translated and edited by Marva J. Dawn and John H. Yoder. Grand Rapids: William B. Eerdmans, 1990.

German original: *Heilige Krieg im alten Israel*

Reventlow, Henning Graf, and Hoffman, Yair, eds. *Justice and Righteousness: Biblical Themes and their Influence.* Journal for the Study of Old Testament Supplement Series, 137. Sheffield: JSOT Press, 1992.

Ringe, Sharon H. *Jesus, Liberation, and the Biblical Jubilee: Images for Ethics and Christology.* Overtures to Biblical Theology, 19. Philadelphia: Fortress Press, 1985.

Sanders, E[d]. P[arish]. *Jewish Law from Jesus to the Mishnah.* London: SCM Press, 1990.

Schilling, Alfred. *Die zehn Gebote. Eine Anleitung zu ihrem rechten Verständnis und zu ihre Verkündigung heute.* Luzern/Stuttgart: Rex-Verlag, 1982.

Schmidt, W.H., H. Delkurt, und A. Graupner, eds. *Die Zehn Gebote im Ramen alttestamentlicher Ethik.* Erträge der Forschung, 281. Darmstadt: Wissenschftliche Buchgesellschaft, 1993.

Schreiner, Josef. *I dieci comandamenti nella vita del popolo di Dio.* Biblioteca biblica, 5. Brescia: Queriniana, 1991.

Translated from the German.

Sentuq, D. "Le Décalogue. Des sources d'un Droit à l'origine du peuple de Dieu." In *L'Ancien Testament, Approches et lecutres,* 173-207. Le point théoloique, 24. Ed. A. Vanel. Paris: Beauschene, 1977.

Sicre, José Luis. *El clamor de los profestas en favor de la justícia.* Curso Fe y Justícia. Madrid: Fundación Santa Maria, 1988.

_____. *Con los pobres de la tierra. La justicia social en los profestas de Israel.* Madrid: Ediciones Cristiandad, 1984.

Spong, John Shelby and Haines, Denise G. *Beyond Moralism: A Contemporary View of the Ten Commandments.* San Francisco: Harper & Row, 1986.

Stamm, J.J., and Andrews, M[ary].E[dith]. *The Ten Commandments in Recent Research.* London: SCM Press; Naperville IL: Allenson, 1967.

Tang, S.Y. "The Ethical Content of Job 31: A Comparative Study." Ph.D. Dissertation for the University of Edinburgh, 1967.

Testa, Emmanuele. *La morale dell'Antico Testamento.* Brescia: Morcelliana, 1981.

Reviewed by Alviero Niccacci in *Rivista di Teologia Morale* 23 (1991): 393-396.

Tomson, Peter J. *Paul and the Jewish Law: Halakha in the Letters of the Apostle to the Gentiles.* Compendia Rerum Iudaicarum ad Novum Testamentum III/2. Assen and Maastricht: Van Gorcum, 1990.

Reviewed by Timothy H. Lim in *Journal of Jewish Studies* 43 (1992): 157-160.

Weems, Renita J. *Battered Love: Marriage, Sex, and Violence in the Hebrew Prophets.* Minneapolis: Fortress Press, 1995.

Investigates ways in which the Hebrew Prophets' descriptions of divine love, compassion, and commitment to the covenant, as well as the prophetic discourse, rhetoric and sexual metaphors used, became linked to violence against women, such as battery, infidelity, rape and mutilation.

Weems teaches Hebrew Bible at Vanderbilt Divinity School.

Weinfeld, Moshe. *Justice and Righteousness in Israel and the Nations: Equality and Freedom in Ancient Israel in Light of Social Justice in the Ancient Near East.* Jerusalem: The Magnes Press. The Hebrew University, 1985.

_____. *Social Justice in Ancient Israel and in the Ancient Near East.* Minneapolis: Fortress Press; Jerusalem: The Magnes Press, The Hebrew University, 1995.

Shows that the biblical expression "to do justice (mishpat) and righteousness (zedekah)" generally refers to acting on behalf of the poor and oppressed. After an analysis of the meaning of the terms, Weinfeld investigates the ideal of justice in relation to social reforms promoted by Israelite monarchy, the implications of the ideal in individual life, and the theological implications of all aspects of the concept.

Wénin, André. *L'homme biblique. Anthropologie et ethique dans le premier Testament.* Paris: Les Editions de Cerf, 1995.

Westbrook, Raymond. *Property and the Family in Biblical Law.* Journal for the Study of the Old Testament Supplement Series, 113. Sheffield: Sheffield Academic Press, 1991.

Contains five previously published essays on this theme, plus two previously unpublished essays.

Whybray, R.N. *Wealth and Poverty in the Book of Proverbs.* Sheffield: Journal for the Study of the Old Testament Press, 1990.

Reviewed by Joseph Mulroney in *The Heythrop Journal* 34 (1993): 187-188.

Winninge, Mikael. *Sinners and the Righteous: A Comparative Study of the Psalms of Solomon and Paul's Letters.* Coniectanea Biblica, New Testament Series 26. Stockholm: Almqvist and Wiskell International, 1995.

Wolff, Hans Walter, Hrsg. *Gottes Recht: Gesammelte Studien zum Recht in Alten Testament.* München: Christian Kaiser Verlag, 1961.

Wright, Christopher J.H. *An Eye for An Eye: The Place of Old Testament Ethics Today.* Downers Grove Il: InterVarsity Press, 1983.

Same book as *Living as the People of God.*

Excellent, very readable approach to a "typology" of Old Testament ethics. Has a good basic bibliography of further books and articles for each chapter of the book.

_____. *Living as the People of God: The Relevance of Old Testament Ethics.* Leicester: Inter-Varsity Press, 1983.

Same book as *An Eye for an Eye.*

____. *Walking in the Ways of the Lord: The Ethical Authority of the Old Testament.* Downers Grove, IL: InterVarsity Press, 1996.

Wright first investigates the perennial issues in approaching Scripture's ethical authority. He then considers the various ways in which the church had understood and lived under the ethical authority of the Old Testament, including a survey of contemporary approaches. Finally he employs his method by exploring the specific issues of land, jubilee, the state, human rights and the struggle against corruption, dishonesty and injustice.

****

NEW TESTAMENT ETHICS

General and Miscellaneous Works in New Testament Ethics

Articles on General New Testament Ethics

Aguirre, R. "El mensaje de Jesús y los ideales del Reino de Dios." *Lumen* 38 (1989): 449-473.

Alvarez-Verdes, Lorenzo, C.Ss.R. "Las éticas bíblicas del Nuevo Testamento." *Estudios Biblicos* 48 (1990): 113-136.

Essentially the same bibliographical article is also found under the title "La etica del Nuevo Testamento, *Panorámica actual*," in *Studia Moralia* 29 (1991): 421-454.

Baden, H.J. "Ethischer Pluralismus im Neuen Testament." *Theologie der Gegenwart* 19 (1976): 13-17.

Becker, Jürgen. "Das Ethos Jesu und die Geltung des Gesetzes." In *Neues Testament und Ethik. Für Rudolf Schnackenburg*, 31-52. Herausgegeben von Helmut Merklein. Freiburg: Herder, 1989.

Blank, Josef. "New Testament Morality and Modern Moral Theology." *Concilium* 5 (1967): 6-12.

In Spanish: "Sobre el problema de las `normas éticas' en el Nuevo Testamento." *Concilium* 25 (1967): 187-201.

Outlines some of the issues in approaching the ethical material of the New Testament, and the methodological concerns these present to the moral theologian. The concept of "norms" as such does not fit well into the ethical discourse of the Bible, and interpretation of the scriptural material is an indispensable requirement for any application to the concrete issues of contemporary moral theology.

106

———. "Unity and Plurality in New Testament Ethics." *Concilium* 150 (1981): 65-71.

In Spanish: "Unidad y pluralidad en la ética del NT." *Concilium* 17 (1981): 526-537.

Outlines an ethos of "itinerant radicalism" and its relation to eschatology visible in the Synoptic tradition coming out of rural Palestine, and contrasts this with the change of ethos to a "love radicalism" seen in the Pauline and Deutero-Pauline literature. Concludes that the constant task facing Christians is "always to confront Jesus' ethical sayings and those of the New Testament traditions/authors with changing socio-cultural circumstances and to put them in practice." p. 70.

———. "Il problema delle norme etiche nel Nuovo Testamento." *Concilium* (5/1967): 23-38.

In German: "Zum Problem ethischer Normen im Neuen Testament." In *Herausforderung und Kritik der Moraltheologie,* ed. Georg Teichtweier and Wilhelm Dreier, 172-83. Würzburg: Echter Verlag, 1971.

Bonora, Antonio. "L'appello alla Scrittura nell'enciclica «Sollicitudo rei socialis»." In *La dottrina sociale della Chiesa,* 242-250. Gianni Ambrosio, et al. Milano: Glossa, 1989.

Bonora, who is a biblical exegete, is not very impressed by either the integration of Scripture in Pope John Paul II's 1988 social encyclical or the level of exegesis of the Biblical citations which are included.

Briend, Jacques. "Honore ton père et ta mère." *Christus* 31 (122, 1984): 203-216.

Jesus' often paradoxical attitude toward this commandment reflected the conflict between the role of parents in transmitting God's word to their children, and Jesus' call to revelation and discipleship.

"Le paradoxe existe, mais il s'explique si on rapelle que le rôle des parents est, entre autres, de transmettre la parole de Dieu à leurs enfants. Or, face à la révélation qu'apporte Jésus comme envoyé du Père, les liens familiaux peuvent constituer des obstacles, car les parents peuvent s'opposer à ce que leurs enfants puissent devenir disciples de Jésus. Dès lors ils ne remplissent plus le rôle qui était le leur avec l'irruption de la Bonne Nouvelle de Jésus-Christ. En passant de l'ancienne à la nouvelle alliance les parents, compris comme ceux qui sont chargés de transmettre la parole de Dieu, sont confrontés eux-mêmes à celui qui est le Verbe fait chair; en fonction des choix qu'ils font des tensions peuvent naître au sein d'une même famille. La croix de Jésus est un signe de contradiction qui peut bouleverser les rapport entre parents et enfants tels qu'ils étaient définis dans le judaïsme." p. 215.

Burrows, Millar. "Old Testament Ethics and the Ethics of Jesus." In *Essays in Old Testament Ethics (J. Philip Hyatt, In Memoriam)*, 215-223. Edited by James L. Crenshaw and John T. Willis. New York: Ktav Publishing House, 1974.

Cahill, Lisa Sowle. "Kingdom and Cross: Christian Moral Community and the Problem of Suffering." *Interpretation* 50 (April 1996): 156-68.

The Bible guides Christian ethics by showing how Jesus and early Christianity transformed the moral conventions of first-century Greco-Roman society by making them more inclusive and compassionate. This is the one side of the coin. The other side, however, is that the Bible also attests to the problem of the existence of evil and suffering in human life. In Paul's theology of cross and resurrection, Christian ethicists confront the ineradicable nature of this problem and the need to identify with those who must suffer.

Cahill is a Roman Catholic and did her doctoral studies at the University of Chicago under the direction of James M. Gustafson. She is Professor of Theological Ethics at Boston College, and past President of both the Catholic Theological Society of America (CTSA) and the Society of Christian Ethics (SCE).

_____. "The New Testament and Ethics: Communities of Social Change." *Interpretation* 44 (1990): 383-395.

Cahill discusses several leading theologians who use Scripture in their ethical analysis: Stanley Hauerwas, John Howard Yoder, Bruce Birch and Larry Rasmussen, Thomas Ogletree, Gustavo Gutiérrez, Halvor Moxnes, Richard A. Horsley, Ched Myers, Michael Crosby, Dan O. Via, Herman C. Waetjen, and Richard J. Cassidy. Her discussion centers on the role of an authoritative Scripture for contemporary ethical reflection, specifically on how the socially radical communities reflected in Scripture may propose authoritative patterns for today. Cahill concludes by posing a number of what she terms "veridical problems" in evaluating both the possibility and use of ethically normative biblical material.

Carrillo, S. "`Amarás al Señor, tu Dios, con todo el corazón...'." *Medellín* 10 (1984): 42-54.

Collins, Raymond F. "Obedience, Children and the Fourth Commandment--A New Testament Perspective." *Louvain Studies* 4 (1972): 157-173.

Collins taught New Testament for many years at Louvain in Belgium, and is now at Catholic University in Washington, D.C.

_____. "Scripture and the Christian Ethic." *Proceedings of the Catholic Theological Society of America* 29 (1974): 215-241.

Collins' presentation is followed by two responses (found in the same volume of the CTSA Proceedings): the first by John Dedek, pp. 243-246; and the second by Val Peter, pp. 247-253.

Dautzenberg, Gerhard. "Neutestamentliche Ethik und autonome Moral." *Tübinger Theologische Quartelschrift* 161 (1981): 43-55.

Italian translation: "Critica della legge e ubbidienza alla legge nella tradizione di Gesù." In *Saggi esegetici sulla legge nel Nuovo Testamento*, 41-64, a cura di Karl Kertelge, (Cinisello Balsamo: Edizioni Paoline, 1990).

De Virgilio, Giuseppe. "Etica del Nuovo Testamento: lo stato della ricerca." *Bibbia e Oriente* 33 (1991): 141-155.

Presents first an overview of some of the principal issues involved in the question of the place of revelation, and especially the New Testament, for moral theology, and then discusses a number of recent works in three sub-areas: general New Testament ethics, ethics in the various gospels, and ethics in the Pauline literature.

_____. "Etica e Scrittura: il Nuovo Testamento." *Rivista di Teologia Morale* 23 (1991): 363-371.

L'articolo traccia un quadro sintetico dello *status questiones* epistemologico circa la relazione tra le due discipline: l'etica e la Scrittura. La selezione bibliografica però manca un grande numero dei titoli più recenti delle lingue *non-italiana*.

Discusses the *status questiones* of relation between ethics and Scriptural studies. However, the bibliography considered in the article omits many recent works which are not in Italian.

Delhaye, Philippe. "Questioning the Specificity of Christian Morality," in Charles E. Curran and Richard A. McCormick, S.J., eds., *Readings in Moral Theology, No. 2: The Distinctiveness of Christian Ethics*, 234-269. New York: Paulist Press, 1980.

French original: "La mise en cause de la spécificité de la morale chrétienne." *Revue Theologique de Louvain* 4 (1973): 308-339.

Discusses the specificity of Christian ethics and the relation Scripture plays to this issue.

Descamps, A[lbert].L. "La morale synoptique." In *Morale chrétienne et reqûetes contemporaines*, 27-45. Tournai-Paris, 1954.

Dilhe, Albrecht. "Ethik." In *Reallexikon für Antike und Christentum. I. Neues Testament*, 701-728. Hrsg. Th. Klauser. Stuttgart, 1966.

Espinel, J.L. "Jesús y los movimientos políticos y sociales de su tiempo. Estado actual de la cuestión." *Ciencia Tomista* 113 (1986): 251-284.

Evans, Craig A. "Jesus' Ethic of Humility." *Trinity Journal* 13 ns (1992): 127-138.

Reviews Jesus' principal statements about the kingdom and messiahship and then traces the origin and understanding of humility in Jesus' ethic.

Fabris, Rinaldo. "Morale del Nuovo Testamento." In *Nuovo Dizionario di Teologia Morale*, 786-800. A cura di Francesco Compagnoni, Giannino Piana, e Salvatore Privitera. Cinisello Balsamo: Edizioni Paoline, 1990.

Fee, Gordon D. "Issues in Evangelical Hermeneutics, Part II: The Crucial Issue--
Authorial Intentionality: A Proposal Regarding New Testament Imperatives."
Crux 26 (3/1990): 35-42.

Following some preliminary observations on hermeneutics and normativity,
Fee raises the question of authorial intent in reference to the New Testament
imperatives. Suggests that these are best understood as part of the gospel,
and not some new form of law.

Fiedler, Peter. "La Tora in Gesù e nella tradizione di Gesù." In *Saggi esegetici sulla
legge nel Nuovo Testamento*, 65-81, a cura di Karl Kertelge, (Cinisello
Balsamo: Edizioni Paoline, 1990).

German original in *Das Gesetz im Neuen Testament*. Herausgegeben von
Karl Kertelge. Questiones Disputatae, 108. Freiburg: Herder, 1986.

Forell, George Wolfgang. "New Testament Ethics." Chapter 1 in *History of
Christian Ethics. Volume 1: From the New Testament to Augustine*, 13-32.
Minneapolis: Augsburg, 1979.

Forell is Carver Distinguished Professor of Religion at the University of Iowa.

Fraijó, M. "Jesús frente al sistema dominante de su época." *Razón y Fe* 219 (1989):
626-638.

Fuller, Reginald H. "The Decalogue in the New Testament." *Interpretation* 43
(1989): 243-255.

Furger, Franz. "Ethische Argumentation und neutestamentliche Aussagen." In *Ethik
im Neuen Testament*, 13-31. Hrsg. Karl Kertelge. Freiburg: Herder, 1984.

Gnilka, Joachim. "Apokalyptik und Ethik. Die Kategorie der Zukunft als Anweisung
für sittliches Handeln." In *Neues Testament und Ethik. Für Rudolf
Schnackenburg*, 464-481. Herausgegeben von Helmut Merklein. Freiburg:
Herder, 1989.

Goffi, Tullo. "L'etica di Gesù di Nazaret." *Rivista di Teologia Morale* 17 (1985): 33-42.

Gómez Dorado, Guillermo. "¿Fue Jesús de Nazaret crítico implacable de las instituciones?" *Moralia* 2 (1980): 32-56.

____. "La Moral del Nuevo Testamento. Boletin Bibliografico." En *Perspectivas de moral bíblica,* 173-192. Estudios de Etica Teologica. Edd. Marciano Vidal, Francisco Lage y Alfosno Ruiz-Mateos. Madrid: Instituto Superior de Ciencas Morales, PS Editorial, 1984.

Grant, F.C. "The Impractibility of the Gospel Ethics." In *Aux sources de la tradition chrétienne,* 86-94. Edited by Oscar Cullman. Paris: Delachaux et Niestle, 1950.

Gräßer, Erich. "Zum Stichwort «Interimsethik». Eine notwendige Korrektur." In *Neues Testament und Ethik. Für Rudolf Schnackenburg,* 16-30. Herausgegeben von Helmut Merklein. Freiburg: Herder, 1989.

Grech, Prosper, O.S.A., Segalla, Giuseppe. "L'etica del N.T." In *Metodologia per uno studio della teologia del Nuovo Testamento,* 143-171. Torino: Marietti, 1978.

Gregorios, Paulos Mar. "New Testament Foundations for Understanding the Creation." In *Liberating Life: Contemporary Approaches to Ecological Theology,* 37-45. Edited by Charles Birch, William Eakin and Jay B. McDaniel. Maryknoll: Orbis Press, 1990.

Gustafson, James M. "The Relation of the Gospels to the Moral Life." Chapter 7 in *Theology and Christian Ethics,* 147-159. Philadelphia: Pilgrim Press, 1974.

This has established itself as a foundational essay in the area of methodology of Scripture and New Testament ethics.

Gustafson is an ordained minister in the United Church of Christ, and currently Henry R. Luce Professor of Humanities and Comparative Studies at Emory University. Previously he taught at Yale and the University of

Chicago. He has studied at the Chicago Theological Seminary, University of Chicago, and his Ph.D. is from Yale (1955), done under H. Richard Niebuhr. He has also taught at Yale and the University of Chicago.

Häring, Bernard, C.Ss.R. "Avenir de la théologie morale, avenir de la morale." *Lumière & vie* 39 (décembre, 1990): 105-16.

"On a proposé le mot «parénèse». Mais il n'a pas de fondement biblique. Il est encore trop moralisant. La Bible parle de *paraclèse*: ce mot rappele immédiatement le *paraclet*, celui qui console, encourage, rend possible (les termes *parakalein, paraklesis,* et *parakletos,* figuerent plus de cent fois dans le Nouveau Testament). C'est le concept-clé d'une intervention éthique pneumatologiquement juste. Il exprime toujours en premier lieu le message de la grâce, de l'action de l'Esprit-Saint, de la vocation «dans le Christ», et cela de telle manière que l'exigence, jamais séparée des paroles de consolation et d'encouragement, signifie exhortation." (p. 116).

Suggests that rather than speaking of "paranesis" (exhortation) in biblical morality one should speak instead of "paraclesis"--the gift and action of the Holy Spirit--as being the key to understanding how Christians live their lives of faith.

Häring (born 1912) is a major Roman Catholic moral theologian who sought to incorporate Scripture into his approach to moral theology, and who taught moral theology for a number of years at the Academia Alphonsianum in Rome.

Hays, Richard B. "New Testament Ethics: The Theological Task." *The Annual of the Society of Christian Ethics* (1995): 97-120.

Hays is professor of New Testament at Duke University Divinity School, and taught for a number of years previously at Yale.

_____. "Recent Books on New Testament Ethics." *Quarterly Review* 6 (4, 1986): 13-30.

_____. "Scripture--Shaped Community: *The Problem of Method in New Testament Ethics.*" *Interpretation* 44 (1990): 42-55.

Also found in *Evangelical Review of Theology* 18 (1994): 234-247.

Gives a good review of the principal problems and principles in using Scripture in moral theology. Hays concentrates on the hermeneutical issues involved in this use of Scripture, and concludes his article with a trial application to a "test case" involving the Christian community's response to the problem of the homeless.

Henning, R. "'Familiensoziologisches' in Neuen Testament." *Jahrbuch für Christliche Sozialwissenschaft* 29 (1988): 175-191.

Hiers, Richard H. "Jesus, Ethics and the Present Situation." In Charles E. Curran and Richard A. McCormick, S.J., eds., *Readings in Moral Theology No. 4: The Use of Scripture in Moral Theology*, 1-20. New York: Paulist Press, 1984.

This article originally appeared in Hiers' *Jesus and Ethics, Four Interpretations*.

Horn, Friederich Wilhelm. "Ethik des Neuen Testaments 1982-1992." *Theologische Rundschau* 60 (1/1995): 32-86.

Iersel, Bas van. "The Normative Anthropology of the Gospel." *Concilium* 5 (8/1972): 48-57.

"The Gospel provides only one fundamental element for a normative view of man, and that is the model of man's absolute involvement with his fellow man in need, the model of complete human solidarity. All the rules of human conduct found in the Gospel can be traced back to this." p. 57.

Johnson, Luke Timothy. "Why Scripture Isn't Enough." *Commonweal* (6 June 1997): 23-25.

Somewhat critical review of Richard B. Hays' *The Moral Vision of the New Testament* (San Francisco: HarperSanFrancisco, 1996).

Johnson is professor of New Testament at the Candler School of Theology at Emory University.

114

de Jonge, Marinus. "Die Paränese in den Schriften des Neuen Testaments und in den Testamenten der Zwölf Patriarchen. Einege Überlegungen." In *Neues Testament und Ethik. Für Rudolf Schnackenburg*, 538-550. Herausgegeben von Helmut Merklein. Freiburg: Herder, 1989.

Keck, Leander E. "Ethos and Ethics in the New Testament." In *Essays in Morality and Ethics*. The Annual Publication of the College Theology Society, 29-49. Edited by James Gaffney. New York: Paulist Press, 1980.

Keck is Winkley Professor of Biblical Theology at Yale Divinity School.

Leonardi, Giovanni. "Introduzione all'etica del Nuovo Testamento." *Studia Patavina* 37 (1990): 601-625.

Review of the book of the same title by Giuseppe Segalla.

Lohfink, Gerhard. "Die Not der Exegese mit der Reich-Gottes-Verkündigung Jesu." *Theologische Quartelschrift* 168 (1988): 1-15.

Lyonnet, Stanislaus, S.J. "Les fondements bibliques de la Constitution pastorale *Gaudium et Spes*." In *L'Eglise dans le monde de ce temps*, 196-212. Edited by G. Baraúna. Bruges, 1967.

Marshall, I. Howard. "New Occasions Teach New Duties? The Use of the New Testament in Christian Ethics." *The Expository Times* 105 (1994): 131-136.

Overview of some the issues and problems associated with the use of Scripture in ethics, focusing primarily on the contributions of Richard Longenecker and Richard B. Hays.

McGrath, Alister E. "In What Way Can Scripture Be a Moral Example for Christians?" *Journal of the Evangelical Theological Society* 34 (1991): 289-298.

Failure to grasp Jesus Christ's gospel relevance results in the acceptance of worldly standards for human behavior. A proper Christian doctrine also will preserve Christian distinctiveness so that it not be lost in the liberal American culture.

McIlhone, James P. "The Gospels: A Source of Morality." *The Bible Today* 31 (1993): 277-282.

Brief overview of the principal moral themes in the Gospels.

McIlhone teaches Scripture at Mundelein Seminary.

Meeks, Wayne A. "Understanding Early Christian Ethics." *Journal of Biblical Literature* 105 (1986): 3-11.

Merk, Otto. "Ethik im Neuen Testament. Zu Wolfgang Schrages Gesamtdarstellung." *Theologische Literaturzietung* 112 (1987): 641-650.

Mott, Stephen Charles. "The Use of the New Testament for Social Ethics." *Journal of Religious Ethics* 15 (1987): 225-260.

Moule, C.F.D. [Charles Francis Digby] "Important Moral Issues: Prolegomena: The New Testament and Moral Decisions." *Expository Times* 74 (1963): 370-373.

Mueller, G. "Der Dekalog im NT." *Theologische Zeitschrift* 38 (1982): 79-97.

Muñoz Iglesias, Salvador. "Old Testament Values superseded by the New." *Concilium* 10 (1967): 50-55.

Oriol, J. "¿Qué significa seguir a Jesús hoy?" *Razón y Fe* 212 (1985): 25-39.

van Ouwerkerk, Conrad. "Gospel Morality and Human Compromise." *Concilium* 5 (1965): 5-12.

116

Penna, Romano. "Nuovo Testamento ed esigenza morale." *Lateranum* 60, no. 1 (1994): 5-27.

Perkins, Pheme. "Jesus and Ethics." *Theology Today* 52 (1995): 49-65.

Discusses reasons why the image of Jesus might be out of focus in both contemporary Christian ethics and popular consciousness, and utilizing the work of many exegetes suggests ways in which some of the problematic elements might be avoided in appropriating ethics based in New Testament biblical texts.

Perkins is professor of New Testament at Boston College.

_____. "New Testament Ethics: Questions and Contexts." *Religious Studies Review*. 10 (1984): 321-327.

Pokorny, P. "Neutestamentliche Ethik und die Probleme ihrer Darstellungen." *Evangelische Theologie* 50 (1990): 357-371.

Rebell, Walter. "Neutestamentliche Ethik--Anmerkungen zum gegenwärtigen Diskussionstand." *Zeitschrift für Evangelische Ethik* 32 (1988): 142-151.

Rodríguez Carmona, A. "Tolerancia e intolerancia en el NT." *Estudios Eclesiásticos* 59 (1984): 265-295.

Roloff, Jürgen. "Themen und Traditionen urchristlicher Amststrägerparänese." In *Neues Testament und Ethik. Für Rudolf Schnackenburg*, 507-526. Herausgegeben von Helmut Merklein. Freiburg: Herder, 1989.

Salguero, José, O.P. "Relazione tra l'Antica e la Nuova Alleanza." *Angelicum* 60 (1983): 165-189.

Sanders, Jack T. "The Question of the Relevance of Jesus for Ethics Today." In Charles E. Curran and Richard A. McCormick, S.J., eds., *Readings in Moral*

Theology No. 4: The Use of Scripture in Moral Theology, 45-65. New York: Paulist Press, 1984.

This article originally appeared in the *Journal of the American Academy of Religion* in 1970.

Schlosser, J. "Le Règne de Dieu, présent et à venir dans la prédication de Jésus." *Revue de Droit Canonique* 33 (1983): 201-212.

Schnackenburg, Rudolf. "Ethische Argumentationsmethoden und neutestamentlich-ethische Aussagen." In *Ethik im Neuen Testament*, 32-49. Hrsg. Karl Kertelge. Freiburg: Herder, 1984.

_____. "Das Ethos des Alten Bundes und die sittliche Botschaft Jesu." In *Der Mensch und sein sittlicher Auftrag*. Hrsg. H. Althaus. Freiburg, 1983.

____. "Neutestamentliche Ethik im Kontext heutiger Wirklichkeit." In *Anspruch der Wirklichkeit und christlicher Glaube: Probleme und Wege theologischer Ethik heute*, 193-207. Hrsg. Helmut Weber und Dietmar Mieth. Düsseldorf: Patmos Verlag, 1980.

Schneider, Gerhard. "Imitatio Dei als Motiv der «Ethik Jesu»." In *Neues Testament und Ethik. Für Rudolf Schnackenburg*, 71-83. Herausgegeben von Helmut Merklein. Freiburg: Herder, 1989.

Schrage, Wolfgang. "Ethische Tendenzen in der Textüberlieferung des Neuen Testaments." In *Studien zum Text und zur Ethik des Neuen Testaments. Festschrift zum 80. Geburtstag von Heinrich Greeven*, 374-396. Herausgegeben von Wolfgang Schrage. Berlin/New York: Walter de Gruyter, 1986.

___. "Komparativ Ethik im Neuen Testament." In *Neues Testament und Ethik. Für Rudolf Schnackenburg*, 482-506. Herausgegeben von Helmut Merklein. Freiburg: Herder, 1989.

_____. "Zum Komparativ in der urchristlichen Ethik." *Evangelische Theologie* 48 (1988): 330-345

Schulz, Siegfried. "Evangelium und Welt. Hauptprobleme einer Ethik des Neuen Testaments." In *Neues Testament und christlicher Existenz*, 483-501. Herausgegeben von Hans Dieter Betz und Luise Schottroff. Tübingen: J.C.B. Mohr, 1973.

Festschrift für Herbert Braun zum 70. Geburtstag.

Festschrift for Herbert Braun on the occasion of his 70th birthday.

Schürmann, Heinz. "How Normative Are the Values and Precepts of the New Testament?" In *Principles of Christian Morality*, 9-44. Translated by Graham Harrison. San Francisco: Ignatius Press, 1986.

Also found under the title, "Report from the International Theological Commission, «The Actual Impact of Moral Norms in the New Testament: *Text by Hans Schürmann, Introduction and Commentary by Philippe Delhaye*,»" in Charles E. Curran and Richard A. McCormick, S.J., eds., *Readings in Moral Theology No. 4: The Use of Scripture in Moral Theology*, (New York: Paulist Press, 1984): 78-104.

Also found in *International Theological Commission: Texts and Documents (1969-1985)*, 121-128. Edited by Michael Sharkey. San Francisco: Ignatius Press, 1989.

German original: "Die Frage nach der Verbindlichkeit der neutestamentlichen Wertungen und Weisungen." In Joseph Ratzinger, Hrsg. *Prinzipien Christlicher Moral*, 9-39. Einsiedeln, 1975.

Italian translation: "Sul problema del contenuto e del fondamento dell'ethos cristiano." In *Prospettive di morale cristiana*. Contributi di teologia, 3. Ed. Joseph Cardinal Ratzinger. Roma: Città Nuova Editrice, 1986.

In French: "Du caractère obligatoire des normes et directives morales du Nouveau Testament." In Joseph Ratzinger et Philippe Delhaye, ed., *Principes d'éthique chrétienne*, 37-71. Le Sycomore. Paris: Editions Lethielleux, 1979.

_____. "L'impact des normes morales du nouveau Testament." *Esprit et Vie* 85 (1975): 593-603.

_____. "Menschenwürde und Menschenrechte im Licht der «Offenbarung Iesu Christi»." *Gregorianum* 65 (1984): 327-336.

Prepared as a Working Paper for the International Theological Commission plenary session in December, 1983.

_____. "Moraltheologische Ansätze in der Mahnungen und Weisungen Jesus. Questiones disputandae." *Theologie und Glaube* 72 (1982): 446-450.

Scroggs, Robin. "The New Testament and Ethics: How Do We Get from There to Here?" *Perspectives in Religious Studies* 11 (4, 1984): 77-93.

Segalla, Giuseppe. "C'è un'etica «cristiana» nel Nuovo Testamento?" *Rivista Biblica* 37 (1989): 461-467.

Critical review of the book by Willi Marxsen, `Christliche' und christliche Ethik im Neuen Testament*, (Gütersloh, 1989). English translation: *New Testament Foundations for Christian Ethics*, (Minneapolis: Fortress Press, 1993).

Segalla is professor of New Testament Exegesis at the Theological Faculty of Milan.

_____. "«Etiche del Nuovo Testamento» (1933-1976): Una rassegna." *Studia Patavina* 24 (1977): 37-54.

English digest version: "'New Testament ethics': a survey (1933--1976)." *Theology Digest* 27 (1979): 3-9.

_____. "Regno di Dio e ordine giuridico nel Nuovo Testamento." In AAVV. *Ordine morale e ordine giuridico. Rapporto e distinzione tra diritto e morale*, 109-172. Bologna: Edizioni Dehoniane Bologna, 1985.

Also in Idem, *Introduzione all'etica del Nuovo Testamento*, 239-289. Biblioteca Biblica, 2. Brescia: Queriniana, 1989.

_____. "La triplice funzione dell'esperienza nell'etica sapienziale di Gesù." *Teologia* 16 (1991): 101-146.

Considers the function of human experience in the sapiential ethics of Jesus. 30 of these sayings are examined both exegetically and theologically, comparing Jesus' sayings with the Law, eschatological message, and finally, with experience used as a metaphor.

Spicq, Ceslas, O.P. "Charité et vie morale selon le NT." *La Vie Spirituelle* 658 (1984): 4-16.

Spohn, William C. "Jesus and Christian Ethics." *Theological Studies* 56 (1995): 92-107.

Part of the annual "Notes on Moral Theology" in which Spohn examines three themes which have had an important impact in recent theological literature: the shift from history to ethics, Jesus as subsversive sage versus eschatological prophet debate, and the use of analogical reasoning in addressing the normativity of Jesus for Christian ethics.

Spohn studied under James Gustafson at the University of Chicago, taught moral theology at the Jesuit School of Theology-Berkeley for many years, and currently teaches Christian ethics at the University of Santa Clara.

_____. "Jesus and Ethics." *Catholic Theological Society of America Proceedings* 49 (1994): 40-57.

Presented as a Plenary Address at the 1994 CTSA Convention.

Strecker, Georg. "Strukturen einer neutestamentlichen Ethik." *Zeitschrift für Theologie und Kirche* 75 (1978): 117-146.

Tettamanzi, Dionigi. "L'etica cristiana `sub luce' Evangelii." *Rivista del Clero Italiano* 55 (1974): 194-205.

Tettamanzi did his doctorate in moral theology under Josef Fuchs, S.J. at the Pontifical Gregorian University in Rome, and later was made a bishop.

Vanni, Ugo, S.J. "Carità e politica nel Nuovo Testamento." *Civiltà Cattolica* 141 (1990): 15-28.

Vanni is professor of New Testament at the Pontifical Gregorian University in Rome.

Vidal, Marciano, C.Ss.R. "El `ethos' juvenil del Evangelio." *Sal Terrae* 73 (1985): 571-583.

_____. "Etica narrativa en los Evangelios. Aproximaciones generales de caracter metodológico y temático." *Moralia* 6 (1984): 145-171.

Tambien en [also found in] *Perspectivas de moral bíblica*, 145-171. Estudios de Etica Teologica. Edd. Marciano Vidal, Francisco Lage y Alfosno Ruiz-Mateos. Madrid: Instituto Superior de Ciencas Morales, PS Editorial, 1984.

Wall, Robert W. "Introduction: New Testament Ethics." *Horizons in Biblical Theology* 5/2 (1983): 49-94.

_____. "New Testament Ethics." In *Christian Ethics: An Inquiry into Christian Ethics from a Biblical Theological Perspective*, 31-75. Edited by Leon O. Hynson and Lane A. Scott. Anderson IN: Warner Press, 1983.

Wall has a Th.D from Dallas Theological Seminary and is associate professor of biblical studies and ethics at Seattle Pacific University.

Wiebe, Ben. "Messianic Ethics: *Response to the Kingdom of God.*" *Interpretation* 45 (1991): 29-42.

Jesus' ethics envisaged not the individual--as so much of modern scholarship has mistakenly supposed--but restored Israel as a community brought into being through appropriate response to Jesus' proclamation of the kingdom.

Wilder, Amos N. "The Basis of Christian Ethics in the New Testament." *Journal of Religious Thought* 15 (1958): 137-146.

Zeller, Dieter. "Wie imperativ ist der Indikativ?" In *Ethik im Neuen Testament*, 190-196. Hrsg. Karl Kertelge. Freiburg: Herder, 1984.

Books on General New Testament Ethics

Baker, Eric W. *The Neglected Factor--The Ethical Element in the Gospel.* New York: Abingdon Press, 1963.

The 1963 Cato Lecture.

Betz, Hans Dieter, und Schottroff, Luise, Hrsgs. *Neues Testament und christlicher Existenz.* Tübingen: J.C.B. Mohr, 1973.

Festschrift für Herbert Braun zum 70. Geburtstag.

Festschrift for Herbert Braun on the occasion of his 70th birthday.

Bonhoeffer, Dietrich. *The Cost of Discipleship.* Translated by Reginald H. Fuller, revised by Irmgard Booth. Rev. ed. New York: Macmillan, 1963.

German original: *Nachfolge.* München: Chr. Kaiser Verlag, 1937.

Translations available in many other languages, including French, *La Prix de la grâce,* and Italian, *Sequela,* Nuovi Saggi Queriniana, 3, (Brescia: Queriniana, 1971).

Classic work of the well-known German Lutheran theologian was imprisoned in April 1943 for his role in the Nazi resistance hanged at the age of 39 by the Gestapo in the Nazi concentration camp at Flossenbürg in April 1945. The book contains a theological discussion of the meaning of Christian discipleship and for this Bonhoeffer devotes an extended discussion of the Call of Levi in Matthew's Gospel and the Sermon on the Mount.

Borg, Marcus J. *Conflict, Holiness & Politics in the Teachings of Jesus.* Studies on the Bible and Early Christianity, 5. New York and Toronto: Edwin Mellen Press, 1984.

Braaten, Carl E. *Eschatology and Ethics: Essays on the Theology and Ethics of the Kingdom of God.* Minneapolis: Augsburg, 1974.

Braaten is a well-known American Lutheran theologian.

Briggs, Charles A. (Charles Augustus), 1841-1913. *The Ethical Teaching of Jesus.* New York: Scribner's, 1904; Chicago: American Theological Library Association, (ATLA monograph preservation program), ATLA fiche, 1985.

Briggs lived from 1841-1913.

Burch, Ernest Ward. *The Ethical Teaching of the Gospels.* New York and Cincinnati: Abingdon Press, 1925.

Carter, Charles W., and Thompson, R. Duane. *The Biblical Ethic of Love.* American University Studies: Series 7, Theology and Religion, 79. Frankfurt-am-Main, Bern, New York, Paris: Peter Lang, 1990.

The authors explore "the relevance of divine love, as revealed in the Judeo-Christian Scripture, to the ethical decisions and moral conduct of mankind." Topic treated include: the inadequacy of humanistic ethics, the Ten Commandments, ethics of the Old Testament Prophets and Wisdom literature, ethics of the New Testament. Attention is also given to the ethics of John Wesley, and Christian ethics in relation to the state, military defense, public education, the family, and other trends in contemporary Christian ethics.

Carter is scholar-in-residence, and Thompson is professor of philosophy and religion at Indiana Wesleyan University.

Cave, Sydney. *The Christian Way: A Study of New Testament Ethics in Relation to Present Problems.* London: Nisbet, 1949.

Chilton, Bruce D. and McDonald, J [ames].I.H. *Jesus and the Ethics of the Kingdom.* Biblical Foundations in Theology. James D.G. Dunn and James P. Mackey, eds. London: SPCK, 1987. Grand Rapids: Eerdmans, 1988.

Collange, Jean François. *De Jésus à Paul: L'éthique du Nouveau Testament.* Le Champ éthique, 3. Genève: Labor et Fides, 1980.

Cook, David. *Living in the Kingdom: The Ethics of Jesus.* London: Hodder & Stoughton, 1992.

Cranfield, C.E.B. *The Bible and Christian Life*. Edinburgh: T. & T. Clark, 1985.

Series of essays which deal with various aspects of New Testament ethics.

Dewar, Lindsay. *An Outline of New Testament Ethics*. Philadelphia: The Westminster Press, 1949.

Dillmann, Rainer. *Das Eigentliche der Ethik Jesu. Ein exegetischer Beitrag zur moraltheologischen Diskussion um das Proprium einer christlichen Ethik*. Tübinger Theologische Studien, 23. Mainz: Matthais-Grünewald Verlag, 1984.

Donahue, John R., S.J. *The Gospel in Parable: Metaphor, Narrative, and Theology in the Synoptic Gospels*. Philadelphia: Fortress Press, 1988.

Discusses much of the ethical material in the gospel parables.

Donahue studied under Norman Perrin at the University of Chicago is Professor of Biblical Studies (New Testament) at the Jesuit School of Theology and Graduate Theological Union, Berkeley.

Farley, Benjamin W. *In Praise of Virtue: An Exploration of the Biblical Virtues in a Christian Context*. Grand Rapids, MI: Wm. B. Eerdmans Publishing Company, 1995.

Farley examines both the Old and the New Testament and applies their teachings on moral character to the Christian life today. In the process, Farley critically reviews the current philosophical and theological interest in virtue, engages the Aristotelian, Thomist, and modern views of virtue, incorporates and responds to feminist concerns, and discusses the importance of the biblical virtues for our pluralistic age.

Fiorenza, Elisabeth Schüssler. *In Memory of Her: A Feminist Theological Reconstruction of Christian Origins*. New York: Crossroad, 1983.

French translation: *En Mémoire d'Elle: Essai de reconstruction des origines chrétiennes selon la théologie féministe*. Cogitatio Fidei, 136. Traduit de l'américain par Macelline Brun. Paris: Editions du Cerf, 1986.

Italian translation: *In memoria di lei: Una recostruzione femminista delle origini cristiane*. Edizione italiana a cura di M. Corsani Comba. Torino: Claudiana, 1990.

Reviewed by Mary Pellauer in *Theology Today* 45 (1989): 472.

Also critically discussed by Giuseppe Segalla in his essay "L'Ermeneutica biblica femminista di E. Schüssler Fiorenza," *Studia Patavina* 37 (1990): 585-599

Flew, R. Newton. *Jesus and His Way: A Study of the Ethics of the New Testament*. London: Epworth Press, 1963.

An expansion of the 1948 Cato Lecture, and published after Flew's death in 1962.

Gallagher, John, C.S.B. *The Basis for Christian Ethics*. New York: Paulist Press, 1985.

See especially in Part II, "The Criteria for Moral Judgment: Sacred Scripture," Chapters 10-12 for Gallagher's treatment of New Testament ethics.

Goldsmith, Dale. *New Testament Ethics*. Elgin IL: Brethren Press, 1988.

Brief consideration of the distinctive "moral personality" of eight "authors" of the New Testament in reference to the Christian life: James, Paul, 1 Peter, Hebrews, as well as the four gospels. Goldsmith's treatment is aimed primarily at the interested lay reader rather than the professional exegete or ethician.

Goldsmith is an ordained minister in the Presbyterian Church.

Golser, Karl, Hrsg. *Christlicher Glaube und Moral*. Innsbruck-Wien, 1986.

Harvey, A.E. [Anthony Ernest]. *Strenuous Commands: The Ethic of Jesus.* London: SCM, 1990.

Harvey is Sub-Dean of Westminster, a former theology lecturer at the University of Oxford, and a New Testament scholar.

Harvey, Nicholas Peter. *The Morals of Jesus.* London: Darton, Longman and Todd, 1991.

States that Jesus did not offer a set of moral commands, and that in fact he was little interested in morals as such. Through an analysis of some of the "hard sayings" of Jesus Harvey intends to show that these should lead us to a creative freedom in which we can explore new dimensions of human life.

Harvey taught Christian ethics at Queen's College in Birmingham and is now a freelance writer and speaker.

Hays, Richard B. *The Moral Vision of the New Testament: Community, Cross, New Creation. A Contemporary Introduction to New Testament Ethics.* San Francisco: Harper San Francisco, 1996.

Hays proposes three central organizing metaphors from the New Testament, Community, Cross, and New Creation, as a basic methodological approach to utilizing the biblical material in Christian ethics. Hays also names and treats four principal "tasks" of using the Bible in ethics: the descriptive task (what is being said); the synthetic task (how does this or that passage, text, etc., fit within the larger biblical text in a coherent manner); the hermeneutical task of interpreting the biblical texts for ethics, and finally the "pragmatic" task of "living under the Word" (applying the biblical texts to concrete moral issues). Hays treats several such issues in individual chapters: non-violence, divorce and remarriage, homosexuality, anti-Judaism and ethnic conflict, and abortion.

Hays is professor of New Testament at Duke University Divinity School, and taught for a number of years previously at Yale.

Reviewed by Luke Timothy Johnson: "Why Scripture Isn't Enough." *Commonweal* (6 June 1997): 23-25.

Herr, Theodor. *Naturrecht aus der kritischen Sicht des Neuen Testamentes.* Abhandlungen zur Sozialethik, Band 11. Paderborn--München--Wien, 1976.

Hiers, Richard H. *Jesus and Ethics, Four Interpretations*. Philadelphia: Westminster Press, 1968.

Hoffmann, Paul.; Eid, Volker. *Jesus von Nazareth und eine christliche Moral. Sittliche Perspektiven der Verkündigung Jesu*. Questiones Disputatae, 66. Freiburg: Herder, 1975.

Horsley, Richard A. *The Liberation of Christmas: The Infancy Narratives in Social Context*. New York: Crossroad, 1989.

Briefly discussed by Lisa Sowle Cahill in her article "The New Testament and Ethics: Communities of Social Change," *Interpretation* 44 (1990): 383-395.

Hoskyns, Edwyn Clement, and Davey, Francis Noel. *Crucifixion--Resurrection: The Pattern of the Theology and Ethics of the New Testament*. Edited, with a biographical introduction by Gordon S. Wakefield. London: SPCK, 1983.

Hoskyns lived from 1884-1937.

Houlden, J.L. *Ethics and the New Testament*. Baltimore and Hammondsworth: Penguin, 1973; and New York and London: Oxford University Press, 1977.

Houlden's basic position is contemporary Christians should not turn to the New Testament for *specific* guidance, but rather should approach moral issues by asking the question, "On the basis of what we know of God through Christ, what should we now do?"

Houlden is Professor of Theology at King's College, University of London.

Johnson, Luke Timothy. *Decision Making in the Church: A Biblical Model*. Philadelphia: Fortress Press, 1983.

See Johnson's *Scripture and Discernment: Decision Making in the Church* for a 1996 revised and expanded edition of this work.

Johnson is professor of New Testament at the Candler School of Theology at Emory University.

_____. *Scripture and Discernment: Decision Making in the Church.* Nashville: Abingdon Press, 1996.

> Argues that the Church should not make decisions according simply to good management policy, but in response to God's activity in the world. Revised and expanded edition of Johnson's *Decision Making in the Church: A Biblical Model,* (Philadelphia: Fortress Press, 1983).

Kahn, Robert I. *The Letter and the Spirit.* Waco TX: Word, 1972.

Kertelge, Karl, Hrsg. *Ethik im Neuen Testament.* Questiones Disputatae, 102. Freiburg: Herder, 1984.

Knox, John. *The Ethics of Jesus in the Teaching of the Church: Its Authority and Relevance.* Nashville: Abingdon Press, 1961.

Koenig, John. *New Testament Hospitality: Partners with Strangers as Promise and Mission.* Overtures to Biblical Theology, 17. Philadelphia: Fortress Press, 1985.

> Examines the ministry of Jesus, Paul and the life-style of the early church depicted in Luke-Acts to show that the early Christians fostered a way of life in which individuals acted as "God's guests and hosts on behalf of the world." Hospitality and openness to strangers are viewed as both crucial to the Christian life and the development of the faith and ethics of the early believers.

Légasse, Simon. *«Et qui est mon prochain?» Etude sur l'agape dans le Nouveau Testament.* Lectio Divina, 136. Paris Editions du Cerf, 1989.

> Italian translation: *E chi è il mio prossimo?.* Roma: Edizioni Dehoniane, 1991.

> Also includes Old Testament background material.

Lillie, William. *Studies in New Testament Ethics.* Edinburgh: Oliver and Boyd, 1961; Philadelphia: Westminster, 1963.

Lohse, Eduard. *Theological Ethics of the New Testament.* Translated by M. Eugene Boring. Minneapolis: Fortress Press, 1991.

German original: *Theologische Ethik des Neuen Testaments.* Stuttgart: Verlag W. Kohlhammer, 1988.

Italian translation: *Etica Teologica del Nuovo Testamento.* Biblioteca di Cultura Religiosa, 57. A cura di Omero Soffriti. Brescia: Paideia, 1991.

Lohse discusses method, and then individual chapters treat The Old Testament and Greek Hellenistic Background, The Christological Grounding of Early Christian ethics, The Kingship of God, The New Righteousness, Directions for Everyday Life of the Christians, The New Creation in the Life of the Believer, The Worldliness of Faith, Law and Commandment, Endurance in Suffering, and Early Christian Ethics in Late Antiquity. Each chapter also ends with a bibliography.

Reviewed by L. John Topel, S.J. in *Theological Studies* 53 (1992): 550-552.

Lohse is a Lutheran bishop and former New Testament professor at the University of Göttingen.

Longenecker, Richard. *New Testament Social Ethics for Today.* Grand Rapids: Eerdmans, 1984.

Malherbe, Abraham J. *Social Aspects of Early Christianity.* 2nd ed. Philadelphia: Fortress Press, 1983.

Manson, T.W. *Ethics and the Gospel.* New York: Scribner's, 1960.

An unrevised version of the Ayer Lectures given at Colgate-Rochester Divinity School and published posthumously.

Marshall, L.H. *The Challenge of New Testament Ethics.* London: Macmillan, 1947.

Marxsen, Willi. *New Testament Foundations for Christian Ethics.* Translated by O.C. Dean. Minneapolis: Fortress Press, 1993.

German Original: `Christliche' und christliche Ethik im Neuen Testament.
Gütersloh: Gütersloher Verlagshaus Gerd Mohn, 1989.

Marxsen maintains that one should not seek a "normative" ethic in the New
Testament, but rather a "Christian" ethic--christological and existential.

Critically reviewed by Giuseppe Segalla: "C'è un'etica «cristiana» nel Nuovo
Testamento?" *Rivista Biblica* 37 (1989): 461-467.

Marxsen is emeritus professor of New Testament at the Protestant
Theological Faculty of the Westphalian Wilhelms-University in Münster.

Matera, Frank J. *New Testament Ethics: The Legacies of Jesus and Paul.* Louisville:
Westminster John Knox Press, 1996.

The author explores the broad range of ethical concerns found in the teachings
of Jesus and Paul and illuminates in identifiable unity that underlies the ethical
teachings of both.

Meeks, Wayne A. *The Moral World of the First Christians.* Library of Early
Christianity, vol. 6. Philadelphia: The Westminster Press, 1986.

Briefly discussed by Lisa Sowle Cahill in her article "The New Testament and
Ethics: Communities of Social Change," *Interpretation* 44 (1990): 383-395.

_____. *The Origins of Christian Morality: The First Two Centuries.* New Haven:
Yale University Press, 1993.

Merklein, Helmut, Hrsg. *Neues Testament und Ethik. Für Rudolf Schnackenburg.*
Freiburg: Herder, 1989.

Festschrift for Rudolf Schnackenburg by a large number of authors. Essays
range on Jesus and the Synoptics (7); Johannine literature (2); Pauline (7) and
Deutero-Pauline literature (4); Letter to James (1); Revelation (2); and
Miscellaneous themes (6).

Reviewed by Denis Müller in *Etudes Théologiques et Religieuses* 66 (1991):
565-568.

Merklein, Helmut. *Die Gottesherschaft als Handlungsprinzip: Untersuchung zur Ethik Jesu. Forschung zur Bibel*, no. 34. Würzburg: Echter Verlag, 1982.

Montagnini, Felice. *Messaggio del regno e appello morale nel Nuovo Testamento.* Brescia: Morcelliana, 1976.

Mott, Stephen Charles. *Jesus and Social Ethics.* Grove Booklets on Ethics, 55. Malden MA: Institute for Christian Renewal, 1984.

Criticizes the view that Jesus' teachings cannot be invoked for contemporary systematic social justice concerns.

Neuhäusler, Engelbert. *Anspruch und Antwort Gottes. Zur Lehre von den Weisungen innerhalb der synoptischen Jesusverkündigung.* Düsseldorf, 1962.

French translation: *Exigence de Dieu et morale chrétienne. Etudes sur les ensegnements moraux de la prédication de Jésus dans les Synoptiques.* Lectio divina, 70. Par F. Schanen. Paris: Editions du Cerf, 1971.

Osborn, Eric. *Ethical Patterns in Early Christian Thought.* Cambridge: Cambridge University Press, 1976, 1978.

French translation: *La morale dans la pensée chrétienne primitive: Description des archétypes de la morale patristique.* Théologie Historique, 68. Traduit de l'anglais par E. Latteur. Paris: Beauchesne, 1984.

Presents the historical background of the New Testament beginnings of the Church and then considers the ethics of Clement of Alexandria, Basil, John Chrysostom and Augustine, using four themes of righteousness, discipleship, faith and love.

Palmer, Earl F. *Old Law--New Life: The Ten Commandments and New Testament Faith.* Nashville: Abingdon Press, 1984.

Pierce, C[laude] A[nthony]. *Conscience in the New Testament: A Study of Syneidesis in the New Testament; in the light of its sources, and with particular reference to St. Paul: with some observations regarding its pastoral relevance today.* Studies in Biblical Theology, 15. London: SCM Press, 1955.

Pinckaers, Servais, O.P. *L'Evangile et la morale.* Etudes d'éthique chrétienne, 29. Paris: Editions du Cerf, 1990.

Italian translation: *La Parola e la coscienza.* Torino: Società Editrice Internazionale, 1991.

Includes articles from a 20 year period which deal with three principal areas of renewal in moral theology: gospel-morality relationship, restoration of hope and love to a central place in moral methodology, and the correction of a false individualism. A key organising theme in Pinckaers' work is *bonheur*, or beatitude and happiness.

[From a review of the 6th edition (1990) by Raphael Gallagher, C.Ss.R. in *Studia Moralia* 29 (1991): 484-488.]

_____. *La Justice évangélique.* Paris: Téqui, 1986.

Petraglio, Renzo. *Obiezione di coscienza: Il Nuovo Testamento provoca i cristiani.* Bologna: Edizioni Dehoniane Bologna, 1984.

Pizirin, Daniel. *Jesus prechait-il une morale?* Paris: Editions de l'Atelier, 1994.

Reumann, John. *Righteousness in the New Testament: "Justification" in the United States Lutheran-Roman Catholic Dialogue. With Responses by Joseph A. Fitzmeyer and Jerome D. Quinn.* Philadelphia: Fortress Press, and New York: Paulist Press, 1982.

Reumann's essay is entitled "'Justification by Grace through Faith' as Expression of the Gospel: The Biblical Witness to the Reformation Emphasis."

Ringe, Sharon H. *Jesus, Liberation, and the Biblical Jubilee: Images for Ethics and Christology.* Overtures to Biblical Theology, 19. Philadelphia: Fortress Press, 1985.

Sanders, Jack T. *Ethics in the New Testament*. Philadelphia: Fortress Press; and London: SCM, 1975, 1986.

Analyzes and critiques the basic ethical perspectives found in the New Testament, with six chapters devoted to "Jesus," the Synoptics and Acts, Paul, Deutero-Pauline Epistles, Johannine Literature, and the Later Epistles and the Apocalypse. Sanders holds that the ethical perspective of Jesus is inseparably linked to his eschatological expectation of the imminent coming of the Kingdom of God, and that New Testament ethics can offer nothing to a contemporary ethics.

Schelkle, Karl Hermann. *Theologie des Neuen Testaments. III. Ethos*. Düsseldorf: Patmos-Verlag, 1970.

Italian translation: *Teologia del Nuovo Testamento. III. Ethos*. A cura di G. Cappelli. Bologna, 1974.

In Spanish: *Teología del Nuevo Testamento. III. Moral*. Sección de Sagrada Escritura, 147. Barcelona: Herder, 1975.

Schnackenburg, Rudolf. *Christian Existence in the New Testament*. Notre Dame: University of Notre Dame Press, 1968.

Original in German, translations (among others) in French and Italian.

French translation: *L'Existence chrétienne selon le Nouveau Testament*. I-II. Paris: Desclée de Brouver, 1971.

_____. *The Moral Teaching of the New Testament*. Translated by J. Holland-Smith and W.J. O'Hara from the second revised German edition (1962). London: Burns and Oates, 1965.

German original: *Die sittliche Botschaft des Neuen Testaments*. München: Max Hüber Verlag, 1962..

Italian translation: *Messaggio morale del Nuovo Testamento*. Alba, 1971.

Also translated into French, Spanish, etc.

134

———. *Die sittliche Botschaft des Neuen Testaments. Band I: Von Jesus zur Urkirche. Band II: Die urchristlichen Verkündiger.* Völlige Neubearbeitung. Herders theologischer Kommentar zum Neuen Testament, Supplementband. Freiburg: Herder, 1986, 1988.

French translation: *Le Message moral du Nouveau Testament.* Lyon, 1963.

Italian translation: *Il messaggio morale del Nuovo Testamento, I. Da Gesù all chiesa primitiva; II. I primi predicatori cristiani.* Supplementi al Commentario teologico del Nuovo Testamento. Brescia: Paideia, 1989, 1990.

Reviewed by Elena Bosetti in *Rivista di Teologia Morale* 23 (1991): 389-399.

In Spanish: *El mensaje moral del Nuevo Testamento. I De Jesús a la Iglesia primitiva; II Los primeros predicadores.* Barcelona: Herder, 1989, 1991.

Schrage, Wolfgang. *The Ethics of the New Testament.* Translated by David E. Green. Philadelphia: Fortress Press, 1988.

German original: *Ethik des Neuen Testaments.* Grundrisse zum Neuen Testament, 4. Göttingen: Vandenhoeck & Ruprecht, 1982.

Spanish translation: *Etica del Nuevo Testamento.* Biblioteca de Estudios Bíiblicos. Salamanca: Sígueme, 1987.

Reviewed by Sharon H. Ringe in *Theology Today* 45 (1989): 355.

Excellent exegetical treatment of the ethical material found throughout the New Testament.

———, Hrsg. *Studien zum Text und zur Ethik des Neuen Testaments. Festschrift zum 80. Geburtstag von Heinrich Greeven.* Berlin/New York: Walter de Gruyter, 1986.

Schramm, Tim und Löwenstein, Kathrin. *Unmoralische Helden. Anstößige Gleichnisse Jesu.* Göttingen: Vandenhoeck & Ruprecht, 1986.

Schulz, Siegfried. *Neutestamentliche Ethik.* Zürcher Grundrisse zur Bibel. Zürich: Theologischer Verlag Zürich, 1987.

Schürmann, Heinz. *Studien zur neutestamentlichen Ethik.* Stuttgarter biblische Aufsatzbäande, 7. Herausgegeben von Thomas Söding. Stuttgart: Verlag Katholisches Bibelwerk, 1990.

Recensione in italiano da [Book review in Italian by] Giuseppe Segalla in *Studia Patavina* 37 (1990): 401-403.

Scott, Charles Archibald Anderson. *New Testament Ethics, An Introduction.* The Hulsean Lectures, 1929. Cambridge: University Press, 1929.

Scott, E. F. (Ernest Findlay). *The Ethical Teaching of Jesus.* New York: Macmillan, 1924, 1936.

Scott lived from 1868 to 1954.

Segalla, Giuseppe. *Introduzione all'etica del Nuovo Testamento.* Biblioteca Biblica, 2. Brescia: Queriniana, 1989.

L'opera raccoglie alcuni articoli pubblicati tra il 1977-1987, rivisti e aggiornati con l'aggiunta di altri, tutti frutto di lezioni al relativo corso di licenza alla Facoltà Teologica Settentrionale--sede centrale di Milano.

This book contains several articles published between 1977-1987, somewhat revised and expanded, in light of the author's courses given in the Licentiate Program at the Facoltà Teologica Settentrionale--sede centrale in Milan, Italy.

See also the review by Giovanni Leonardi in *Studia Patavina* 37 (1990): 601-625; and the review by Elena Bosetti in *Rivista di Teologia Morale* 23 (1991): 400-402.

Segalla is professor of New Testament Exegesis at the Theological Faculty of Milan.

Spicq, Ceslas, O.P. *Théologie morale du Nouveau Testament.* Paris, 1965, 1970.

Strecker, Georg. *Handlungsorientierter Glaube. Vorstudien zu einer des N.T. Ethik.* Stuttgart-Berlin, 1972.

Theissen, Gerd. *Social Reality and the Early Christians: Theology, Ethics, and the World of the New Testament.* Translated by Margaret Kohl. Minneapolis: Fortress Press, 1992.

Discusses the correlation between the theological and ethical convictions of the first Christians, as well as the social realities of the world in which they lived.

Verhey, Allen. *The Great Reversal: Ethics and the New Testament.* Grand Rapids: Eerdmans, 1984.

Verhey considers first the ethic of Jesus, and then analyzes the various in which the early church handed down this teaching until its ultimate development of a moral tradition. The final part of the book focuses on the use of the New Testament in the context of the contemporary Church's Christian ethics.

Reviewed by Robert W. Wall in *Theology Today* 42 (1986): 125.

Verhey is the Evert J. and Hattie E. Blekkink Professor of Religion at Hope College.

Vögtle, Anton. *Was ist Frieden? Orientierungshilfen aus dem Neuen Testament.* Freiburg i. B.: Herder, 1984.

Italian translation: *La pace. Le fonti nel Nuovo Testamento.* Brescia: Morcelliana, 1984.

Wakefield, Gordon S. *See* Hoskyns, Edwin Clement.

Walters, John R. *Perfection in New Testament Theology: Ethics and Eschatology in Relational Dynamic.* Mellen Biblical Press Series 25. Lewiston NY: Mellen, 1995.

The author's wide-ranging survey of NT perfection includes modern theologians (from Schleiermacher to Cullman), second temple Judaism, Hebrews, 1 John, and the Pauline epistles. The cardinal result: NT perfection (more akin to Judaism than to Hellenism) is an endowment which pertains to moral behavior both now (faith, obedience, endurance, etc.) and in the eschatological future (the consummation of such acts), rather than some static, unchanging, absolute state of being as the ontological norm against which all else is measured. Perfection, thus equated with the Christian life itself, becomes a matter of degree.

Wendland, Heinz-Dietrich. *Ethik des Neuen Testaments: Eine Einführung von Heinz-Dietrich Wendland.* Grundrisse zum Neuen Testament, 4. Göttingen: Vandenhoeck & Ruprecht, 1970.

In French: *Ethique du Nouveau Testament. Introduction aux problèmes.* Nouvelle série théologique. Genève: Labor et Fides, 1972.

Italian translation: *Etica del Nuovo Testamento.* Nuovo Testamento, supplementi, 4. Brescia: Paideia, 1975.

Reviewed by Elena Bosetti in *Rivista di Teologia Morale* 23 (1991): 396-397.

Wiebe, Ben. *Messianic Ethics: Jesus' Proclamation of the Kingdom of God and the Church in Response.* Waterloo, Ontario: Herald Press, 1992.

Wiebe argues that Jesus' ethical teachings are comprehensible only with the double context of his own consciousness as messianic king, and his intent to restore a faithful community. In this context Jesus' ethics are best interpreted as an ethics for a repentent and restored people of God, i.e., for the church.

Wilder, Amos N. *Eschatology and Ethics in the Teaching of Jesus.* New York: Harper, 1939, 1950.

Yoder, John Howard. *The Politics of Jesus.* 2nd Ed. Grand Rapids: Eerdmans, 1972, 1994.

In Portuguese: *A politica de Jesus.* Serie Estudos Biblicos. Sao Leopoldo: Ed. Sinodal, 1988.

Author argues that Jesus did teach a specific Christian ethics of non-violence, and that the New Testament is directly normative in this respect for contemporary Christians.

Yoder is a well-known ethicist in the Mennonite tradition who teaches at the University of Notre Dame.

_____. *The Priestly Kingdom: Social Ethics as Gospel.* Notre Dame: University of Notre Dame Press, 1984.

Yoder examines first the theoretical and scriptural foundations of Christian social ethics, then he reviews the historical efforts of the Anabaptists to "return" to the fundamental ethics of the New Testament, before concluding with an analysis of democracy and civil religion in the contemporary world.

****

Sermon on the Mount

Articles on the Sermon on the Mount

AA.VV. "'Et moi, je vous dis'. Le sermon sur la montagne dans l'évangile de Matthieu." *Lumière et Vie* 36 (1987) n. 183.

Beasley-Murray, G.R. "Matthew 6:33: The Kingdom of God and the Ethics of Jesus, «Seek first his kingdom and righteousness, and all these things will be added to you»." In *Neues Testament und Ethik. Für Rudolf Schnackenburg*, 31-52. Edited by Helmut Merklein. Freiburg: Herder, 1989.

Betz, Hans Dieter. "The Hermeneutical Principles of the Sermon on the Mount." *Journal of Theology for Southern Africa* 42 (1983): 17-28.

Also found in *Essays on the Sermon on the Mount*, Philadelphia: Fortress Press, 1985).

German original: "Die hermeneutischen Prinzipien in der Bergpredigt (Mt 5, 17-20)." In *Verifikationen, Festschrift für Gerhard Ebeling zum 70. Geburtstag*, 27-41. Herausgegeben von Eberhard Jüngel, Johannes Wallmann, und Wilfrid Werbeck. Tübingen: J.C.B. Mohr, 1982.

Betz is professor of New Testament at the University of Chicago.

_____. "Kosmogonie und Ethik in der Bergpredigt." *Zeitschrift für Theologie und Kirche* 81 (1984): 139-171.

Buechekle, H. "Bergpredigt und Gewaltfreiheit." *Stimmen der Zeit* 199 (1981): 632-640.

Burchard, Charles. "Le thème du Sermon de la Montagne." *Etudes Théologiques et Religieuses* 62 (1987): 1-17.

Burkhardt, H. "Die Bergpredigt--eine allgemeine Handlungsanweisung? *Kritische Erwägungen zu dem Aufsatz von A. Strobel: Die Bergpredigt als ethische Weisung heute.*" *Theologische Beiträge* 15 (1984): 137-140.

Cahill, Lisa Sowle. "The Ethical Implications of the Sermon on the Mount." *Interpretation* 41 (1987): 144-156.

Cahill is a Roman Catholic and did her doctoral studies at the University of Chicago under the direction of James M. Gustafson. She is Professor of Theological Ethics at Boston College, and past President of both the Catholic Theological Society of America (CTSA) and the Society of Christian Ethics (SCE).

Camacho, F. "Las Bienaventuranzas de Mateo (5, 3-10). Análisis semántico y comentario exegético." *Communio* (Sevilla) 16 (1983): 151-181.

Carrón, J. "«Bienaventurados los que tienen hambre y sed de justicia porque ellos serán saciados» (Mt 5,6)." *Revista Católica Internacional* 12 (1990): 521-541.

Collins, Raymond F. "Christian Personalism and the Sermon on the Mount." Chapter 10 in *Christian Morality: Biblical Foundations,* 223-237. Notre Dame: University of Notre Dame Press, 1986.

Collins taught New Testament for many years at Louvain in Belgium, and is now at Catholic University in Washington, D.C.

Dautzenberg, Gerhard. "Ist das Schwerberbot Mt 5, 33-37; Jak 5, 12 ein Beispiel für die Toralkritik Jesu?" *Biblische Zeitschrift* 25 (1980): 47-66.

Davies, W.D., and Allison, Dale G., Jr. "Reflections on the Sermon on the Mount." *Scottish Journal of Theology* 44 (1991): 283-309.

Descamps, A[lbert].L. "Le discours sur la montagne." *Ephemerides Theologicae Lovanienses* 12 (1981): 5-39.

Dietzfelbinger, Ch. "Die Frömmigkeitsregeln von Mt 6, 1-18 als Zeugnisse frühchristlicher Geschichte." *Zeitschrift für die Neutestamentliche Wissenschaft* 75 (1984): 184-201.

Dumbrell, W.J. "The Logic of the Role of the Law in Matthew V 1-20." *Novum Testamentum* 23 (1,1981): 1-21.

Egger, Wilhelm. "Handlungsorientierte Auslegung der Antithesen Mt 5, 21-48." In *Ethik im Neuen Testament*, 119-144. Hrsg. Karl Kertelge. Freiburg: Herder, 1984.

Falcke, H. "Die Seligpreisungen der Bergpredigt und das gesellschaftliche Zeugnis der Kirche." *Zeitschrift für Evangelische Ethik* 28 (1984): 376-401.

Frankenmoelle, H. "Neue Literatur zur Bergpredigt." *Theologische Revue* 79 (1983): 62-74.

Freisen, B. "Approaches to the Interpretation and Application of the Sermon on the Mount." *Direction* 10 (2, 1981): 19-25.

Giavini, Giovanni. "Il discorso della montagna nella problematica attuale circa il valore delle norme etiche del Nuovo Testamento." AA.VV., *Fondamenti biblici della teologia morale: Atti della XXII Settimana Biblica*, 253-272. Brescia, 1973.

Sostanzialmente lo stesso testo pubblicato come seconda parte dell'articolo in *La Scuola Cattolica* 100 (1972): 83-97, però aggiornato bibliograficamente e modificato anche in base ad alcuni suggerimenti avuti durante la Settimana Biblica della Associazione biblica italiana.

This is essentially the same article originally published as part two of an article in *La Scuola Cattolica* 100 (1972): 83-97, though with some bibliographic additions, and slight revisions suggested during the Italian "Settimana Biblica" (Biblical Week) meeting.

Hall, Douglas John. "The Theology and Ethics of the Lord's Prayer." *Princeton Seminary Bulletin* Supplementary Issue, 2 (1992): 125-136.

One of a series of articles in this issue devoted to various aspects of the Lord's Prayer.

Hall is Professor of Christian Theology on the Faculty of Religious Studies at McGill University.

Hanssler, B. "Das Jünger-Ethos der Bergpredigt im Verhältnis zu den allgemeinen Moralprinzipen." *Renovatio* 40 (1984): 82-95.

Hauerwas, Stanley. "Living the Proclaimed Reign of God: *A Sermon on the Sermon on the Mount*." *Interpretation* 47 (1993): 152-158.

One of a series of articles on the Kingdom of God in this issue.

Hauerwas is a well-known Methodist ethician who taught for many years at the University of Notre Dame and is now Gilbert T. Rowe Professor of Theological Studies at Duke University.

_____. "The Sermon on the Mount: Just War and the Quest for Peace." *Concilium* 195 (1988): 36-43.

Hengel, Martin. "Das Ende aller Politik. *Die Bergpredigt in der Diskussion*." *Evangelische Kommentare* 14 (1981): 686-690.

142

Hoerber, R.G. "Implication of the Imperative in the Sermon on the Mount." *Concordia Journal* 7 (3, 1981): 100-103.

Kertelge, Karl. "Handeln aus glauben--Zum Verständnis der Bergpredigt." *Renovatio* 40 (1984): 73-81.

Kirchschläger, W. "Die Friedenbotschaft der Bergpredigt. *Zu Mt 5.9.17-48; 7,1-5.*" *Kairos* 25 (1983): 223-237.

Légasse, Simon. "L'amore dei nemici nei vangeli. Matteo." Capitolo 5 di *E chi è il mio prossimo?*, 99-112. Roma: Edizioni Dehoniane, 1991.

French original in: *«Et qui est mon prochain?» Etude sur l'agape dans le Nouveau Testament*. Lectio Divina, 136. Paris Editions du Cerf, 1989.

Linskens, J. "A Pacifist Interpretation of Peace in the Sermon on the Mount?" *Concilium* 164 (1983): 16-25.

Lohfink, Gerhard. "Der präexistente Heilsplan. Sinn und Hintergrund der dritten Vaterunserbitte." In *Neues Testament und Ethik. Für Rudolf Schnackenburg*, 110-133. Herausgegeben von Helmut Merklein. Freiburg: Herder, 1989.

———. "Wem gilt die Bergpredigt? Eine redaktionskritische Untersuchung von Mt 4, 23--5,2 und 7,28f." In *Ethik im Neuen Testament*, 145-167. Hrsg. Karl Kertelge. Freiburg: Herder, 1984.

In Italian: *Per chi vale il discorso della montagna? Contribuiti per un'etica cristiana*. Biblioteca biblica, 3. Brescia: Queriniana, 1990.

In Spanish: *El sermon de la montaña, ¿para quién?*. Barcelona: Herder, 1989.

McEleney, Neil J. "The Principles of the Sermon on the Mount." *Catholic Biblical Quarterly* 41 (1979): 552-570.

Römelt, Josef. "Normativität, Ethische Radikalität und Christlicher Glaube. Zur theologisch-ethischen Hermeneutik der Bergpredigt." *Zeitschrift für Katholische Theologie* 114 (1992): 293-303.

Schedl, Cl. "Zur Ehebruchklausel der Bergpredigt in Lichte der neugefundenen Tempelrolle." *Theologisch-praktische Quartelschrift* 130 (1982): 34-49.

Schnackenburg, Rudolf. "Die Seligpreisung der Friedenstifter (Mt 5,9) im matthäischem Kontext." *Biblische Zeitschrift* 104 (1982): 161-178.

Schuele, Frederick E. "Living Up to Matthew's Sermon on the Mount: An Approach." In *Christian Biblical Ethics: From Biblical Revelation to Contemporary Christian Praxis: Method and Content*, 200-210. New York: Paulist Press, 1984.

Sicre, José Luis. "El Sermón del Monte: La actitud cristiana ante las obras de piedad." *Proyección* 39 (1992): 95-102.

_____. "El Sermón del Monte: La actitud cristiana ante el dinero y el prójimo." *Proyección* 39 (1992): 193-204.

Simoens, Y. "Une lecture du discours sur la montagne pour éclairer la conscience chrétienne." *Lumen Vitae* 40 (1980): 415-432.

Strecker, Georg. "Compliance--Love of One's Enemy--The Golden Rule." *Australian Biblical Review* 29 (1981): 38-46.

_____. "The Law in the Sermon on the Mount, and the Sermon on the Mount as Law." In *The Promise and Practice of Biblical Theology*, 35-49. Edited by John H.P. Reumann. Minneapolis: Fortress Press, 1991.

Strobel, August. "Die Bergpredigt als ethische Weisung heute. *Vier Thesen für Nachfolger Jesu Christi in einer modernen Welt.*" *Theologische Beiträge* 15 (1984): 3-16.

144

Vögtle, Anton. "Ein «unablässiger Stachel» (Mt 5,39b-42 par Lk 6,29-30)." In *Neues Testament und Ethik. Für Rudolf Schnackenburg*, 53-70. Herausgegeben von Helmut Merklein. Freiburg: Herder, 1989.

Wambacq, B.N. "Mattieu 5, 31-32. Possibilité de divorce ou obligation de rompre une union illégitime." *Nouvelle Revue Théologique* 104 (1982): 154-190.

Weder, H. "Die `Rede der Reden'. *Beobachtungen zum Verständnis der Bergpredigt Jesu.*" *Evangelische Theologie* 45 (1985): 45-60.

Williams, James G. "Paraenesis, Ethics, and Excess: Matthew's Rhetoric in the Sermon on the Mount." *Semeia* 50 (1990): 163-187.

The Matthean rites of passage or initiation introduce the disciples to a vision in which the passion of Christ and eschatological reward are translated into a new ethical mode that encourages concrete acts of love and non-violence as the re-enactment of redemption. The general and typical elements of paraenesis are subsumed by this transformational process into a rhetorical mode of "excess" (Frank Kermode).

Wink, Walter. "Beyond Just War and Pacifism: Jesus' Nonviolent Way." *Review and Expositor* 89 (1992): 197-214.

Argues for non-violence and though not non-resistance to evil. Bases his arguments largely on an exegesis of Mt 5:38-42.

Wolbert, Werner. "Bergpredigt und Gewaltlosigkeit." *Theologie und Philosophie* 57 (1982): 498-525.

Books on the Sermon on the Mount

Alt, Franz. *Peace is Possible: The Politics of the Sermon on the Mount*. New York: Schocken Books, 1985.

In German: *Liebe ist möglich. Die Bergpredigt im Atomzeitalter.* Serie Piper, 284. München: Piper, 1985.

Betz, Hans Dieter. *Essays on the Sermon on the Mount.* Translated by L.L. Welborn. Philadelphia: Fortress Press, 1985.

German original: *Studien zur Bergpredigt.* Tübingen: J.C.B. Mohr, 1985.

Reviewed by Richard A. Edwards in *Theology Today* 43 (1987): 132.

Betz is professor of New Testament at the University of Chicago.

Bonhoeffer, Dietrich. *The Cost of Discipleship.* Translated by Reginald H. Fuller, revised by Irmgard Booth. Rev. ed. New York: Macmillan, 1963.

German original: *Nachfolge.* München: Chr. Kaiser Verlag, 1937.

Translations available in many other languages, including French, *La Prix de la grâce,* and Italian, *Sequela,* Nuovi Saggi Queriniana, 3, (Brescia: Queriniana, 1971).

Classic work of the well-known German Lutheran theologian was imprisoned in April 1943 for his role in the Nazi resistance hanged at the age of 39 by the Gestapo in the Nazi concentration camp at Flossenbürg in April 1945. The book contains a theological discussion of the meaning of Christian discipleship and for this Bonhoeffer devotes an extended discussion of the Call of Levi in Matthew's Gospel and the Sermon on the Mount.

Broer, Ingo. *Die Seligpreisungen der Bergpredigt. Studien au ihrer Überlieferung und Interpretation.* Bonner biblische Beitrage. Bonn: Peter Hanstein, 1986.

Brooks, Oscar Stephen. *The Sermon on the Mount: Authentic Human Values.* Washington D.C.: University Press, 1985.

Carter, Warren. *What Are They Saying About Matthew's Sermon on the Mount?.* New York: Paulist Press, 1994.

Focuses on scholarship published since 1960.

Coste, René. *Le grand secret des béatitudes. Une théologie et une spiritualité pour aujourd'hui*. Coll. Théologie de la Charité. Paris: Ed. S.O.S., 1985.

Crosby, Michael H., O.F.M. *Spirituality of the Beatitudes: Matthew's Challenge for First World Christians*. Maryknoll: Orbis Books, 1981.

Intended as a further Matthean reflection in line with the author's earlier work, *Thy Will Be Done: Praying the Our Father as Subversive Activity*.

_____. *Thy Will Be Done: Praying the Our Father as Subversive Activity*. Maryknoll: Orbis Books, 1977.

Crosby's contention is that many Christians pray the Our Father inauthentically when they fail to ask what changes should be brought about in their lives and their world. An authentic praying of the Our Father will involve Christian conversion, and then a "subversion" of the cultural idols of our time.

Davenport, Gene. *Into the Darkness: Discipleship in the Sermon on the Mount*. Nashville: Abingdon Press, 1988.

DeVulder, Gérard, a cura di. *Il vangelo della felicità. Le beatitudini*. Brescia: Queriniana, 1990.

Dornreich, Monica, ed. *Vater-Unser Bibliographie--The Lord's Prayer, a Bibliography*. Veröffentlichungen der Stiftung Oratio Dominica. Freiburg im Breisgau: Herder, 1982.

Häring, Bernard, C.Ss.R. *The Beatitudes: Their Personal and Social implications*. Slough: St. Paul Publications, 1976.

Häring (born 1912) is a major Roman Catholic moral theologian who sought to incorporate Scripture into his approach to moral theology, and who taught moral theology for a number of years at the Academia Alphonsianum in Rome.

Hendrickx, Hermann. *El Sermón de la Montaña*. Madrid: Ediciones Paulinas, 1986.

Translated from the Dutch.

Hochgrebe, Volker, ed. *Il discorso della montagna. Una provocazione per la coscienza moderna*. Roma: Città Nuova, 1986.

Hunter, A.M. *Un idéal de vie, le Sermon sur la montagne*. Lire la Bible, 44. Paris: Editions de Cerf, 1973.

Jeremias, Joachim. *The Sermon on the Mount*. Facet Books Biblical Series, no. 2. Translated by Norman Perrin. Philadelphia: Fortress Press, 1963.

Jeremias outlines three traditional approaches to the ethical material of the Sermon: perfectionist code, impossible ideal, or interim ethic. He sees certain values in each, but notes they share a common failing in viewing the Sermon as Law rather than Gospel, in other words, an indicative depiction of incipient life in the Kingdom of God, which presupposes as its condition of possibility the experience of conversion.

German original: *Die Bergpredigt*. Calwer Hefte, no. 27. Stuttgart: Calwer Verlag, 1959.

French translation: *Paroles de Jésus: La Sermon sur la montagne, le Notre-Père dans l'exégèse actuelle*. Lectio Divina, 38. Traduction de Dom Marie Mailhé, O.S.B. Paris: Editions du Cerf, 1963.

Lambrecht, Jan, S.J. *Ich aber sage euch. Die Bergpredigt als programmatische Rede Jesu (Mt 5-7; Lk 6, 20-49)*. Stuttgart: Kath. Bibelwerk, 1984.

Lambrecht is a New Testament exegete.

Lapide, Pinchas. *The Sermon on the Mount: Utopia or Program for Action?* Translated by Arlene Swidler. Maryknoll: Orbis Books, 1986.

German original: *Die Bergpredigt—Utopie oder Program?* Mainz: Matthias-Grunewald Verlag, 1982.

Portuguese translation: *O Sermão da monthanha. Utopio ou programa?*
Pertropolis: Vozes, 1986.

———. *Wie liebt man seine Feinde? Mit einer Neuübersetzung der Bergpredigt (Mt 5-7) unter Berücksichtigung der rabbinischen Lehrmethoden und der judischen Muttersprache Jesu.* Mainz: Matthias-Grünewald Verlag, 1984.

Lohfink, Gerhard. *Wem gilt die Bergpredigt? Beiträge zu einer christlichen Ethik.* Freiburg: Herder, 1988.

Italian translation: *Per chi vale il discorso della montagna? Contribuiti per un'etica cristiana.* Biblioteca biblica, 3. Brescia: Queriniana, 1990.

Spanish translation: *El sermon de la montaña, ¿para quién?.* Barcelona: Herder, 1989.

Reviewed by Elena Bosetti in *Rivista di Teologia Morale* 23 (1991): 406.

Lohse, Eduard. *Die Ethik der Bergpredigt und was sie uns heute zu sagen hat.* Vorlagen, 21. Hannover: Lutherhaus Verlag, 1984.

Lohse is a Lutheran bishop and former New Testament professor at the University of Göttingen.

Patte, Daniel. *Discipleship According to the Sermon on the Mount: Four Legitimate Readings, Four Plausible Views of Discipleship and Their Relative Values.* Valley Forge PA: Trinity Press, 1996.

Pobee, John S. *Who Are the Poor? The Beatitudes As a Call to Community.* The Risk Book Series. Geneva: World Council of Churches, 1987.

Schmidt, K.O. *Die Religion der Bergpredigt als Grundlage rechten Lebens.* München/Engelberg: Drei Eichen Verlag, 1987.

Schnackenburg, Rudolf, Hrsg. *Die Bergpredigt: Utopische Vision oder Handlungsanweisung?* Schriften der Katholischen Akademie in Bayern 107. Dusseldorf: Patmos, 1982.

_____. *Alles kann wer glaubt. Bergpredigt und Vaterunser in der Absicht Jesu.* Freiburg: Herder, 1985.

Schweizer, Eduard. *Il discorso della montagna (Matteo cap. 5-7).* Torino: Claudiana, 1991.

Translated from German.

Siker, Jeffrey S. *Scripture and Ethics: Twentieth-Century Portraits.* New York: Oxford University Press, 1997.

Analyzes eight twentieth-century Protestant and Catholic theologians' use of Scripture in their respective works: Reinhold Niebuhr, H. Richard Niebuhr, Bernhard Häring, Paul Ramsey, Stanley Hauerwas, Gustavo Gutiérrez, James Cone, and Rosemary Radford Ruether. Siker addresses five questions to each author's work: 1) which biblical texts are used; 2) how are the texts used; 3) how does the author envision biblical authority; 4) what kind of hermeneutics are employed; and 5) what does the respective author's approach to the Bible yield in terms of Christian ethics. A concluding chapter focusses on the authors' respective appropriations of the Sermon on the Mount.

Siker is an ordained Presbyterian minister and Associate Professor of Theology at Loyola Marymount University in Los Angeles.

Six, Jean-François. *Les Béatitudes aujourd'hui.* Paris: Editions du Seuil, 1984.

In Italian: *Le beatitudini oggi.* Bologna: Edizioni Dehoniane Bologna, 1986.

Speyr, Adrienne von. *Le sermon sur la montagne.* Paris: P. Lethielleuz; Namur: Culture et Vérité, 1989.

Translated from the German.

150

Stoll, Brigitta. *De Virtute in Virtutem. Zur Auslegungs und Wirkungsgeschicte der Bergpredigt in Kommentaren, Predigten und hagiographischer Literatur von der Merovingerzeit bis um 1200.* Beiträge zur Geschichte der biblischen Exegese, 30. Tübingen: J.C.B. Mohr, 1988.

Stramare, Tarcisio. *Matteo divorzista? Studio su Mt. 5,3 e 19,9.* Brescia: Paideia, 1986.

Strecker, Georg. *Die Bergpredigt. Ein exegetischer Kommentar.* Göttingen: Vandenhoeck & Ruprecht, 1984.

In English: *The Sermon on the Mount: An Exegetical Commentary.* Translated by O.C. Dean, Jr. Nashville: Abingdon Press, 1988.

Talec, Pierre. *Le beatitudini. Messagio di felicità.* Roma: Città Nuova, 1991.

Translated from French.

Thompson, Ernest Trice. *The Sermon on the Mount and Its Meaning for Today.*

Reviewed by Irvin W. Batdorf in *Theology Today* 4 (1948): 288.

Thompson lived from 1894 to 1985.

Vaught, Carl. *The Sermon on the Mount: A Theological Interpretation.* SUNY Series in Religious Studies. Albany: SUNY Press, 1986.

Author is not an exegete or theologian, but rather a philosophy professor at Pennsylvania State University. He presents both an exposition of the meaning of the Sermon on Mount as well as a commentary which deals with the central issues of Jesus' teaching and their relevance today.

Venetz, Hermann-Josef. *Die Bergpredigt. Biblische Anstöße.* Düsseldorf: Patmos Verlag; Freiburg/Schweiz: Kanisius Verlag, 1987.

Ward, K. *The Rule of Love: Reflections on the Sermon on the Mount*. London: Darton, Longman and Todd, 1989.

A meditation on Christian ethics.

****

Other Works on the Gospel of Matthew

Articles on the Gospel of Matthew

Baltensweiler, Heinrich. "Die Ehebruchklauseln bei Matthäus." *Theologische Zeitschrift* 15 (1959): 340-356.

Barth, Gerhard. "Matthew's Understanding of the Law." In *Tradition and Interpretation in Matthew*, 58-164. With Günther Bornkamm and Heinz Joachim Held. The New Testament Library. Translated by Percy Scott. Philadelphia: The Westminster Press, 1963.

Broer, Ingo. "Osservazione sull'interpretazione della legge in Matteo." In *Saggi esegetici sulla legge nel Nuovo Testamento*, 121-214. A cura di Karl Kertelge. Cinisello Balsamo: Edizioni Paoline, 1990.

Original version in: *Das Gesetz im Neuen Testament*. Herausgegeben von Karl Kertelge. Questiones Disputatae, 108. Freiburg: Herder, 1986.

Crouzel, Henri, S.J. "Le sens de `porneia' dans les incises mathéennes." *Nouvelle Revue Théologique* 110 (1988): 903-910.

Donahue, John R., S.J. "The 'Parable' of the Sheep and the Goats: A Challenge to Christian Ethics." *Theological Studies* 47 (1986): 3-31.

Treats the Last Judgment Parable found in Mt 25:31-46, the present debate on the meaning of the parable, and offers an interpretation which posits the parable as a radical challenge to the Christian community.

Donahue studied under Norman Perrin at the University of Chicago is Professor of Biblical Studies (New Testament) at the Jesuit School of Theology and Graduate Theological Union, Berkeley.

Feuillet, A. "Le caractère universel du jugement et la charité sans frontières en Mt 25, 31-46." *Nouvelle Revue Théologique* 102 (1980): 179-196.

Frahier, Louis-Jean. *Le jugement dernier. Implications éthiques pour le bonheur de l'homme (Mt 25, 31-46)*. Recherches morales, Synthèses. Paris: Editions du Cerf, 1992.

Reviewed by Henri Wattiaux in *Revue Théologique de Louvain* 24 (1993): 493-498.

Giesen, Heinz. "`Herrschaft der Himmel' und Gericht. *Zum Gerichtverständnis des Matthäusevangeliums.*" *Studia Moralia* 18 (1980): 195-220.

Herranz Marco, Mariano. "Las espigas arrancadas en sábado (Mt. 12, 1-8 par.). Tradición y elaboración redaccional." In *La Etica Bíblica*, 289-322. XXIX Semana Bíblica Española. Madrid: Consejo Superior de Investigaciones Científicas, 1971.

Keck, Leander E. "Ethics in the Gospel According to Matthew." *Iliff Review* 41 (1984): 39-56.

Keck is Winkley Professor of Biblical Theology at Yale Divinity School.

Kotva, Joseph J., Jr. "Biblical Connections." Chapter 5 in Id. *The Christian Case for Virtue Ethics*, 103-142. Moral Traditions and Moral Arguments Series. Washington, D.C.: Georgetown University Press, 1996.

Discusses Paul and the Gospel of Matthew as part of a larger for a discussion of how the Bible can figure in the development of a Christian approach to virtue ethics. See also Ch. 6 "Theological and Biblical Objections" (pp. 143-166).

Revised version of Kotva's doctoral dissertation done at Fordham University.

Kotva is pastor of the First Mennonite Church in Allentown, Pennsylvania.

Little, David, and Twiss, Sumner B. "Religion and Morality in the Gospel of Matthew." Chapter 7 in Id. *Comparative Religious Ethics*, 156-209. New York: Harper & Row, 1978.

Lohfink, Gerhard. "Der präexistente Heilsplan. Sinn und Hintergrund der dritten Vaterunserbitte." In *Neues Testament und Ethik. Für Rudolf Schnackenburg*, 110-133. Herausgegeben von Helmut Merklein. Freiburg: Herder, 1989.

Marguerat, D. "L'avenir de la loi: Matthieu à l'épreuve de Paul." *Etudes Théologiques et Religieuses* 57 (1982): 361-374.

Matera, Frank J. "The Ethics of the Kingdom in the Gospel of Matthew." *Listening* 24 (1989): 241-250.

The Law is bound up with righteousness, and this means an undivided commitment to Jesus' teachings on mercy and compassion.

McMahon, Michael. "Paralysis of the Heart." *The Bible Today* 31 (1993): 85-88.

Focuses on the cure of the paralytic in Matthew 9:2-8 to show Jesus' attitude toward sin. One of several articles in this issue on the theme of "The Bible on Sin."

Oates, Wayne E. "A Biblical Perspective on Addiction." *Review and Expositor* 91 (1994): 71-75.

Treats Dt 5:6-7; Mt 22:340-40; and Gal 4:3,8.

Pikaza, X. "'Limpios de corazón'. Reflexión bíblica sobre Mt 5,8." *Communio: Revista Católica Internacional* 10 (1988): 502-520.

154

Popkes, W. "Die Gerechtigkeitstradition im Matthäus-Evangelium." *Zeitschrift für die Neutestamentliche Wissenschaft* 80 (1989): 1-23.

Salas, Antonio, O.S.A. "El mensaje del Bautista. Estudio histórico-redaccional de Mt 3, 7-12." In *La Etica Bíblica*, 271-287. XXIX Semana Bíblica Española. Madrid: Consejo Superior de Investigaciones Científicas, 1971.

Snodgrass, Klyne R. "Matthew's Understanding of the Law." *Interpretation* 46 (1992): 368-378.

Via, Dan O. "Narrative World and Ethical Response: The Marvelous and Righteousness in Matthew 1-2." *Semeia* 12 (1978): 123-149.

Via is Professor of New Testament at The Divinity School of Duke University.

_____. "Ethical Responsibility and Human Wholeness in Matthew 25:31-46." *Harvard Theological Review* 80 (1987): 79-100.

_____. "Structure, Christology and Ethics in Matthew." In *Orientation by Disorientation: Studies in Literary Criticism and Biblical Literary Criticism*, 199-215. Pittsburgh Theological Monograph Series, 35. Edited by Richard A. Spencer. Pittsburgh: Pickwick Press, 1980.

Part of a *Festschrift* for William A. Beardslee.

Wattiaux, Henri. "La théologie morale entre l'Ecriture et la raison." *Revue Théologique de Louvain* 24 (1993): 493-498.

Review of Louis-Jean Frahier's *Le jugement dernier. Implications éthiques pour le bonheur de l'homme (Mt 25, 31-46)*. Recherches morales, Synthèses. Paris: Editions du Cerf, 1992.

Whelan, Caroline F. "Suicide in the Ancient World: A Re-examination of Matthew 27:3-10." *Laval Théologique et Philosophique* 49 (1993): 505-522.

Re-examines the death of Judas in a more positive light, through a consideration of suicide in the context of the honor-shame culture of the ancient world.

Books on the Gospel of Matthew

Bonhoeffer, Dietrich. *The Cost of Discipleship*. Translated by Reginald H. Fuller, revised by Irmgard Booth. Rev. ed. New York: Macmillan, 1963.

German original: *Nachfolge*. München: Chr. Kaiser Verlag, 1937.

Translations available in many other languages, including French, *La Prix de la grâce*, and Italian, *Sequela*, Nuovi Saggi Queriniana, 3, (Brescia: Queriniana, 1971).

Classic work of the well-known German Lutheran theologian was imprisoned in April 1943 for his role in the Nazi resistance hanged at the age of 39 by the Gestapo in the Nazi concentration camp at Flossenbürg in April 1945. The book contains a theological discussion of the meaning of Christian discipleship and for this Bonhoeffer devotes an extended discussion of the Call of Levi in Matthew's Gospel and the Sermon on the Mount.

Buckley, Thomas W. *Seventy Times Seven: Sin, Judgment, and Forgiveness in Matthew*. Zacchaeus Studies. Collegeville: Liturgical Press/ Michael Glazier, 1991.

Examines Matthean notions of sin and judgment and discusses the Gospel's portrayal of Jesus as Savior, in that through this self-offering sin is forgiven, guilt expiated, and humanity renewed in hope.

Crosby, Michael H., O.F.M. *House of Disciples: Church, Economics, and Justice in Matthew*. New York: Paulist Press, 1988.

Briefly discussed by Lisa Sowle Cahill in her article "The New Testament and Ethics: Communities of Social Change," *Interpretation* 44 (1990): 383-395.

Giesen, Heinz. *Christliches Handeln: eine redaktionskritische Untersuchung zum [dikaiosyne]-Begriff im Matthaus-Evangelium.* Europaische Hochschulschriften, Reihe 23 Theologie Bd. 181. Frankfurt am Main: Peter Lang, 1982.

Thesis (doctoral)--Papstliches Bibelinstitut in Rom, 1979.

Doctoral dissertation done in 1979 at the Pontifical Biblical Institute in Rome.

Meier, John P. *The Vision of Matthew: Christ, Church, and Morality in the First Gospel.* Theological Inquiries. New York: Paulist Press, 1979; New York: Crossroad, 1991.

Reviewed by Cain Hope Felder in *Theology Today* 37 (1981): 145.

Meier is professor of New Testament at the Catholic University of America.

Mohrlang, Roger. *Matthew and Paul: A Comparison of Ethical Perspectives.* Society for New Testament Studies, Monograph Series, 48. London: Cambridge University Press, 1984.

Reviewed by Hans Dieter Betz in *Journal of Religion* 66 (1986): 206.

Neuhäusler, Engelbert. *Anspruch und Antwort Gottes. Zur Lehre von den Weisungen innerhalb der synoptischen Jesusverkündigung.* Düsseldorf, 1962.

French translation: *Exigence de Dieu et morale chrétienne. Etudes sur les ensegnements moraux de la prédication de Jésus dans les Synoptiques.* Lectio divina, 70. Par F. Schanen. Paris: Editions du Cerf, 1971.

Powell, Mark Allan. *God With Us: A Pastoral Theology of Matthew's Gospel.* Minneapolis: Augsburg Fortress, 1995.

Powell inquires into the direction and thrust of Matthew's Gospel in categories related to pastoral theology rather than systematic theology. In successive chapters, Matthew's understanding of mission, worship, teaching, stewardship, and social justice are described in such a way as to assist the reader in understanding the theology of Matthew as a whole.

Przybylski, Benno. *Righteousness in Matthew and His World of Thought.* Society for New Testament Studies, Monograph Series, 41. Cambridge: Cambridge University Press, 1980.

Segundo, Juan Luis. *El caso Mateo: Los comienzos de una etica judeo-cristiana.* Presencia teologica, 74. Santandar: Sal Terrae, 1994.

Stramare, Tarcisio. *Matteo divorzista? Studio su Mt. 5,3 e 19,9.* Brescia: Paideia, 1986.

Via, Dan O. *Self-Deception and Wholeness in Paul and Matthew.* Minneapolis: Fortress Press, 1990.

> Treats the concepts of sin (self-deception) and salvation (recovery of wholeness), in the context of the anthropology, soteriology and ethics of Paul and Matthew.

> Via is Professor of New Testament at The Divinity School of Duke University.

****

Gospel of Mark

Barr, Steve. "The Eye of the Needle--Power and Money in the New Community: A Look at Mark 10:17-31." *Andover Newton Review* 3 (1992): 31-44.

Beck, Robert B. *Nonviolent Story: Narrative Conflict Resolution in the Gospel of Mark.* Maryknoll: Orbis Books, 1996.

> Beck argues that Mark portrays Jesus as one who does not avoid conflict, but who enters into it without resorting to violence himself, and which Gospel message therefore challenges our cultural myth of "constructive violence."

Berger, Klaus. *Die Gesetzesauslegung Jesu. Ihr historischer Hintergrund im Alten Testament. Teil I: Markus und die Parallelen.* WMANT, 40. Neukirchen, 1972.

Black, C. Clifton. "Christ crucified in Paul and in Mark: Reflections on an Intracanonical Conversation." Part II, Chapter 3 in *Theology and Ethics in Paul and His Interpreters: Essays in Honor of Victor Paul Furnish,* 184-206. Ed. Eugene H. Lovering, Jr. and Jerry L. Sumney. Nashville: Abingdon Press, 1996.

Brooten, B. "Konnten Frauen im alten Judentum die Scheidung betrieben? *Überlegungun zu Mk 10, 11-12 und 1 Cor 7, 10-11. Evangelische Theologie* 42 (1982): 65-69.

Collange, Jean François. "La déroute de L'aveugle (Mc 8, 22-26): Ecriture et pratique chrétienne." *Revue d'Histoire et de Philosophie Religieuses* 66 (1986): 21-28.

Dillmann, Rainer. "Aufbruch zu einer neuen Sittlichkeit: Biblisch-narrative Begründung ethischen Handelns." *Theologie und Glaube* 82 (1992): 34-35.

Considers Mk 7: 31-35; Lk 13:10-17, and 1 Kings 21:17-19.

Dunn, James D.G. *Jesus, Paul, and the Law: Studies in Mark and Galatians.* Louisville: Westminster/John Knox Press; London: SPCK, 1990.

One-volume collection of journal articles which have previously appeared from 1982 to 1988. Dunn also includes some additional notes responding to various critiques made to his articles.

Gräßer, Erich. "*KAI EN META THOE THERIOE* (Mk 1, 13b). Ansätze einer theologischen Tierschutzethik." In *Studien zum Text und zur Ethik des Neuen Testaments. Festschrift zum 80. Geburtstag von Heinrich Greeven,* 144-157. Herausgegeben von Wolfgang Schrage. Berlin/New York: Walter de Gruyter, 1986.

LaVerdière, Eugene. "Marriage and Divorce in the Gospel According to Mark." *The Way* 34 (1994): 54-63.

Matera, Frank J. "Ethics for the Kingdom of God: The Gospel According to Mark." *Louvain Studies* 20 (Summer-Fall 1995): 187-200.

Myers, Ched. *Binding the Strong Man: A Political Reading Mark's Story of Jesus.* Maryknoll: Orbis Books, 1988.

Briefly discussed by Lisa Sowle Cahill in her article "The New Testament and Ethics: Communities of Social Change," *Interpretation* 44 (1990): 383-395.

Also reviewed by Frank J. Matera in *Theology Today* 46 (1990): 354.

Neuhäusler, Engelbert. *Anspruch und Antwort Gottes. Zur Lehre von den Weisungen innerhalb der synoptischen Jesusverkündigung.* Düsseldorf, 1962.

French translation: *Exigence de Dieu et morale chrétienne. Etudes sur les ensegnements moraux de la prédication de Jésus dans les Synoptiques.* Lectio divina, 70. Par F. Schanen. Paris: Editions du Cerf, 1971.

O'Grady, John F. "Evil and Sin in Mark." *Chicago Studies* 34 (1995): 42-52.

Soending, Thomas. "Die Nachfolgeforderung Jesus im Markus-Evangelium." *Trier Theologische Zeitschrift* 94 (1985): 292-310.

Via, Dan O. *The Ethics of Mark's Gospel: In the Middle of Time.* Philadelphia: Fortress Press, 1985.

Via uses a hermeneutical approach to analyze the Gospel of Mark in order to inform both New Testament and "constructive" ethics. Via focuses on narrative method and considers a number of significant Gospel motifs, such as eschatology, revelation, faith, and the messianic secret. The "Middle of Time" refers both to Mark 10 and to the paradoxical position of the disciple who is placed in the period of the overlapping of the Kingdom of God and the age of the hardness of heart.

Briefly discussed by Lisa Sowle Cahill in her article "The New Testament and Ethics: Communities of Social Change," *Interpretation* 44 (1990): 383-395.

Via is Professor of New Testament at The Divinity School of Duke University.

Waetjen, Herman C. *A Reordering of Power: A Socio-Political Reading of Mark's Gospel*. Minneapolis: Augsburg Fortress, 1989.

Briefly discussed by Lisa Sowle Cahill in her article "The New Testament and Ethics: Communities of Social Change," *Interpretation* 44 (1990): 383-395.

Waetjen is professor emeritus of New Testament at San Francisco Theological Seminary in San Anselmo, California.

****

Luke/Acts

Articles on Luke/Acts

Bartchy, S. Scott. "Community of Goods in Acts: Idealization or Social Reality?" In *The Future of Early Christianity: Essays in Honor of Helmut Koester*, 309-318. Edited by Birger A. Pearson. Minneapolis: Fortress Press, 1991.

Baergen, Rudy. "The Motif of Renunciation of Possessions in the Gospel of Luke." *Conrad Grebel Review* 11 (1993): 233-248.

Baergen is pastor of the First Mennonite Church in Kitchener, Ontario.

Crowe, Jerome. "Wealth and Poverty in Luke's Writings." *Australasian Catholic Record* 69 (1992): 343-355.

Exegetical comments in line with the 1991 draft paper of the Australian Bishops' statement, "Common Wealth and Common Good."

Dillmann, Rainer. "Aufbruch zu einer neuen Sittlichkeit: Biblisch-narrative Begründung ethischen Handelns." *Theologie und Glaube* 82 (1992): 34-35.

Considers Mk 7: 31-35; Lk 13:10-17, and 1 Kings 21:17-19.

Donahue, John R., S.J. "Two Decades of Research on the Rich and Poor in Luke-Acts." In *Justice and the Holy: Essays in Honor of Walter Harrelson*, 129-144. Edited by D.A. Knight and P.J. Paris. Atlanta: Scholars Press, 1989.

Donahue studied under Norman Perrin at the University of Chicago and is Professor of Biblical Studies (New Testament) at the Jesuit School of Theology and Graduate Theological Union, Berkeley.

_____. "Who Is My Enemy? The Parable of the Good Samaritan and the Love of Enemies." In *The Love of Enemy and Nonretaliation in the New Testament*, 137-156. Edited by Willard M. Swartley. Louisville: Westminster/John Knox Press, 1992.

Dupont, Jacques. "Community of Goods in the Early Church." In *The Salvation of the Gentiles: Studies in the Acts of the Apostles*, 85-102. New York: Paulist Press, 1979.

_____. "The Poor and Poverty in the Gospels." In *Gospel Poverty: Essays in Biblical Theology*, 25-52. Edited by A. George. Chicago: Franciscan Herald Press, 1977.

D'Sa, Thomas. "The Salvation of the Rich in the Gospel of Luke." *Vidyajoti* 52 (1988): 170-180.

von Eckert, Jost. "The Realisation of Fellowship in the Earliest Christian Communities." *Concilium* 130 (1979): 21-28.

Treats the material in Acts and Paul, as one of a series of articles under the general theme, "The Dignity of the Despised of the Earth."

Giesen, Heinz. "Verantwortung des Christen in der Gegenwart und Heilsvollendung. *Ethik und Eschatologie nach Lk 13,23 und 16,16.*" *Theologie der Gegenwart* 31 (1988): 218-228.

Hamel, Edouard, S.J. "Le Magnificat et le Renversement des Situations: Réflexion théologico-biblique." *Gregorianum* 60 (1979): 55-84.

Examines the theme of the "overview of situations" in the Old and New Testament, as well as Hellenistic literature, and then proceeds to a hermeneutical consideration of the Magnificat for the contemporary Church, concluding that the prayer should be interpreted as an incentive to the promotion of justice.

Hamel was professor of moral theology at the Pontifical Gregorian University until 1986.

Heard, Warren. "Luke's Attitude Toward the Rich and the Poor." *Trinity Journal* 9 (1988): 47-80.

Argues that Luke attacks greed while counselling a carefree attitude towards riches, yet still demanding good stewardship.

Karris, Robert J., O.F.M. "Poor and Rich, the Lukan *Sitz-im-Leben.*" In *Perspectives in Luke-Acts*, 112-125. Edited by C.H. Talbert. Edinburgh: T. & T. Clark; Danville VA: Association of Baptist Professors of Religion, 1978.

Légasse, Simon. "L'amore dei nemici nei vangeli. Luca." Capitolo 6 di *E chi è il mio prossimo?*, 113-129. Roma: Edizioni Dehoniane, 1991.

French original: *«Et qui est mon prochain?» Etude sur l'agape dans le Nouveau Testament.* Lectio Divina, 136. Paris Editions du Cerf, 1989.

Lohfink, Gerhard. "Der präexistente Heilsplan. Sinn und Hintergrund der dritten Vaterunserbitte." In *Neues Testament und Ethik. Für Rudolf Schnackenburg*, 110-133. Herausgegeben von Helmut Merklein. Freiburg: Herder, 1989.

Nickelsburg, George W. "Riches, the Rich, and God's Judgment in 1 Enoch 92-105 and the Gospel According to Luke." *New Testament Studies* 25 (1978-79): 324-344.

O'Leary, Anthony, C.P. "The Role of Possessions in the Journey Narrative of Luke 9:51-19:27." *Milltown Studies* 28 (1991): 41-60.

O'Toole, Robert F., S.J. "Poverty and Wealth in Luke-Acts." *Chicago Studies* 30 (1991): 29-41.

Using a composition-criticism methodological approach to the study of Luke-Acts, O'Toole argues that the disposition of possessions in Luke's theology symbolizes the disposition of oneself. Makes reference to other contemporary literature in the field.

O'Toole is a member of the faculty and the rector of the Pontifical Biblical Institute in Rome.

Ramaroson, L. "'Le premier, c'est l'amour' (Lc 7,47a)." *Science et Esprit* 39 (1988): 319-329.

Reid, Barbara E., O.P. "The Ethics of Luke." *The Bible Today* 31 (1993): 283-287.

Brief overview of some of the principal moral themes in Luke's Gospel.

Reid teaches New Testament at the Catholic Theological Union in Chicago.

____. "Reading Luke with the Poor." *The Bible Today* 32 (1994): 283-289.

One of several articles on biblical economic justice in this issue.

Sanders, J. A. "The Ethic of Election in Luke's Great Banquet Parable." In *Essays in Old Testament Ethics (J. Philip Hyatt, In Memoriam)*, 245-271. Edited by James L. Crenshaw and John T. Willis. New York: Ktav Publishing House, 1974.

Segalla, Giuseppe. "L'ambiente sociocomunitario di `luca-atti'." *Rivista del Clero Italiano* 73 (1992): 104-114.

> Segalla is professor of New Testament Exegesis at the Theological Faculty of Milan.

_____. "L'etica narrativa di Luca-Atti," *Teologia* 20 (1995): 34-74.

Stegemann, Wolfgang. "The Following of Christ as Solidarity Between Rich, Respected Christians and Poor, Despised Christians (Gospel of Luke)." In *Jesus and the Hope of the Poor*, 67-120. Edited by Luise Schottroff and Wolfgang Stegemann. Maryknoll: Orbis Press, 1986.

Topel, L. John, S.J. "The Christian Ethics of the Lukan Sermon." In *Christian Biblical Ethics: From Biblical Revelation to Contemporary Christian Praxis: Method and Content*, 179-199. New York: Paulist Press, 1984.

> Topel is professor of theology at Seattle University in Seattle, Washington.

Tumbarello, Giacomo. "La Parabola del Buon Samaritano: Lettura etico-morale." *Bibbia e Oriente* 33 (1991): 223-231.

Tyson, Joseph B. "Authority in Acts." *Bible Today* 30 (1992): 279-283.

> One of several articles in this issue on the theme of "Power and Authority."

Books on Luke/Acts

Bassler, Jouette M. *God and Mammon: Asking for Money in the New Testament.* Nashville: Abingdon, 1991.

> Treats the cultural context of the ancient world, and then considers perspectives in light of the Gospels, Paul, and Acts.

Beck, B. *Christian Character in Luke's Gospel.* London: Epworth Press, 1989.

Cassidy, Richard J. *Jesus, Politics, and Society: A Study of Luke's Gospel.* Maryknoll: Orbis Books, 1978.

Has a good bibliography on both Lucan and related materials.

_____. *Society and Politics in the Acts of the Apostles.* Maryknoll: Orbis Books, 1987.

Briefly discussed by Lisa Sowle Cahill in her article "The New Testament and Ethics: Communities of Social Change," *Interpretation* 44 (1990): 383-395.

Esler, Philip F. *Community and Gospel in Luke-Acts: The Social and Political Motivations of Lucan Theology.* Society for New Testament Studies, Monograph Series, 57. Cambridge: Cambridge University Press, 1987.

Uses sociology and anthropology to re-examine Lucan theology in terms of a response to social and political pressures of the Christian community of the time. Special attention is given to Lucan themes such as table-fellowship, the law, the Temple, poverty and riches and politics.

Ford, Josephine Massyngbaerde. *My Enemy is My Guest: Jesus and Violence in Luke.* Maryknoll: Orbis Books, 1984.

Gillman, John. *Possessions and the Life of Faith: A Reading of Luke-Acts.* Zacchaeus Studies. Collegeville: Liturgical Press/Michael Glazier, 1991.

Argues that the reader is challenged to make faith decisions about one's money and personal resources. The study includes literary features of Luke-Acts, three approaches to possessions, the privileged place of the poor, the theme of possessions as it relates to discipleship, and the use of possessions in the early Church.

Girardet, Giorgio. *Il Vangelo della liberazione: letture politica di Luca.*

166

In French: *Lecture politique de l'Evangile de Luc.* Preface de François Houtart. Traduit de l'italien par le Centre Communautaire International. Bruxelles: Vie Ouvriere, 1978.

Horn, Friederich Wilhelm. *Glaube und Handeln in der Theologie des Lukas.* Göttinger Theologische Arbeiten, 26. Göttingen: Vandenhoeck und Ruprecht, 1983, 1986.

Johnson, Luke Timothy. *The Literary Function of Possessions in Luke-Acts.* Society of Biblical Literature Dissertation Series 39. Missoula MT: Scholars Press, 1977.

Very readable, excellent treatment of the theme of wealth and possessions in the Lukan Christian community, and its implications for a contemporary biblical perspective on wealth.

Johnson is professor of New Testament at the Candler School of Theology at Emory University.

_____. *Sharing Possessions: Mandate and Symbol of Faith.* Overtures to Biblical Theology. Philadelphia: Fortress Press, 1981.

Klein, Hans. *Barmherzigkeit gegenüber den Elenden und Geächteten. Studien zur Botschaft des lukanischen Sondergutes.* Biblisch-theologische Studien, 10. Neukirchen-Vluyn: Neukirchener Verlag, 1987.

Koenig, John. *New Testament Hospitality: Partners with Strangers as Promise and Mission.* Overtures to Biblical Theology, 17. Philadelphia: Fortress Press, 1985.

Examines the ministry of Jesus, Paul and the life-style of the early church depicted in Luke-Acts to show that the early Christians fostered a way of life in which individuals acted as "God's guests and hosts on behalf of the world." Hospitality and openness to strangers are viewed as both crucial to the Christian life and the development of the faith and ethics of the early believers.

Lambrecht, Jan, S.J. *Ich aber sage euch. Die Bergpredigt als programmatische Rede Jesu (Mt 5-7; Lk 6, 20-49).* Stuttgart: Kath. Bibelwerk, 1984.

Lambrecht is a New Testament exegete.

Moxnes, Halvor. *The Economy of the Kingdom: Social Conflict and Economic Relations in Luke's Gospel.* Overtures to Biblical Theology. Philadelphia: Fortress Press, 1988.

In addition to exegesis and discussion of ancient economics, Moxnes uses some concepts developed by cultural anthropologists, such as Mary Douglas, to analyze the socio-economic conflict between the Pharisees and other traditional social groups in First Century Palestine. Moxnes argues for the so-called rural-based "moral values of the Magnificat" against the urban -centered Pharisees' love of money.

Reviewed by David L. Balch in *Interpretation* 45 (1991): 84, 86. Also briefly discussed by Lisa Sowle Cahill in her article "The New Testament and Ethics: Communities of Social Change," *Interpretation* 44 (1990): 383-395.

Mueller, Joan. *Why Can't I Forgive you: A Christian Reflection.* Allen TX: Thomas More, 1996.

Mueller reflects upon Jesus' prayers of forgiveness (Lk 23:34) and surrender (Lk 23:46) as they appear in the Gospel of Luke, using the example of a couple whose young on is killed by an unrepentant and unreformed drunk driver. The text is written in a manner readily accessible to undergraduates and adult education classes.

Neuhäusler, Engelbert. *Anspruch und Antwort Gottes. Zur Lehre von den Weisungen innerhalb der synoptischen Jesusverkündigung.* Düsseldorf, 1962.

French translation: *Exigence de Dieu et morale chrétienne. Etudes sur les ensegnements moraux de la prédication de Jésus dans les Synoptiques.* Lectio divina, 70. Par F. Schanen. Paris: Editions du Cerf, 1971.

Ossanna, Tullio Faustino. *Il Magnificat progetto etico di vita. Analisi etico-strutturale di Lc 46b-55.* Roma: Borla, 1984.

168

Pilgrim, Walter E. *Good News to the Poor: Wealth and Poverty in Luke-Acts.*
Minneapolis: Augsburg Press, 1981.

Prior, Michael. *Jesus the Liberator: Nazareth Liberation Theology (Luke 4:16-30).*
The Biblical Seminar 26. Sheffield: Sheffield Academic Press, 1995.

Uses Luke 4:16-30 to introduce different methods in Gospel study and as an
entry into Luke's gospel in particular, as well as to explore ways to connect
Luke's "liberation theology" with contemporary liberation theologies.

Sanders, Jack T. *Ethics in the New Testament.* Philadelphia: Fortress Press; and
London: SCM, 1975, 1986.

Analyzes and critiques the basic ethical perspectives found in the New
Testament, with six chapters devoted to "Jesus," the Synoptics and Acts, Paul,
Deutero-Pauline Epistles, Johannine Literature, and the Later Epistles and the
Apocalypse. Sanders holds that the ethical perspective of Jesus is inseparably
linked to his eschatological expectation of the imminent coming of the
Kingdom of God, and that New Testament ethics can offer nothing to a
contemporary ethics.

Talbert, C.H., ed., *Perspectives in Luke-Acts.* Edinburgh: T. & T. Clark; Danville
VA: Association of Baptist Professors of Religion, 1978.

Wilson, S.G. *Luke and the Law.* Society for New Testament Studies, Monograph
Series, 50. Cambridge: Cambridge University Press, 1983.

Wilson treats Luke's view of the law and the way in which the relevant
material would most probably have been understood at the time of Luke's
writing.

****

Johannine Literature

Anthonysamy, S.J. "An Eco-theology Foreshadowed in the Gospel of John." *Bible Bhashyam* 19 (1993): 188-204.

One of several articles in this issue on various theological aspects of ecology.

Angelini, Giuseppe. "Morale e civiltà alla luce del Vangelo di Giovanni." In AA.VV. *Fede e cultura dal Vangelo di Giovanni,* 111-139. Bologna: Edizioni Dehoniane Bologna, 1986.

Bahr, Ann Marie B. "God's Family and Flocks: Remarks on Ownership in the Fourth Gospel." In *Covenant for a New Creation: Ethics, Religion, and Public Policy,* 91-104. Edited by Carol S. Robb and Carl S. Casebolt. Maryknoll: Orbis Books, 1991.

Balz, Horst. "Johanneische Theologie und Ethik im Licht der «letzen Stunde»." In *Studien zum Text und zur Ethik des Neuen Testaments. Festschrift zum 80. Geburtstag von Heinrich Greeven,* 35-56. Herausgegeben von Wolfgang Schrage. Berlin/New York: Walter de Gruyter, 1986.

Beutler, Johannes. "Il comandamento fondamentale nel vangelo di Giovanni." In *Saggi esegetici sulla legge nel Nuovo Testamento,* 215-229. A cura di Karl Kertelge. Cinisello Balsamo: Edizioni Paoline, 1990.

Original version in *Das Gesetz im Neuen Testament.* Herausgegeben von Karl Kertelge. Questiones Disputatae, 108. Freiburg: Herder, 1986.

Casabó Suqué, J.M., S.J. *La teología moral en san Juan.* Madrid: Ediciones Fax, 1970.

Collange, Jean François. "'Faire la vérité': considérations éthiques sur Jean 3, 21." *Revue d'Histoire et de Philosophie Religieuses* 62 (1982): 415-424.

Collins, Thomas. "Moral Guidance in the Apocalypse." *Emmanuel* 95 (1989): 502-509.

_____. *Apocalypse 22:6-21 as the Focal Point of Moral Teaching in the Apocalypse*. Dissertatio ad Doctoratum in Facultate Theologiae Pontificiae Universitatis Gregorianae. Romae, 1986.

Concentrates on Rev 22:6-21 as a summary of the moral theology of the Apocalypse.

STD dissertation done under Ugo Vanni, S.J.

De la Potterie, Ignazio [Ignace], S.J. "I precetti morali e Cristo secondo S. Giovanni." In *Fondamenti biblici della teologia morale*, 329-344. Atti della XXII Settimana Biblica. Associazione biblica italiana. Brescia: Paideia, 1973.

Ignace De la Potterie is on the faculty of the Pontifical Biblical Institute in Rome.

Dorado, G.G. *Moral y existencia cristianas en el IV Evangelio y en las Cartas de Juan*. Colección Estudios de Etica Teológica. Madrid: Ed. PS, 1989.

Fernández Ramos, F. "Seguimiento y persecución. Reflexiones en torno a la comunidad joánica." *Studium Legionense* 24 (1983): 81-135.

Fiorenza, Elisabeth Schüssler. *The Book of Revelation: Justice and Judgment*. Philadelphia: Fortress Press, 1985.

_____. *Revelation: Vision of a Just World*. Minneapolis: Fortress Press, 1991.

Grob, Francis. *Faire l'oeuvre de Dieu: Christologie et éthique dans l'évangile de Jean*. Etudes d'histoire et de philosophie religieuses, 68. Paris: Paris: Presses Universitaires de France, 1986.

Holtz, Traugott. "Die «Werke» in der Johannesapokalypse." In *Neues Testament und Ethik. Für Rudolf Schnackenburg*, 426-441. Herausgegeben von Helmut Merklein. Freiburg: Herder, 1989.

Karris, Robert J., O.F.M. *Jesus and the Marginalized in John's Gospel.* Collegeville: The Liturgical Press, 1990.

Klauck, Hans-Josef. "Brudermord und Bruderliebe. Ethische Paradigmen in 1 Joh 3,11-17." In *Neues Testament und Ethik. Für Rudolf Schnackenburg*, 151-169. Herausgegeben von Helmut Merklein. Freiburg: Herder, 1989.

Lazure, Noël, O.M.I. *Les valeurs morales de la théologie johannique.* Paris: Gabalda, 1965.

Légasse, Simon. "Agape interumana. Dall'apertura al ripiegamento." Capitolo 1 di *E chi è il mio prossimo?*, 9-34. Roma: Edizioni Dehoniane, 1991.

French Original: *«Et qui est mon prochain?»* Etude sur l'agape dans le *Nouveau Testament.* Lectio Divina, 136. Paris Editions du Cerf, 1989.

Treats the theme of agape in both the Epistles and the Johannine writings.

Lona, Horacio E. "«Treu bis zum Tod». Aum Ethos des Martyriums in der Offenbarung des Johannes." In *Neues Testament und Ethik. Für Rudolf Schnackenburg*, 442-461. Herausgegeben von Helmut Merklein. Freiburg: Herder, 1989.

Manns, F. "'Le péché, c'est Bélial' (1 Jn 3,4) à la lumière du judaïsme." *Revue des Sciences Religieuses* 62 (1988): 1-9.

Marshall, I. Howard. "Using the Bible in Ethics." In *Essays in Evangelical Social Ethics*, 39-55. Edited by David F. Wright. Exeter: Paternoster Press, 1973; Wilton CT: Morehouse-Barlow Co., Inc., 1983.

Marshall's essay comes out of the September, 1978 National Evangelical Conference in Hertfordshire, England. He gives a brief overview of the problematic, as well as some traditional approaches to the Bible in ethics. Marshall then concludes with what he terms an "evangelical approach" which is based on a hermeneutical reading of the Bible. To illustrate his approach Marshall employs the Foot-Washing command of John 13:14ff.

Martin, Francis. "The Integrity of Christian Moral Activity: The First Letter of John and *Veritatis Splendor*." *Communio* 21 (1994): 265-285.

Discusses the use of Scripture in Pope John Paul II's 1993 Encyclical *Veritatis Splendor* on fundamental moral theology.

Muñoz León, Domingo. "El novedad del Mandamiento del amor en los escritos de San Juan: Intentos modernos de solución." In *La Etica Bíblica*, 193-231. XXIX Semana Bíblica Española. Madrid: Consejo Superior de Investigaciones Científicas, 1971.

Neal, B.S. *The Concept of Character in the Apocalypse with Implications for Character Education.* Washington, D.C.: University Press of America, 1983.

Prunet, Olivier. *La morale chrétienne d'après les écrits johanniques.* Paris: Presses Universitaires de France, 1957.

Raja, R. J., S.J. "As It Was in the Beginning: *Eco-Spirituality in the Book of Revelation.*" *Vidyajyoti* 60 (1991): 681-697.

Rese, M. "Das Gebot der Bruderliebe in den Johannesbriefen." *Theologische Zeitschrift* 41 (1985): 44-58.

Ritt, Hubert. "Der christologische Imperativ. Zur Weinstock-Metapher in der testamentarischen Mahnrede Joh 15,1-17." In *Neues Testament und Ethik. Für Rudolf Schnackenburg*, 136-150. Herausgegeben von Helmut Merklein. Freiburg: Herder, 1989.

Russo, Giovanni, S.D.B. "Libertà nella filiazione." *Palestra del Clero* 70 (1991): 593-614.

Considerazioni etiche sulla nozione di libertà nel Quattro Vangelo e della teologia della libertà.

Ethical consideration of the concept of freedom in the Fourth Gospel, and in the theology of freedom (liberty).

Russo è professore di Etica sessuale all' Univ. Pont. Salesiana di Messina.

Russo is professor of sexual ethics at the Pontifical Salesian University in Messina, Sicily.

Sanders, Jack T. *Ethics in the New Testament.* Philadelphia: Fortress Press; and London: SCM, 1975, 1986.

Analyzes and critiques the basic ethical perspectives found in the New Testament, with six chapters devoted to "Jesus," the Synoptics and Acts, Paul, Deutero-Pauline Epistles, Johannine Literature, and the Later Epistles and the Apocalypse. Sanders holds that the ethical perspective of Jesus is inseparably linked to his eschatological expectation of the imminent coming of the Kingdom of God, and that New Testament ethics can offer nothing to a contemporary ethics.

Santa Maria, Miguel Saenz de. "La Sexualidad. Aporte del cuarto evangelico." *Biblia y Fe* 18 (1992): 114-135.

One of several articles under this number's general theme of "La Sexualidad: *Aproximacion Biblica.*"

Smith, D. Moody. "The Love Command: John and Paul?" Part II, Chapter 4 in *Theology and Ethics in Paul and His Interpreters: Essays in Honor of Victor Paul Furnish,* 207-217. Ed. Eugene H. Lovering, Jr. and Jerry L. Sumney. Nashville: Abingdon Press, 1996.

Verhey, Allen. "The Revelation to John: Patient Endurance." In *The Great Reversal: Ethics and the New Testament,* 147-152. Grand Rapids: Eerdmans, 1984.

Verhey is the Evert J. and Hattie E. Blekkink Professor of Religion at Hope College.

Von Wahlde, Urban C. *The Johannine Commandments: 1 John and the Struggle for the Johannine Tradition.* New York: Paulist Press, 1990.

174

Von Wahlde is professor of New Testament at Loyola University, Chicago.

****

Pauline Ethics

**N.B.   *For purposes of this bibliography Deutero-Pauline literature and the Letter to the Hebrews are included in this section on Pauline Ethics*

Articles on Pauline Ethics

AA.VV. "La liberté chrétienne. L'épître aux Galates." *Lumière et Vie* 38 (1989) n. 192.

Achtmeier, Paul J. "The Continuing Quest for Coherence in St. Paul: An Experiment in Thought." Part I, Chapter 9 in *Theology and Ethics in Paul and His Interpreters: Essays in Honor of Victor Paul Furnish*, 132-145. Edited by Eugene H. Lovering, Jr. and Jerry L. Sumney. Nashville: Abingdon Press, 1996.

Alvarez-Verdes, Lorenzo, C.Ss.R. "La Función del a 'Razón en el pensamiento ético de S. Pablo." *Studia Moralia* 34 (1996): 7-42.

In the Pauline ethic 'reason' is a theme of fundamental importance. An in-depth analysis of the text shows that voûs has a positive human application in Paul. The renewal of voûs in the believer does not signify either its abandonment or rejection: rather, it is developed through acquiring a new horizon of understanding. The mediating role of voûs is, for Paul, an essential condition so that the fundamental imperative can be translated into the concrete imperatives of a positive ethic.

Alvarez- Verdes is Professor of Sacred Scripture at the Academia Alphonsianum in Rome.

Arróniz, J.M. "Ley y libertad cristiana en S. Pablo." *Lumen* 33 (1984): 385-411.

Attridge, Harold W. "Paul and the Domestication of Thomas." Part II, Chapter 5 in *Theology and Ethics in Paul and His Interpreters: Essays in Honor of Victor Paul Furnish*, 218-231. Edited by Eugene H. Lovering, Jr. and Jerry L. Sumney. Nashville: Abingdon Press, 1996.

Auneau, Joseph. "De la justice d'Amos à la justice de Paul." *La Vie Spirituelle* 72 (1992): 307-322.

Badini, Giuseppe. "Sin in the Theology of St. Paul." In *Sin: Its Reality and Nature: A Historical Survey*, 79-100. Edited by Pietro Palazzini. Translated by Brendan Devlin. Dublin: Scepter Publishers, 1964.

Baird, William. "The Fate of Paul in Nineteenth-Century Liberalism: Ritschl and Harnack." Part III, Chapter 2 in *Theology and Ethics in Paul and His Interpreters: Essays in Honor of Victor Paul Furnish*, 254-274. Edited by Eugene H. Lovering, Jr. and Jerry L. Sumney. Nashville: Abingdon Press, 1996.

Barrett, C[harles]. K[ingsley]. "Deuteropauline Ethics: Some Observations." Part II, Chapter 1 in *Theology and Ethics in Paul and His Interpreters: Essays in Honor of Victor Paul Furnish*, 161-172. Edited by Eugene H. Lovering, Jr. and Jerry L. Sumney. Nashville: Abingdon Press, 1996.

Bartow, Charles L. "Speaking the Text and Preaching the Gospel." In *Homosexuality and Christian Community*, 86-98. Edited by Choon-Leong Seow. Louisville: Westminister/John Knox Press, 1996.

Looks at how the Bible might be read in a congregation and uses Romans 1:18-32 as an illustrative case. One of a series of essays in Part II, "How Do the Scriptures Inform Our Theological Reflection?". The other two sections are Part I, "What Do the Scriptures Say?" and Part III, "How Do We Live Faithfully?". All the contributors are members of the Princeton Theological Faculty.

Bartow is the Carl and Helen Egner Professor of Speech Communication in Ministry at Princeton Theological Seminary and an ordained minister of the Presbyterian Church.

176

Bassler, Jouette M. "'He remains faithful' (2 Tim 2:13a)." Part II, Chapter 2 in *Theology and Ethics in Paul and His Interpreters: Essays in Honor of Victor Paul Furnish*, 173-183. Edited by Eugene H. Lovering, Jr. and Jerry L. Sumney. Nashville: Abingdon Press, 1996.

Betz, Hans Dieter. "Das Problem der Grundlagen der paulinischen Ethik (Röm 12, 1-2)." *Zeitschrift für Theologie und Kirche* 85 (1988): 199-218.

Betz is professor of New Testament at the University of Chicago.

Black, C. Clifton. "Christ crucified in Paul and in Mark: Reflections on an Intracanonical Conversation." Part II, Chapter 3 in *Theology and Ethics in Paul and His Interpreters: Essays in Honor of Victor Paul Furnish*, 184-206. Edited by Eugene H. Lovering, Jr. and Jerry L. Sumney. Nashville: Abingdon Press, 1996.

Black, David Alan. "The Pauline Love Command: Structure, Style, and Ethics in Romans 12:9-21." *Filologia Neotestamentaria* 2 (1989): 3-22.

Blank, Josef. "Unity and Plurality in New Testament Ethics." *Concilium* 150 (1981): 65-71.

In Spanish: "Unidad y pluralidad en la ética del NT." *Concilium* 17 (1981): 526-537.

Outlines an ethos of "itinerant radicalism" and its relation to eschatology visible in the Synoptic tradition coming out of rural Palestine, and contrasts this with the change of ethos to a "love radicalism" seen in the Pauline and Deutero-Pauline literature. Concludes that the constant task facing Christians is "always to confront Jesus' ethical sayings and those of the New Testament traditions/authors with changing socio-cultural circumstances and to put them in practice." p. 70.

Blank, Rudolph H. "Six Theses Concerning Freedom in Christ and Liberation: Liberation in Galatians, Luther, and Liberation Theology." *Concordia Journal* 20 (1994): 236-260.

Critiques Liberation theology's understanding of liberation, and suggests that it differs considerably from Paul's understanding of liberation as presented in the Letter to the Galatians. This problem leads to further difficulties in Christology, anthropology, soteriology, and missiology.

Blount, Brian K. "Reading and Understanding the New Testament on Homosexuality." In *Homosexuality and Christian Community*, 28-38. Edited by Choon-Leong Seow. Louisville: Westminister/John Knox Press, 1996.

Examines the Pauline references to homoerotic activity, and argues that these pronouncements are socially and historically conditioned, and therefore should be distinguished from Paul's faith pronouncements. One of a series of essays in Part I, "What Do the Scriptures Say?". The other two sections are Part II, "How Do the Scriptures Inform Our Theological Reflection?" and Part III, "How Do We Live Faithfully?". All the contributors are members of the Princeton Theological Faculty.

Blount is Asst. Professor of New Testament at Princeton Theological Seminary and an ordained minister of the Presbyterian Church.

Bosetti, Elena. "Quale etica nei codici domestici (*Haustafeln*) del Nuovo Testamento? *Rivista di Teologia Morale* 18 (1986).

Bosetti is professor of New Testament at the Pontifical Gregorian University in Rome.

Broer, Ingo. "«Darum: Wer da meint zu stehen, der sehe zu, daß er nicht falle». 1 Kor 10,12f im Kontext von 1 Kor 10,1-13." In *Neues Testament und Ethik. Für Rudolf Schnackenburg*, 299-325. Herausgegeben von Helmut Merklein. Freiburg: Herder, 1989.

Brooten, B. "Konnten Frauen im alten Judentum die Scheidung betrieben? *Überlegungun zu Mk 10, 11-12 und 1 Cor 7, 10-11. Evangelische Theologie* 42 (1982): 65-69.

Byron, Brian. "1 Cor 7:10-15: A Basis for Future Catholic Discipline on Marriage and Divorce." *Theological Studies* 34 (1973): 429-445.

Cahill, Lisa Sowle. "Kingdom and Cross: Christian Moral Community and the Problem of Suffering." *Interpretation* 50 (April 1996): 156-68.

The Bible guides Christian ethics by showing how Jesus and early Christianity transformed the moral conventions of first-century Greco-Roman society by making them more inclusive and compassionate. This is the one side of the coin. The other side, however, is that the Bible also attests to the problem of the existence of evil and suffering in human life. In Paul's theology of cross and resurrection, Christian ethicists confront the ineradicable nature of this problem and the need to identify with those who must suffer.

Cahill is a Roman Catholic and did her doctoral studies at the University of Chicago under the direction of James M. Gustafson. She is Professor of Theological Ethics at Boston College, and past President of both the Catholic Theological Society of America (CTSA) and the Society of Christian Ethics (SCE).

Cavina, A. "Etica e battesimo nella teologia paolina." *Protestantesimo* 45 (1990): 162-172.

For Paul baptism establishes an ethic of renouncement of sin (Rm 6), and is also the unifying factor of all the baptized in the one savior, Jesus Christ.

Clark, Elizabeth A. "Comment: Chrysostom and Pauline Social Ethics." In *Paul and the Legacies of Paul*, 193-200. Edited by William S. Babcock. Dallas: Southern Methodist University Press, 1990.

Clark is Professor of Religion at Duke University.

Collins, Raymond F. "Paul's First Reflections on Love." Chapter 6 in *Christian Morality: Biblical Foundations*, 137-148. Notre Dame: University of Notre Dame Press, 1986.

Collins taught New Testament for many years at Louvain in Belgium, and is now at Catholic University in Washington, D.C.

_____. "The Unity of Paul's Paranesis in 1 Thess 4:3-8: 1 Cor 7:1-7, A Significant Parallel." Chapter 9 in *Christian Morality: Biblical Foundations*, 211-222. Notre Dame: University of Notre Dame Press, 1986.

Dacquino, Pietro. "La vita morale e l'azione dello Spirito secondo S. Paolo." In *Fondamenti biblici della teologia morale*, 357-373. Atti della XXII Settimana Biblica. Associazione biblica italiana. Brescia: Paideia, 1973.

Dautzenberg, Gerhard. "*Pheugete ten porneian* (1 Kor 6, 18). Eine Fallstudie zur paulinischen Sexualethik in ihrem Verhältnis zur Sexualethik des Frühjudentums." In *Neues Testament und Ethik. Für Rudolf Schnackenburg*, 271-298. Herausgegeben von Helmut Merklein. Freiburg: Herder, 1989.

Davies, Margaret. "New Testament Ethics and Ours: Homosexuality and Sexuality in Romans 1:26-27." *Biblical Interpretation* 3 (1995): 315-31.

The article contains one major argument and one minor argument. The major argument is that Paul's strictures against homosexual practice were taken over from Leviticus and expressed concern of Hellenistic Judaism. The Pauline subversion of the web of relations which make sense of the exclusion of homosexual practice within the jewish tradition, however, leaves the Pauline strictures without warrant. The minor argument is that we in the twentieth century should subvert the Pauline assumption of difference between males and females, again adopted from the Jewish tradition, and that we should recognize a continuum and variety. Such a subversion would allow us to see ourselves primarily as people rather than primarily as either men or women.

Davis, J.A. "The Interaction Between Individual Ethical Conscience and Community Ethical Consciousness in 1 Corinthians." *Horizons in Biblical Theology* 10 (1989): 1-18.

Centers on 1 Cor 8-9 and the relation between the individual's conscience and community norms.

Dawes, Gregory W. "'But If You Can Gain Your Freedom' (1Cor 7:17-29)." *Catholic Biblical Quarterly* 52 (1990): 681-697.

De Virgilio, Giuseppe. "Etica del Nuovo Testamento: lo stato della ricerca." *Bibbia e Oriente* 33 (1991): 141-155.

Presents first an overview of some of the principal issues involved in the question of the place of revelation, and especially the New Testament, for moral theology, and then discusses a number of recent works in three sub-areas: general New Testament ethics, ethics in the various gospels, and ethics in the Pauline literature.

Delhaye, Philippe. "L'apport paulinien à deux traités de morale fondamentale." In *Studiorum Paulinorum Congressus*, 187-197. Roma, 1963.

_____. "Les quatres forces de la vie morale d'après S. Paul et S. Thomas." *Esprit et Vie* 94 (1984): 4-11; 57-60.

Donelson, Lewis R. "The Structure of Ethical Argument in the Pastorals." *Biblical Theology Bulletin* 18 (1988): 108-113

Dunn, James D.G. "'The Law of Faith,' 'the Law of the Spirit' and 'the Law of Christ.'" Part I, Chapter 5 in *Theology and Ethics in Paul and His Interpreters: Essays in Honor of Victor Paul Furnish*, 62-82. Edited by Eugene H. Lovering, Jr. and Jerry L. Sumney. Nashville: Abingdon Press, 1996.

von Eckert, Jost. "Indikativ und Imperativ bei Paulus." In *Ethik im Neuen Testament*, 168-189. Hrsg. Karl Kertelge. Freiburg: Herder, 1984.

_____. "The Realisation of Fellowship in the Earliest Christian Communities." *Concilium* 130 (1979): 21-28.

Treats the material in Acts and Paul, as one of a series of articles under the general theme, "The Dignity of the Despised of the Earth."

Eid, Volker. "Die Verbindlichkeit der paulinischen Freiheitsbotschaft für die christliche Lebensgestaltung." In *Herausforderung und Kritik der Moraltheologie*, ed. Georg Teichtweier and Wilhelm Dreier, 184-205. Würzburg: Echter Verlag, 1971.

Elliott, J.K. "Paul's Teaching on Marriage in I Corinthians: Some Problems Considered." *New Testament Studies* 19 (1972-1973): 219-225.

Ellis, E.E. "*Soma* in First Corinthians." *Interpretation* 44 (1990): 132-144.

The notion of *soma* runs through all of Paul's theology: his ethics, sacraments, ministry, ecclesiology, and eschatology.

Elorriaga, C. "La vida cristiana como camino progresivo según Rom 1-8." *Anales Valentinos* 9 (1983): 1-22.

Emslie, B.L. "The Methodology of Proceeding from Exegesis to an Ethical Decision." *Neotestamentica* 19 (1985): 87-91.

Using the problem of citizen-state relations in Rom 13:1-7, Emslie argues that Paul is not formulating general principles but rather addresses an *ad hoc* situation. The historico-socio-political ethos of the audience provides an important interpretive key to the text. In terms of using Scripture in ethics there should *not* be a direct move from biblical imperatives or analogies to a specific application.

Feuillet, A. "Les fondements de la morale chrétienne d'après l'épître aux Romains." *Revue Thomiste* 70 (1970): 357-386.

Fischer, James A., C.M. "1 Cor 7:8-24--Marriage and Divorce." In *Christian Biblical Ethics: From Biblical Revelation to Contemporary Christian Praxis: Method and Content*, 245-255. New York: Paulist Press, 1984.

_____. "Dissent within a Religious Community: Romans 9-11." In *Christian Biblical Ethics: From Biblical Revelation to Contemporary Christian Praxis: Method and Content*, 256-265. New York: Paulist Press, 1984.

_____. "Politics and Biblical Ethics: Romans 13:1-7." In *Christian Biblical Ethics: From Biblical Revelation to Contemporary Christian Praxis: Method and Content*, 266-277. New York: Paulist Press, 1984.

Fowl, Stephen E. "Some Uses of Story in Paul's Moral Discourse." *Modern Theology* 4 (1988).

Fowl is professor of biblical theology at Loyola College, Baltimore.

182

Friedrich, J., Pöhlmann, W., Stuhlmacher, P. "Zur historischen Situation und Intention von Röm 13:1-7." *Zeitschrift für Theologie und Kirche* 73 (1976): 131-166.

Fuchs, Eric. "De la soumission des femmes. Une lecture d'Ephésiens 5, 21-33." *Le Supplément* 161 (1987): 73-81.

Fuchs, Josef, S.J. "Early Christianity in Search of a Christian Morality: 1 Cor 7." Chapter 7 in *Christian Morality: The Word Became Flesh*, 83-101. Translated by Brian McNeil. Washington, D.C.: Georgetown University Press; Dublin: Gill and Macmillan, 1987.

German original: "Die frühe Christenheit auf der Suche nach einer christlichen Moral: 1 Kor 7." In *Für eine menschliche Moral. Grundfragen der theologischen Ethik. Band 2: Ethische Konkretisierungen*, 9-28. Studien zur theologischen Ethik, 26. Freiburg: Universitätsverlag-Herder, 1989.

Italian translation: "I Cor 7: Temi di teologia morale fondamentale." Cap. 2 in *Essere del Signore. Un corso di teologia morale fondamentale*, 28-45. Trascirzioni per gli studenti 1981. Roma: Pontificia Università Gregoriana, 1981.

Fuchs is Professor Emeritus of Moral Theology at the Pontifical Gregorian University in Rome.

Furnish, Victor Paul. "A Paradigm for Ethics in First Corinthians." *Interpretation* 44 (1990): 145-157.

Furnish argues that Paul's ethical reflection and moral judgments in 1 Corinthians are largely based not on citations from Scripture, nor by teachings attributed to the Lord, nor by insights ascribed to the Spirit's leading, but rather these "have been informed primarily by the truth of the gospel, as he understands that." p. 157.

Gaventa, Beverly Roberts. "Mother's Milk and Ministry in 1 Corinthians 3." Part I, Chapter 7 in *Theology and Ethics in Paul and His Interpreters: Essays in Honor of Victor Paul Furnish*, 101-113. Edited by Eugene H. Lovering, Jr. and Jerry L. Sumney. Nashville: Abingdon Press, 1996.

Getty, Mary Ann. "Sin and Salvation in Romans." *The Bible Today* 31 (1993): 89-93.

One of several articles in this issue on the theme of "The Bible on Sin."

Gooch, Paul W. "Authority and Justification in Theological Ethics: A Study in 1 Corinthians 7." *Journal of Religious Ethics* 11 (1983): 62-74.

Considers the ways in which Paul grounds his ethical advice in 1 Corinthians 7, noting that he invokes his own authority as well as the Lord's rulings and the commands of God. Gooch's thesis is that theological ethics in this case at least cannot be reduced to simple obedience to religious authority.

_____. "Conscience in 1 Corinthians 8 and 10." *New Testament Studies* 33 (1987): 244-254.

Grabska, Stanislawa. "Comment lire les lettres de Saint Paul pour utiliser son enseignement dans la théologie morale contemporaine." *Studia Moralia* 13 (1975): 41-65.

Hahn, Ferdinand. "Prophetie und Lebenswandel. Bemerkungen zu Paulus und zu zwei Texten der Apostolischen Väter." In *Neues Testament und Ethik. Für Rudolf Schnackenburg*, 527-537. Herausgegeben von Helmut Merklein. Freiburg: Herder, 1989.

Hamel, Edouard, S.J. : "Scripture, the Soul of Moral Theology?" In *Readings in Moral Theology No. 4: The Use of Scripture in Moral Theology*, 105-132. Edited by Charles E. Curran and Richard A. McCormick, S.J. New York: Paulist Press, 1984.

French original: "L'Ecriture âme de la Théologie." *Gregorianum* 52 (1971): 511-535.

Unpacks the metaphors of "soul" and "nourishment" used by Vatican II to indicate possible roles and applications of Scripture to moral theology. Concludes with a brief look at Pauline morality to illustrate the relationship between a moral theology rooted in both the faith kerygma and human reason.

The text was given as a lecture at the University of Sydney (Australia), and follows upon another study published in *Fondamenti biblici della teologia morale* (Brescia: Paideia, 1973.)

Hamel was professor of moral theology at the Pontifical Gregorian University until 1986.

_____. "La théologie morale entre l'Ecriture et la raison." *Gregorianum* 56 (1975): 273-319.

Texte d'un rapport rédigé pour la Commission Théologique Internationale.

Paper prepared for the International Theological Commission, of which Hamel was a member at the time.

Hamel considers the proper role and relationship of Scripture to moral theology, outlining some of the methodological problems, stressing the need for an ongoing hermeneutical application, and discussing in brief how St. Paul utilized both Scripture and contemporary Greek moral philosophy in his Letters.

Hays, Richard B. "Awaiting the redemption of our bodies: drawing on Scripture and tradition in the church debate on homosexuality." *Sojourners* 20 (July 1991): 17-21.

Discusses Romans 1:18-32.

Hays is professor of New Testament at Duke University Divinity School, and taught for a number of years previously at Yale.

_____. "Christology and Ethics in Galatians: The Law of Christ." *Catholic Biblical Quarterly* 49 (1987): 268-290.

_____. "Relations Natural and Unnatural: A Response to John Boswell's Exegesis of Romans 1." *Journal of Religious Ethics* 14 (1986): 184-215.

See Chapter 4, "The Scriptures," of John Boswell's *Christianity, Social Tolerance, and Homosexuality: Gay People in Western Europe from the Beginning of the Christian Era to the Fourteenth Century*, (Chicago: University of Chicago Press, 1980): 91-117 for the treatment discussed in this article, as well as for a listing of other works which deal with Boswell's position.

_____. "The Role of Scripture in Paul's Ethics." Part I, Chapter 3 in *Theology and Ethics in Paul and His Interpreters: Essays in Honor of Victor Paul Furnish*, 30-47. Edited by Eugene H. Lovering, Jr. and Jerry L. Sumney. Nashville: Abingdon Press, 1996.

Hoffmann, Paul. "Paul as a Witness to Dissent." *Concilium* 158 (1982): 75-80.

One of a series of articles on various aspects of this issue.

Hooker, Morna D. "A Partner in the Gospel: Paul's Understanding of His Ministry." Part I, Chapter 6, in *Theology and Ethics in Paul and His Interpreters: Essays in Honor of Victor Paul Furnish*, 83-100. Edited by Eugene H. Lovering, Jr. and Jerry L. Sumney. Nashville: Abingdon Press, 1996.

Humbert, Alphonse, C.Ss.R. "La morale de St. Paul: morale du plan de salut." *Mélanges de Sciences Religieuses* 15 (1958): 257-266.

Keck, Leander E. "The Accountable Self." Part I, Chapter 1, in *Theology and Ethics in Paul and His Interpreters: Essays in Honor of Victor Paul Furnish*, 1-13. Edited by Eugene H. Lovering, Jr. and Jerry L. Sumney. Nashville: Abingdon Press, 1996.

Keck is Winkley Professor of Biblical Theology at Yale Divinity School.

Keegan, Terence J., O.P. "Paul's Dying/Rising Ethics in 1 Corinthians." In *Christian Biblical Ethics: From Biblical Revelation to Contemporary Christian Praxis: Method and Content*, 220-244. New York: Paulist Press, 1984.

Kertelge, Karl. "Freiheitsbotschaft und Liebesgebot im Galaterbrief." In *Neues Testament und Ethik. Für Rudolf Schnackenburg*, 326-337. Herausgegeben von Helmut Merklein. Freiburg: Herder, 1989.

_____. "Gesetz und Freiheit im Galaterbrief." *New Testament Studies* 30 (1984): 382-394.

_____. "The Sin of Adam in the Light of Christ's Redemptive Act according to Romans 5: 12-21." *Communio* 18 (1991): 502-513.

In Spanish: "El pecado de Adán a la luz de la obra redentora de Cristo según Rm 5, 12-21." *Communio* 13 (1991): 508-517.

One of a series of articles on various aspects of this theme.

Kilner, John F. "A Pauline Approach to Ethical Decision-Making." *Interpretation* 43 (1989): 366-379.

Kilner describes Paul's approach to moral dilemmas as God-centered, reality-bounded, and love-impelled. For Paul ethical living is seen as a response to and empowerment by God, while at the same time moral living involves both faith in God and fidelity to Him. Also discusses the roles of freedom and discernment in Pauline ethics. For Paul the right action is the most loving one, provided that no God-given moral realities are violated.

Kotva, Joseph J., Jr. "Biblical Connections." Chapter 5 in Id. *The Christian Case for Virtue Ethics*, 103-142. Moral Traditions and Moral Arguments Series. Washington, D.C.: Georgetown University Press, 1996.

Discusses Paul and the Gospel of Matthew as part of a larger for a discussion of how the Bible can figure in the development of a Christian approach to virtue ethics. See also Ch. 6 "Theological and Biblical Objections" (pp. 143-166).

Revised version of Kotva's doctoral dissertation done at Fordham University.

Kotva is pastor of the First Mennonite Church in Allentown, Pennsylvania.

Kroger, Daniel. "Paul and the Civil Authorities: An Exegesis of Romans 13:1-7." *Asia Journal of Theology* 7 (1993): 344ff.

Lafon, G. "La pensée du social et la théologie. Loi et grâce en Romains 4, 13-16." *Recherches de Science Religieuse* 75 (1987): 9-38.

_____. "Une loi de foi. La pensée de la loi en Romains 3, 19-31." *Revue des Sciences Religieuses* 61 (1987): 32-53.

Lage, Francisco. "Nuevas perspectivas sobre la valorición de la ley en la moral de san Pablo (I)." *Moralia* 13 (1991): 357-392.

Part One.

_____. "Nuevas perspectivas sobre la valorición de la ley en la moral de san Pablo (II)." *Moralia* 14 (1992): 3-28.

Part Two.

Lambrecht, Jan, S.J. "La comprensione della legge in Paolo." In *Saggi esegetici sulla legge nel Nuovo Testamento*, 82-120. A cura di Karl Kertelge. Cinisello Balsamo: Edizioni Paoline, 1990.

German original in *Das Gesetz im Neuen Testament*. Herausgegeben von Karl Kertelge. Questiones Disputatae, 108. Freiburg: Herder, 1986.

Lambrecht is a New Testament exegete.

Lance, H. Darell. "The Bible and Homosexuality." *American Baptist Quarterly* 8 (1989): 140-151.

Reviews some of the major changes that have occurred in the understanding of some biblical texts traditionally used in reference to homosexuality, such as Gn 19; Jg 19; Lv 18-20; Dt 23:17-18; 1 Cor 6:9-11; Rm 1:26-27; and Jde 6-7. Raises hermeneutical questions which these texts present, and includes bibliography for further study.

Lee, Page. "Conscience in Romans 13:5." *Faith and Mission* 8 (1990): 85-93.

Légasse, Simon. "Agape interumana. Dall'apertura al ripiegamento." Capitolo 1 di *E chi è il mio prossimo?*, 9-34. Roma: Edizioni Dehoniane, 1991.

French original: *«Et qui est mon prochain?» Etude sur l'agape dans le Nouveau Testament*. Lectio Divina, 136. Paris Editions du Cerf, 1989.

Treats the theme of agape in both the Epistles and the Johannine writings.

Lindemann, Andreas. "Die biblischen Toragebote und die paulinische Ethik." In *Studien zum Text und zur Ethik des Neuen Testaments. Festschrift zum 80. Geburtstag von Heinrich Greeven*, 242-265. Herausgegeben von Wolfgang Schrage. Berlin/New York: Walter de Gruyter, 1986.

_____. "Pauline Mission and Religious Pluralism." Part III, Chapter 3 in *Theology and Ethics in Paul and His Interpreters: Essays in Honor of Victor Paul Furnish*, 275-288. Edited by Eugene H. Lovering, Jr. and Jerry L. Sumney. Nashville: Abingdon Press, 1996.

Lodge, John G. "The Apostle's Appeal and Reader's Response: 2 Corinthians 8 and 9." *Chicago Studies* 30 (1991): 59-75.

Lodge's thesis is that the generosity urged by Paul to the Corinthians was crucial to building unity within the entire early Church.

Lohse, Eduard. "Die Berufung auf das Gewissen in der paulinischen Ethik." In *Neues Testament und Ethik. Für Rudolf Schnackenburg*, 207-219. Herausgegeben von Helmut Merklein. Freiburg: Herder, 1989.

Lohse is a Lutheran bishop and former New Testament professor at the University of Göttingen.

_____. "Changes of Thought in Pauline Theology? Some Reflections on Paul's Ethical Teaching in the context of His Theology." Part I, Chapter 10 in *Theology and Ethics in Paul and His Interpreters: Essays in Honor of Victor Paul Furnish*, 146-160. Edited by Eugene H. Lovering, Jr. and Jerry L. Sumney. Nashville: Abingdon Press, 1996.

Luck, Ulrich. "Das Gute und das Böse in Römer 7." In *Neues Testament und Ethik.*
   Für Rudolf Schnackenburg, 220-237. Herausgegeben von Helmut Merklein.
   Freiburg: Herder, 1989.

Luz, Ulrich. "Überlegungen zum Epheserbrief und seiner Paränese." In *Neues*
   Testament und Ethik. Für Rudolf Schnackenburg, 376-396. Herausgegeben
   von Helmut Merklein. Freiburg: Herder, 1989.

Lyonnet, Stanislaus, S.J. "St. Paul: Liberty and Law." In *Readings in Biblical*
   Morality, 62-83. Edited by C. Luke Salm. Englewood Cliffs: Prentice Hall,
   1967.

MacDonald, M.Y. "Women Holy in Body and Spirit: The Social Setting of 1
   Corinthians 7." *New Testament Studies* 36 (1990): 161-181.

Mainville, Odette. "L'éthique paulinienne." *Eglise et théologie* 24 (1993): 391-412.

Malick, David E. "The Condemnation of Homosexuality in Romans 1:26-27."
   Bibliotheca Sacra 150 (1993): 327-340.

   Argues that the Pauline prohibition against homosexuality is both transcultural
   and transhistorical, and therefore holds for today. Homosexuality represents
   a reversal of God's created order according to Malick.

Marguerat, D. "L'avenir de la loi: Matthieu à l'épreuve de Paul." *Etudes*
   Théologiques et Religieuses 57 (1982): 361-374.

Martin, Dale B. "Heterosexism and the Interpretation of Romans 1:18-32." *Biblical*
   Interpretation 3 (1995): 332-55.

   This article, concentrating on two articles by Richard B. Hays, critiques recent
   interpretation of Rom. 1:18-32. Modern interpreters, influenced more by
   particularly modern forms of heterosexism and its construction of
   homosexuality, desire, and "nature" than by a straightforward historical-
   critical reading of Paul's letter, portray Paul as referring to the "Fall" of
   Genesis 1-3 in Romans 1. Paul, it is assumed, takes homosexuality to be a

sign of "humanity's fallen state." These interpreters, therefore, ascribe homosexual desire to universal fallen humanity in a way that Paul does not do. Paul is referring not to the Fall in Romans 1 but to the invention of idolatry and polytheism by the Gentiles; homosexual intercourse is therefore not a symptom of "the Fall" but of Gentile polytheism. Paul also is not giving an etiology of homosexual desire, which for him as for most ancients was not different from heterosexual desire, but an etiology of homosexual intercourse. Furthermore, modern scholars misconstrue Paul's references to "nature" and acts "contrary to nature" because they import into Paul's discourse particularly modern notions of "natural" and "unnatural" not available in the ancient world. Heterosexist scholars interpret Paul the way they do not because they are simply and objectively "reading the text," as they claim, but because of their implication in homophobia, a particularly modern ideological system that construes desire, "nature," and sexuality in particular ways.

Martin, Leonard M., C.Ss.R. "Moral Sexual missionária de Paulo: *Subsidios para uma moral do matrimônio no Brasil.*" *Revista Eclesiástica Brasileira* 50 (1990): 515-536.

In Portuguese.

Martyn, J. Louis. "The Crucial Event in the History of the Law (Gal 5:14)." Part I, Chapter 4 in *Theology and Ethics in Paul and His Interpreters: Essays in Honor of Victor Paul Furnish*, 48-61. Edited by Eugene H. Lovering, Jr. and Jerry L. Sumney. Nashville: Abingdon Press, 1996.

Matera, Frank J. "Moral Exhortation: The Relation between Moral Exhortation and Doctrinal Exposition in the Letter to the Hebrews." *Toronto Journal of Theology* 10 (1994): 169-182.

McCarthy, J., S.J. "Le Christ cosmique et l'âge de l'écologie. Une lecture de Col 1, 15-20." *Nouvelle Revue Théologique* 116 (1994): 27-47.

McGuire, Anne. "Equality and Subordination in Christ: Displacing the Powers of the Household Code in Colossians." In *Religion and Economic Ethics*, 65-86. The Annual Publication of the College Theology Society, 31 (1985). Lanham: University Press of America, 1990.

McGuire teaches New Testament at Haverford College.

Meeks, Wayne A. "The 'Haustafeln' and American Slavery: A Hermeneutical Challenge." Part III, Chapter 1 in *Theology and Ethics in Paul and His Interpreters: Essays in Honor of Victor Paul Furnish*, 232-253. Edited by Eugene H. Lovering, Jr. and Jerry L. Sumney. Nashville: Abingdon Press, 1996.

_____. "The Polyphonic Ethics of the Apostle Paul." *The Annual of the Society of Christian Ethics 1988*. (1988): 17-29.

Merk, Otto. "Nachahmung Christi. Zu ethischen Perspektiven in der paulinischen Theologie." In *Neues Testament und Ethik. Für Rudolf Schnackenburg*, 172-206. Herausgegeben von Helmut Merklein. Freiburg: Herder, 1989.

Merklein, Helmut. "Sinn und Zweck von Röm 13,1-7. Zur semantischen und pragmatischen Struktur eines umstrittenen Textes." In *Neues Testament und Ethik. Für Rudolf Schnackenburg*, 238-270. Herausgegeben von Helmut Merklein. Freiburg: Herder, 1989.

Miller, James E. "The Practices of Romans 1:26: Homosexual or Heterosexual?" *Novum Testamentum* 37, no. 1 (1995): 1-11.

Maintains that while Romans 1:27 clearly condemns male homosexual practice, 1:26 is best understood as not describing female homosexual activity, but unnatural heterosexual intercourse such as contraception.

Moule, C.F.D. "Obligation in the Ethics of Paul." In *Christian History and Interpretation: Studies Presented to John Knox*, 389-406. Edited by WW.R. Farmer et al. Cambridge: Cambridge University Press, 1967.

Munro, Winsome. "Romans 13:1-7; Apartheid's Last Biblical Refuge." *Biblical Theology Bulletin* 20 (1990): 161-168.

Apartheid advocates have often used this Pauline passage as a biblical warrant. This view has been criticized by signers of the 1985-1986 *Kairos Document*, who relativize the passage's applicability by referring to both situational and total biblical context. This approach is critiqued in turn by Munro, who suggests that the passage is part of an overall redaction of Pauline letters connected with the Pastoral Epistles. Munro suggests a hermeneutical method of applying the passage in the sense of identifying a "kindred struggle" among 2nd Century Christians in Asia Minor.

Ms. Munro is a South African who teaches religion at St. Olaf's College in Northfield, MN.

Nebe, Gottfried. "Righteousness in Paul." In *Justice and Righteousness: Biblical Themes and their Influence*, 131-153. Edited by Henning Graf Reventlow and Yair Hoffman. Sheffield: JSOT Press, 1992.

Neidhart, W. "Das paulinische Verständnis der Liebe und die Sexualität." *Theologische Zeitschrift* 40 (1984): 245-250.

Oates, Wayne E. "A Biblical Perspective on Addiction." *Review and Expositor* 91 (1994): 71-75.

Treats Dt 5:6-7; Mt 22:340-40; and Gal 4:3,8.

Ogden, Schubert M. "Paul in Contemporary Theology and Ethics: Presuppositions of Critically Appropriating Paul's Letters Today." Part III, Chapter 4 in *Theology and Ethics in Paul and His Interpreters: Essays in Honor of Victor Paul Furnish*, 289-305. Edited by Eugene H. Lovering, Jr. and Jerry L. Sumney. Nashville: Abingdon Press, 1996.

Outka, Gene. "On Harming Others." *Interpretation* 34 (1980): 381-393.

Using several Pauline texts Outka uses the case of personal harm done to others to consider how the norm of love should function as guide to Christian action and discernment.

Padron, Diego. "Romanos 2, 14-16: datos sobre la interpretación del texto. Recto actuar moral y salvación de Dios." *Teologia IUSI* 12 (1994): 88-100.

One of several articles in this issue devoted to an analysis of *Veritatis Splendor*, Pope John Paul II's 1993 Encyclical on fundamental moral theology.

Pastor Ramos, Felix. "La ética paulina. El fundamento de la vida cristiana según San Pablo." *Moralia* 6 (1984): 129-144.

Tambien en [also found in] *Perspectivas de moral bíblica*, 129-144. Estudios de Etica Teologica. Edd. Marciano Vidal, Francisco Lage y Alfosno Ruiz-Mateos. Madrid: Instituto Superior de Ciencas Morales, PS Editorial, 1984.

Pérez Gordo, A. "¿Es el velo en 1 Cor 11, 2-16 síimbolo de libertad o de sumisión? *Burgense* 29 (1988): 337-366.

Perkins, Pheme. "Paul and Ethics." *Interpretation* 38 (1984): 268-280.

Perkins is professor of New Testament at Boston College.

Peterson, David. "Worship and Ethics in Romans 12." *Tyndale Bulletin* 44 (1993): 271-288.

Working against Käsemann's thesis that the mystical tradition of Hellenism is the principal inspiration for Paul's thinking, Peterson fleshes out Paul's thinking in reference to its theological background in the Hebrew Scriptures and development within the body of the Letter itself. According to Peterson, "the function of the worship terminology in Romans 12:1 is to proclaim the possibility of a new kind of service to God and to summon believers to respond to God's gracious initiative by the daily offering of themselves, in a whole-person commitment" (p. 281).

Phipps, William E. "Is Paul's Attitude toward Sexual Relations Contained in 1 Cor 7:1 ?" *New Testament Studies* 28 (1982): 125-131.

Price, R.M. "The Distinctiveness of Early Christian Sexual Ethics." *Heythrop Journal* 31 (1990): 257-276.

Paul's supposedly negative and strict sexual ethics arose out of his desire to preserve the purity of the whole Christian community by means of the purity of its individual members.

Priess, Theodore. "Life in Christ and Social Ethics in the Epistle to Philemon." In *Life in Christ*, 32-42. London: SCM, 1954.

Reichke, Bo. "Paulus und das Gesetz." *Theologische Zeitschrift* 41 (1985): 237-257.

Ricart, I. "El `discernimento cristià' en la Carta als Gàlates." *Revista Catalana de Teologia* 13 (1988): 1-22.

Richardson, Peter, and Gooch, Paul W. "Accomodation Ethics." *Tyndale Bulletin* 29 (1978): 89-142.

Richardson, William J. "Principle and Context in the Ethics of the Epistle to Philemon." *Interpretation* 22 (1968): 301-316.

Rossano, Piero. "Morale ellenistica e morale paolina." In *Fondamenti biblici della teologia morale*, 173-185. Atti della XXII Settimana Biblica. Associazione biblica italiana. Brescia: Paideia, 1973.

Russell, K.C. "The Embarrassing Verse in First Corinthians." *The Bible Today* (September 1980): 338-341.

Deals with masturbation.

Sacchi, Alessandro. "La legge naturale nella Lettera ai Romani." In *Fondamenti biblici della teologia morale*, 375-389. Atti della XXII Settimana Biblica. Associazione biblica italiana. Brescia: Paideia, 1973.

Salas, Antonio, O.S.A. "La Sexualidad. Aporte del «corpus» paulino." *Biblia y Fe* 18 (1992): 67-91.

One of several articles under this number's general theme of "La Sexualidad: *Aproximacion Biblica.*"

Sampley, J. Paul. "Reasoning From the Horizons of Paul's Thought World: A Comparison of Galatians and Philippians." Part I, Chapter 8 in *Theology and Ethics in Paul and His Interpreters: Essays in Honor of Victor Paul Furnish*, 114-131. Edited by Eugene H. Lovering, Jr. and Jerry L. Sumney. Nashville: Abingdon Press, 1996.

Sauer, J. "Traditionsgeschichtliche Erwägungen zu den synoptischen und paulinischem Aussagen über Feindesliebe und Wiedervergeltungsverzicht." *Zeitschrift für die Neutestamentliche Wissenschaft* 76 (1985): 1-28.

Schrage, Wolfgang. "Zur Ethik der neutestamentlichen Haustafeln." *New Testament Studies* 21 (1975): 3-22.

Schulz, Siegfried. "Der frühe und der Späte Paulus. Überlegungen zur Entwurf seiner Theologie und Ethik. *Theologische Zeitschrift* 41 (1985): 228-236.

Schweizer, Eduard. "Askese nach Kol1,24 oder 2,20f?" In *Neues Testament und Ethik. Für Rudolf Schnackenburg*, 340-348. Herausgegeben von Helmut Merklein. Freiburg: Herder, 1989.

_____. "Traditional Ethical Patterns in the Pauline and Post-Pauline Letters and Their Development (List of Vices and House-Tables)." In *Text and Interpretation*, 195-209. Matthew Black *Festschrift*. Edited by E. Best and R. McL. Wilson. Cambridge: Cambridge University Press, 1979.

Scroggs, Robin. "Ethics: Eschatological Action." Chapter 4 in Id. *Paul for a New Day*, 57-74. Philadelphia: Fortress Press, 1977.

_____. "Paul and the Eschatological Body." Part I, Chapter 2 in *Theology and Ethics in Paul and His Interpreters: Essays in Honor of Victor Paul Furnish*, 14-29. Edited by Eugene H. Lovering, Jr. and Jerry L. Sumney. Nashville: Abingdon Press, 1996.

Sklba, Bishop Richard J. "Living the truth in love (Eph 4:15): reflections on the ministry of teaching in the church." In *Theology toward the third millennium*, 125-144. Edited by G. Schultenover. 1991.

Sklba is a biblical theologian and auxiliary bishop of Milwaukee, Wisconsin.

Smith, Abraham. "The New Testament and Homosexuality." *Quarterly Review* 11 (1991): 18-32.

Examines three New Testament texts, 1 Cor 6:9; Rm 1:26-27; and 1 Tm 1:10, in the light of the Greco-Roman cultural milieu and the literary design of each passage.

Smith, Mark D. "Ancient Bisexuality and the Interpretation of Romans 1:26-27. *Journal of the American Academy of Religion* 64 (1996): 223-256.

Smith is Associate Professor of History at Albertson College in Caldwell, Idaho.

Smith, D. Moody. "The Love Command: John and Paul?" Part II, Chapter 4 in *Theology and Ethics in Paul and His Interpreters: Essays in Honor of Victor Paul Furnish*, 207-217. Edited by Eugene H. Lovering, Jr. and Jerry L. Sumney. Nashville: Abingdon Press, 1996.

Soending, Thomas. "Gottesliebe bei Paulus." *Theologie und Glaube* 79 (1989): 219-242.

Spohn, William C. "St.Paul on Apostolic Celibacy and the Body of Christ." *Studies in the Spirituality of the Jesuits* 17 (January 1985).

Written while Spohn was a Roman Catholic priest in the Society of Jesus.

Spohn studied under James Gustafson at the University of Chicago, taught moral theology at the Jesuit School of Theology-Berkeley for many years, and currently teaches Christian ethics at the University of Santa Clara.

Stachowiak, L. "Die Erforschung der paulinischen Paränesen in 20. Jahrhundert." *Collectanea Theologica* 53 (1983): 177-194.

Strecker, Georg. "Die neutestamentlichen Haustafeln (Kol 3,18-4,1 und Eph 5,22- 6.9)." In *Neues Testament und Ethik. Für Rudolf Schnackenburg*, 349-375. Herausgegeben von Helmut Merklein. Freiburg: Herder, 1989.

Thériault, Jean-Yves. "La portée écologique de la notion paulinienne de création." *Eglise et théologie* 23 (1991): 293-314.

Thickstun, Margaret Olofson. "Writing the Spirit: Margaret Fell's Feminist Critique of Pauline Theology." *Journal of the American Academy of Religion* 63 (Summer 1995): 269-79.

Thomas, Carolyn, S.C.N. "Economic Issues in Paul." *The Bible Today* 32 (1994): 290-294.

One of several articles on biblical economic justice in this issue.

Vanhoye, Albert, S.J. "The Apostle Paul as Moral Teacher and Guide." In *The Catholic Priest as Moral Teacher and Guide*, 21-38. San Francisco: Ignatius Press, 1990.

Given at a symposium held at St. Charles Borromeo Seminary in Overbrook, Pennsylvania held on 17-20 January 1990.

Vanhoye is former rector of the Pontifical Biblical Institute in Rome, and member of the Pontifical Biblical Commission.

Varó, F. "El léxico del pecado en la Epíistola de S. Pablo a los Romanos." *Scripta Theologica* 21 (1989): 99-116.

Vassiliadis, Petros. "Equality and Justice in Classical Antiquity and in Paul: The Social Implications of the Pauline Collection." *St. Vladimir's Theological Quarterly* 36 (1992): 51-59.

Ward, R.B. "Musonius and Paul on Marriage." *New Testament Studies* 36 (1990): 281-289.

Weiser, Alfons. "Titus 2 als Gemeindeparänese." In *Neues Testament und Ethik. Für Rudolf Schnackenburg*, 397-414. Herausgegeben von Helmut Merklein. Freiburg: Herder, 1989.

White, Leland J. "Biblical Texts and Contemporary Gay People: A Response to Boswell and Boughton." *Irish Theological Quarterly* 59 (1993): 286-301.

Argues that neither Boughton nor Boswell uses "sufficiently elaborated models of culture and cultural variation to address the issue of whether the actions proscribed in the Bible are equivalent in meaning (p. 286)."

See Lynne C. Boughton's "Biblical Texts and Homosexuality: A Response to John Boswell." *Irish Theological Quarterly* 58 (1992): 141-153, as well as Chapter 4, "The Scriptures," of John Boswell's *Christianity, Social Tolerance, and Homosexuality: Gay People in Western Europe from the Beginning of the Christian Era to the Fourteenth Century*, (Chicago: University of Chicago Press, 1980): 91-117 for the treatment discussed in this article, as well as for a listing of other works which deal with Boswell's position.

_____. "Does the Bible Speak about Gays or Same-Sex Orientation? A Test Case in Biblical Ethics: Part I." *Biblical Theological Bulletin* (1995): 14-23.

Examines the biblical texts of Genesis 19, Leviticus 18-20, Romans 1:1, 1 Corinthians 6, and 1 Timothy 1 in light of three traditional core values of Mediterranean culture: honor, reproductivity, and holiness. White's thesis is that these texts frame the ethical issue of "homosexuality" in terms of fulfilling traditional cultural roles, and therefore these texts do not address the contemporary issues of same-sex orientation.

Wilson, Kenneth T. "Should Women Wear Headcoverings?" *Bibliotheca Sacra* 148 (1991): 442-462.

Wilson offers an extended exegesis of 1 Cor 11:2-16, and concludes that the theological point made by Paul is that the female/male distinction, ordained by God, is what must be preserved. The actual choice of the appropriate cultural symbol (e.g. headcoverings) to show such distinction may well change from epoch to epoch, or culture to culture.

Wilson is Pastor-Teacher of the Anchorage Bible Fellowship.

Winter, Bruce. "The Entries and Ethics of Orators and Paul (1 Thessolonians 2:1-12)." *Tyndale Bulletin* 44 (1993): 55-74.

Wolbert, Werner. "Vorbild und paränetische Autorität. *Zum problem der 'Nachahmung' des Paulus.*" *Münchener Theologische Zeitschrift* 32 (1981): 249-270.

Zeller, Dieter. "Zur neuereren Diskussion über das Gesetz bei Paulus." *Theologie und Philosophie* 62 (1987): 481-499.

Books on Pauline Ethics

Alexander, Archibald Browning Drysdale. *The Ethics of St. Paul.* Glasgow: Maclehose and Sons, 1910.

Alvarez-Verdes, Lorenzo, C.Ss.R. *El Imperativo cristiano en san Pablo: La tensión indicativo-imperativo en Rom 6, Análisis estructural.* Institución San Jerónimo, 11. Valencia: Institución San Jerónimo, 1980.

Andrews, Mary Edith. *The Ethical Teaching of Paul: A Study in Origin.* Chapel Hill: The University of North Carolina press, 1934.

Barclay, John. *Obeying the Truth: A Study of Paul's Ethics in Galatians.* Studies of the New Testament and Its World. Edinburgh: T. & T. Clark, 1988.

Barclay's thesis is that the hortatory section of Galatians (5:13--6:10) is a continuation of Paul's central argument with the Galatian community, and therefore should not be "detached" from the interpretation of the rest of the

Letter. Barclay discusses Paul's pneumatology here in its various aspects and concludes with a broad-ranging survey of the relationship to other questions of Pauline interpretation, such as the Lutheran position that Paul is arguing against dependence on works to merit salvation.

Reviewed by Robert G. Hall in *Interpretation* 45 (1991): 94.

Barclay lectures in biblical studies at the University of Glasgow, Scotland.

Barrett, Charles Kingsley. *Freedom and Obligation: A Study of the Epistle to the Galatians.* Philadelphia: Westminster Press, 1985.

Bassler, Jouette M. *God and Mammon: Asking for Money in the New Testament.* Nashville: Abingdon, 1991.

Treats the cultural context of the ancient world, and then considers perspectives in light of the Gospels, Paul, and Acts.

Benz, Karl. *Die Ethik des Apostels Paulus.* Freiburg i. B.: Herder, 1912.

Burthchaell, James Tunstead, C.S.C. *Philemon's Problem: The Daily Dilemma of the Christian.* Chicago: ACTA [Foundation for Adult Catechetical Teaching Aids], 1973.

Using the *Letter to Philemon* as a touchstone for an approach to contemporary moral issues Burthchaell discusses peace and violence, sex and ritual, prayer and penance--in an attempt to fashion a Christian vision of the world. Written in a popular, rather than academic style.

Collange, Jean François. *De Jésus à Paul: L'éthique du Nouveau Testament.* Le Champ éthique, 3. Genève: Labor et Fides, 1980.

Corriveau, R. *The Liturgy of Life: A Study of the Ethical Thought of St. Paul in his Letters to the Early Christian Communities.* Studia, 25. Bruxelles, Paris, Montréal: Desclée de Brouwer, 1970.

Cruz, Hieronymus. *Christological Motives and Motivated Actions in Pauline Paranesis.* Europäische Hochschulschriften, 23; Theologie, 396. Frankfurt-am-Main: Peter Lang, 1990.

Deidun, T.J. *New Covenant Morality in Paul.* Analecta Biblica, vol 89. Rome: Biblical Institute Press: 1981.

The intention of this study is to relate Pauline ethics to its proper theological context and within that context to examine certain important problems of a more special nature, among them the indicative-imperative relationship in Paul, the specifically religious character of Christian love, the status of Paul's ethical "directives," and the role of external law in Christian living.

Deming, Will. *Paul on Marriage and Celibacy. The Hellenistic Backgrounds of 1 Corinthians 7.* Cambridge (UK): Cambridge University Press, 1995.

This book challenges the traditional interpretation of Paul's thinking on marriage and celibacy, by looking at the established theories about the main influences on Paul's theology and by reconstructing the Stoic and Cynic discourse on marriage that formed its context, Deming offers a reassessment of both Paul's understanding of marriage and his place in the history of Christian asceticism, while also providing new information for discussions of Christian sexuality and feminist evaluations of the Bible.

Diaz-Rodelas, Juan Miguem. *Pablo y la ley. La novedad de Rom 7,7-8,4 en el conjunto de la reflexion pauliana sobre la ley.* Estella: Verbo Divino, 1994.

Donelson, Lewis R. *Pseudoepigraphy and Ethical Argument in the Pastoral Epistles.* Hermeneutische Untersuchungen zur Theologie, 22. Tübingen: J.C.B. Mohr, 1986.

Dunn, James D.G. *Jesus, Paul, and the Law: Studies in Mark and Galatians.* Louisville: Westminster/John Knox Press; London: SPCK, 1990.

One-volume collection of journal articles which have previously appeared from 1982 to 1988. Dunn also includes some additional notes responding to various critiques made to his articles.

Reviewed by C.R.A. Morray-Jones in *Journal of Jewish Studies* 43 (1992): 147-150.

Eliott, Neil. *Liberating Paul: The Justice of God and the Politics of the Apostle.* Maryknoll: Orbis Press, 1993.

For centuries the apostle Paul has been invoked to justify oppression-whether on behalf of slavery, to enforce unquestioned obedience to the state, to silence women, or to legitimate anti-Semitism. Elliott argues that the struggle to liberate human beings from the power of death and oppression requires "liberating Paul" from the unfortunate consequence of the way he has usually been read, or rather misread, in the churches.

Enslin, Morton Scott. *The Ethics of Paul.* New York: Harper & Brothers, 1930.

Forrell, George Wolfgang. *The Christian Lifestyle: Reflections on Romans 12-15.* Philadelphia: Fortress Press, 1975.

Fowl, Stephen E. *The Story of Christ in the Ethics of Paul: An Analysis of the Function of the Hymnic Material in the Pauline Corpus.* Journal for the Study of the New Testament Supplement Series, 36. Sheffield: JSOT Press, 1990.

Reviewed by Marion L. Soards in *Theology Today* 48 (1992): 262.

Fowl is professor of theology at Loyola College, Baltimore.

Furnish, Victor Paul. *The Moral Teaching of Paul: Selected Issues*, 2nd ed. Nashville: Abingdon, 1985.

Treats sexual questions, such as marriage and divorce, homosexuality, as well as other issues, such as the place of women in the Church, and the relationship between Christians and governing authorities.

_____. *Theology and Ethics in Paul: Selected Issues.* Nashville: Abingdon, 1978.

An earlier version of Furnish's 1985 book.

Georgi, Dieter. *Remembering the Poor: The History of Paul's Collection for Jerusalem*. Nashville: Abingdon Press, 1992.

German original: *Die Geschicte der Kollekte des Pauls für Jerusalem*. Theologische Forschung, 28. Hamburg: Herbert Reich Evangelischer Verlag GMBH, 1965.

An exegetical and historical analysis of the history of the Pauline collection for the church at Jerusalem which raises the question of socio-political responsibility of biblical hermeneutics in a concluding reflection on Paul's understanding of the nature of money and the consequences for contemporary economic arrangements.

Gielen, Marlis. *Tradition und Theologie neutestamentlicher Haustafelethik: Ein Beitrag zur Frage einer christlichen Auseinandersetzung mit gesellschaftlichen Normen*. Bonner Biblische Beiträge, 75. Frankfurt-am-Main: Hain, 1990.

Considers both Pauline texts (Colossians and Ephesians), as well as 1 Peter.

Goldsmith, Dale. *New Testament Ethics*. Elgin IL: Brethren Press, 1988.

Brief consideration of the distinctive "moral personality" of eight "authors" of the New Testament in reference to the Christian life: James, Paul, 1 Peter, Hebrews, as well as the four gospels. Goldsmith's treatment is aimed primarily at the interested lay reader rather than the professional exegete or ethician.

Goldsmith is an ordained minister in the Presbyterian Church.

Grabner-Haider, Anton. *Paraklese und Eschatologie bei Paulus. Mensch und Welt in Anspruch der Zukunft Gottes*. NTAb, NF, 4. Münster: Aschendorff, 1968.

Halter, Hans. *Taufe und Ethos. Paulinische Kriterien für das Proprium Christlicher Moral*. FreibThSt, 106. Freiburg i. B.: Herder, 1977.

Hasenstab, Rudolf. *Modelle paulinischer Ethik. Beiträge zu einem Autonomie-Modell aus paulinischem Geist.* Tübinger Theologische Studien, 11. Mainz: Grünewald Verlag, 1977.

Hübner, Hans. *Law in Paul's Thought.* Studies of the New Testament and Its World. Edinburgh: T. & T. Clark, 1984.

German Original: *Das Gesetz bei Paulus. Ein Beitrag zum Werden der paulinischen Theologie.* FRLANT, 119. Göttingen: Vandenhoeck & Ruprecht, 1978.

Italian translation: *La legge in Paolo. Contributo allo svillupo della teologia paolina.* Studi Biblici, 109. Brescia: Paideia, 1995.

Jones, F. Stanley. *"Freiheit" in den Briefen des Apostels Paulus. Eini historische, exegetische und religionsgeschichte Studie.* Göttinger theologische Arbeiten, 34. Göttingen: Vandenhoeck & Ruprecht, 1987.

Keener, Craig S. *Paul, Women and Wives: Marriage and Women's Ministry in the Letters of Paul.* Peabody MA: Hendrickson, 1991.

Kidd, Reggie M. *Wealth and Beneficence in the Pastoral Epistles: A "Bourgeois Form of Early Christianity.* SBL Dissertation Series, 122. Atlanta: Scholars Press, 1990.

Kirchhoff, R. *Die Sünde gegen den eigenen Leib. Studien zu "porne" und "porneia" in 1 Kor 6, 12-20 und dem sozio-kulturellen Kontext der paulinischen Adressaten.* Göttingen: Vandenhoeck & Ruprecht, 1994.

Koenig, John. *New Testament Hospitality: Partners with Strangers as Promise and Mission.* Overtures to Biblical Theology, 17. Philadelphia: Fortress Press, 1985.

Examines the ministry of Jesus, Paul and the life-style of the early church depicted in Luke-Acts to show that the early Christians fostered a way of life in which individuals acted as "God's guests and hosts on behalf of the world."

Hospitality and openness to strangers are viewed as both crucial to the Christian life and the development of the faith and ethics of the early believers.

Longenecker, Richard N. *Paul, Apostle of Liberty*. New York: Harper and Row, 1964.

Lovering, Eugene H., Jr., and Sumney, Jerry L., eds. *Theology & Ethics in Paul and His Interpreters. Essays in Honor of Victor Paul Furnish*. Nashville: Abingdon Press, 1996.

Festschrift in honor of Victor Paul Furnish, with contributions by Paul Achtmeier, Harold W. Attridge, William Baird, C.K. Barrett, Jouette M. Bassler, C. Clifton Black, James D.G. Dunn, Beverly Roberts Gaventa, Richard B. Hays, Morna D. Hooker, Leander E. Keck, Andreas Lindemann, Eduard Lohse, J. Louis Martyn, Wayne A. Meeks, Schubert M. Ogden, J. Paul Sampley, Robin Scroggs, and D. Moody Smith.

Martin, Brice L. *Christ and the Law in Paul*. Novum Testamentum Supplement, 62. Leiden: E.J. Brill, 1990.

Matera, Frank J. *New Testament Ethics: The Legacies of Jesus and Paul*. Louisville: Westminster John Knox Press, 1996.

The author explores the broad range of ethical concerns found in the teachings of Jesus and Paul and illuminates in identifiable unity that underlies the ethical teachings of both.

Meeks, Wayne A. *The First Urban Christians: The Social World of the Apostle Paul*. New Haven: Yale University Press, 1983.

Merk, Otto. *Handeln aus Glauben. Die Motivierungen der paulinischen Ethik*. Marburg: Elwert, 1968.

Merritt, H. Wayne. *In Word and Deed: Moral Integrity in Paul*. Emory Studies in Early Christianity, 1. New York: Peter Lang, 1993.

Focuses on an analysis of 2 Cor 10-13 and suggests that the Pauline phrase of "in word and deed" at 2 Cor 10:11 is the key to Paul's vision of the moral life.

Mohrlang, Roger. *Matthew and Paul: A Comparison of Ethical Perspectives.* Society for New Testament Studies, Monograph Series, 48. London: Cambridge University Press, 1984.

Reviewed by Hans Dieter Betz in *Journal of Religion* 66 (1986): 206.

Murphy-O'Connor, Jerome, O.P. *L'existence chrétienne selon Saint Paul.* Lectio divina, 80. Paris: Editions du Cerf, 1974.

Newton, Michael. *The Concept of Purity at Qumran and in the Letters of Paul.* Society for New Testament Monograph Series, 53. Cambridge: Cambridge University Press, 1985.

Contradicts the view that traditional Jewish attitudes toward purity and impurity have no place in Christianity. By using a concept of purity also found in the Qumranic literature and Pharisaic Judaism, Paul was able to elucidate his views on the church, the divine presence, the basis of ethical behavior, and the significance of the death of Jesus.

Nickle, Keith. *The Collection: A Study of Paul's Strategy.* Studies in Biblical Theology, 48. Naperville: Allenson, 1966.

Nieder, Lorenz, C.Ss.R. *Die Motive der religiös-sittlichen Paränese in den paulinischen Gemeindebriefen.* München: Zink, 1956.

O'Toole, Robert F., S.J. *Who Is a Christian?: A Study in Pauline Ethics.* Collegeville: Liturgical Press/Michael Glazier: 1990.

O'Toole uses the method of compositional redaction criticism to investigate the sources Paul employed in those passages which related directly to ethical matters of Christian living. The book's four sections are devoted to Paul's sources for Christian ethics, his moral directives, his understanding of morality in light of the Parousia, and the contemporary relevance of Pauline ethics.

O'Toole is a member of the faculty and the rector of the Pontifical Biblical Institute in Rome.

Penna, Romano. *Essere Cristiano secondo Paolo.* "Fame della Parola," 2. 2 ed. Torino: Marietti, 1979, 1982.

Perkins, Pheme. *Ministering in the Pauline Churches.* New York: Paulist Press, 1982.

Perkins is professor of New Testament at Boston College.

Pierce, C[laude]. A[nthony]. *Conscience in the New Testament: A Study of Syneidesis in the New Testament; in the light of its sources, and with particular reference to St. Paul: with some observations regarding its pastoral relevance today.* Studies in Biblical Theology, 15. London: SCM Press, 1955.

Räisänen, H. *Paul and the Law.* Wissenschaftliche Untersuchungen zum Neuen Testament, 29. Rev. ed. Tübingen: J.C.B. Mohr, 1987.

_____. *Jesus, Paul and the Torah: Collected Essays.* Journal for the Study of the New Testament Supplement Series, 43. Sheffield: JSOT Press, 1990.

Rebell, Walter. *Gehorsam und Unabhängigkeit. Eine sozialpsychologische Studie zu Paulus.* München: Christian Kaiser Verlag, 1986.

Redalié, Yann. *Paul après Paul. Le temps, le salut, la morale selon les épîtres à Thimothée et à Tite.* Monde de la Bible, 31. Genève: Labor et Fides, 1994.

Reinmuth, Eckart. *Geist und Gesetz. Studien zu Voraussetzungen und Inhalt der paulinishcen Paränese.* Theologische Arbeiten, 44. Berlin: Evangelische Verlagsanstalt, 1985.

Reumann, John. *Righteousness in the New Testament: "Justification" in the United States Lutheran-Roman Catholic Dialogue. With Responses by Joseph A.*

Fitzmeyer and Jerome D. Quinn. Philadelphia: Fortress Press, and New York: Paulist Press, 1982.

See especially Chapter 3, "The Pauline School," pp. 41-123 of Reumann's essay "'Justification by Grace through Faith' as Expression of the Gospel: The Biblical Witness to the Reformation Emphasis," and also Jerome D. Quinn's "Response" entitled "The Pastoral Epistles on Righteousness," pp. 229-238.

Richardson, Peter. *Paul's Ethic of Freedom.* Philadelphia: Westminster Press, 1979.

Rosner, Brian S., ed. *Understanding Paul's Ethics: Twentieth-Century Approaches.* Grand Rapids, MI: Wm. B. Eerdmans Publishing Company, 1995.

To introduce the study of Paul's ethics, Rosner has drawn together fourteen essays--including work by Adolf von Harnack, Traugott Holtz, Edwin Judge, Bruce Winter, Gerd Theissen, Gerald Harris, Alfred Seeberg, Lars Hartman, Rudolf Bultmann, Michael Parsons, Eduard Lohse, Eckhard Schnabel, Wolfgang Schrage, and Richard Longenecker--to consider the origin, context, social dimension, shape, logic, foundations, and relevance of Paul's ethics.

Rosner, Brian S. *Paul, Scripture, and Ethics. A Study of 1 Corinthians 5-7.* Arbeiten zur Geschichte des antiken Judentums und des Urchristentums. Leiden: E.J. Brill, 1994.

Sampley, J. Paul. *Pauline Partnership in Christ: Christian Community and Commitment in Light of Roman Law.* Philadelphia: Fortress Press, 1980.

Discusses the presence and function of the Roman legal "partnership," the consensual *societas,* in several Pauline epistles: Galatians, Philippians, Corinthians, and Philemon. Paul adapted these legal traditions and terminology of *societas (koinonia)* for theological purposes.

_____. *Walking Between the Times: Paul's Moral Reasoning.* Minneapolis: Fortress Press, 1991.

Sampley explores early Christian ethics as developed by Paul's understanding of his own times.

Reviewed by Richard C. Sparks in *Religious Studies Review* 18 (1992): 317.

Sanders, E[d].P[arish]. *Paul, the Law and the Jewish People*. London: SCM Press, 1985.

Italian translation: *Paolo, le legge e il popolo giudaico*. Studi Biblici, 86. Brescia: Paideia, 1986.

Reviewed by Alviero Niccacci in *Rivista di Teologia Morale* 23 (1991): 404-405.

Sanders, Jack T. *Ethics in the New Testament*. Philadelphia: Fortress Press; and London: SCM, 1975, 1986.

Analyzes and critiques the basic ethical perspectives found in the New Testament, with six chapters devoted to "Jesus," the Synoptics and Acts, Paul, Deutero-Pauline Epistles, Johannine Literature, and the Later Epistles and the Apocalypse. Sanders holds that the ethical perspective of Jesus is inseparably linked to his eschatological expectation of the imminent coming of the Kingdom of God, and that New Testament ethics can offer nothing to a contemporary ethics.

Schnabel, Eckhard J. *Law and Wisdom from Ben Sira to Paul: A Tradition Historical Enquiry into the Relation of Law, Wisdom and Ethics*. Wissenschaftliche Untersuchungen zum N.T. 2. Reihe, 16. Tübingen: J.C.B. Mohr, 1985.

Schrage, Wolfgang. *Die konkreten Einzelgebote in der paulinischen Paränese. Ein Beitrag zur neutestamentlicher Ethik*. Gütersloh, 1961.

Soending, Thomas. *Das Liebesgebot bei Paulus. Die Mahnung zur Agape im Rahmen der paulinischen Ethik*. Münster: Aschendorff, 1995.

Spicq, Ceslas, O.P. *The Trinity and Our Moral Life according to St. Paul*. Westminster MD: The Newman Press, 1963.

French original: *Vie morale et Trinité Sainte selon Saint Paul.* Lectio Divina, 19. Paris: Editions du Cerf, 1957.

Stowers, Stanley Kent. *A Rereading of Romans: Justice, Jews, and Gentiles.* New Haven: Yale University Press, 1994.

Theissen, Gerd. *Psychological Aspects of Pauline Theology.* Translated by John Galvin. Edinburgh: T. & T. Clark, 1987.

Original in German.

Combines a psychological-historical approach to the New Testament with a theological perspective to show how belief in Christ enables previously unconscious aspects of life to become conscious.

Therrien, G. *Le discerniment dans les écrits pauliniencs.* Paris: Gabalda, 1973.

Thielman, Frank. *From Plight to Solution: A Jewish Framework for Understanding Paul's View of the Law in Galatians and Romans.* Supplements to Novum Testamentum, 61. Leiden and New York: E.J. Brill, 1989.

____. *Paul and the Law: A Contextual Approach.* Downers Grove Il: InterVarsity Press, 1994.

Tobin, Thomas H., S.J. *The Spirituality of Paul.* Message of Biblical Spirituality, 12. Wilmington: Michael Glazer, 1987.

See especially Chapter 5: "Ethical Perspectives: The Spirit and Sin"; and Chapter 6: "Ethics in Practice: Freedom and Community."

Tomson, Peter J. *Paul and the Jewish Law: Halakha in the Letters of the Apostle to the Gentiles.* Compendia Rerum Iudaicarum ad Novum Testamentum III/2. Assen and Maastricht: Van Gorcum, 1990.

Reviewed by Timothy H. Lim in *Journal of Jewish Studies* 43 (1992): 157-160.

Towner, Philip H. *The Goal of Our Instruction: The Structure of Theology and Ethics in the Pastoral Epistles.* Journal for the Study of the New Testament Supplement Series, 34. Sheffield: JSOT Press, 1990.

Verner, D.C. *The Household of God: The Social World of the Pastoral Epistles.* SBL Dissertation Series, 71. Chico CA: Scholars Press, 1983.

Via, Dan O. *Self-Deception and Wholeness in Paul and Matthew.* Minneapolis: Fortress Press, 1990.

Treats the concepts of sin (self-deception) and salvation (recovery of wholeness), in the context of the anthropology, soteriology and ethics of Paul and Matthew.

Via is Professor of New Testament at The Divinity School of Duke University.

Vollenweider, Samuel. *Freiheit als neue Schöpfung. Eine Untersuchung zur Eleutheria bei Paulus und in seiner Umwelt.* Forschungen zur Religion und Literatur des Alten und Neuen Testaments, 147. Göttingen: Vandenhoeck & Ruprecht, 1989.

Wagener, Ulrike. *Die Ordnung des "Hauses Gottes": Der Ort von Frauen in der Ekklesiologie und Ethik der Pastoralbriefe.* Wissenschaftliche Untersuchungen zum Neuen Testament, 2.65. Tübingen: J. C. B. Mohr (Paul Siebeck), 1994.

Among Wagener's conclusions: for the Pastorals, the church is the "house of God," with its own proper male head of the family (along civil lines); wealth meant power, even for women; hence the letter's injunctions against ostentatious dress are a male power-play to keep women subordinate in the church. On the positive side, the Pastorals exalt marriage and family at the expense of a misunderstood encratism.

Westerholm, Stephen. *Israel's Law and the Church's Faith: Paul and His Recent Interpreters.* Grand Rapids: William B. Eerdmans, 1988.

Winninge, Mikael. *Sinners and the Righteous: A Comparative Study of the Psalms of Solomon and Paul's Letters.* Coniectanea Biblica, New Testament Series 26. Stockholm: Almqvist and Wiskell International, 1995.

Wolbert, Werner. *Ethische Argumentation und Paränese in 1 Kor 7.* Düsseldorf: Patmos Verlag, 1981.

Wright, N.T. *The Climax of the Covenant: Christ and the Law in Pauline Theology.* Minneapolis: Fortress Press, 1991.

Wright is Fellow, Tutor in Theology, and Chaplain of Worcester College, Oxford, and University Lecturer in New Testament Studies.

Yang, You-Sub. *Vollkommenheit nach paulinischem und konfuzianischem Verstandnis: Ein Vergleich des Begriffs "téleios" bei Paulus und "Ch`eng" beim Verfasser des Buches "Chung-yung".* Dissertationen Theologische Reighe, 4. Sankt Ottilien: EOS-Verlag, 1984.

Discusses the pauline and confucian notions of perfection and moral self-cultivation, comparing Paul's usage of *téleios* with the confucian notion of *ch'eng* (sincerity) in the confucian classic, the Doctrine of the Mean (*Chung-yung*).

Zedda, Silverio. *Relativo e assoluto nella morale di san Paolo.* Biblioteca di cultura religiosa, 43. Brescia: Paideia, 1984.

Reviewed by Alviero Niccacci in *Rivista di Teologia Morale* 23 (1991): 402-403.

****

The Epistle of James

Baker, William R. *Personal Speech-Ethics in the Epistle of James.* Wissenschaftliche Untersuchungen zum Neuen Testament. Tübingen: J.C.B. Mohr, 1995.

Author's revised thesis done at King's College, University of Aberdeen.

Reviewed by Vincent L. Wimbush in *Theological Studies* 57 (1996): 343-344.

Dautzenberg, Gerhard. "Ist das Schwerberbot Mt 5, 33-37; Jak 5, 12 ein Beispiel für die Toralkritik Jesu?" *Biblische Zeitschrift* 25 (1980): 47-66.

Goldsmith, Dale. *New Testament Ethics.* Elgin IL: Brethren Press, 1988.

Brief consideration of the distinctive "moral personality" of eight "authors" of the New Testament in reference to the Christian life: James, Paul, 1 Peter, Hebrews, as well as the four gospels. Goldsmith's treatment is aimed primarily at the interested lay reader rather than the professional exegete or ethician.

Goldsmith is an ordained minister in the Presbyterian Church.

Humbert, Alphonse, C.Ss.R. "Examen des principales motivations religieuses dans l'enseignement moral de l'Epitre de Jacques." *Studia Moralia* 15 (1977): 385-400.

Published on the occasion of the *Festschrift* given to Bernard Häring, C.Ss.R. in this volume of *Studia Moralia*.

Maynard-Reid, Pedrito-V. *Poverty and Wealth in James.* Maryknoll: Orbis Books, 1987.

The author, who comes from Jamaica, gives a sociological reading to an exegesis of the Letter of James in order to show how the community is summoned to an ethic with strong public and economic implications.

Mußner, Franz. "Die ethische Motivation im Jakobusbrief." In *Neues Testament und Ethik. Für Rudolf Schnackenburg*, 416-423. Herausgegeben von Helmut Merklein. Freiburg: Herder, 1989.

Tamez, Elsa. *The Scandalous Message of James: Faith Without Works Is Dead.* New York: Crossroad, 1990.

Via, Dan O. "The Right Strawy Epistle Reconsidered: A Study in Biblical Ethics and Hermeneutics." *Journal of Religion* 49 (1969).

Study of the Epistle of James.

Villar, E. "Radicalismo evangélico en la carta de Santiago." *Misión Abierta* 73 (1980): 273-278.

****

The Epistles of Peter

Elliott, John H. *A Home for the Homeless: A Sociological Exegesis of 1 Peter, Its Situation and Strategy.* Philadelphia: Fortress Press, 1981.

According to Elliott, the theology of 1 Peter was aimed to counteract those forces which threatened to undermine the religious commitment and social solidarity of believers who were alienated from society. Thus the epistle asserts the distinctive communal identity, internal cohesion, and embracing sectarian ideology which should characterize and sustain the worldwide Christian brotherhood.

Elliott is Professor of Theology and Religious Studies at the University of San Francisco.

Frattallone, Raimondo, S.D.B. *Fondamenti dell'agire morale secondo la 1ª Pt. Il battezzato sulle orme di Cristo.* Studi e ricerche, 11. Bologna: Edizioni Dehoniane Bologna, 1971.

Gielen, Marlis. *Tradition und Theologie neutestamentlicher Haustafelethik: Ein Beitrag zur Frage einer christlichen Auseinandersetzung mit gesellschaftlichen Normen.* Bonner Biblische Beiträge, 75. Frankfurt-am-Main: Hain, 1990.

Considers both Pauline texts (Colossians and Ephesians), as well as 1 Peter.

Goldsmith, Dale. *New Testament Ethics.* Elgin IL: Brethren Press, 1988.

Brief consideration of the distinctive "moral personality" of eight "authors" of the New Testament in reference to the Christian life: James, Paul, 1 Peter, Hebrews, as well as the four gospels. Goldsmith's treatment is aimed primarily at the interested lay reader rather than the professional exegete or ethician.

Goldsmith is an ordained minister in the Presbyterian Church.

Green, Gene L. "The Use of the Old Testament for Christian Ethics in 1 Peter." *Tyndale Bulletin* 41 (1990): 276-289.

Légasse, Simon. "La soumission aux autorités d'après 1 Pierre 2, 13-17: version spécifique d'une parènese traditionelle." *New Testament Studies* 34 (1988): 378-396.

Prostmeier, Ferdinand-Rupert. *Handlungsmodelle im ersten Petrusbrief.* Würzburg: Echter Verlag, 1990.

****

Law and Gospel in the New Testament

Ahern, Barnabas M., C.P. "Law and Gospel." In *Law for Liberty: The Role of Law in the Church Today,* 93-108. Edited by James E. Biechler. Baltimore: Helicon Press, 1967.

Essay written for the Canon Law Society of America's seminar on The Role of Law in the Church.

216

Alvarez-Verdes, Lorenzo, C.Ss.R. *El Imperativo cristiano en san Pablo: La tensión indicativo-imperativo en Rom 6, Análisis estructural.* Institución San Jerónimo, 11. Valencia: Institución San Jerónimo, 1980.

Arróniz, J.M. "Ley y libertad cristiana en S. Pablo." *Lumen* 33 (1984): 385-411.

Barth, Gerhard. "Matthew's Understanding of the Law." In *Tradition and Interpretation in Matthew*, 58-164. With Günther Bornkamm and Heinz Joachim Held. The New Testament Library. Translated by Percy Scott. Philadelphia: The Westminster Press, 1963.

Berger, Klaus. *Die Gesetzesauslegung Jesu. Ihr historischer Hintergrund im Alten Testament. Teil I: Markus und die Parallelen.* WMANT, 40. Neukirchen, 1972.

Broer, Ingo. "Osservazione sull'interpretazione della legge in Matteo." In *Saggi esegetici sulla legge nel Nuovo Testamento*, 121-214. A cura di Karl Kertelge. Cinisello Balsamo: Edizioni Paoline, 1990.

Original version in: *Das Gesetz im Neuen Testament.* Herausgegeben von Karl Kertelge. Questiones Disputatae, 108. Freiburg: Herder, 1986.

Cranfield, C.E.B. "'The Works of the Law' in the Epistle to the Romans." *Journal for the Study of the New Testament* 43 (September, 1991): 89-101.

Questions as being unduly narrow James D.G. Dunn's thesis that Paul's use of the term, "works of the Law," refers specifically to Jewish practices which would distinguish them from their Gentile neighbors.

Diaz-Rodelas, Juan Miguem. *Pablo y la ley. La novedad de Rom 7,7-8,4 en el conjunto de la reflexion pauliana sobre la ley.* Estella: Verbo Divino, 1994.

Dodd, C.H. *Gospel and Law: The Relation of Faith and Ethics in Early Christianity.* Cambridge: Cambridge University Press, 1951.

Dumbrell, W.J. "The Logic of the Role of the Law in Matthew V 1-20." *Novum Testamentum* 23 (1,1981): 1-21.

Dunn, James D.G. *Jesus, Paul, and the Law: Studies in Mark and Galatians.* Louisville: Westminster/John Knox Press; London: SPCK, 1990.

One-volume collection of journal articles which have previously appeared from 1982 to 1988. Dunn also includes some additional notes responding to various critiques made to his articles.

See also C.E.B. Cranfield's critical article on Dunn's interpretation: "'The Works of the Law' in the Epistle to the Romans." *Journal for the Study of the New Testament* 43 (September, 1991): 89-101.

Fee, Gordon D. "Issues in Evangelical Hermeneutics, Part II: The Crucial Issue-- Authorial Intentionality: A Proposal Regarding New Testament Imperatives." *Crux* 26 (3/1990): 35-42.

Following some preliminary observations on hermeneutics and normativity, Fee raises the question of authorial intent in reference to the New Testament imperatives. Suggests that these are best understood as part of the gospel, and not some new form of law.

Fiedler, Peter. "La Tora in Gesù e nella tradizione di Gesù." In *Saggi esegetici sulla legge nel Nuovo Testamento*, 65-81, a cura di Karl Kertelge, (Cinisello Balsamo: Edizioni Paoline, 1990).

German original in *Das Gesetz im Neuen Testament.* Herausgegeben von Karl Kertelge. Questiones Disputatae, 108. Freiburg: Herder, 1986.

Hübner, Hans. *Das Gesetz in der synoptischen Tradition. Studien zur These einer progressiven Qumranisierung und Judaisierung innerhalb der synoptischer Tradition.* Witten: Luther Verlag, 1973.

Habilitationschrift Ruhr-Universität Bocum.

The author's "Habilitation" dissertation.

_____. *Law in Paul's Thought*. Studies of the New Testament and Its World. Edinburgh: T. & T. Clark, 1984.

German Original: *Das Gesetz bei Paulus. Ein Beitrag zum Werden der paulinishcen Theologie*. FRLANT, 119. Göttingen: Vandenhoeck & Ruprecht, 1978.

Jeremias, Joachim. *The Sermon on the Mount*. Facet Books Biblical Series, no. 2. Translated by Norman Perrin. Philadelphia: Fortress Press, 1963.

Jeremias outlines three traditional approaches to the ethical material of the Sermon: perfectionist code, impossible ideal, or interim ethic. He sees certain values in each, but notes they share a common failing in viewing the Sermon as Law rather than Gospel, in other words, an indicative depiction of incipient life in the Kingdom of God, which presupposes as its condition of possibility the experience of conversion.

German original: *Die Bergpredigt*. Calwer Hefte, no. 27. Stuttgart: Calwer Verlag, 1959.

French translation: *Paroles de Jésus: La Sermon sur la montagne, le Notre-Père dans l'exégèse actuelle*. Lectio Divina, 38. Traduction de Dom Marie Mailhé, O.S.B. Paris: Editions du Cerf, 1963.

von Eckert, Jost. "Indikativ und Imperativ bei Paulus." In *Ethik im Neuen Testament*, 168-189. Hrsg. Karl Kertelge. Freiburg: Herder, 1984.

Kalusche, M. "`Das Gesetz als Thema biblischer Theologie?' *Anmerkungen zu einem Entwurf Peter Stuhlfmachers*." *Zeitschrift für die Neutestamentliche Wissenschaft* 77 (1986): 194-205.

Kampling, R. "Zur Diskussion um das Verständnis des Gesetzes in NT." *Theologische Revue* 83 (1987): 441-448.

Kertelge, Karl, Hrsg. *Das Gesetz im Neuen Testament*. Questiones Disputatae, 108. Freiburg: Herder, 1986.

In Italian: *Saggi esegetici sulla legge nel Nuovo Testamento*. Parola di Dio, seconda serie. Cinisello Balsamo: Edizioni Paoline, 1990.

Reviewed by Alviero Niccacci in *Rivista di Teologia Morale* 23 (1991): 407-409.

Kertelge, Karl. "Gesetz und Freiheit im Galaterbrief." *New Testament Studies* 30 (1984): 382-394.

Lafon, G. "La pensée du social et la théologie. Loi et grâce en Romains 4, 13-16." *Recherches de Science Religieuse* 75 (1987): 9-38.

_____. "Une loi de foi. La pensée de la loi en Romains 3, 19-31." *Revue des Sciences Religieuses* 61 (1987): 32-53.

Lage, Francisco. "Nuevas perspectivas sobre la valorición de la ley en la moral de san Pablo (I)." *Moralia* 13 (1991): 357-392.

Part One.

_____. "Nuevas perspectivas sobre la valorición de la ley en la moral de san Pablo (II)." *Moralia* 14 (1992): 3-28.

Part Two.

Lambrecht, Jan, S.J. "La comprensione della legge in Paolo." In *Saggi esegetici sulla legge nel Nuovo Testamento*, 82-120. A cura di Karl Kertelge. Cinisello Balsamo: Edizioni Paoline, 1990.

German original in *Das Gesetz im Neuen Testament*. Herausgegeben von Karl Kertelge. Questiones Disputatae, 108. Freiburg: Herder, 1986.

Lambrecht is a New Testament exegete.

Lyonnet, Stanislaus, S.J. "St. Paul: Liberty and Law." In *Readings in Biblical Morality*, 62-83. Edited by C. Luke Salm. Englewood Cliffs: Prentice Hall, 1967.

Marguerat, D. "L'avenir de la loi: Matthieu à l'épreuve de Paul." *Etudes Théologiques et Religieuses* 57 (1982): 361-374.

Martin, Brice L. *Christ and the Law in Paul*. Novum Testamentum Supplement, 62. Leiden: E.J. Brill, 1990.

Martyn, J. Louis. "The Crucial Event in the History of the Law (Gal 5:14)." Part I, Chapter 4 in *Theology and Ethics in Paul and His Interpreters: Essays in Honor of Victor Paul Furnish*, 48-61. Edited by Eugene H. Lovering, Jr. and Jerry L. Sumney. Nashville: Abingdon Press, 1996.

Matera, Frank J. "The Ethics of the Kingdom in the Gospel of Matthew." *Listening* 24 (1989): 241-250.

The Law is bound up with righteousness, and this means an undivided commitment to Jesus' teachings on mercy and compassion.

Molldrem, Mark J. "A Hermeneutic of Pastoral Care and the Law/Gospel Paradigm Applied to the Divorce Texts of Scripture." *Interpretation* 45 (1991): 43-54.

Looks at the primary Scriptural texts through the Law/Gospel dialectic in order to develop a hermeneutic of pastoral care in dealing with the contemporary context on divorce.

Molldrem is the pastor of the First Evangelical Lutheran Church in Beaver Dam, Wisconsin.

Mueller, U.B. "Zur Rezeption gesetzkritischer Jesusüberlieferung in frühen Christentum." *New Testament Studies* 27 (1981): 158-185.

Noll, Peter. *Jesus und das Gesetz. Rechtliche Analyse der Normenkritik in der Lehre Jesu*. SgV, 253. Tübingen: J.C.B. Mohr, 1968.

Räisänen, H. *Paul and the Law*. Wissenschaftliche Untersuchungen zum Neuen Testament, 29. Rev. ed. Tübingen: J.C.B. Mohr, 1987.

Reichke, Bo. "Paulus und das Gesetz." *Theologische Zeitschrift* 41 (1985): 237-257.

Reinmuth, Eckart. *Geist und Gesetz. Studien zu Voraussetzungen und Inhalt der paulinishcen Paränese.* Theologische Arbeiten, 44. Berlin: Evangelische Verlagsanstalt, 1985.

Ruh, U. "Gesetz im Neuen Testament." *Herder Korrespondenz* 39 (1985): 233-235.

Sanders, E[d].P[arish]. *Paul, the Law and the Jewish People.* London: SCM Press, 1985.

Italian translation: *Paolo, le legge e il popolo giudaico.* Studi Biblici, 86. Brescia: Paideia, 1986.

Schnabel, Eckhard J. *Law and Wisdom from Ben Sira to Paul: A Tradition Historical Enquiry into the Relation of Law, Wisdom and Ethics.* Wissenschaftliche Untersuchungen zum N.T. 2. Reihe, 16. Tübingen: J.C.B. Mohr, 1985.

Sleeper, C. Freeman. *The Bible and the Moral Life.* Louisville: Westminster/John Knox Press, 1992.

Looks at how various churches use the Bible to address contemporary ethical issues, particularly nuclear war and abortion, and also considers the issue of biblical authority in terms of four major styles of moral reflection, i.e., law, prophecy, apocalypse, and wisdom. The book is designed for adult study groups and contains practical exercises.

Sleeper is Professor of Religion at Roanoke College in Salem, Virginia.

Snodgrass, Klyne R. "Matthew's Understanding of the Law." *Interpretation* 46 (1992): 368-378.

Strecker, Georg. "The Law in the Sermon on the Mount, and the Sermon on the Mount as Law." In *The Promise and Practice of Biblical Theology*, 35-49. Edited by John H.P. Reumann. Minneapolis: Fortress Press, 1991.

Strickland, Wayne G., ed. *The Law, the Gospel, and the Modern Christian: Five Views*. Grand Rapids: Zondervan Publishing House, 1993.

This volume seeks to present an objective and well-argued "presentation of major alternatives regarding the Mosaic Law, its relationship to the Gospel, and the role it plays in personal sanctification as well as in ethical systems." Willem A. VanGemeren presents a non-theonomic Reformed view of the use of the Law. Greg L. Bahnsen argues for a theonomic Reformed approach. Walter C. Kaiser, Jr., maintains that the weightier matters of the Law of Moses are binding on believers today. Wayne G. Strickland treats the dispensational view of the Law-Gospel question. Douglas J. Moo proposes a modified Lutheran approach with a clear antithesis between Law and Gospel. Each author's presentation is followed by responses from the other four contributors.

Stuhlmacher, Peter. *Reconciliation, Law and Righteousness: Essays on Biblical Theology*. Philadelphia: Fortress Press, 1986.

Translated from the German.

Thielman, Frank. *From Plight to Solution: A Jewish Framework for Understanding Paul's View of the Law in Galatians and Romans*. Supplements to Novum Testamentum, 61. Leiden and New York: E.J. Brill, 1989.

____. *Paul and the Law: A Contextual Approach*. Downers Grove Il: InterVarsity Press, 1994.

Tomson, Peter J. *Paul and the Jewish Law: Halakha in the Letters of the Apostle to the Gentiles*. Compendia Rerum Iudaicarum ad Novum Testamentum III/2. Assen and Maastricht: Van Gorcum, 1990.

Reviewed by Timothy H. Lim in *Journal of Jewish Studies* 43 (1992): 157-160.

Welker, M. "Zur Lehre von Gesetz und Evangelium." *Evangelische Kommentare* 18 (1985): 680-684.

Westerholm, Stephen. *Israel's Law and the Church's Faith: Paul and His Recent Interpreters*. Grand Rapids: William B. Eerdmans, 1988.

Wilson, S.G. *Luke and the Law*. Society for New Testament Studies, Monograph Series, 50. Cambridge: Cambridge University Press, 1983.

Wilson treats Luke's view of the law and the way in which the relevant material would most probably have been understood at the time of Luke's writing.

Wright, N.T. *The Climax of the Covenant: Christ and the Law in Pauline Theology*. Minneapolis: Fortress Press, 1991.

Zeller, Dieter. "Zur neuereren Diskussion über das Gesetz bei Paulus." *Theologie und Philosophie* 62 (1987): 481-499.

****

The Love Command in the New Testament

**See also War, Peace, and Non-violence section of the Bibliography*

AA.VV. *Essays on the Love Commandment*. Philadelphia: Fortress Press, 1978.

Black, David Alan. "The Pauline Love Command: Structure, Style, and Ethics in Romans 12:9-21." *Filologia Neotestamentaria* 2 (1989): 3-22.

Carter, Charles W., and Thompson, R. Duane. *The Biblical Ethic of Love*. American University Studies: Series 7, Theology and Religion, 79. Frankfurt-am-Main, Bern, New York, Paris: Peter Lang, 1990.

The authors explore "the relevance of divine love, as revealed in the Judeo-Christian Scripture, to the ethical decisions and moral conduct of mankind." Topic treated include: the inadequacy of humanistic ethics, the Ten Commandments, ethics of the Old Testament Prophets and Wisdom literature, ethics of the New Testament. Attention is also given to the ethics of John Wesley, and Christian ethics in relation to the state, military defense, public education, the family, and other trends in contemporary Christian ethics.

Carter is scholar-in-residence, and Thompson is professor of philosophy and religion at Indiana Wesleyan University.

Collins, Raymond F. "Paul's First Reflections on Love." Chapter 6 in *Christian Morality: Biblical Foundations*, 137-148. Notre Dame: University of Notre Dame Press, 1986

Collins taught New Testament for many years at Louvain in Belgium, and is now at Catholic University in Washington, D.C.

Daly, Robert J., S.J. "The New Testament Love Command and the Call to Non-violence." In *Christian Biblical Ethics: From Biblical Revelation to Contemporary Christian Praxis: Method and Content*, 211-219. New York: Paulist Press, 1984.

Daly is professor of theology at Boston College.

Donahue, John R., S.J. "Who Is My Enemy? The Parable of the Good Samaritan and the Love of Enemies." In *The Love of Enemy and Nonretaliation in the New Testament*, 137-156. Edited by Willard M. Swartley. Louisville: Westminster/John Knox Press, 1992.

Donahue studied under Norman Perrin at the University of Chicago and is Professor of Biblical Studies (New Testament) at the Jesuit School of Theology and Graduate Theological Union, Berkeley.

Feuillet, A. "Le caractère universel du jugement et la charité sans frontières en Mt 25, 31-46." *Nouvelle Revue Théologique* 102 (1980): 179-196.

Furnish, Victor Paul. *The Love Command in the New Testament*. Nashville: Abingdon Press, 1972.

_____. "The Love Commandment in New Testament Perspective." *Journal of Religious Ethics* 10 (1982): 327-334.

Hallet, Garth L., S.J. *Christian Neighbor-Love: An Assessment of Six Rival Positions*. Washington, D.C.: Georgetown University Press, 1989.

Reviewed by Stephen J. Pope in *Theological Studies* 51 (1989).

Hallet analyzes six positions on agapaic neighbor-love: self-preference, parity, other-preference, self-subordination, self-forgetfulness, and self-denial. He argues that the fourth type, self-subordination, is most in line with the Christian tradition.

Hoffmann, Paul. "Tradition und Situation: *Zur `Verbindlichkeit' des Gebots der Feindesliebe in der synoptischen Überlieferung und in der gegenwärtigen Friedensdiskussion*." In *Ethik im Neuen Testament*, 50-118. Hrsg. Karl Kertelge. Freiburg: Herder, 1984.

Horsley, Richard A. "Ethics and Exegesis: `Love Your Enemies' and the Doctrine of Non-Violence." *Journal of the American Academy of Religion* 54 (1986): 3-31.

Kertelge, Karl. "Freiheitsbotschaft und Liebesgebot im Galaterbrief." In *Neues Testament und Ethik. Für Rudolf Schnackenburg*, 326-337. Herausgegeben von Helmut Merklein. Freiburg: Herder, 1989.

Légasse, Simon. "Interhuman love: New Testament limits and promise." *Theology Digest* 27 (1979): 9-13.

MacNamara, Vincent. "The Issue of the Specificity of Agape," Chapter 6 in *Faith and Ethics*, 146-176. Dublin: Gill and Macmillan; and Washington, D.C.: Georgetown University Press, 1985.

____. "The Truth in Love." Chapter 4 in *The Truth in Love: Reflections on Christian Morality*, 62-85. Dublin: Gill and Macmillan, 1988.

Outka, Gene. *Agape: An Ethical Analysis*. New Haven CT: Yale University Press, 1972.

____. "On Harming Others." *Interpretation* 34 (1980): 381-393.

Using several Pauline texts Outka uses the case of personal harm done to others to consider how the norm of love should function as guide to Christian action and discernment.

Perkins, Pheme. *Love Commands in the New Testament*. New York: Paulist Press, 1982.

Perkins is professor of New Testament at Boston College.

Piper, John. *Love Your Enemies: Jesus' Love Command in the Synoptic Gospels and the Early Christian Paranesis*. Society for New Testament Studies Monograph Series, 38. Cambridge: Cambridge University Press, 1979; Grand Rapids: Baker Book House 1991.

Pesch, Rudolf. "Jesus und das Hauptgebot." In *Neues Testament und Ethik. Für Rudolf Schnackenburg*, 99-109. Herausgegeben von Helmut Merklein. Freiburg: Herder, 1989.

Post, Stephen G. *A Theory of Agape: On the Meaning of Christian Love*. Lewisburg PA: Bucknell University Press, 1990.

Reviewed by William Werpehowski in *The Journal of Religion* 72 (1992): 463-464.

Ramaroson, L. "'Le premier, c'est l'amour' (Lc 7,47a)." *Science et Esprit* 39 (1988): 319-329.

Rese, M. "Das Gebot der Bruderliebe in den Johannesbriefen." *Theologische Zeitschrift* 41 (1985): 44-58.

Sauer, J. "Traditionsgeschichtliche Erwägungen zu den synoptischen und paulinischem Aussagen über Feindesliebe und Wiedervergeltungsverzicht." *Zeitschrift für die Neutestamentliche Wissenschaft* 76 (1985): 1-28.

Schottroff, Luise. "Non-Violence and the Love of One's Enemies." In *Essays on the Love Commandment*, 9-39. Philadelphia: Fortress Press, 1978.

Argues that true love of enemies might involve actions which confront and change the "enemy."

Schottroff is professor of New Testament at the University of Kassel, Germany.

Six, Jean-François. *Le Chant de 'amour. Eros dans la Bible.* Paris: Desclee de Brouwer / Flammarion, 1995.

Smith, D. Moody. "The Love Command: John and Paul?" Part II, Chapter 4 in *Theology and Ethics in Paul and His Interpreters: Essays in Honor of Victor Paul Furnish*, 207-217. Edited by Eugene H. Lovering, Jr. and Jerry L. Sumney. Nashville: Abingdon Press, 1996.

Soending, Thomas. *Das Liebesgebot bei Paulus: Die Mahnung zur Agape in Rahmen der paulinischen Ethik.* Neutestamentliche Abhandlungen. Neue Folge, Band 26. Munster: Aschendorff, 1995.

Swartley, Willard M., ed. *The Love of Enemy and Nonretaliation in the New Testament.* Louisville: Westminster/John Knox Press, 1992.

Reviewed by David Gill, S.J. in *Horizons* 20 (1993): 346-347.

Ward, K. *The Rule of Love: Reflections on the Sermon on the Mount.* London: Darton, Longman and Todd, 1989.

A meditation on Christian ethics.

****

SPECIAL QUESTIONS IN SCRIPTURE AND ETHICS

Ecology and Nature

Anderlini, Gianpaolo. "Bibbia e Natura: Appunti per una lettura ecologica della Bibbia." *Bibbia e Oriente* 33 (1991): 193-209.

Testo ampliato della conferenza tenuta a Villaminozzo (RE) il 18 gennaio 1989, nell'ambito del convegno "Pace, non violenza, salvaguardia del creato. Il punto di vista di alcune dottrine religiose."

This is a revised text of a talk given in Villaminozzo, Italy on 18 January 1989 in a conference on "Peace, Non-Violence, Safe-guarding of Creation: Perspectives from Some Religious Doctrines."

Anthonysamy, S.J. "An Eco-theology Foreshadowed in the Gospel of John." *Bible Bhashyam* 19 (1993): 188-204.

One of several articles in this issue on various theological aspects of ecology.

Baker, John Austin. "Biblical Views of Nature." In *Liberating Life: Contemporary Approaches to Ecological Theology*, 9-26. Edited by Charles Birch, William Eakin and Jay B. McDaniel. Maryknoll: Orbis Press, 1990.

Originally appeared in the World Council of Churches' publication *Anticipation* 25 (January, 1979): 40-46.

Clifford, Richard J., S.J. "The Bible and the Environment." In *Preserving the Creation: Environmental Theology and Ethics*, 1-26. Edited by Kevin W. Irwin and Edmund D. Pellegrino. Washington, D.C.: Georgetown University Press, 1994.

See also the response to Clifford's article by Bernhard W. Anderson, "The Sacredness of the Earth," in the same volume, pp. 27-32.

Clifford is Professor of Old Testament at the Weston Jesuit School of Theology in Cambridge, Massachusetts.

David, Robert. "Prolégomènes à l'étude écologique des récits de Gn 1-11." *Eglise et théologie* 22 (1991): 275-292.

Duchrow, Ulrich and Liedke, Gerhard. *Shalom: Biblical Perspectives on Creation, Justice and Peace*. Geneva: WCC Publications, 1989.

German original: *Schalom: Der Schöpfung Befreiung, den Menschen Gerechtigkeit, den Völkern Frieden*. Stuttgart: Kreuz Verlag, 1987.

Written in part for the 1990 Seoul WCC Conference on Peace, Justice, and the Integrity of Creation.

Reviewed by Newton B. Fowler, Jr. in *Mid-Stream* 29 (1990): 442-444.

George, P.G. "Ecological Agenda in the Book of Psalms." *Bible Bhashyam* 19 (1993): 169-175.

Gottwald, Norman K. "The Biblical Mandate for Eco-justice Action." In *For Creation's Sake: Preaching, Ecology, and Justice*, 32-44. Edited by Dieter T. Hessel. Philadelphia: Geneva Press, 1985.

Paper given at the Institute for Pastors on Eco-Justice Preaching, held in Stony Point, N.Y., 14-16 February 1984.

Granberg-Michaelson, Wesley. "Covenant and Creation." In *Liberating Life: Contemporary Approaches to Ecological Theology*, 27-36. Edited by Charles Birch, William Eakin and Jay B. McDaniel. Maryknoll: Orbis Press, 1990.

Gräßer, Erich. "*KAI EN META THOE THERIOE* (Mk 1, 13b). Ansätze einer theologischen Tierschutzethik." In *Studien zum Text und zur Ethik des Neuen Testaments. Festschrift zum 80. Geburtstag von Heinrich Greeven*, 144-157. Herausgegeben von Wolfgang Schrage. Berlin/New York: Walter de Gruyter, 1986.

Gregorios, Paulos Mar. "New Testament Foundations for Understanding the Creation." In *Liberating Life: Contemporary Approaches to Ecological*

Theology, 37-45. Edited by Charles Birch, William Eakin and Jay B. McDaniel. Maryknoll: Orbis Press, 1990.

Grelot, Pierre. "L'idée de nature en théologie morale: le témoignage de l'Ecriture." *La Vie Spirituelle* 20 (1967): 208-229.

Gulick, Walter B. "The Bible and Ecological Spirituality." *Theology Today* 48 (1991): 182-194.

Consideration of "nature" in the abstract is largely foreign to the Bible. In order to tap the Bible for an ecological spirituality it is necessary to see how the former might support the qualities described by the latter.

Gulick is Professor of Philosophy, Humanities, and Religious Studies at Eastern Montana College in Billings, Montana.

Mathew, K.V. "Ecological Perspectives in the Book of Psalms." *Bible Bhashyam* 19 (1993): 159-168.

One of several articles in this issue on various theological aspects of ecology.

McCarthy, J., S.J. "Le Christ cosmique et l'âge de l'écologie. Une lecture de Col 1, 15-20." *Nouvelle Revue Théologique* 116 (1994): 27-47.

Murray, Robert. *The Cosmic Covenant: Biblical Themes of Justice, Peace and the Integrity of Creation.* Heythrop Monographs, 7. London: Sheed and Ward, 1992.

Reviewed by John W. Rogerson in *The Heythrop Journal* 34 (1993): 184-185.

Raja, R. J., S.J. "As It Was in the Beginning: *Eco-Spirituality in the Book of Revelation.*" *Vidyajyoti* 60 (1991): 681-697.

Sharp, D.B. "A Biblical Foundation for an Environmental Theology: A New Perspective on Genesis 1: 26-28 and 6: 11-13," *Science et Esprit* 47 (1995): 305-313.

Trible, Phyllis. "A Tempest in a Text: ecological soundings in the book of Jonah." *Theology Digest* 43 (4/1996): 303-312.

Trible finds in Jonah not entertainment and humor, but rather dissonances of sovereignty and freedom, mercy and caprice, leaving readers with unsettling questions regarding both theology and ecology.

Sharp, D.B. "A Biblical Foundation for an Environmental Theology: A New Perspective on Genesis 1: 26-28 and 6: 11-13," *Science and Esprit* Vol. XLVII (Décembre 1995): 305-313.

Thériault, Jean-Yves. "La portée écologique de la notion paulinienne de création." *Eglise et théologie* 23 (1991): 293-314.

Van Dyke, Fred, David C. Mahan, Joseph K. Sheldon, and Raymond H. Brand. *Redeeming Creation: The Biblical Basis for Environmental Stewardship.* Downers Grove, IL: InterVarsity Press, 1996.

Wink, Walter. "Ecobible: The Bible and Ecojustice." *Theology Today* 49 (1993): 465-477.

Essay adapted from Wink's *Engaging the Powers: Discernment and Resistence in a World of Domination,* (Minneapolis: Augsburg Fortress Press, 1992).

Wink is a biblical scholar at Auburn Theological Seminary in New York City.

****

Economic Issues

Baergen, Rudy. "The Motif of Renunciation of Possessions in the Gospel of Luke." *Conrad Grebel Review* 11 (1993): 233-248.

Baergen is pastor of the First Mennonite Church in Kitchener, Ontario.

Bahr, Ann Marie B. "God's Family and Flocks: Remarks on Ownership in the Fourth Gospel." In *Covenant for a New Creation: Ethics, Religion, and Public Policy*, 91-104. Edited by Carol S. Robb and Carl S. Casebolt. Maryknoll: Orbis Books, 1991.

Barr, Steve. "The Eye of the Needle--Power and Money in the New Community: A Look at Mark 10:17-31." *Andover Newton Review* 3 (1992): 31-44.

Bartchy, S. Scott. "Community of Goods in Acts: Idealization or Social Realty?" In *The Future of Early Christianity: Essays in Honor of Helmut Koester*, 309-318. Edited by Birger A. Pearson. Minneapolis: Fortress Press, 1991.

Bassler, Jouette M. *God and Mammon: Asking for Money in the New Testament*. Nashville: Abingdon, 1991.

Treats the cultural context of the ancient world, and then considers perspectives in light of the Gospels, Paul, and Acts.

Beals, Art, with Larry, Libby. *Beyond Hunger: A Biblical Mandate for Social Responsibility*. A Critical Concern Book. Portland OR: Multnomah Press, 1985.

Bergant, Dianne, C.S.A. "Stewards of the Household of God." In *Economic Justice: CTU's Pastoral Commentary on The Bishops' Letter on the Economy*, 3-10. Edited by John Pawlikowski, O.S.M. and Donald Senior, C.P. Washington, D.C.: The Pastoral Press, 1988.

Book includes the text of the Bishops' Letter on the Economy, plus 12 essays organized into three sections: 1) The Biblical Perspective; 2) The Ethical Perspective; and 3) The Pastoral Perspective.

Biggar, Nigel, and Donald Hay. "The Bible, Christian Ethics and the Provision of Social Security." *Studies in Christian Ethics* 7 (1994): 43-64.

Boerma, C. *Rich Man, Poor Man--and the Bible*. Translated by J. Bowden. London: SCM Press, 1979.

Collins, John J. "The Biblical Vision of the Common Good." In *The Common Good and U.S. Capitalism*, 50-69. Edited by Oliver F. Williams and John W. Houck. Lanham MD: University Press of America, 1987.

Crosby, Michael H., O.F.M. *House of Disciples: Church, Economics, and Justice in Matthew*. New York: Paulist Press, 1988.

Briefly discussed by Lisa Sowle Cahill in her article "The New Testament and Ethics: Communities of Social Change," *Interpretation* 44 (1990): 383-395.

Crowe, Jerome. "Wealth and Poverty in Luke's Writings." *Australasian Catholic Record* 69 (1992): 343-355.

Exegetical comments in line with the 1991 draft paper of the Australian Bishops' statement, "Common Wealth and Common Good."

Daly, Herman E. "A Biblical Economic Principle and the Steady-State Economy." In *Covenant for a New Creation: Ethics, Religion, and Public Policy*, 47-60. Edited by Carol S. Robb and Carl S. Casebolt. Maryknoll: Orbis Books, 1991.

Dearman, John Andrew. *Property Rights in the Eighth-Century Prophets*. Society for Biblical Literature Dissertation Series, 106. Atlanta: Scholars Press, 1988.

Dempsey, Carol J., O.P. "Economic Injustice in Micah." *The Bible Today* 32 (1994): 272-276.

One of several articles on biblical economic justice in this issue.

Donahue, John R., S.J. "Two Decades of Research on the Rich and Poor in Luke-Acts." In *Justice and the Holy: Essays in Honor of Walter Harrelson*, 129-144. Edited by D.A. Knight and P.J. Paris. Atlanta: Scholars Press, 1989.

Donahue is Professor of Biblical Studies (New Testament) at the Jesuit School of Theology and Graduate Theological Union, Berkeley.

Dupont, Jacques. "Community of Goods in the Early Church." In *The Salvation of the Gentiles: Studies in the Acts of the Apostles*, 85-102. New York: Paulist Press, 1979.

____. "The Poor and Poverty in the Gospels." In *Gospel Poverty: Essays in Biblical Theology*, 25-52. Edited by A. George. Chicago: Franciscan Herald Press, 1977.

D'Sa, Thomas. "The Salvation of the Rich in the Gospel of Luke." *Vidyajoti* 52 (1988): 170-180.

von Eckert, Jost. "The Realisation of Fellowship in the Earliest Christian Communities." *Concilium* 130 (1979): 21-28.

Treats the material in Acts and Paul, as one of a series of articles under the general theme, "The Dignity of the Despised of the Earth."

Fabris, Rinaldo. "Valutazione e uso dei beni nella prospettiva biblica." In AA.VV. *Economia, politica e morale nelle società dell'occidentale*, 53-72. Bologna: Edizioni Dehoniane Bologna, 1990.

Fager, Jeffrey A. *Land Tenure and the Biblical Jubilee: Uncovering Hebrew Ethics through the Sociology of Knowledge*. Journal for the Study of the Old Testament; Supplement Series, 155. Sheffield: JSOT, 1993.

This volume addresses the perennial questions concerning the legislation in Leviticus 25 on the Jubilee with the method of the sociology of knowledge, especially as articulated by Berger and Luckmann. An earlier version of this work was the author's dissertation (1987).

Fensham, F.C. "Widow, Orphan and the Poor in Ancient Near Eastern Legal and Wisdom Literature." *Journal of Near Eastern Studies* 21 (1962): 129-139.

Gamoran, H. "The Biblical Law against Loans on Interest." *Journal of Near Eastern Studies* 30 (1971): 127-134.

Gelin, Albert. *The Poor of Yahweh.* Collegeville: Liturgical Press, 1964.

George, A., ed. *Gospel Poverty: Essays in Biblical Theology.* Chicago: Franciscan Herald Press, 1977.

Georgi, Dieter. *Remembering the Poor: The History of Paul's Collection for Jerusalem.* Nashville: Abingdon Press, 1992.

German original: *Die Geschicte der Kollekte des Pauls für Jerusalem.* Theologische Forschung, 28. Hamburg: Herbert Reich Evangelischer Verlag GMBH, 1965.

An exegetical and historical analysis of the history of the Pauline collection for the church at Jerusalem which raises the question of socio-political responsibility of biblical hermeneutics in a concluding reflection on Paul's understanding of the nature of money and the consequences for contemporary economic arrangements.

Getz, Gene A. *A Biblical Theology of Material Possessions.* Chicago: Moody Press, 1990.

Getz has taught at the Moody Bible Institute and Dallas Theological Seminary, and is now senior pastor of the Fellowship Bible Church in North Plan, Texas.

Gill, B. *Stewardship: The Biblical Basis for Living.* Arlington TX: Summit, 1996.

Gillingham, Sue. "The Poor in the Psalms." *Expository Times* 100 (1989): 15-19.

Gillman, John. *Possessions and the Life of Faith: A Reading of Luke-Acts.* Zacchaeus Studies. Collegeville: Liturgical Press/Michael Glazier, 1991.

Reader is challenged to make faith decisions about one's money and personal resources. Study includes literary features of Luke-Acts, three approaches to possessions, the privileged place of the poor, the theme of possessions as it relates to discipleship, and the use of possessions in the early Church.

Ginsberg, E. "Studies in the Economics of the Bible." *Jewish Quarterly Review* 22 (1932): 343-408.

Gnuse, Robert. *You Shall Not Steal: Community and Property in the Biblical Tradition.* Maryknoll: Orbis Books, 1985.

Spanish translation: *Comunidad y propiedad en la tradición bíblica.* Col. Buena Noticia, 16. Estella: Ed. Verbo Divino, 1987.

Traces the biblical attitudes on possessions from the Old Testament through the New Testament.

Gonzalez, Justo L. *Faith and Wealth: A History of Early Christian Ideas on the Origin, Significance, and Use of Money.* San Francisco: Harper and Row, 1990.

Gordon, Barry. *The Economic Problem in Biblical and Patristic Thought.* Supplements to Vigiliae Christianae, 9. Leiden: E.J. Brill, 1989.

Focuses especially on the economic problem of scarcity, tracing its treatment in both the Old and New Testaments, then continuing on with the early Christian communities and the Church Fathers up to Augustine.

Gowan, Donald E. "Wealth and Poverty in the Old Testament: The Case of the Widow, the Orphan and the Sojourner." *Interpretation* 41 (1987): 341-353.

Guinan, Michael D., O.F.M. *Gospel Poverty: Witness to the Risen Christ.* New York: Paulist Press, 1981.

> Surveys the theme of poverty in the Old Testament, Qumran texts, and the New Testament, stressing how poverty becomes a witness to the risen Christ.

> Guinan is professor of Old Testament at the Franciscan School of Theology in Berkeley, California.

Habecker, Eugene B. "Biblical guidelines for asking and giving." *Christianity Today* 31 (15 May 1987): 32-34.

Hengel, Martin. *Property and Riches in the Early Church: Aspects of a Social History of Early Christianity.* Translated by John Bowden. London: SCM Press; Philadelphia: Fortress Press, 1974.

_____. "Property and Riches in the Old Testament and Judaism." In Id. *Property and Riches in the Early Church: Aspects of a Social History of Early Christianity,* 12-22. Translated by John Bowden. London: SCM Press; Philadelphia: Fortress Press, 1974.

> Shorter version also found in *On Moral Business: Classical and Contemporary Resources for Ethics in Economic Life,* 67-68. Edited by Max L. Stackhouse, et. al. Grand Rapids: Wm. B. Eerdmans Publishing Co., 1995.

Herring, Basil F. "Truth and Deception in the Marketplace." Chapter 6 in *Jewish Ethics and Halakhah for Our Time: Sources and Commentary, Vol. 2,* 221-274. The Library of Jewish Law and Ethics, 11. New York: KTAV, 1984.

Hoppe, Leslie J., O.F.M. *Being Poor: A Biblical Study.* Wilmington: Michael Glazier, 1987.

_____. "Community and Justice: *A Biblical Perspective.*" In *Economic Justice: CTU's Pastoral Commentary on The Bishops' Letter on the Economy,* 11-17.

Edited by John Pawlikowski, O.S.M. and Donald Senior, C.P. Washington, D.C.: The Pastoral Press, 1988.

Book includes the text of the Bishops' Letter on the Economy, plus 12 essays organized into three sections: 1) The Biblical Perspective; 2) The Ethical Perspective; and 3) The Pastoral Perspective.

_____. "The Torah Responds to the Poor." *The Bible Today* 32 (1994): 277-282.

One of several articles on biblical economic justice in this issue.

Johnson, Luke Timothy. *The Literary Function of Possessions in Luke-Acts*. Society of Biblical Literature Dissertation Series 39. Missoula MT: Scholars Press, 1977.

Very readable, excellent treatment of the theme of wealth and possessions in the Lukan Christian community, and its implications for a contemporary biblical perspective on wealth.

Johnson is now professor of New Testament at the Candler School of Theology at Emory University. This work was his doctoral dissertation.

_____. *Sharing Possessions: Mandate and Symbol of Faith*. Overtures to Biblical Theology. Philadelphia: Fortress Press, 1981.

Karris, Robert J., O.F.M. "Poor and Rich, the Lukan *Sitz-im-Leben*." In *Perspectives in Luke-Acts*, 112-125. Edited by C.H. Talbert. Edinburgh: T. & T. Clark; Danville VA: Association of Baptist Professors of Religion, 1978.

Keck, Leander E. "The Poor Among the Saints in Jewish Christianity and Qumran." *Zeitschrift für Neutestamentliche Wissenschaft* 57 (1966): 54-78.

_____. "The Poor Among the Saints in the New Testament." *Zeitschrift für Neutestamentliche Wissenschaft* 56 (1965): 100-129.

Keeling, Michael. *The Foundations of Christian Ethics*. Edinburgh: T. & T. Clark, 1990.

240

Concentrating on three themes: sexuality, property, and political power, Keeling examines the foundations of Christian ethics in the Bible and their embodiment in the Church. Follows a chronological structure and considers the influence of liberation theology on perceptions of social justice.

Kidd, Reggie M. *Wealth and Beneficence in the Pastoral Epistles: A "Bourgeois Form of Early Christianity.* SBL Dissertation Series, 122. Atlanta: Scholars Press, 1990.

Lage, Francisco. "La crítica del comercio en los profetas de Israel." *Moralia* 8 (1986): 3-28.

Lohfink, Norbert. "The Kingdom of God and the Economy in the Bible." *Communio* 13 (1986): 216-231.

Argues that the Kingdom of God should evoke a "contrast society" to secular values.

Lohfink is professor of Old Testament Exegesis at Sankt Georgen in Frankfurt-am-Main.

_____. "Poverty in the Laws of the Ancient Near East and of the Bible." *Theological Studies* 52 (1991): 34-50.

Lohfink finds that the law codes of ancient Mesopotamia and Israel evidence a better care for the poor than our modern societies.

Originally given as a paper at the 53rd General Meeting of the Catholic Biblical Association of America on 14 August 1990 at the University of Notre Dame.

Malina, Bruce J. "Wealth and Poverty in the New Testament and Its World." *Interpretation* 41 (1987): 354-366.

Shorter version also found in *On Moral Business: Classical and Contemporary Resources for Ethics in Economic Life*, 88-93. Edited by Max L. Stackhouse, et. al. Grand Rapids: Wm. B. Eerdmans Publishing Co., 1995.

Mattai, Giuseppe. "Indicazioni assiologiche in tema di vita economica alla luce della Bibbia." Parte Seconda, Capitolo Secondo in *Corso di morale*, 353-366. Vol. 3. A cura di Tullo Goffi e Giannino Piana. Brescia: Queriniana, 1984.

Maynard-Reid, Pedrito-V. *Poverty and Wealth in James*. Maryknoll: Orbis Books, 1987.

The author, who comes from Jamaica, gives a sociological reading to an exegesis of the Letter of James in order to show how the community is summoned to an ethic with strong public and economic implications.

McClelland, William Robert. *Worldly Spirituality: Biblical Reflections on Money, Politics, and Sex*. St. Louis: CBP Press, 1990.

Reviewed by Dwight E. Stevenson in *Mid-Stream* 29 (1990): 444-446.

McFayden, J.E. "Poverty in the Old Testament." *Expository Times* 37 (1925): 184-189.

Mealand, David L. *Poverty and Expectation in the Gospels*. London: SPCK, 1980.

Nakanose, Shigeyuki. *Josiah's Passover: Sociology and the Liberating Bible*. Bible & Liberation Series. Maryknoll: Orbis Press, 1993.

Shigeyuki Nakanose, a Catholic priest born in Japan, now works with base communities in Brazil. He shows how "the so-called Deuteronomic reform spearheaded by King Josiah - including a revamped Passover festival as one of its cardinal features - decisively strengthened the small ruling elite of Judah to the detriment of the economic, social, political, and religious well-being of the majority of Israelites." He then goes on to show "how his understanding of biblical Passover was shared with leaders and lay participants in Brazilian basic ecclesial communities in and around Sâo Paulo, as well as how they responded to it."

Nickelsburg, George W. "Riches, the Rich, and God's Judgment in 1 Enoch 92-105 and the Gospel According to Luke." *New Testament Studies* 25 (1978-79): 324-344.

Nickle, Keith. *The Collection: A Study of Paul's Strategy.* Studies in Biblical Theology, 48. Naperville: Allenson, 1966.

Patterson, R. "The Widow, the Orphan and the Poor in the Old Testament and Extra-Biblical Literature." *Bibliotheca Sacra* 130 (1973): 223-235.

Pawlikowski, John, O.S.M., and Senior, Donald, C.P., eds. *Economic Justice: CTU's Pastoral Commentary on The Bishops' Letter on the Economy.* Washington, D.C.: The Pastoral Press, 1988.

Includes the text of the Bishops' Letter on the Economy, plus 12 essays organized into three sections: 1) The Biblical Perspective; 2) The Ethical Perspective; and 3) The Pastoral Perspective. Suggestions for further reading, and short discussion questions follow most sections.

Pilgrim, Walter E. *Good News to the Poor: Wealth and Poverty in Luke-Acts.* Minneapolis: Augsburg Press, 1981.

Pleins, J. David. "How Ought We Think about Poverty?--Rethinking the Diversity of the Hebrew Bible." *Irish Theological Quarterly* 60 (1994): 280-286.

_____. "Poverty in the Social World of the Wise." *Journal for the Study of the Old Testament* 37 (1987): 61-78.

Porteous, N.W. "The Care of the Poor in the Old Testament." In *Living the Mystery*, 143-155. Blackwell, 1967.

Ravasi, Gianfranco. "«Tra di voi no vi sia nessun bisogno!». Solidarietà nel popolo di Dio dell'Antico Testamento." *Communio* 125 (settembre-ottobre 1992).

One of a series of articles on various aspects of the theme of solidarity.

Reid, Barbara E., O.P. "Reading Luke with the Poor." *The Bible Today* 32 (1994): 283-289.

One of several articles on biblical economic justice in this issue.

Rosenblatt, Marie-Eloise, R.S.M. "Mission and Money in the New Testament." *Chicago Studies* 30 (1991): 77-98.

Starting from an analysis of the current financial situation of the Church, Rosenblatt then argues that contemporary church administrators may profit from a consideration of the early Church's fragile economic structure as portrayed in the New Testament and the underlying spiritual values and ideals which nourished philanthropy and the sharing of resources.

Rossé, Gérard. "L'insegnamento della Scrittura come premessa all'«economia di comunione»." *Nuova Umanità* 14 (marzo-giugno 1992): 21-32.

Non mancano, nei libri dell'Antico Testamento, e specialmente nei profeti, riflessioni che costituiscono le radici per la comprensione di una «una economia di comunione». Dopo avervi fatto riferimento l'A. sintetizza l'insegnamento di Gesù in merito alla povertà e alla ricchezza e spiega la concezione e l'esperienza della comunione dei beni nella prima comunità cristiana. Ne emerge che l'economia di comunione tende a superare l'«economia di sopravvivenza» che caratterizzava la comunità primitiva, per trovare applicazione anche in una società nella quale non ci siano più «poveri in mezza a voi».

Discusses the concept of "economy of communion" in the Old Testament, the teachings of Jesus as presented in the Gospels, and the experience of the early Christian community, in order to apply this concept to contemporary society so that there would no longer be "poor among you."

Ruiz, Gregorio. "La ética profética: frente a la pobreza desde la justicia." *Moralia* 6 (1984): 79-101.

Tambien en [also found in] *Perspectivas de moral bíblica,* 79-101. Estudios de Etica Teologica. Edd. Marciano Vidal, Francisco Lage y Alfosno Ruiz-Mateos. Madrid: Instituto Superior de Ciencas Morales, PS Editorial, 1984.

Schmidt, T.E. *Hostility to Wealth in the Synoptic Gospels.* Journal for the Study of the New Testament Supplement Series, 15. Sheffield: JSOT Press, 1987.

Senior, Donald, C.P. "Called To Be Disciples." In *Economic Justice: CTU's Pastoral Commentary on The Bishops' Letter on the Economy*, 29-36. Edited by John Pawlikowski, O.S.M. and Donald Senior, C.P. Washington, D.C.: The Pastoral Press, 1988.

Book includes the text of the Bishops' Letter on the Economy, plus 12 essays organized into three sections: 1) The Biblical Perspective; 2) The Ethical Perspective; and 3) The Pastoral Perspective.

Sicre, José Luis. "El Sermón del Monte: La actitud cristiana ante el dinero y el prójimo." *Proyección* 39 (1992): 193-204.

Sider, Ronald J., ed. *Cry Justice! The Bible on Hunger and Poverty*. New York: Paulist Press, 1980.

Soares-Prabhu, G. "Class in the Bible: The Biblical Poor a Social Class?" *Vidyajoti* 49 (1985): 322-346.

Sobrino, Jon, S.J. "Jesus' Relationship with the Poor and Outcasts: Its Importance for Fundamental Moral Theology. *Concilium* 130 (1979): 12-20.

One of a series of articles under the general theme, "The Dignity of the Despised of the Earth."

Sobrino is a Spanish Jesuit who has worked for many years in Central America and is a noted Liberation theologian.

Spicq, Ceslas, O.P. "Charité et vie morale selon le NT." *La Vie Spirituelle* 658 (1984): 4-16.

Stackhouse, Max L. "Jesus and Economics: A Century of Reflection." In *The Bible in American Law, Politics, and Political Rhetoric*, 107-151. Edited by James Turner Johnson. Philadelphia: Fortress Press; Chico, CA: Scholars Press, 1985.

____. "The Ten Commandments: Economic Implications." In *On Moral Business: Classical and Contemporary Resources for Ethics in Economic Life*, 59-62.

Edited by Max L. Stackhouse, et. al. Grand Rapids: Wm. B. Eerdmans Publishing Co., 1995.

Adpated from an address given to the Convocation of the National Council of Churches of Christ held in Cleveland in 1982.

_____. "What Then Shall We Do? On Using Scripture in Economic Ethics." *Interpretation* 41 (1987): 382-397.

Shorter version also found in *On Moral Business: Classical and Contemporary Resources for Ethics in Economic Life*, 109-113. Edited by Max L. Stackhouse, et. al. Grand Rapids: Wm. B. Eerdmans Publishing Co., 1995.

Stegemann, Wolfgang. "The Following of Christ as Solidarity Between Rich, Respected Christians and Poor, Despised Christians (Gospel of Luke)." In *Jesus and the Hope of the Poor*, 67-120. Edited by Luise Schottroff and Wolfgang Stegemann. Maryknoll: Orbis Press, 1986.

____. *The Gospel and the Poor.* Philadelphia: Fortress Press, 1984.

Stein, S. "The Laws on Interest in the Old Testament." *Journal of Theological Studies* 4 (1953): 161-170.

Stuhlmueller, Carroll, C.P. "Option for the Poor: *Old Testament Directives*." In *Economic Justice: CTU's Pastoral Commentary on The Bishops' Letter on the Economy*, 19-27. Edited by John Pawlikowski, O.S.M. and Donald Senior, C.P. Washington, D.C.: The Pastoral Press, 1988.

Book includes the text of the Bishops' Letter on the Economy, plus 12 essays organized into three sections: 1) The Biblical Perspective; 2) The Ethical Perspective; and 3) The Pastoral Perspective.

Tamez, Elsa. *The Scandalous Message of James: Faith Without Works Is Dead.* New York: Crossroad, 1990.

Taylor, Richard K. *Economics and the Gospel: A Primer on Shalom as Economic Justice*. Philadelphia: United Church Press, 1973.

Thomas, Carolyn, S.C.N. "Economic Issues in Paul." *The Bible Today* 32 (1994): 290-294.

One of several articles on biblical economic justice in this issue.

Wee, Paul A. "Biblical Ethics and Lending to the Poor." *Ecumenical Review* 38 (1986): 416-430.

Westbrook, Raymond. "Jubilee Laws." *Israel Law Review* 6 (1971): 209-225.

Also found as Chapter Two in his *Property and the Family in Biblical Law*, 36-57. Journal for the Study of the Old Testament Supplement Series, 113. Sheffield: Sheffield Academic Press, 1991.

_____. *Property and the Family in Biblical Law*. Journal for the Study of the Old Testament Supplement Series, 113. Sheffield: Sheffield Academic Press, 1991.

Contains five previously published essays on this theme, plus two previously unpublished essays.

Westbrook teaches at Johns Hopkins University.

Wheeler, Sondra Ely. *Wealth as Peril: The New Testament on Possessions*. Grand Rapids, MI: Wm B. Eerdmans Publishing Company, 1995.

Whybray, R.N. "Poverty, Wealth, and Point of View in Proverbs." *Expository Times* 100 (1988-89): 332-336.

_____. *Wealth and Poverty in the Book of Proverbs*. Sheffield: Journal for the Study of the Old Testament Press, 1990.

Reviewed by Joseph Mulroney in *The Heythrop Journal* 34 (1993): 187-188.

Justice, Rights and Righteousness

**See also Scripture and Economic Issues, and Liberation Theology sections*

Ahern, Barnabas M., C.P. "Biblical Doctrine on the Rights and Duties of Man."
Gregorianum 65 (1984): 301-317.

> Gives an overview of scriptural support and understanding of "human rights."
> Prepared as a Working Paper for the International Theological Commission
> plenary session in December, 1983.

Ahituv, Shmuel. "Land and Justice." In *Justice and Righteousness: Biblical Themes
and their Influence*, 11-28. Edited by Henning Graf Reventlow and Yair
Hoffman. Sheffield: JSOT Press, 1992.

Amit, Yairah. "The Jubilee Law--An Attempt at Instituting Social Justice." In
Justice and Righteousness: Biblical Themes and their Influence, 47-59.
Edited by Henning Graf Reventlow and Yair Hoffman. Sheffield: JSOT Press,
1992.

Auneau, Joseph. "De la justice d'Amos à la justice de Paul." *La Vie Spirituelle* 72
(1992): 307-322.

Barton, John. "Natural Law and Poetic Justice in the Old Testament." *Journal of
Theological Studies* 39 (1979): 1-14.

Berkovits, Eliezer. "The Biblical Meaning of Justice." *Judaism* 18 (1969): 188-209.

> Survey of various meanings of the term "justice" in Hebrew Scriptures.

Birch, Bruce C. *Let Justice Roll Down: The Old Testament, Ethics, and Christian
Life*. Louisville: Westminster/John Knox, 1991.

Discusses methodological questions, the importance of the Hebrew narratives as a moral resource, and specific texts and themes which might inform Christian ethics.

Reviewed by Dennis T. Olson in *Theology Today* 50 (1994): 148.

Blank, Josef. "The Justice of God as the Humanisation of Man--the Problem of Human Rights in the New Testament." *Concilium* 124 (1979): 27-38.

One of a series of articles on various aspects of the theological meaning and significance of human rights.

Boecker, H.J. *Law and the Administration of Justice in the Old Testament and Ancient Near East.* London: SPCK, 1981.

Bloom, A. "Human Rights in Israel's Thought." *Interpretation* 8 (1954): 422-432.

Casabó Suqué, J.M. "La justicia en el Antiguo Testamento." *Stromata* 25 (1969): 3-20.

Collins, John J. "The Biblical Vision of the Common Good." In *The Common Good and U.S. Capitalism*, 50-69. Edited by Oliver Williams and John W. Houck. Lanham MD: University Press of America, 1987.

Co-published by arrangement with the Notre Dame Center for Ethics and Religious Values in Business.

Cook, Michael L., S.J. "Jesus' Parables and the Faith That Does Justice." *Studies in the Spirituality of Jesuits* 24 (November, 1992).

Cook is professor of theology at Gonzaga University in Spokane, Washington.

Crosby, Michael H., O.F.M. *House of Disciples: Church, Economics, and Justice in Matthew.* New York: Paulist Press, 1988.

Briefly discussed by Lisa Sowle Cahill in her article "The New Testament and Ethics: Communities of Social Change," *Interpretation* 44 (1990): 383-395.

Donahue, John R., S.J. "Biblical Perspectives on Justice." In *The Faith That Does Justice: Examining the Christian Sources for Social Change.* Woodstock Studies: Occasional Papers from the Woodstock Theological Center, vol. 2, 68-112. New York: Paulist Press, 1977.

Donahue is Professor of Biblical Studies (New Testament) at the Jesuit School of Theology and Graduate Theological Union, Berkeley.

_____. "What Does the Lord Require? *A Bibliographical Essay on the Bible and Social Justice.*" *Studies in the Spirituality of Jesuits* 25 (March, 1993).

Excellent introductory essay to the major themes of biblical social ethics, plus an annotated bibliography 211 titles thematically arranged, complete with index.

Doorly, William J. *Obsession with Justice: The Story of the Deuteronomists.* New York: Paulist Press, 1994.

_____. *Prophet of Justice: Understanding the Book of Amos.* New York: Paulist Press, 1989.

Short introductory book on Amos, with discussion of economic justice, including ten homiletic themes drawn this topic in Amos.

Duchrow, Ulrich, and Liedke, Gerhard. *Shalom: Biblical Perspectives on Creation, Justice and Peace.* Geneva: WCC Publications, 1989.

German original: *Schalom: Der Schöpfung Befreiung, den Menschen Gerechtigkeit, den Völkern Frieden.* Stuttgart: Kreuz Verlag, 1987.

Written in part for the 1990 Seoul WCC Conference on Peace, Justice, and the Integrity of Creation.

Reviewed by Newton B. Fowler, Jr. in *Mid-Stream* 29 (1990): 442-444.

250

Epsztein, Léon. *Social Justice in the Ancient Near East and the People of the Bible.* London: SCM Press, 1986.

French original: *La justice sociale dans le Proche-Orient ancien et le peuple de la Bible.* Paris: Editions du Cerf, 1983.

Helpful background study on Israel's social legislation.

Escobar, Donoso S. "Social Justice in the Book of Amos," *Review and Expositor* 92 (1995): 169-174.

Fohrer, Georg. "The Righteous Man in Job 31." In *Essays in Old Testament Ethics (J. Philip Hyatt, In Memoriam),* 23-55. Edited by James L. Crenshaw and John T. Willis. New York: Ktav Publishing House, 1974.

Frey, Christofer. "The Impact of the Biblical Idea of Justice on Present Discussions of Social Justice." In *Justice and Righteousness: Biblical Themes and their Influence,* 91-104. Edited by Henning Graf Reventlow and Yair Hoffman. Sheffield: JSOT Press, 1992.

Frey is Professor on the Evangelisch-Theologische Fakultät of the Ruhr-Universität in Bochum.

Gossai, Hemchand. *Justice, Righteousness and the Social Critique of the Eighth-Century Prophets.* American University Studies, Series 7, Theology and Religion, 141. New York: Peter Lang, 1993.

Hamm, Dennis, S.J. *Preaching Biblical Justice: To Nurture the Faith That Does It.* Studies in the Spirituality of Jesuits Series. St. Louis MO: The Seminar on Jesuit Spirituality, 1997.

Hamm is professor of New Testament at Creighton University in Omaha, Nebraska.

Hendrickx, Hermann. *Social Justice in the Bible.* Quezon City: Dilliman, 1985.

Henshaw, Richard A. "Justice and Righteousness in the Bible and the Ancient Near East: A Recapituation in Dialogue with Confucian Thought." In *Confucian-Christian Encounters in Historical and Contemporary Perspective*, 339-352. Edited by Peter K. H. Lee. New York: The Edwin Mellen Press, 1991.

Hollyday, Joyce. *Clothed with the Sun: Biblical Women, Social Justice and Us.* Louisville, KY: Westminster John Knox Press, 1994.

Humphrey, Lorie A., and Oordt, Ruth M. "Ethic of Justice and Ethic of Care as Compared to Biblical Concepts of Justice and Mercy." *Journal of Pastoral Care* 10 (1991): 300-305.

Discusses the concepts of "ethics of justice" (Kohlberg) with "ethics of care" (e.g. Gilligan) and examines these two versions of moral theory in light of biblical themes of justice and mercy. The authors emphasize the paradoxical relationship between justice and mercy in morality.

Lebacqz, Karen. *Justice in an Unjust World: Foundations for a Christian Approach to Justice.* Minneapolis: Augsburg, 1987.

Using biblical images and models the author portrays divine justice and God's call for us to heed the cry of suffering and to work for justice in an unjust world.

Lebacqz is professor of Christian ethics at the Pacific School of Religion in Berkeley, California.

Limburg, James. "Human Rights in the Old Testament." *Concilium* 124 (1979): 20-26.

One of a series of articles on various aspects of the theological meaning and significance of human rights.

Malchow, Bruce. *Social Justice in the Hebrew Bible: What is New and What is Old.* Collegeville MN: Liturgical Press, 1996.

_____. "Social Justice in the Israelite Law Codes." *Word and Word* 4 (1984): 293-306.

Overview of this theme.

_____. "Social Justice in the Wisdom Literature." *Biblical Theological Bulletin* 12 (1982): 120-124.

Marchadour, Alain. "Justice et paix dans la Bible." *La Vie Spirituelle* 72 (1992): 293-306.

Mays, James L. "Justice: Perspectives from the Prophetic Tradition." In *Prophecy in Israel*, 144-158. Edited by David L. Petersen. Philadelphia: Fortress Press, 1987.

Originally appeared in *Interpretation* 37 (1983): 5-17.

Menzes, Ruiz de. "Social Justice in Israel's Law." *Bible Bhashyam* 11 (1985): 10-46.

Survery of social concerns in Israel's legal traditions.

Moreno Rejón, Francisco. "Seeking the Kingdom and its Justice: the Development of the Ethic of Liberation." *Concilium* 172 (1984): 35-41.

One of a series of articles devoted to the ethics of liberation.

Murray, Robert. *The Cosmic Covenant: Biblical Themes of Justice, Peace and the Integrity of Creation*. Heythrop Monographs, 7. London: Sheed and Ward, 1992.

Reviewed by John W. Rogerson in *The Heythrop Journal* 34 (1993): 184-185.

Nahmani, H.S. *Human Rights in the Old Testament*. Tel Aviv, 1964.

Nebe, Gottfried. "Righteousness in Paul." In *Justice and Righteousness: Biblical Themes and their Influence*, 131-153. Edited by Henning Graf Reventlow and Yair Hoffman. Sheffield: JSOT Press, 1992.

Oakham, Douglas. *Jesus and the Economic Questions of His Day*. Toronto: Edward Mellen Press, 1986.

Doctoral dissertation which offers a good source of information on the economic life of ancient Palestine.

Penna, Angelo. "I diritti umani nel Vecchio Testamento." In *I Diritti Umani: Dottrina e Prassi*, 61-95. A cura di Gino Concetti. Roma: AVE, 1982.

Pinckaers, Servais, O.P. *La Justice évangélique*. Paris: Téqui, 1986.

Pinckaers is a moral theologian.

Popkes, W. "Die Gerechtigkeitstradition im Matthäus-Evangelium." *Zeitschrift für die Neutestamentliche Wissenschaft* 80 (1989): 1-23.

Przybylski, Benno. *Righteousness in Matthew and His World of Thought*. Society for New Testament Studies, Monograph Series, 41. Cambridge: Cambridge University Press, 1980.

Ramsey, Paul. "The Biblical Norm of Righteousness." *Interpretation* 24 (1970): 419-429.

Ramsey was a very well-known American Protestant ethician who lived from 1913-1988.

Rebić', Adalbert."Righteousness in the Old Testament." *Theology Digest* 39 (1992): 139-142.

Digested version of   "Der Gerechtigkeitsbegriff im Alten Testament." *Communio* 19 (1990): 390-396.

The Occidental Christian concepts of retributive and punitive justice are inadequate for understanding the Hebrew concept of righteousness (*zedaqah*). In the Hebrew Scriptures righteousness refers above all to God's relationship

254

with God's people. Several Old Testament texts, plus the opinion of many biblical exegetes are marshalled to support the author's thesis.

Reumann, John. *Righteousness in the New Testament: "Justification" in the United States Lutheran-Roman Catholic Dialogue. With Responses by Joseph A. Fitzmeyer and Jerome D. Quinn.* Philadelphia: Fortress Press, and New York: Paulist Press, 1982.

See especially Chapter 3, "The Pauline School," pp. 41-123 of Reumann's essay "'Justification by Grace through Faith' as Expression of the Gospel: The Biblical Witness to the Reformation Emphasis," and also Jerome D. Quinn's "Response" entitled "The Pastoral Epistles on Righteousness," pp. 229-238.

Reventlow, Henning Graf, and Hoffman, Yair, eds. *Justice and Righteousness: Biblical Themes and their Influence.* Journal for the Study of Old Testament Supplement Series, 137. Sheffield: JSOT Press, 1992.

Reventlow, Henning Graf. "Righteousness as Order of the World: Some Remarks towards a Programme." In *Justice and Righteousness: Biblical Themes and their Influence,* 163-172. Edited by Henning Graf Reventlow and Yair Hoffman. Sheffield: JSOT Press, 1992.

Ruiz, Gregorio. "La ética profética: frente a la pobreza desde la justicia." *Moralia* 6 (1984): 79-101.

Tambien en [also found in] *Perspectivas de moral bíblica,* 79-101. Estudios de Etica Teologica. Edd. Marciano Vidal, Francisco Lage y Alfosno Ruiz-Mateos. Madrid: Instituto Superior de Ciencas Morales, PS Editorial, 1984.

Sandeen, Ernest, ed. *The Bible and Social Reform.* Chico: Scholars Press, 1982.

Schofield, J.N. "Righteousness in the Old Testament." *Bible Translator* 16 (1965): 112-116.

Schüssler Fiorenza, Elisabeth. *The Book of Revelation: Justice and Judgment.* Philadelphia: Fortress Press, 1985.

____. *Revelation: Vision of a Just World.* Minneapolis: Fortress Press, 1991.

Sicre, José Luis. *El clamor de los profetas en favor de la justícia.* Curso Fe y Justícia. Madrid: Fundación Santa Maria, 1988.

____. *Con los pobres de la tierra. La justicia social en los profestas de Israel.* Madrid: Ediciones Cristiandad, 1984.

____. "La precoupación por la justicia en el Antiguo Oriente (I y II)." *Proyección* 28 (1981): 3-19; 91-104.

Sider, Ronald J., ed. *Cry Justice: The Bible on Hunger and Poverty.* New York: Paulist, 1980.

Stek, J.H. "Salvation, Justice and Liberation in the Old Testament." *Calvin Theological Journal* 13 (1978): 133-165.

Stowers, Stanley Kent. *A Rereading of Romans: Justice, Jews, and Gentiles.* New Haven: Yale University Press, 1994.

Stuhlmacher, Peter. *Reconciliation, Law and Righteousness: Essays on Biblical Theology.* Philadelphia: Fortress Press, 1986.

Translated from the German.

Vanoni, Gottfried. "Schalom als zentrale biblische Botschaft." *Theologisch-praktische Quartalschrift* 141 (1993): 3-12.

English digest: "Shalom and the Bible." *Theology Digest* 41 (1994): 171-121.

Shalom means more than peace and its opposite is not merely war, but evil and calamity. Shalom is closely related to biblical righteousness, and is God's gift to humankind. For Christians shalom is also understood as the offering of mutual forgiveness.

Vassiliadis, Petros. "Equality and Justice in Classical Antiquity and in Paul: The Social Implications of the Pauline Collection." *St. Vladimir's Theological Quarterly* 36 (1992): 51-59.

Weinfeld, Moshe. "`Justice and Righteousness'--The Expression and its Meaning." In *Justice and Righteousness: Biblical Themes and their Influence*, 228-246. Edited by Henning Graf Reventlow and Yair Hoffman. Sheffield: JSOT Press, 1992.

_____. *Justice and Righteousness in Israel and the Nations: Equality and Freedom in Ancient Israel in Light of Social Justice in the Ancient Near East.* Jerusalem: The Magnes Press. The Hebrew University, 1985.

_____. *Social Justice in Ancient Israel and in the Ancient Near East.* Minneapolis: Augsburg Fortress; Jerusalem: The Magnes Press, The Hebrew University, 1995.

Shows that the biblical expression "to do justice (*mishpat*) and righteousness (*zedekah*)" generally refers to acting on behalf of the poor and oppressed. After an analysis of the meaning of the terms, Weinfeld investigates the ideal of justice in relation to social reforms promoted by Israelite monarchy, the implications of the ideal in individual life, and the theological implications of all aspects of the concept.

Wénin, André. "Foi et justice dans l'Ancien Testament." *Lumen Vitae* 46 (1991): 380-392.

Chercher à articuler sans cesse foi et justice est une constante du message biblique; encore faut-il étudier de près la *manière* dont la Bible s'y prend. A partir d'un texte précis (Dt 26), finement analysé, l'auteur montre comment la Loi de Moïse contient une exigence de justice; puis il en présente les échos dans l'A.T. (Dieu et le prochain; injustice et idôlatrie; les prophètes) et les prolongements dan le N.T. Ainsi est dégagé, non sans clarté, un message central, très éloquent pour notre temps.

Maintains that faith and justice are constant terms in the biblical message, and that it is necessary to investigate the manner in which the Bible takes up these terms.

Wright, Christopher J.H. *Human Rights: A Study in Biblical Themes.* Grove
Booklet on Ethics, 31. Downers Grove IL: Grove Books, 1979.

Yoder, Perry B. *Shalom: The Bible's Word for Salvation, Justice, and Peace.*
Newton KA: Faith and Life Press, 1990.

Uses the concept of *shalom* in both Old and New Testament in application to
themes of justice, freedom, liberation, law, salvation and atonement.

****

Liberation Themes and Scripture

Baker, Christopher J., SSC. *Covenant and Liberation: Giving New Heart to God's
Endangered Family.* New York: Peter Lang, 1991.

Based in part on his eleven years' experience of working in Lima, Baker aims
to present a continuous and unified story of covenant as it emerges from the
beginning to the end of the Bible. The final chapter deals specifically with the
"Covenant Dimension in Liberation Theology."

Blank, Rudolph H. "Six Theses Concerning Freedom in Christ and Liberation:
Liberation in Galatians, Luther, and Liberation Theology." *Concordia
Journal* 20 (1994): 236-260.

Critiques Liberation theology's understanding of liberation, and suggests that
it differs considerably from Paul's understanding of liberation as presented in
the Letter to the Galatians. This problem leads to further difficulties in
Christology, anthropology, soteriology, and missiology.

Cahill, Lisa Sowle. "The New Testament and Ethics: Communities of Social
Change." *Interpretation* 44 (1990): 383-395.

Cahill discusses several leading theologians who use Scripture in their ethical
analysis, including Gustavo Gutiérrez. Her discussion centers on the role of
an authoritative Scripture for contemporary ethical reflection, specifically on
how the socially radical communities reflected in Scripture may propose
authoritative patterns for today. Cahill concludes by posing a number of what

she terms "veridical problems" in evaluating both the possibility and use of ethically normative biblical material.

Cahill is a Roman Catholic and did her doctoral studies at the University of Chicago under the direction of James M. Gustafson. She is Professor of Theological Ethics at Boston College, and past President of both the Catholic Theological Society of America (CTSA) and the Society of Christian Ethics (SCE).

Carroll, M. Daniel. "The Prophetic Text and the Literature of Dissent in Latin America: Amos, García Márquez, and Cabrera Infante Dismantle Militarism." *Biblical Interpretation* 4 (1996): 76-100.

Gives a reading of the prophet Amos within the framework of some novels of dissent in Latin America in order to give a perspective on dealing with militarism in Latin America.

Cook, Michael L., S.J. "Jesus' Parables and the Faith That Does Justice." *Studies in the Spirituality of Jesuits* 24 (November, 1992).

Cook is professor of theology at Gonzaga University in Spokane, Washington.

Federici, Tommaso. "Aspetti Biblici della Solidarietà." *Per La Filosofia: Filosofia e insegnamento* 7 (1990): 13-25.

Fullenbach, John, S.V.D. *The Kingdom of God: The Heart of Jesus' Message for Us Today*. Manila: Divine Word Publications, 1989.

Fullenbach served as a missionary in the Philippines and teaches theology at the Pontifical Gregorian University in Rome.

Garcia Cordero, Maximiliano, O.P. "Teologia biblica de la liberación." En *Teologia de la liberación*, 135-180. Conversaciones de Toledo (Junio 1973). Burgos: Ediciones Aldecoa, 1974.

Girardet, Giorgio. *Lecture politique de l'Evangile de Luc.* Preface de François Houtart. Traduit de l'italien par le Centre Communautaire International. Bruxelles: Vie Ouvriere, 1978.

Italian original: *Il Vangelo della liberazione: letture politica di Luca.*

Gottwald, Norman K., and Horsley, Richard A., eds. *The Bible and Liberation: Political and Social Hermeneutics.* Rev. ed. Maryknoll: Orbis Books, 1983, 1993.

Gottwald is the sole editor of the original 1983 edition.

Divided into five sections: 1) Social Scientific Method in Biblical Studies; 2) Social Class as a Hermeneutical Factor; 3) Sociological Readings of the Old Testament; 4) Sociological Readings of the New Testament; and 5) The Bible in Political Theology and Marxist Thought.

Gudorf, Christine E. "Liberation Theology's Use of Scripture," *Interpretation* 41 (1987): 5-18.

Discusses the impact of differences in the social context between North and South America upon the reading of Scripture in reference to the use of Scripture in Liberation Theology.

Hennelly, Alfred T. "The Biblical Hermeneutics of Juan Luis Segundo." In *Readings in Moral Theology No. 4,* 303-320. Edited by Charles E. Curran and Richard A. McCormick, S.J. New York and Ramsey: Paulist Press, 1984.

Originally appeared in Hennelly's *Theologies in Conflict: The Challenge of Juan Luis Segundo.* Maryknoll: Orbis Books, 1979.

Keeling, Michael. *The Foundations of Christian Ethics.* Edinburgh: T. & T. Clark, 1990.

Concentrating on three themes: sexuality, property, and political power, Keeling examines the foundations of Christian ethics in the Bible and their embodiment in the Church. Follows a chronological structure and considers the influence of liberation theology on perceptions of social justice. His second chapter specifically addresses the Bible as the source of authority in Christian ethics.

Koch, Kurt. "Befreiungstheoligische Lektüre der Bibel." *Stimmen der Zeit* 207 (1989): 771-784.

Lochman, Jan Milic. *Wegweisung der Freiheit. Abriss der Ethik in der Perspektive des Dekalogs.* Gütersloh: Gütersloher Verlagshaus Gerd Mohn, 1979.

In French: *Faut-il parler encore des commandements?.* Paris: Editions du Cerf, 1981.

Italian translation: *I comandamenti, segnali verso la libertà.* Torino: Elle Di Ci, 1986.

Reviewed, in French, by Jean Desclos in *Studia Moralia* 36 (1989): 309-311.

Lochman is a Czechoslovakian Protestant (Reformed) theologian. His work considers not only the Bible, but also the Protestant tradition as well as Marxism.

Lohfink, Norbert. *Option for the Poor: The Basic Principle of Liberation Theology in Light of the Bible.* Berkeley: BIBAL Press, 1987.

Lohfink is professor of Old Testament Exegesis at Sankt Georgen in Frankfurt-am-Main.

Meier, John P. "The Bible as a Source for Theology." *Proceedings of the Forty-Third Annual Convention.* Catholic Theological Society of America. 43 (1988): 1-14.

Critiques two key liberation theologians' (Jon Sobrino and Juan Luis Segundo) use of Scripture in their theology in terms of their exegesis and interpretation.

Meier is professor of New Testament at the Catholic University of America.

Miller, William R. "Liberation Theology and Homophobia." *American Baptist Quarterly* 8 (1989): 124-139.

Searches for the biblical sources for liberation and justice concerns which have implications for how the church should deal with a range of issues such as homosexuality, abuse of women, and the use of power. Uses Thomas Kuhn's concept of a "paradigm shift" to argue that white males need to reevaluate their roles in contemporary social structures. Miller proposes that Liberation Theology provides a framework for such a paradigm shift.

Miranda, José Porfirio. *Communism in the Bible.* Maryknoll: Orbis Books, 1982.

____. *Marx and the Bible: A Critique of the Philosophy of Oppression.* Translated by John Eagleson. Maryknoll: Orbis Books, 1974.

Spanish original: *Marx y la biblia, Crítica a la filosofia de la opresión.* Salamanca: Ediciones Sígueme, 1971.

Nakanose, Shigeyuki. *Josiah's Passover: Sociology and the Liberating Bible.* Bible & Liberation Series. Maryknoll: Orbis Press, 1993.

Shigeyuki Nakanose, a Catholic priest born in Japan, now works with base communities in Brazil. He shows how "the so-called Deuteronomic reform spearheaded by King Josiah - including a revamped Passover festival as one of its cardinal features - decisively strengthened the small ruling elite of Judah to the detriment of the economic, social, political, and religious well-being of the majority of Israelites." He then goes on to show "how his understanding of biblical Passover was shared with leaders and lay participants in Brazilian basic ecclesial communities in and around Sâo Paulo, as well as how they responded to it."

Prior, Michael. *Jesus the Liberator: Nazareth Liberation Theology (Luke 4:16-30).* The Biblical Seminar 26. Sheffield: Sheffield Academic Press, 1995.

Uses Luke 4:16-30 to introduce different methods in Gospel study and as an entry into Luke's gospel in particular, as well as to explore ways to connect Luke's "liberation theology" with contemporary liberation theologies.

Ravasi, Gianfranco. "«Tra di voi no vi sia nessun bisogno!». Solidarietà nel popolo di Dio dell'Antico Testamento." *Communio* 125 (settembre-ottobre 1992).

One of a series of articles on various aspects of the theme of solidarity.

Reimer, Ivoni Richter. *Women in the Acts of the Apostles: A Feminist Liberation Perspective.* Minneapolis: Fortress Press, 1995.

Considers the women portrayed in the Book of Acts, such as Sapphira (marriage property issue), Lydia (dye seller), Candace (queen of Ethiopia), Tabitha (disciple), Priscilla (co-apostle with her husband, Aquila), and others.

Ringe, Sharon H. *Jesus, Liberation, and the Biblical Jubilee: Images for Ethics and Christology.* Overtures to Biblical Theology, 19. Philadelphia: Fortress Press, 1985.

Rowland, Christopher and Corner, Mark. *Liberating Exegesis: The Challenge of Liberation Theology to Biblical Studies.* Louisville: Westminster/John Knox Press, 1989.

Reviewed by Ronald D. Witherup in *Theology Today* 48 (1992): 93.

Rowland, Christopher. "How the Poor can Liberate the Bible." *Priests and People* 6 (1992): 367-371.

Rowland is Dean Ireland Professor of New Testament Exegesis at the University of Oxford.

Schottroff, Luise. "Experiences of Liberation. Liberty and Liberation according to Biblical Testimony." *Concilium* 172 (1984): 67-73.

In Spanish: "Experiencias de liberación. Libertad y liberación según la Biblia." *Concilium* 192 (1984): 263-274.

Schottroff is professor of New Testament at the University of Kassel, Germany.

_____. *Let the Oppressed Go Free: Feminist Perspectives on the New Testament.* Louisville: Westminster/John Knox Press, 1993.

These exegetical studies are contributions to feminist liberation theology. They treat Freedom and Liberation According to Biblical Evidence; How Justified Is the Feminist Critique of Paul?; "Leaders of the Faith" or "Just Some Pious Women-folk"?; Women as Disciples of Jesus; Lydia: A New Quality of Power; The Woman Who Loved Much and the Pharisee Simon; The Virgin Birth; Mary Magdalene and the Women at Jesus' Tomb.

Schüssler Fiorenza, Elisabeth. "Toward a Feminist Biblical Hermeneutics: Biblical Interpretation and Liberation Theology." In *Readings in Moral Theology No. 4*, 354-382. Edited by Charles E. Curran and Richard A. McCormick, S.J. New York and Ramsey: Paulist Press, 1984.

Originally appeared in *The Challenge of Liberation Theology: A First-World Response.* Edited by Brian Mahan and L. Dale Richesin. Maryknoll: Orbis, 1981.

Segundo, Juan Luis. *El caso Mateo. Los comienzos de una ética judeo-cristiana.* Santander: Sal Terrae, 1994.

Segundo is a well-known Latin American liberation theologian.

Sievernich, Michael, S.J. "Von der Utopie zur Ethik. Zur Theologie von Gustavo Gutiérrez." *Theologie und Philosophie* 71 (1996): 33-46.

Siker, Jeffrey S. *Scripture and Ethics: Twentieth-Century Portraits.* New York: Oxford University Press, 1997.

Analyzes eight twentieth-century Protestant and Catholic theologians' use of Scripture in their respective works: Reinhold Niebuhr, H. Richard Niebuhr, Bernhard Häring, Paul Ramsey, Stanley Hauerwas, Gustavo Gutiérrez, James Cone, and Rosemary Radford Ruether. Siker addresses five questions to each author's work: 1) which biblical texts are used; 2) how are the texts used; 3) how does the author envision biblical authority; 4) what kind of hermeneutics are employed; and 5) what does the respective author's approach to the Bible yield in terms of Christian ethics. A concluding chapter focuses on the authors' respective appropriations of the Sermon on the Mount.

264

Siker is an ordained Presbyterian minister and Associate Professor of Theology at Loyola Marymount University in Los Angeles.

_____. "Uses of the Bible in the Theology of Gustavo Gutiérrez: Liberating Scriptures of the Poor." *Biblical Interpretation* 4 (1996): 40-71.

Sleeper, Charles Freeman. *Black Power and Christian Responsibility: Some Biblical Foundations for Social Ethics.* Nashville: Abingdon, 1968.

Spohn, William C. Chapter 3, "Call to Liberation," in *What Are They Saying About Scripture and Ethics?*, 54-69. New York: Paulist Press, 1984.

Treats primarily the work of Gustavo Gutiérrez and his use of Scriptural themes in liberation theology. Mention also made of other liberation theologians such as Juan Luis Segundo, as well as two feminist theologians, Letty Russell and Phyllis Trible.

Spohn studied under James Gustafson at the University of Chicago, taught moral theology at the Jesuit School of Theology-Berkeley for many years, and currently teaches Christian ethics at the University of Santa Clara.

Stek, J.H. "Salvation, Justice and Liberation in the Old Testament." *Calvin Theological Journal* 13 (1978): 133-165.

Stuhlmueller, Carroll, C.P. "Option for the Poor: *Old Testament Directives.*" In *Economic Justice: CTU's Pastoral Commentary on The Bishops' Letter on the Economy*, 19-27. Edited by John Pawlikowski, O.S.M. and Donald Senior, C.P. Washington, D.C.: The Pastoral Press, 1988.

Book includes the text of the Bishops' Letter on the Economy, plus 12 essays organized into three sections: 1) The Biblical Perspective; 2) The Ethical Perspective; and 3) The Pastoral Perspective.

Sugirtharajah, R.S., ed. *Voices from the Margin: Interpreting the Bible in the Third World.* Maryknoll: Orbis Press, 1991.

Collection of essays which focus on the contribution of Latin American, Asian and Black authors to biblical exegesis. Critiques the European dominance of this field.

Tambasco, Anthony J. *The Bible for Ethics: Juan Luis Segundo and First-World Ethics.* Washington, D.C.: University Press of America, 1981.

Concentrates on Segundo's use of Scripture in his treatment of the ethical concerns of liberation. Special attention is given to Segundo's use of the hermeneutical circle in his efforts to demonstrate how the Bible can be normative for Christian ethics.

_____. "A Critical Appraisal of Segundo's Biblical Hermeneutics." In *Readings in Moral Theology No. 4*, 321-336. Edited by Charles E. Curran and Richard A. McCormick, S.J. New York and Ramsey: Paulist Press, 1984.

Originally appeared in Tambasco's *The Bible for Ethics: Juan Luis Segundo and First-World Ethics.* Washington, D.C.: University Press of America, 1981.

Topel, L. John, S.J. *The Way to Peace: Liberation through the Bible.* Maryknoll: Orbis Books, 1979.

Italian translation: *La via della Pace. La liberazione attraverso la Bibbia.* Orizzonti biblici. Assisi: Cittadella, 1984.

Reviewed by Frederick Herzog in *Theology Today* 36 (1980): 617.

Topel is professor of Seattle University in Seattle, Washington.

de Villiers, Pieter G.R., ed. *Liberation Theology and the Bible.* Miscellanea Congregalia, 31. Pretoria : University of South Africa, 1987.

Yoder, John Howard. "Exodus and Exile: The Two Faces of Liberation." In *Readings in Moral Theology No. 4*, 337-353. Edited by Charles E. Curran and Richard A. McCormick, S.J. New York and Ramsey: Paulist Press, 1984.

Originally appeared in *Cross Currents* in 1973.

Critiques liberation theology's use of Scripture in ethics.

Yoder is a well-known ethicist in the Mennonite tradition who teaches at the University of Notre Dame.

****

Medical Issues and Scripture

Anderson, J. Kerby. "Euthanasia: a biblical appraisal." *Bibliotheca Sacra* 144 (1987): 208-217.

Bishop, Marilyn E. *Religion and Disability: Perspectives in Scripture, Theology and Ethics*. Kansas City, MO: Sheed & Ward, 1995.

Key presentations from the national symposium, "Ministry Perspectives on Disability." Scripture scholar Donald Senior identifies themes often associated with scripture--such as the notion that sin and guilt somehow cause sickness and disability--that contribute to non-welcoming attitudes toward disabled persons. Presentations by John Macquarrie and Stanley Hauerwas emphasize the dignity of all persons and the responsibility of the community to respond in love to those with disabilities.

Granberg-Michaelson, Wesley. "The Authorship of Life [a biblical look at genetic engineering]." *Sojourners* 12 (June-July 1983): 18-22.

Herring, Basil F. "The Definition and Determination of Death." Chapter 2 in *Jewish Ethics and Halakhah for Our Time: Sources and Commentary, Vol. 2*, 39-84. The Library of Jewish Law and Ethics, 11. New York: KTAV, 1984.

_____. "Euthanasia." Chapter 3 in *Jewish Ethics and Halakhah for Our Time: Sources and Commentary, Vol. I*, 67-90. The Library of Jewish Law and Ethics, 11. New York: KTAV, 1984.

_____. "Medical Practice, Research, and Self-Endangerment." Chapter 1 in *Jewish Ethics and Halakhah for Our Time: Sources and Commentary, Vol. 2*, 1-38. The Library of Jewish Law and Ethics, 11. New York: KTAV, 1984.

____. "Organ Transplantation." Chapter 3 in *Jewish Ethics and Halakhah for Our Time: Sources and Commentary, Vol. 2*, 85-128. The Library of Jewish Law and Ethics, 11. New York: KTAV, 1984.

____. "Truth and the Dying Patient." Chapter 2 in *Jewish Ethics and Halakhah for Our Time: Sources and Commentary, Vol. I*, 47-66. The Library of Jewish Law and Ethics, 11. New York: KTAV, 1984.

Hiltner, S. "The Bible Speaks to the Health of Man." In *Dialogue in Medicine and Theology*, 51-68. Edited by D. White. New York: Abingdon, 1967.

Mouw, Richard J. "Biblical Revelation and Medical Decisions." In *Revisions: Changing Perspectives in Moral Philosophy*, 182-202. Edited by Stanley M. Hauerwas and Alasdair MacIntyre. Notre Dame: University of Notre Dame Press, 1983.

Originally appeared in the *Journal of Medicine and Philosophy* 4 (1979): 367-382.

Mouw writes out of the Calvinist tradition and is professor of Christian Philosophy and Ethics and President at Fuller Theological Seminary.

Mullen, Alyce Miller. "A Study of the Relationship of Sin, Distress, and Health in the Old Testament Psalms: As a Basis for a Biblical Theology of Wholeness in Pastoral Ministry. Thesis (doctoral)--Wesley Theological Seminary, 1985.

Nelson, J. Robert. *Human Life: A Biblical Perspective for Bioethics*. Philadelphia: Fortress Press, 1984.

Reviewed by E. Clinton Gardner in *Journal of Religion* 66 (1986): 214-215.

Oates, Wayne E. "A Biblical Perspective on Addiction." *Review and Expositor* 91 (1994): 71-75.

Treats Dt 5:6-7; Mt 22:340-40; and Gal 4:3,8.

Palmer, B., ed. *Medicine and the Bible*. Exeter: Paternoster Press, 1986.

Payne, F.E. *Biblical/Medical Ethics*. Milford, MI: Mott Media, 1985.

Schenk, Elizabeth Anne. "Care of the Person with HIV/AIDS: The Biblical Mandate." *Ashland Theological Journal* 25 (1993): 68-84.

Verhey, Allen. "Scripture and Medical Ethics: Psalm 51:10a, the Jarvik VII, and Psalm 50:9." In *Religious Methods and Resources in Bioethics*, 261-288. Edited by Paul F. Camenisch. Dordrecht: Kluwer Academic Publishers, 1994.

> Verhey is the Evert J. and Hattie E. Blekkink Professor of Religion at Hope College.

****

Miscellaneous Questions

Beestermöller, Gerhard. "Lex naturalis--Stolperstein einer ökumenischen Ethik?" *Theologie und Philosophie* 71 (1996): 47-62.

Bohr, David. "Evangelization: Proclaiming the Good News: Biblical Perspectives." Chapter 1 in Idem. *Evangelization in America: Proclamation, Way of Life and the Catholic Church in the United States*. New York: Paulist Press, 1977.

> Published version of the author's doctoral dissertation in moral theology done under Bernard Häring, C.Ss.R. at the Accademia Alfonsiana in Rome.

Clemons, James T. *What Does the Bible Say about Suicide?* Minneapolis: Fortress Press, 1990.

> Reviewed by Roland M. Kawano in *Anglican Theological Review* 74 (1992): 257-258.
> Reviewed by Lloyd R. Bailey in *Theology Today* 48 (1992): 262.

Clemons is Professor of New Testament at Wesley Theological Seminary in Washington, D.C.

Forrell, George Wolfgang, ed. *Christian Social Teaching: A Reader in Christian Social Ethics from the Bible to the Present.* Garden City: Doubleday, 1966.

Gardner, E[dward] Clinton. *Biblical Faith and Social Ethics.* New York: Harper & Row, 1963.

Gonzalez-Ruiz, José-Maria. "Che cosa dice la Scrittura sulla libertà religiosa?" In AA.VV., *Cattolicesimo e libertà: La coscienza individuale criterio inviolabile,* 93-108. IDO-C Documentinuovi, 2. Verona: Arnoldo Mondadori Editore, 1967.

Greenspahn, Frederick E., ed. *Contemporary Ethical Issues in the Jewish and Christian Traditions.* Hoboken: KTAV, 1986.

Harris, J. Gordon. *Biblical Perspectives on Aging: God and the Elderly.* Overtures to Biblical Theology 11. Philadelphia: Fortress Press, 1987.

Hays, Richard B. "Anti-Judaism and Ethnic Conflict." Chapter 17 in Idem. *The Moral Vision of the New Testament: Community, Cross, New Creation. A Contemporary Introduction to New Testament Ethics,* 407-443. San Francisco: Harper San Francisco, 1996.

Hays treats anti-Judaism and ethnic conflict as a "pragmatic" task (and test) of his proposed approach to New Testament ethics. He proposes three central organizing metaphors from the New Testament, Community, Cross, and New Creation, as a basic methodological approach to utilizing the biblical material in Christian ethics. Hays also names and treats four principal "tasks" of using the Bible in ethics: the descriptive task (what is being said); the synthetic task (how does this or that passage, text, etc., fit within the larger biblical text in a coherent manner); the hermeneutical task of interpreting the biblical texts for ethics, and finally the "pragmatic" task of "living under the Word" (applying the biblical texts to concrete moral issues). Hays treats several such issues in individual chapters: non-violence, divorce and remarriage, homosexuality, and abortion.

270

Hays is professor of New Testament at Duke University Divinity School, and taught for a number of years previously at Yale.

Hoyles, J. Arthur. *Punishment in the Bible*. London: Epworth Press, 1986.

Book is divided into three parts: punishment in the Old Testament, punishment in the New Testament, and biblical insights and penal history.

Hoyles is a retired Methodist minister who spent much of his time as a prison chaplain.

Jodock, Darrell. "The Reciprocity Between Scripture and Theology: The Role of Scripture in Contemporary Theological Reflection." *Interpretation* 44 (1990): 369-382.

Considers the issue in light of a critical need for dialogue not only within the community of faith, and between the community of faith and the larger society, but also between people of faith and the Scriptures.

Kysar, Robert. *Called to Care: Biblical Images for Social Ministry*. Minneapolis: Fortress Press, 1991.

Survey of biblical images of God and their relation to social ministry, as well as pastoral reflections on such ministry.

Long, Thomas G. "The Use of Scripture in Contemporary Preaching." *Interpretation* 44 (1990): 341-352.

It is at the juncture between human imagination and textual interpretation that biblical hermeneutics will aid the preacher.

MacArthur, Kathleen W. *The Bible and Human Rights*. Rev. ed. New York: A Woman's Press Publication, 1949.

Pinckaers, Servais, O.P. *La quête du bonheur*. Paris: Téqui, 1979.

Pinckaers is a moral theologian.

Sapp, Stephen. *Full of Years: Aging and the Elderly in the Bible and Today.* Nashville: Abingdon Press, 1987.

Sleeper, C. Freeman. *The Bible and the Moral Life.* Louisville: Westminster/John Knox Press, 1992.

Looks at how various churches use the Bible to address contemporary ethical issues, particularly nuclear war and abortion, and also considers the issue of biblical authority in terms of four major styles of moral reflection, i.e., law, prophecy, apocalypse, and wisdom. The book is designed for adult study groups and contains practical exercises.

Sleeper is Professor of Religion at Roanoke College in Salem, Virginia.

Stagg, Frank. *The Bible Speaks on Aging.* Nashville: Broadman Press, 1981.

Whelan, Caroline F. "Suicide in the Ancient World: A Re-examination of Matthew 27:3-10." *Laval Théologique et Philosophique* 49 (1993): 505-522.

Re-examines the death of Judas in a more positive light, through a consideration of suicide in the context of the honor-shame culture of the ancient world.

****

Politics, Power, Authority, and/or Dissent in Scripture

> *N.B., See also sections dealing with Liberation Theology, Economy, Justice, and War and Peace.*

Articles on Power and Politics

Barr, James. "The Bible as a Political Document." *Bulletin of the John Rylands University Library of Manchester* 62 (1980): 268-298.

Offers certain cautions about the use of the Bible for social ethics.

Barr, Steve. "The Eye of the Needle--Power and Money in the New Community: A Look at Mark 10:17-31." *Andover Newton Review* 3 (1992): 31-44.

Bergant, Dianne, C.S.A. "Power: A Blessing or a Curse?" *Bible Today* 30 (1992): 260-266.

One of several articles in this issue on the theme of "Power and Authority."

Blank, Josef. "The Concept of Power in the Church: New Testament." *Concilium* 197 (1988): 3-12.

Blank's central thesis is "The decisive factor in the New Testament understanding of the concepts of `power, sovereignty', etc., is that all exercise of power in Christ's Church is understood fundamentally as *diakonia* [ministry/service] and not as *arché* [power/sovereignty]." p. 8.

Crüsemann, Frank. "Dominion, Guilt, and Reconciliation: The Contribution of the Jacob Narrative in Genesis to Political Ethics." *Semeia*, no. 66 (1995): 67-77.

One of several articles on Old Testament ethics in this issue.

Emslie, B.L. "The Methodology of Proceeding from Exegesis to an Ethical Decision." *Neotestamentica* 19 (1985): 87-91.

Using the problem of citizen-state relations in Rom 13:1-7, Emslie argues that Paul is not formulating general principles but rather addresses an *ad hoc* situation. The historico-socio-political ethos of the audience provides an important interpretive key to the text. In terms of using Scripture in ethics there should *not* be a direct move from biblical imperatives or analogies to a specific application.

Espinel, J.L. "Jesús y los movimientos políticos y sociales de su tiempo. Estado actual de la cuestión." *Ciencia Tomista* 113 (1986): 251-284.

Fiorenza, Francis Schüssler. "The Crisis of Scriptural Authority: Interpretation and Reception." *Interpretation* 44 (1990): 353-368.

> Because the current crisis of scriptural authority is not simply a crisis of Scriptures but also a crisis of modernity, any understanding of this crisis must consider the current intellectual environment as well as the way in which the Scriptures are viewed.

Fischer, James A., C.M. "Dissent within a Religious Community: Romans 9-11." In *Christian Biblical Ethics: From Biblical Revelation to Contemporary Christian Praxis: Method and Content*, 256-265. New York: Paulist Press, 1984.

_____. "Politics and Biblical Ethics: Romans 13:1-7." In *Christian Biblical Ethics: From Biblical Revelation to Contemporary Christian Praxis: Method and Content*, 266-277. New York: Paulist Press, 1984.

Furnish, Victor Paul. "Christians and the Governing Authorities." Chapter 5 in Idem. *The Moral Teaching of Paul: Selected Issues*, 115-139. 2nd ed. Nashville: Abingdon, 1985.

Gooch, Paul W. "Authority and Justification in Theological Ethics: A Study in 1 Corinthians 7." *Journal of Religious Ethics* 11 (1983): 62-74.

> Considers the ways in which Paul grounds his ethical advice in 1 Corinthians 7, noting that he invokes his own authority as well as the Lord's rulings and the commands of God. Gooch's thesis is that theological ethics in this case at least cannot be reduced to simple obedience to religious authority.

Gudorf, Christine E. "The magisterium and the Bible: North American experience." In *The Bible and its readers*, 79-90. Edited by W. Beuken, et al. 1991.

Hauerwas, Stanley. "The Moral Authority of Scripture: The Politics and Ethics of Remembering." *Interpretation* 34 (1980): 356-370.

> Also found as Chapter 3 in *A Community of Character: Toward a Constructive Christian Social Ethic*, 53-71. Notre Dame and London: University of Notre Dame Press, 1981.

274

Also found in *Readings in Moral Theology No. 4: The Use of Scripture in Moral Theology*, 242-275. Edited by Charles E. Curran and Richard A. McCormick, S.J. New York: Paulist Press, 1984.

The moral authority of Scripture depends ultimately about what kind of community the church must be, a life centered on a faithful remembering based on the narratives of Scripture.

Hauerwas (born 1940) is a Methodist who currently is Gilbert T. Rowe Professor of ethics at the Divinity School of Duke University in North Carolina. He studied under James M. Gustafson and for over a dozen years was on the faculty of the University of Notre Dame.

Hengel, Martin. "Das Ende aller Politik. *Die Bergpredigt in der Diskussion.*" *Evangelische Kommentare* 14 (1981): 686-690.

Hoffmann, Paul. "Paul as a Witness to Dissent." *Concilium* 158 (1982): 75-80.

One of a series of articles on various aspects of this issue.

Kroger, Daniel. "Paul and the Civil Authorities: An Exegesis of Romans 13:1-7." *Asia Journal of Theology* 7 (1993): 344ff.

Lampe, Stephen J. "Authority and Power in the Synoptics." *Bible Today* 30 (1992): 271-278.

One of several articles in this issue on the theme of "Power and Authority."

Légasse, Simon. "La soumission aux autorités d'après 1 Pierre 2, 13-17: version spécifique d'une parènese traditionelle." *New Testament Studies* 34 (1988): 378-396.

Lindemann, Andreas. "Gottesherrschaft und Menschenherrschaft: Beobachtungen zum neutestamentlichen Basileia-Zeugnis und zum Problem einer theologischen Ethik des Politischen." *Theologie und Glaube* 76 (1986): 69-94.

Morin, A. "Biblia y política." *Medellín* 11 (1985): 3-16.

Murphy, Roland E. "Prophets and Wise Men as Provokers of Dissent." *Concilium* 158 (1982): 61-66.

One of a series of articles on various aspects of this issue.

Perrot, Charles. "Jésus et le pouvoir impérial." *Laval Philosophique et Théologique* 39 (1983): 283-294.

Petraglio, Renzo. "Il riferimento alla Scrittura per l'agire politico." In AA.VV. *Economia, politica e morale nelle società dell'occidentale*, 199-235. Bologna: Edizioni Dehoniane Bologna, 1990.

Schulte, Hannelis. "The End of the Omride Dynasty: Social-Ethical Observations on the Subject of Power and Violence." *Semeia*, no. 66 (1995): 133-48.

Sider, Ronald J. "An Evangelical Vision for Public Policy." *Transformation* 2 (3/1985): 1-9.

Abstract: The author urges evangelicals to adopt a new vision for public life, based not upon the secular, materialistic vision that currently dominates western thought, but upon the scriptures. He argues that because the Bible 1) supplies the Christian's basic perspective on all reality and 2) provides normative paradigms for problem solving, it must be the Christian's foundation for shaping public policy, a foundation rendered inoperative without a sophisticated understanding of contemporary society. While defending the necessity and virtue of separation of church and state, the author maintains that the idea of separating public life from religiously-grounded ethical values is both impossible and immoral. Thus, the Christian public policy maker should lobby for programs shaped by Christian ethical norms. However, not all ethical norms should be legislated; rather, only when the infraction of these norms violates the rights of others should the state assess criminal penalties. This biblically shaped approach to public policy abandons ideologies of left and right and formulates a consistent "pro-life" stance that cuts across current political party lines.

_____. "Toward a Biblical Perspective on Equality. Steps on the Way toward Christian Political Engagement." *Interpretation* 43 (1989): 156-169.

Sklba, Bishop Richard J. "Living the truth in love (Eph 4:15): reflections on the ministry of teaching in the church." In *Theology toward the third millennium*, 125-144. Edited by G. Schultenover. 1991.

Sklba is a biblical theologian and auxiliary bishop of Milwaukee, Wisconsin.

Sleeper, C. Freeman. "The Use of Jesus in Church Social Policy Statements." *Theology and Public Policy* 2 (1990): 47-60.

Tyson, Joseph B. "Authority in Acts." *Bible Today* 30 (1992): 279-283.

One of several articles in this issue on the theme of "Power and Authority."

Vanni, Ugo, S.J. "Carità e politica nel Nuovo Testamento." *Civiltà Cattolica* 141 (1990): 15-28.

Vanni is professor of New Testament at the Pontifical Gregorian University in Rome.

Valeri, Mark, and Wilson, John F. "Scripture and Society: From Reform in the Old World to Revival in the New." In *The Bible in American Law, Politics, and Political Rhetoric*, 13-38. Edited by James Turner Johnson. Philadelphia: Fortress Press; Chico, CA: Scholars Press, 1985.

Venetz, Hermann-Josef. "Dealing with Dissenters in the New Testament Communities." *Concilium* 158 (1982): 67-74.

One of a series of articles on various aspects of this issue.

Wilch, John R. "The Use and Misuse of Scripture in Ethics." *Consensus* 11 (July 1985): 15-31.

Abstract: Christian ethics is founded upon three major hermeneutical principles: *sola scriptura*, the distinction between law and Gospel, and *solus Christus*. Scripture has been misused, e.g., in respect to: not treating a human fetus as a human being and its father not assuming his parental responsibility, men and women not accepting the roles assigned them by God in this world, the church engaging in politics or denying her principles because of political expediency, and building Christian ethics upon so-called inherent human rights. Providing everything Christians need physically and spiritually, God as Creator and Saviour calls them to responsibility and sacrificial service.

Books on Politics and Power

Alt, Franz. *Peace is Possible: The Politics of the Sermon on the Mount*. New York: Schocken Books, 1985.

In German: *Liebe ist möglich. Die Bergpredigt im Atomzeitalter*. Serie Piper, 284. München: Piper, 1985.

Bauckham, Richard. *The Bible in Politics: How to Read the Bible Politically*. Louisville: Westminster/John Knox Press, 1989.

Discusses how to use the Scriptures to bring political and ethical guidance to modern cultures, while still being aware of the distinctive nature of the biblical texts and their own historico-cultural milieu.

Bauckham is lecturer in the History of Christian Thought at the University of Manchester.

Borg, Marcus J. *Conflict, Holiness & Politics in the Teachings of Jesus*. Studies on the Bible and Early Christianity, 5. New York and Toronto: Edwin Mellen Press, 1984.

Cassidy, Richard J. *Jesus, Politics, and Society: A Study of Luke's Gospel*. Maryknoll: Orbis Books, 1978.

Has a good bibliography on both Lucan and related materials.

_____. *Society and Politics in the Acts of the Apostles.* Maryknoll: Orbis Books, 1987.

Briefly discussed by Lisa Sowle Cahill in her article "The New Testament and Ethics: Communities of Social Change," *Interpretation* 44 (1990): 383-395.

Eliott, Neil. *Liberating Paul: The Justice of God and the Politics of the Apostle.* Maryknoll: Orbis Press, 1993.

For centuries the apostle Paul has been invoked to justify oppression-whether on behalf of slavery, to enforce unquestioned obedience to the state, to silence women, or to legitimate anti-Semitism. Elliott argues that the struggle to liberate human beings from the power of death and oppression requires "liberating Paul" from the unfortunate consequence of the way he has usually been read, or rather misread, in the churches.

Esler, Philip F. *Community and Gospel in Luke-Acts: The Social and Political Motivations of Lucan Theology.* Society for New Testament Studies, Monograph Series, 57. Cambridge: Cambridge University Press, 1987.

Uses sociology and anthropology to re-examine Lucan theology in terms of a response to social and political pressures of the Christian community of the time. Special attention is given to Lucan themes such as table-fellowship, the law, the Temple, poverty and riches and politics.

Furger, Franz, Hrsg. *Biblische Ethik: Fragen und Antworten.* Freiburg Schweiz: Kanisius Verlag, 1974.

Short booklet, with contributions from Furger, Fredrich Beutter, Eugen Ruckstuhl and Hermann-Josef Venetz. Topics include: Freiheit, Gebote, Verschiedene Wertung biblischer Forderungen, Fordert Jesus die Revolution?, Sklaven, Arme, Ehelosigkeit, Unkeuschheit, Ehebruch, and Onanie.

Girardet, Giorgio. *Il Vangelo della liberazione: letture politica di Luca.*

In French: *Lecture politique de l'Evangile de Luc.* Preface de François Houtart. Traduit de l'italien par le Centre Communautaire International. Bruxelles: Vie Ouvriere, 1978.

Johnson, James Turner, ed. *The Bible in American Law, Politics, and Political Rhetoric.* Centennial publications (Society of Biblical Literature) Bible in American Culture, 4. Philadelphia: Fortress Press; Chico CA: Scholars Press, 1985.

Johnson, Luke Timothy. *Decision Making in the Church: A Biblical Model.* Philadelphia: Fortress Press, 1983.

See Johnson's *Scripture and Discernment: Decision Making in the Church* for a 1996 revised and expanded edition of this work.

Johnson is professor of New Testament at the Candler School of Theology at Emory University.

_____. *Scripture and Discernment: Decision Making in the Church.* Nashville: Abingdon Press, 1996.

Argues that the Church should not make decisions according simply to good management policy, but in response to God's activity in the world. Revised and expanded edition of Johnson's *Decision Making in the Church: A Biblical Model,* (Philadelphia: Fortress Press, 1983).

Kaye, B.N., and Wenham, G.J. *Law, Morality and the Bible.* Downers Grove IL: Intervaristy Press, 1978.

Keeling, Michael. *The Foundations of Christian Ethics.* Edinburgh: T. & T. Clark, 1990.

Concentrating on three themes: sexuality, property, and political power, Keeling examines the foundations of Christian ethics in the Bible and their embodiment in the Church. Follows a chronological structure and considers the influence of liberation theology on perceptions of social justice.

L'Hour, Jean. *La moral de l'alliance.* Traditions chrétienne, 19. Paris: Editions du Cerf, 1966, 1985.

McClelland, William Robert. *Worldly Spirituality: Biblical Reflections on Money, Politics, and Sex.* St. Louis: CBP Press, 1990.

Reviewed by Dwight E. Stevenson in *Mid-Stream* 29 (1990): 444-446.

Myers, Ched. *Binding the Strong Man: A Political Reading Mark's Story of Jesus.* Maryknoll: Orbis Books, 1988.

Briefly discussed by Lisa Sowle Cahill in her article "The New Testament and Ethics: Communities of Social Change," *Interpretation* 44 (1990): 383-395.

Also reviewed by Frank J. Matera in *Theology Today* 46 (1990): 354.

Neuhaus, Richard John, ed. *The Bible, Politics and Democracy.* Encounter Series, 3. Grand Rapids: William B. Eerdmans, 1987.

Sampley, J. Paul. *Pauline Partnership in Christ: Christian Community and Commitment in Light of Roman Law.* Philadelphia: Fortress Press, 1980.

Discusses the presence and function of the Roman legal "partnership," the consensual *societas,* in several Pauline epistles: Galatians, Philippians, Corinthians, and Philemon. Paul adapted these legal traditions and terminology of *societas* (*koinonia*) for theological purposes.

Sider, Ronald J., und Taylor, Richard K. *Abkehr von Götzen. Biblische Hoffnung als Wegweiser aus dem atomaren Wahnsinn.* Neukirchen-Vluyn: Aussaat Verlag, 1984.

Translation from English.

Waetjen, Herman C. *A Reordering of Power: A Socio-Political Reading of Mark's Gospel.* Minneapolis: Augsburg Fortress, 1989.

Briefly discussed by Lisa Sowle Cahill in her article "The New Testament and Ethics: Communities of Social Change," *Interpretation* 44 (1990): 383-395.

Waetjen is professor emeritus of New Testament at San Francisco Theological Seminary in San Anselmo, California.

Wagener, Ulrike. *Die Ordnung des "Hauses Gottes": Der Ort von Frauen in der Ekklesiologie und Ethik der Pastoralbriefe.* Wissenschaftliche Untersuchungen zum Neuen Testament, 2.65. Tübingen: J. C. B. Mohr (Paul Siebeck), 1994.

Among Wagener's conclusions: for the Pastorals, the church is the "house of God," with its own proper male head of the family (along civil lines); wealth meant power, even for women; hence the letter's injunctions against ostentatious dress are a male power-play to keep women subordinate in the church. On the positive side, the Pastorals exalt marriage and family at the expense of a misunderstood encratism.

Walsh, J.P.M. *The Mighty From Their Throne: Power in the Biblical Tradition.* Overtures to Biblical Theology. Philadelphia: Fortress Press, 1987.

Yoder, John Howard. *The Politics of Jesus.* 2nd Ed. Grand Rapids: Eerdmans, 1972, 1994.

In Portuguese: *A politica de Jesus.* Serie Estudos Biblicos. Sao Leopoldo: Ed. Sinodal, 1988.

Author argues that Jesus did teach a specific Christian ethics of non-violence, and that the New Testament is directly normative in this respect for contemporary Christians.

Yoder is a well-known ethicist in the Mennonite tradition who teaches at the University of Notre Dame.

****

Sexual Ethics and/or Gender Issues

General and/or Miscellaneous Sexual Ethics

Barton, Stephen C. "Is the Bible Good News for Human Sexuality? Reflections on Method in Biblical Interpretation." *Theology & Sexuality* 1 (1994): 42-54.

Beckwith, Francis J. "Arguments from Theology and the Bible." Chapter 8 in Id. *Politically Correct Death: Answering the Arguments for Abortion Rights,* 137-150. Grand Rapids: Baker Book House, 1993.

Beckwith's general thesis is that the pro-life position often has not responded adequately to the pro-choice position, and thus Beckwith offers what he feels are stronger arguments. In this chapter he considers some of the illustrative biblical texts usually employed in arguing against abortion.

Beckwith teaches philosophy at the University of Nevada.

Bosgra, Tj. *Abortion, the Bible and the Church.* Honolulu: Right to Life Educational Foundation, 1981.

A survey of 150 denominational views.

Burthchaell, James Tunstead, C.S.C. *Philemon's Problem: The Daily Dilemma of the Christian.* Chicago: ACTA [Foundation for Adult Catechetical Teaching Aids], 1973.

Using the *Letter to Philemon* as a touchstone for an approach to contemporary moral issues Burthchaell discusses peace and violence, sex and ritual, prayer and penance--in an attempt to fashion a Christian vision of the world. Written in a popular, rather than academic style.

Cahill, Lisa Sowle. "Biblical Sources of Ethics." In *Women and Sexuality,* 15-44. New York: Paulist Press, 1992.

Part of the 1992 Madeleva Lecture in Spirituality.

Cahill is a Roman Catholic and did her doctoral studies at the University of Chicago under the direction of James M. Gustafson. She is Professor of Theological Ethics at Boston College, and past President of both the Catholic Theological Society of America (CTSA) and the Society of Christian Ethics (SCE).

_____. "Is Catholic Ethics Biblical? The Example of Sex and Gender." *Warren Lecture Series in Catholic Studies* 20 (1992).

Using the example of sexual ethics, Cahill gives an overview of the traditional approaches of Roman Catholic moral theology, contrasts these with various Protestant usages of Scripture in ethics, and then concludes by outlining a revised approach to sexuality and gender issues which would be more sensitive to the creative use of the Bible.

Lecture presented at the University of Tulsa on 15 March 1992.

_____. "New Testament Perspectives on Community, Sex, and the Sexes." Ch. 4 in *Between the Sexes: Foundations for a Christian Ethics of Sexuality*, 59-82. New York: Paulist Press; and Philadelphia: Fortress Press, 1985.

_____. *Sex, Gender, and Christian Ethics.* Cambridge: Cambridge University Press, 1996.

The author addresses the ethics of sexuality, marriage, parenthood and family from a feminist standpoint. She wants to reaffirm the traditional unity of sex, love and parenthood as a guiding framework, not as an absolute norm. She also develops the significance of New Testament models of community and of moral formation, to argue that the human values associated with sex and family should be embodied in a context of concern for society's poor and marginalized.

Reviewed by Christine Gudorf in *Theological Studies* 58 (1997): 385-387

_____. "Sexual Ethics: A Feminist Biblical Perspective." *Interpretation* 49 (1995): 5-16.

Collins, Raymond F. "The Bible and Sexuality." Part Four, chs 7-8, in *Christian Morality: Biblical Foundations*, 151-207. Notre Dame: University of Notre Dame Press, 1986.

Chapter 7: "Human Sexuality in the Jewish Scriptures," pp. 151-182. Chapter 8: "Human Sexuality in the Christian Scriptures," pp. 183-207.

After many years teaching New Testament at Louvain, Collins is now Dean of the Catholic University of America.

Cornes, Andrew. *Divorce and Remarriage. Biblical Principles and Pastoral Practice.* Grand Rapids MI: Eerdmans, 1993.

Corley, Kathleen E. *Private Women, Public Meals: Social Conflict in the Synoptic Tradition.* Peabody MA: Hendrickson, 1993.

Examines how women's various roles, and their social changes, in the ancient Greco-Roman world are portrayed in the gospel accounts which deal with women.

Countryman, L. William. *Dirt, Greed and Sex: Sexual Ethics in the New Testament and Their Implications for Today.* Philadelphia: Fortress Press, 1988.

Countryman teaches New Testament at the Church Divinity School of the Pacific in Berkeley, California.

_____. "New Testament Sexual Ethics and Today's World." In *Sexuality and the Sacred: Sources for Theological Reflection,* 28-53. Edited by James B. Nelson and Sandra P. Longfellow. Louisville: Westminster/John Knox Press, 1994.

Crouzel, Henri, S.J. "Le sens de `porneia' dans les incises mathéennes." *Nouvelle Revue Théologique* 110 (1988): 903-910.

Daly, Robert J., S.J., et. al. "Human Sexuality and Christian Biblical Revelation." In *Christian Biblical Ethics: From Biblical Revelation to Contemporary Christian Praxis: Method and Content,* 278-285. New York: Paulist Press, 1984.

Dautzenberg, Gerhard. "*Pheugete ten porneian* (1 Kor 6, 18). Eine Fallstudie zur paulinischen Sexualethik in ihrem Verhältnis zur Sexualethik des Frühjudentums." In *Neues Testament und Ethik. Für Rudolf Schnackenburg,* 271-298. Herausgegeben von Helmut Merklein. Freiburg: Herder, 1989.

Deming, Will. *Paul on Marriage and Celibacy. The Hellenistic Backgrounds of 1 Corinthians 7.* Cambridge (UK): Cambridge University Press, 1995.

Furger, Franz, Hrsg. *Biblische Ethik: Fragen und Antworten.* Freiburg Schweiz: Kanisius Verlag, 1974.

Short booklet, with contributions from Furger, Fredrich Beutter, Eugen Ruckstuhl and Hermann-Josef Venetz. Topics include: Freiheit, Gebote, Verschiedene Wertung biblischer Forderungen, Fordert Jesus die Revolution?, Sklaven, Arme, Ehelosigkeit, Unkeuschheit, Ehebruch, and Onanie.

Furnish, Victor Paul. *The Moral Teaching of Paul: Selected Issues,* 2nd ed. Nashville: Abingdon, 1985.

Treats sexual questions, such as marriage and divorce, homosexuality, as well as other issues, such as the place of women in the Church, and the relationship between Christians and governing authorities.

_____. *Theology and Ethics in Paul: Selected Issues.* Nashville: Abingdon, 1978.

An earlier version of Furnish's 1985 book.

Gilbert, Maurice, S.J. "La procréation: ce qu'en sait le Livre de la Sagesse." *Nouvelle Revue Théologique* (1989): 824-841.

Biblical texts examined from the Book of Wisdom consider the human embryo as a person, especially in view of the relation with God, seen as a vivifying spirit, who gives life to the embryo.

Gilbert is on the faculty and former rector of the Pontifical Biblical Institute in Rome.

_____. "'Une seule chair' (Gn 2,24)." *Nouvelle revue théologique* 100 (1978): 66-89.

Grenz, Stanley. *Sexual Ethics: A Biblical Perspective.* Dallas: Word Pub., 1990.

Hays, Richard B. "Abortion." Chapter 18 in Idem. *The Moral Vision of the New Testament: Community, Cross, New Creation. A Contemporary Introduction to New Testament Ethics*, 444-461. San Francisco: Harper San Francisco, 1996.

Hays treats abortion as a "pragmatic" task (and test) of his proposed approach to New Testament ethics. He proposes three central organizing metaphors from the New Testament, Community, Cross, and New Creation, as a basic methodological approach to utilizing the biblical material in Christian ethics. Hays also names and treats four principal "tasks" of using the Bible in ethics: the descriptive task (what is being said); the synthetic task (how does this or that passage, text, etc., fit within the larger biblical text in a coherent manner); the hermeneutical task of interpreting the biblical texts for ethics, and finally the "pragmatic" task of "living under the Word" (applying the biblical texts to concrete moral issues). Hays treats several other such issues in individual chapters: non-violence, divorce and remarriage, homosexuality, anti-Judaism and ethnic conflict.

Hays is professor of New Testament at Duke University Divinity School, and taught for a number of years previously at Yale.

Humbert, Alphonse, C.SS.R. "Les péchés de sexualité dans le Nouveau Testament." *Studia Moralia* 8 (1970): 149-183.

Jensen, Joseph, O.S.B. "Human Sexuality in the Scriptures." In *Human Sexuality and Personhood: Proceedings of the Workshop for the Hierarchies of the United States and Canada Sponsored by the Pope John Center through a Grant from the Knights of Columbus*, 15-35. Rev. ed. St. Louis: Pope John Center, 1981, 1990.

Johnson, James R. "Toward a Biblical Approach to Masturbation." *Journal of Psychology and Theology* 10 (Summer 1982): 137-146.

Within the context of evangelical theology the author evaluates six traditional objections to masturbation based on biblical texts. The author concludes that the biblical texts provide limiting principles but do not support a universal condemnation of the practice.

Juárez, Miguel A. Martín, O.S.A. "La Sexualidad. Aporte de los escritos sapiensiales." *Biblia y Fe* 18 (1992): 51-66.

One of several articles under this number's general theme of "La Sexualidad: *Aproximacion Biblica.*"

Keeling, Michael. *The Foundations of Christian Ethics.* Edinburgh: T. & T. Clark, 1990.

Concentrating on three themes: sexuality, property, and political power, Keeling examines the foundations of Christian ethics in the Bible and their embodiment in the Church. Follows a chronological structure and considers the influence of liberation theology on perceptions of social justice.

Kirchhoff, R. *Die Sünde gegen den eigenen Leib. Studien zu "porne" und "porneia" in 1 Kor 6, 12-20 und dem sozio-kulturellen Kontext der paulinischen Adressaten.* Göttingen: Vandenhoeck & Ruprecht, 1994.

Koester, Craig R. "The Bible and Sexual Boundaries." *Lutheran Quarterly* 7 (1993): 375-390.

Kurz, William S., S.J. "Genesis and Abortion: An Exegetical Test of a Biblical Warrant in Ethics." *Theological Studies* 47 (1986): 668-680.

Kurz is professor of New Testament at Marquette University in Milwaukee, Wisconsin.

Lang, B. "'Du sollst nicht der Frau eines anderen verlangen'. *Eine neue Deutung des 9. und 10. Gebots.*" *Zeitschrift für die Alttestamentliche Wissenschaft* 93 (1981): 216-224.

Lindemann, Andreas. "Do Not Let a Woman Destroy the Unborn Babe in Her Belly: Abortion in Ancient Judaism and Christianity." *Studia Theologica* 49 (1995): 253-271.

Mattioli, Anselmo. *Le realtà sessuali nella Bibbia. Storia e dottrina.* Casale Monferrato: Ed. Piemme, 1987.

McClelland, William Robert. *Worldly Spirituality: Biblical Reflections on Money, Politics, and Sex.* St. Louis: CBP Press, 1990.

Reviewed by Dwight E. Stevenson in *Mid-Stream* 29 (1990): 444-446.

McKeating, H. "Sanctions against Adultery in Ancient Israelite with some Reflections on Methodology in the Study of Old Testament Ethics." *Journal for the Study of the Old Testament* 11 (1979): 57-72.

Neidhart, W. "Das paulinische Verständnis der Liebe und die Sexualität." *Theologische Zeitschrift* 40 (1984): 245-250.

Newton, Michael. *The Concept of Purity at Qumran and in the Letters of Paul.* Society for New Testament Monograph Series, 53. Cambridge: Cambridge University Press, 1985.

Contradicts the view that traditional Jewish attitudes toward purity and impurity have no place in Christianity. By using a concept of purity also found in the Qumranic literature and Pharisaic Judaism, Paul was able to elucidate his views on the church, the divine presence, the basis of ethical behavior, and the significance of the death of Jesus.

Nobuko, Morimura. "The Story of Tamar: A Feminist Interpretation of Genesis 38." *The Japan Christian Review* 59 (1993): 55-68.

One of several articles dealing with feminist issues in Japan.

Parra, Constantino Quelle. "La Sexualidad. Aporte de la tradución sinóptica." *Biblia y Fe* 18 (1992): 92-113.

One of several articles under this number's general theme of "La Sexualidad: *Aproximacion Biblica.*"

Phipps, William E. "Is Paul's Attitude toward Sexual Relations Contained in 1 Cor 7:1?" *New Testament Studies* 28 (1982): 125-131.

Price, R.M. "The Distinctiveness of Early Christian Sexual Ethics." *Heythrop Journal* 31 (1990): 257-276.

> Paul's supposedly negative and strict sexual ethics arose out of his desire to preserve the purity of the whole Christian community by means of the purity of its individual members.

Rae, Scott B. *Brave New Families: Biblical Ethics and Reproductive Technologies.* Grand Rapids, MI: Baker Book House, 1996.

Raurell, F. "El plaer erotic en el Càntic dels Càntics." *Revista Catalana de Teología* 6 (1981): 257-298.

Russell, K.C. "The Embarrassing Verse in First Corinthians." *The Bible Today* (September 1980): 338-341.

> Deals with masturbation.

Salas, Antonio, O.S.A. "La Sexualidad. Aporte del «corpus» paulino." *Biblia y Fe* 18 (1992): 67-91.

> One of several articles under this number's general theme of "La Sexualidad: *Aproximacion Biblica.*"

Santa Maria, Miguel Saenz de. "La Sexualidad. Aporte del cuarto evangelico." *Biblia y Fe* 18 (1992): 114-135.

> One of several articles under this number's general theme of "La Sexualidad: *Aproximacion Biblica.*"

Seitz, Christopher R. "Human Sexuality: Viewed from the Bible's Understanding of the Human Condition." *Theology Today* 52 (1995): 236-246.

> Seitz is Professor of Old Testament at Yale Divinity School.

Six, Jean-François. *Le chant de l'amour. Eros dans la Bible.* Paris: Desclée De Brouwer/Flammarion, 1995.

_____. *Le chant de l'amour. Eros dans la Bible.* Paris: Desclée De Brouwer/Flammarion, 1995.

Sleeper, C. Freeman. *The Bible and the Moral Life.* Louisville: Westminster/John Knox Press, 1992.

Looks at how various churches use the Bible to address contemporary ethical issues, particularly nuclear war and abortion, and also considers the issue of biblical authority in terms of four major styles of moral reflection, i.e., law, prophecy, apocalypse, and wisdom. The book is designed for adult study groups and contains practical exercises.

Sleeper is Professor of Religion at Roanoke College in Salem, Virginia.

Spohn, William C., S.J. "St.Paul on Apostolic Celibacy and the Body of Christ." *Studies in the Spirituality of the Jesuits* 17 (January 1985).

Written while Spohn was a Roman Catholic priest in the Society of Jesus.

Spohn studied under James Gustafson at the University of Chicago, taught moral theology at the Jesuit School of Theology-Berkeley for many years, and currently teaches Christian ethics at the University of Santa Clara.

Sprinkle, Joe M. "The Interpretation of Exodus 21:22-25 (*lex talionis*) and Abortion." *Westminster Theological Journal* 55 (1993): 233-253.

The Theology Forum Adult Sunday School Class, The First Baptist Church, Redlands, California. "The Bible and Human Sexuality." *American Baptist Quarterly* 12 (1993): 300-322.

Report of an adult Baptist study group's year-long discussion of sexuality undertaken in response to the 1991 American Baptist Church's resolution on "Human Sexuality." This discussion was initially centered on Bruce J. Malina's *The New Testament World: Insights from Cultural Anthropology* (Atlanta: John Knox Press, 1981), and L. William Countryman's *Dirt, Greed and Sex: Sexual Ethics in the New Testament and Their Implications for*

Today, (Philadelphia: Fortress Press, 1988). See responses by several individuals which are published in the same issue.

Weber, Joseph C. "Human sexuality: the biblical witness." *Religion in Life* 49 (1980): 336-348.

Westbrook, Raymond. "Adultery in Ancient Near Eastern Law." *Revue Biblique* 97 (1990): 542-580.

Wilch, John R. "The Use and Misuse of Scripture in Ethics." *Consensus* 11 (July 1985): 15-31.

Abstract: Christian ethics is founded upon three major hermeneutical principles: *sola scriptura*, the distinction between law and Gospel, and *solus Christus*. Scripture has been misused, e.g., in respect to: not treating a human fetus as a human being and its father not assuming his parental responsibility, men and women not accepting the roles assigned them by God in this world, the church engaging in politics or denying her principles because of political expediency, and building Christian ethics upon so-called inherent human rights. Providing everything Christians need physically and spiritually, God as Creator and Saviour calls them to responsibility and sacrificial service.

Gender Issues

Bird, Phyliss A. "'Male and Female He Created Them': Gen. 1:27b in the Context of the Priestly Account of Creation." *Harvard Theological Review* 74 (1981): 129-159.

Cahill, Lisa Sowle. "Is Catholic Ethics Biblical? The Example of Sex and Gender." *Warren Lecture Series in Catholic Studies* 20 (1992).

Using the example of sexual ethics, Cahill gives an overview of the traditional approaches of Roman Catholic moral theology, contrasts these with various Protestant usages of Scripture in ethics, and then concludes by outlining a revised approach to sexuality and gender issues which would be more sensitive to the creative use of the Bible.

Lecture presented at the University of Tulsa on 15 March 1992.

Cahill is a Roman Catholic and did her doctoral studies at the University of Chicago under the direction of James M. Gustafson. She is Professor of Theological Ethics at Boston College, and past President of both the Catholic Theological Society of America (CTSA) and the Society of Christian Ethics (SCE).

_____. "'Male and Female': Sexual Differentiation in Genesis." Chapter 3 in Idem. *Between the Sexes: Foundations for a Christian Ethics of Sexuality.* New York: Paulist Press; and Philadelphia: Fortress Press, 1985.

_____. "New Testament Perspectives on Community, Sex, and the Sexes." Ch. 4 in *Between the Sexes: Foundations for a Christian Ethics of Sexuality*, 59-82. New York: Paulist Press; and Philadelphia: Fortress Press, 1985.

_____. *Sex, Gender, and Christian Ethics.* Cambridge: Cambridge University Press, 1996.

The author addresses the ethics of sexuality, marriage, parenthood and family from a feminist standpoint. She wants to reaffirm the traditional unity of sex, love and parenthood as a guiding framework, not as an absolute norm. She also develops the significance of New Testament models of community and of moral formation, to argue that the human values associated with sex and family should be embodied in a context of concern for society's poor and marginalized.

Reviewed by Christine Gudorf in *Theological Studies* 58 (1997): 385-387

_____. "Sexual Ethics: A Feminist Biblical Perspective." *Interpretation* 49 (1995): 5-16.

Cheney, Emily. *She Can Read: Feminist Reading Strategies for Biblical Narrative.* Valley Forge PA: Trinity Press, 1996.

Cheney develops three "reading strategies" specifically for women whose church traditions would expect them to base sermons on biblical texts, and yet who wish their sermons to reflect a feminist consciousness.

Douglass, Jane Dempsey, and Kay, James F., eds. *Women, Gender, and Christian Community*. Louisville: Westminster/John Knox Press, 1997.

Raises the question, in light of contemporary gender issues in the church, of whether the Bible speaks good news to women, or only the bad news of subjection to men. Essays are by the members of the Princeton Theological Seminary faculty.

Fewell, Danna Nolan, and David M. Gunn. *Gender, Power & Promise*. Nashville, TN: Abingdon Press, 1993.

The authors explore ways in which the Bible's "first story" (Genesis through Kings) presents images of gender, and how this story, with its embedded legal codes, affects our understanding of the theological motifs of power and promise. They contend that reading Scripture is each time an exercise of power: interpretation is always invested in ideology, whether spoken or unspoken. By according special attention to the construction and depiction of character, the authors examine and seek to understand these ideologies. They demonstrate that the reader's choice of a character's perspective as a basis for his or her reading and understanding of the text is a crucial interpretive decision.

Fiorenza, Elisabeth Schüssler. *Bread Not Stone*. Boston: Beacon Press, 1984.

Briefly discussed by Lisa Sowle Cahill in her article "The New Testament and Ethics: Communities of Social Change," *Interpretation* 44 (1990): 383-395. Reviewed by Pheme Perkins in *Theology Today* 42 (1986): 368.

____. *But She Said: Feminist Practices of Biblical Interpretation*. Boston: Beacon Press, 1993.

Reviewed by Kristine A. Culp in *Theology Today* 50 (1994): 619.

294

_____. "Commitment and Critical Inquiry." *Harvard Theological Review* 82 (1989): 1-11.

_____. "The Ethics of Decentering Biblical Scholarship." *Journal of Biblical Literature* 107 (1988): 3-17.

_____. *In Memory of Her: A Feminist Theological Reconstruction of Christian Origins*. New York: Crossroad, 1983.

French translation: *En Mémoire d'Elle: Essai de Reconstruction des origenes chrétiennes selon la théologie féministe*. Cogitatio Fidei, 136. Traduit de l'americain par Macelline Brun. Paris: Editions du Cerf, 1986.

Italian translation: *In memoria di lei: Una recostruzione femminista delle origini cristiane*. Edizione italiana a cura di M. Corsani Comba. Torino: Claudiana, 1990.

Reviewed by Mary Pellauer in *Theology Today* 45 (1989): 472.

Also critically discussed by Giuseppe Segalla in his essay "L'Ermeneutica biblica femminista di E. Schüssler Fiorenza," *Studia Patavina* 37 (1990): 585-599

_____. "Toward a Feminist Biblical Hermeneutics: Biblical Interpretation and Liberation Theology." In Charles E. Curran and Richard A. McCormick, S.J., eds., *Readings in Moral Theology No. 4: The Use of Scripture in Moral Theology*, 354-382. New York: Paulist Press, 1984.

Fuchs, Eric. "De la soumission des femmes. Une lecture d'Ephésiens 5, 21-33." *Le Supplément* 161 (1987): 73-81.

Furnish, Victor Paul. "Women in the Church." Chapter 4 in Idem. *The Moral Teaching of Paul: Selected Issues*, 83-114. 2nd ed. Nashville: Abingdon, 1985.

Gaventa, Beverly Roberts. "Mother's Milk and Ministry in 1 Corinthians 3." Part I, Chapter 7 in *Theology and Ethics in Paul and His Interpreters: Essays in Honor of Victor Paul Furnish*, 101-113. Ed. Eugene H. Lovering, Jr. and Jerry L. Sumney. Nashville: Abingdon Press, 1996.

Gerstenberger, Erhard S. and Schrage, Wolfgang. *Woman and Man*. Nashville: Abingdon Press, 1981.

Groothuis, Rebecca Merrill. *Good News for Women: A Biblical Picture of Gender Equality*. Grand Rapids MI: Baker Book House, 1997.

The author looks at the overall outline of biblical teaching on relationships between men and women which in turn provides the foundation for examining selected biblical passages specifically relating to gender issues.

Hollyday, Joyce. *Clothed with the Sun: Biblical Women, Social Justice and Us*. Louisville, KY: Westminster John Knox Press, 1994.

Hurley, James B. *Man and Woman in Biblical Perspective*. Grand Rapids: Zondervan/Academie Books,1981.

Jacobs-Malina, Diane. "Gender, Power, and Jesus' Identity in the Gospels." *Biblical Theology Bulletin* 24 (1994): 158-166.

Keener, Craig S. *Paul, Women and Wives: Marriage and Women's Ministry in the Letters of Paul*. Peabody MA: Hendrickson, 1991.

Kroeger, Catherine, and James R. Beck, eds. *Women, Abuse, and the Bible: How Scripture Can Be Used to Hurt or to Heal*. Grand Rapids, MI: Baker Book House, 1996.

A 1994 conference on "Women, Abuse, and the Bible" looked for answers, and fifteen select papers appear in this collection. This book analyzes statistics and tells personal stories, showing how Bible concepts can be misused to feed tendencies toward control and violence.

McGuire, Anne. "Equality and Subordination in Christ: Displacing the Powers of the Household Code in Colossians." In *Religion and Economic Ethics*, 65-86. The Annual Publication of the College Theology Society, 31 (1985). Lanham: University Press of America, 1990.

McGuire teaches New Testament at Haverford College.

Ramey-Mollenkott, Virginia. *Women, Men and the Bible*. Nashville: Abingdon Press, 1977.

Reimer, Ivoni Richter. *Women in the Acts of the Apostles: A Feminist Liberation Perspective*. Minneapolis: Fortress Press, 1995.

Considers the women portrayed in the Book of Acts, such as Sapphira (marriage property issue), Lydia (dye seller), Candace (queen of Ethiopia), Tabitha (disciple), Priscilla (co-apostle with her husband, Aquila), and others.

Rooke, Margaret. "Beyond the Bible." *Faith and Freedom* 41 (1988): 73-82.

Examines sexual ethics in biblical times and the double-standards that existed against women. Simple recourse to biblical injunctions will not solve the problems connected with sexual ethics, and in this sense the Christian community must go "beyond the Bible" for its norms and laws.

Scanzoni, Letha, and Hardesty, Nancy A. *All We're Meant to Be: Biblical Feminism for Today*. Nashville: Abingdon Press, 1986; 3rd, rev. ed. Grand Rapids: W.B. Eerdmans, 1992.

Schenker, A. "Der Monotheismus im ersten Gebot, die Stellung der Frau im Sabbatgebot und zwei andere Sachfragen zum Dekalog." *Freiburger Zeitschrift für Philosophie und Theologie* 32 (1985): 323-341.

Schottroff, Luise. *Let the Oppressed Go Free: Feminist Perspectives on the New Testament*. Translated by Annemarie S. Kidder. Louisville: Westminster/John Knox Press, 1993.

These exegetical studies are contributions to feminist liberation theology. They treat Freedom and Liberation According to Biblical Evidence; How Justified Is the Feminist Critique of Paul?; "Leaders of the Faith" or "Just Some Pious Women-folk"?; Women as Disciples of Jesus; Lydia: A New Quality of Power; The Woman Who Loved Much and the Pharisee Simon; The Virgin Birth; Mary Magdalene and the Women at Jesus' Tomb.

Schottroff teaches New Testament at the University of Kassel in Germany.

Schüssler Fiorenza, Elisabeth. *See* Fiorenza, Elizabeth Schüssler.

Selvidge, Marla J. *Woman, Violence, and the Bible.* Lewiston NY: Mellen Press, 1996.

This book is a collection of Biblical investigations which focus on the role of violence and women as they are represented in Genesis, the Gospels, the Acts of the Apostles, and the Book of Revelation. It explores new interpretations of Biblical violence as well as the roles women played in leadership in the Gospels.

Stendahl, Krister. *The Bible and the Role of Women: A Case Study in Hermeneutics.* Philadelphia: Fortress Press, 1966.

Streete, Gail P. Corrington. *The Strange Woman: Power and Sex in the Bible.* Louisville: Westminster/John Knox Press, 1997.

Considers women who engaged in prostitution, adultery, and other "sexual crimes" as creating independence for themselves and producing options not open generally to women who were limited by the political and religious laws of ancient Israel and early Christianity. The actions of these women subverted the social system and led to punishment for some, but power for others.

The author is Associate Professor of Religious Studies at Rhodes College.

Swartley, Willard M. *Slavery, Sabbath, War and Women: Case Issues in Biblical Interpretation.* Scottdale PA: Herald Press, 1983.

Tetlow, Elisabeth M. *Women and Ministry in the New Testament.* New York: Paulist Press, 1980.

Trible, Phyllis. *God and the Rhetoric of Sexuality.* Philadelphia: Fortress Press, 1978.

298

_____. *Texts of Terror: Literary-Feminist Readings of Biblical Narratives*. Overtures to Biblical Theology. Philadelphia: Fortress Press, 1984.

Wagener, Ulrike. *Die Ordnung des "Hauses Gottes": Der Ort von Frauen in der Ekklesiologie und Ethik der Pastoralbriefe*. Wissenschaftliche Untersuchungen zum Neuen Testament, 2.65. Tübingen: J. C. B. Mohr (Paul Siebeck), 1994.

Among Wagener's conclusions: for the Pastorals, the church is the "house of God," with its own proper male head of the family (along civil lines); wealth meant power, even for women; hence the letter's injunctions against ostentatious dress are a male power-play to keep women subordinate in the church. On the positive side, the Pastorals exalt marriage and family at the expense of a misunderstood encratism.

Weems, Renita J. *Battered Love: Marriage, Sex, and Violence in the Hebrew Prophets*. Minneapolis: Fortress Press, 1995.

Investigates ways in which the Hebrew Prophets' descriptions of divine love, compassion, and commitment to the covenant, as well as the prophetic discourse, rhetoric and sexual metaphors used, became linked to violence against women, such as battery, infidelity, rape and mutilation.

Weems teaches Hebrew Bible at Vanderbilt Divinity School.

Wilson, Kenneth T. "Should Women Wear Headcoverings?" *Bibliotheca Sacra* 148 (1991): 442-462.

Wilson offers an extended exegesis of 1 Cor 11:2-16, and concludes that the theological point made by Paul is that the female/male distinction, ordained by God, is what must be preserved. The actual choice of the appropriate cultural symbol (e.g. headcoverings) to show such distinction may well change from epoch to epoch, or culture to culture.

Wilson is Pastor-Teacher of the Anchorage Bible Fellowship.

Homosexuality

Adam, A.K.M. "Disciples Together, Constantly." In *Homosexuality and Christian Community*, 123-132. Edited by Choon-Leong Seow. Louisville: Westminister/John Knox Press, 1996.

Discusses Christian sexual ethics as being based on a theological understanding of the relationships between God and Jesus, Israel, and the Church. One of a series of essays in Part III, "How Do We Live Faithfully?". The other two sections are Part I, "What Do the Scriptures Say?" and Part II, "How Do the Scriptures Inform Our Theological Reflection?". All the contributors are members of the Princeton Theological Faculty.

Adam is Asst. Professor of New Testament at Princeton Theological Seminary and an ordained Episcopal priest.

Bahnsen, Greg L. *Homosexuality: A Biblical View*. Grand Rapids: Baker Book House, 1978.

Bahnsen sees the homosexual orientation as intrinsically sinful, but holds that homosexuals themselves are not beyond the power of God's transforming love.

Bahnsen teaches apologetics and ethics at the Reformed Theological Seminary in Jackson, Mississippi.

Bartlett, David L. "A Biblical Perspective on Homosexuality." In *Homosexuality and the Christian Faith*, 23-40. Edited by H.L. Twiss. Valley Forge: Judson Press, 1978.

Bartow, Charles L. "Speaking the Text and Preaching the Gospel." In *Homosexuality and Christian Community*, 86-98. Edited by Choon-Leong Seow. Louisville: Westminister/John Knox Press, 1996.

Looks at how the Bible might be read in a congregation and uses Romans 1:18-32 as an illustrative case. One of a series of essays in Part II, "How Do the Scriptures Inform Our Theological Reflection?". The other two sections are Part I, "What Do the Scriptures Say?" and Part III, "How Do We Live

Faithfully?". All the contributors are members of the Princeton Theological Faculty.

Bartow is the Carl and Helen Egner Professor of Speech Communication in Ministry at Princeton Theological Seminary and an ordained minister of the Presbyterian Church.

Blount, Brian K. "Reading and Understanding the New Testament on Homosexuality." In *Homosexuality and Christian Community*, 28-38. Edited by Choon-Leong Seow. Louisville: Westminister/John Knox Press, 1996.

Examines the Pauline references to homoerotic activity, and argues that these pronouncements are socially and historically conditioned, and therefore should be distinguished from Paul's faith pronouncements. One of a series of essays in Part I, "What Do the Scriptures Say?". The other two sections are Part II, "How Do the Scriptures Inform Our Theological Reflection?" and Part III, "How Do We Live Faithfully?". All the contributors are members of the Princeton Theological Faculty.

Blount is Asst. Professor of New Testament at Princeton Theological Seminary and an ordained minister of the Presbyterian Church.

Boswell, John. *Christianity, Social Tolerance, and Homosexuality: Gay People in Western Europe from the Beginning of the Christian Era to the Fourteenth Century*. Chicago: University of Chicago Press, 1980.

See especially Chapter 4, "The Scriptures," pp. 91-117, is a treatment of homosexuality in the Bible. See also the following texts: Lynne C. Boughton, "Biblical Texts and Homosexuality: A Response to John Boswell," *Irish Theological Quarterly* 58 (1992): 141-153, and a response by Leland J. White, "Biblical Texts and Contemporary Gay People: A Response to Boswell and Boughton," *Irish Theological Quarterly* 59 (1993): 286-301. See also Richard B. Hays, "Relations Natural and Unnatural: A Response to John Boswell's Exegesis of Romans 1," *Journal of Religious Ethics* 14 (1986): 184-215. See also Donald J. Wold's *Out of Order: Homosexuality in the Bible and the Ancient Near East* (Grand Rapids: Baker Books, 1997).

Boughton, Lynne C. "Biblical Texts and Homosexuality: A Response to John Boswell." *Irish Theological Quarterly* 58 (1992): 141-153.

See reply to this article by Leland J. White, "Biblical Texts and Contemporary Gay People: A Response to Boswell and Boughton." *Irish Theological Quarterly* 59 (1993): 286-301. For Boswell's own position see his Chapter 4, "The Scriptures," of John Boswell's *Christianity, Social Tolerance, and Homosexuality: Gay People in Western Europe from the Beginning of the Christian Era to the Fourteenth Century*, (Chicago: University of Chicago Press, 1980): 91-117, as well as for a listing of other works which deal with Boswell's position.

Brawley, Robert L., ed. *Biblical Ethics and Homosexuality: Listening to Scripture*. Louisville, KY: Westminster John Knox Press, 1996.

Nine papers are compiled here from a 1995 Consultation on Biblical Ethics and Human Sexuality, which brought primarily Presbyterian biblical scholars together to discuss the relevance of the Bible to contemporary reflection on sexual ethics. Most of the papers are exegetical or descriptively ethical in focus. Authors employ historical, sociological, philological, and literary methods of biblical interpretation to illuminate the moral worlds of biblical authors.

Dailey, Timothy J. "The Use of Scripture in Normative Christian Ethics: The Limit Case of Homosexuality as Viewed in the Contemporary Debate (1955-1984)." PhD Dissertation, Marquette University, 1985.

Davies, Margaret. "New Testament Ethics and Ours: Homosexuality and Sexuality in Romans 1:26-27." *Biblical Interpretation* 3 (1995): 315-31.

The article contains one major argument and one minor argument. The major argument is that Paul's strictures against homosexual practice were taken over from Leviticus and expressed concern of Hellenistic Judaism. The Pauline subversion of the web of relations which make sense of the exclusion of homosexual practice within the jewish tradition, however, leaves the Pauline strictures without warrant. The minor argument is that we in the twentieth century should subvert the Pauline assumption of difference between males and females, again adopted from the Jewish tradition, and that we should recognize a continuum and variety. Such a subversion would allow us to see ourselves primarily as people rather than primarily as either men or women.

302

Duff, Nancy J. "How to Discuss Moral Issues Surrounding Homosexuality When You Know Your Are Right." In *Homosexuality and Christian Community*, 144-159. Edited by Choon-Leong Seow. Louisville: Westminister/John Knox Press, 1996.

Using the 1993 "Princeton Declaration" on the non-ordination of practicing homosexuals as her illustrative text, Duff argues that one must consider contrary arguments to one's moral position, even when one is absolutely convinced of the correctness of one's moral position. One of a series of essays in Part III, "How Do We Live Faithfully?". The other two sections are Part I, "What Do the Scriptures Say?" and Part II, "How Do the Scriptures Inform Our Theological Reflection?". All the contributors are members of the Princeton Theological Faculty.

Duff is Associate Profess or New Testament at Princeton Theological Seminary and an ordained minister of the Presbyterian Church.

Dresner, Samuel H. "Homosexuality and the Order of Creation." *Judaism* 40 (1991): 309-321.

Condemns homosexuality as a violation of the order of creation and marshalls biblical evidence for this position.

Field, David. *Omosessualità*. Collana di etica biblica, 1. Roma: Edizioni Gruppi Biblici Universitari.

Furnish, Victor Paul. "The Bible and Homosexuality: Reading the Texts in Context." In *Homosexuality in the Church: Both Sides of the Debate*, 18-35. Edited by Jeffrey S. Siker. Louisville: Westminster/John Knox Press, 1994.

_____. "Homosexuality." Chapter 3 in Idem. *The Moral Teaching of Paul: Selected Issues*, 52-82. 2nd ed. Nashville: Abingdon, 1985.

Gillespie, Thomas W. "The Pastoral Dilemma." In *Homosexuality and Christian Community*, 113-122. Edited by Choon-Leong Seow. Louisville: Westminister/John Knox Press, 1996.

Considers the dilemma between dealing with homosexual persons and maintaining fidelity the gospel which the pastor faces in dealing with homosexuality. One of a series of essays in Part III, "How Do We Live Faithfully?". The other two sections are Part I, "What Do the Scriptures Say?" and Part II, "How Do the Scriptures Inform Our Theological Reflection?". All the contributors are members of the Princeton Theological Faculty.

Gillespie is President and Professor of New Testament at Princeton Theological Seminary and an ordained minister of the Presbyterian Church.

Hays, Richard B. "Awaiting the Redemption of Our Bodies: The Witness of Scripture Concerning Homosexuality." In *Homosexuality in the Church: Both Sides of the Debate*, 3-17. Edited by Jeffrey S. Siker. Louisville: Westminster/John Knox Press, 1994.

Hays is professor of New Testament at Duke University Divinity School, and taught for a number of years previously at Yale.

_____. "Awaiting the redemption of our bodies: drawing on Scripture and tradition in the church debate on homosexuality." *Sojourners* 20 (July 1991): 17-21.

Discusses Romans 1:18-32.

_____. "Homosexuality." Chapter 16 in Idem. *The Moral Vision of the New Testament: Community, Cross, New Creation. A Contemporary Introduction to New Testament Ethics*, 379-407. San Francisco: Harper San Francisco, 1996.

Hays treats and condemns homosexual activity as a "pragmatic" task (and test) of his proposed approach to New Testament ethics. He proposes three central organizing metaphors from the New Testament, Community, Cross, and New Creation, as a basic methodological approach to utilizing the biblical material in Christian ethics. Hays also names and treats four principal "tasks" of using the Bible in ethics: the descriptive task (what is being said); the synthetic task (how does this or that passage, text, etc., fit within the larger biblical text in a coherent manner); the hermeneutical task of interpreting the biblical texts for ethics, and finally the "pragmatic" task of "living under the Word" (applying the biblical texts to concrete moral issues). Hays treats several other such issues in individual chapters: non-violence, divorce and remarriage, anti-Judaism and ethnic conflict, and abortion.

304

_____. "Relations Natural and Unnatural: A Response to John Boswell's Exegesis of Romans 1." *Journal of Religious Ethics* 14 (1986): 184-215.

See Chapter 4, "The Scriptures," of John Boswell's *Christianity, Social Tolerance, and Homosexuality: Gay People in Western Europe from the Beginning of the Christian Era to the Fourteenth Century,* (Chicago: University of Chicago Press, 1980): 91-117 for the treatment discussed in this article, as well as for a listing of other works which deal with Boswell's position..

Herring, Basil F. "Homosexuality." Chapter 7 in *Jewish Ethics and Halakhah for Our Time: Sources and Commentary, Vol. I,* 175-196. The Library of Jewish Law and Ethics, 11. New York: KTAV, 1984.

Horner, Tom. *Jonathan Loved David: Homosexuality in Biblical Times.* Philadelphia: Westminster Press, 1978.

Kay, James F. "Homosexuality--What Then Shall We Preachers Say?" In *Homosexuality and Christian Community,* 99-109. Edited by Choon-Leong Seow. Louisville: Westminister/John Knox Press, 1996.

Examines both traditionalist and reformist preachers on the subject of homosexuality. One of a series of essays in Part II, "How Do the Scriptures Inform Our Theological Reflection?". The other two sections are Part I, "What Do the Scriptures Say?" and Part III, "How Do We Live Faithfully?". All the contributors are members of the Princeton Theological Faculty.

Kay is Associate Profess or Homiletics and Liturgics at Princeton Theological Seminary and an ordained minister of the Presbyterian Church.

Kotva, Joseph J., Jr. "Scripture, Ethics, and the Local Church: Homosexuality as a Test Case." *Conrad Grebel Review* 7 (1989): 41-61.

As a rule the New Testament presents morality in terms of the Christians' new identity in God's eschatological act in Christ, and locates specific moral issues in the context of the local church community where moral discernment is to take place.

Kotva is pastor of the First Mennonite Church in Allentown, Pennsylvania.

Lance, H. Darell. "The Bible and Homosexuality." *American Baptist Quarterly* 8 (1989): 140-151.

> Reviews some of the major changes that have occurred in the understanding of some biblical texts traditionally used in reference to homosexuality, such as Gn 19; Jg 19; Lv 18-20; Dt 23:17-18; 1 Cor 6:9-11; Rm 1:26-27; and Jde 6-7. Raises hermeneutical questions which these texts present, and includes bibliography for further study.

Loader, J.A. *A Tale of Two Cities: Sodom and Gomorrah in the Old Testament, Early Jewish and Early Christian Traditions.* Contributions to Biblical Exegesis and Theology, 1. Kampen: J.H. Kok Publishing House, 1990.

> Details how the Sodom and Gomorrah account has been used in the Bible as well as in extra-biblical literature and traditions.

Long, Thomas G. "Living with the Bible." In *Homosexuality and Christian Community*, 64-73. Edited by Choon-Leong Seow. Louisville: Westminister/John Knox Press, 1996.

> Reflects on how the Bible might be read in ordinary congregations, and uses a story of an American family dealing with the death of their gay son. One of a series of essays in Part II, "How Do the Scriptures Inform Our Theological Reflection?". The other two sections are Part I, "What Do the Scriptures Say?" and Part III, "How Do We Live Faithfully?". All the contributors are members of the Princeton Theological Faculty.

> Long is the Francis Landey Patton Professor of Preaching and Worship at Princeton Theological Seminary and an ordained minister of the Presbyterian Church.

Malick, David E. "The Condemnation of Homosexuality in Romans 1:26-27." *Bibliotheca Sacra* 150 (1993): 327-340.

> Argues that the Pauline prohibition against homosexuality is both transcultural and transhistorical, and therefore holds for today. Homosexuality represents a reversal of God's created order according to Malick.

Martin, Dale B. "Heterosexism and the Interpretation of Romans 1:18-32." *Biblical Interpretation* 3 (1995): 332-55.

This article, concentrating on two articles by Richard Hays, critiques recent interpretation of Rom. 1:18-32. Modern interpreters, influenced more by particularly modern forms of heterosexism and its construction of homosexuality, desire, and "nature" than by a straightforward historical-critical reading of Paul's letter, portray Paul as referring to the "Fall" of Genesis 1-3 in Romans 1. Paul, it is assumed, takes homosexuality to be a sign of "humanity's fallen state." These interpreters, therefore, inscribe homosexual desire into universal fallen humanity in a way that Paul does not do. For one thing, Paul is referring not to the Fall in Romans 1 but to the invention of idolatry and polytheism by the Gentiles; homosexual intercourse is therefore not a symptom of "the Fall" but of Gentile polytheism. For another, Paul is not giving an etiology of homosexual desire, which for him as for most ancients was not different from heterosexual desire, but an etiology of homosexual intercourse. Furthermore, modern scholars misconstrue Paul's references to "nature" and acts "contrary to nature" because they import int Paul's discourse particularly modern notions of "natural" and "unnatural" not available in the ancient world. Heterosexist scholars interpret Paul the way they do not because they are simply and objectively "reading the text," as they claim, but because of their implication in homophobia, a particularly modern ideological system that construes desire, "nature," and sexuality in particular ways.

Mauser, Ulrich W. "Creation, Sexuality, and Homosexuality in the New Testament." In *Homosexuality and Christian Community*, 39-49. Edited by Choon-Leong Seow. Louisville: Westminister/John Knox Press, 1996.

Argues that the issue of homosexuality cannot be separated from the larger understanding of sexuality, and asserts that the New Testament perspective on sexual ethics is significantly shaped by the sexual gender differentiation found in the book of Genesis. One of a series of essays in Part I, "What Do the Scriptures Say?". The other two sections are Part II, "How Do the Scriptures Inform Our Theological Reflection?" and Part III, "How Do We Live Faithfully?". All the contributors are members of the Princeton Theological Faculty.

Mauser is the Otto A. Piper Professor of Biblical Theology and Culture at Princeton Theological Seminary and an ordained minister in the Presbyterian Church.

McClain-Taylor, Mark. "But Isn't 'It' a Sin?" In *Homosexuality and Christian Community*, 74-85. Edited by Choon-Leong Seow. Louisville: Westminister/John Knox Press, 1996.

Questions whether homosexuality should be termed a sin, and suggests looking at the issue from a "theo-ethical hermeneutic of grace and sin" in order to ask if homosexual activity in fact contravenes God's will and action in and through Jesus Christ. One of a series of essays in Part II, "How Do the Scriptures Inform Our Theological Reflection?". The other two sections are Part I, "What Do the Scriptures Say?" and Part III, "How Do We Live Faithfully?". All the contributors are members of the Princeton Theological Faculty.

McClain-Taylor is Associate Professor of Theology and Culture at Princeton Theological Seminary and an ordained minister of the Presbyterian Church.

McNeill, John J. *The Church and the Homosexual*. Kansas City: Sheed Andrews and McMeel, Inc., 1976.

Discusses approaches to homosexuality in Scripture, Church Tradition, the human sciences, before moving on to outline a more positive moral and pastoral theological consideration of homosexuality and the homosexual community.

McNeill is a former Jesuit, who left the Order in protest over the 1986 CDF document on the Pastoral Care of Homosexual Persons.

Miller, James E. "The Practices of Romans 1:26: Homosexual or Heterosexual?" *Novum Testamentum* 37 (1995): 1-11.

Maintains that while Romans 1:27 clearly condemns male homosexual practice, 1:26 is best understood as not describing female homosexual activity, but unnatural heterosexual intercourse such as contraception.

Miller, Patrick D. "What the Scriptures Principally Teach." In *Homosexuality and Christian Community*, 53-63. Edited by Choon-Leong Seow. Louisville: Westminister/John Knox Press, 1996.

Argues that one must distinguish between the "core" of what the Bible teaches from the specifics which each generation of believers must work out for itself in resolving the tension between the "rule of faith" and the "rule of love." One of a series of essays in Part II, "How Do the Scriptures Inform Our Theological Reflection?". The other two sections are Part I, "What Do the Scriptures Say?" and Part III, "How Do We Live Faithfully?". All the contributors are members of the Princeton Theological Faculty.

Miller is Charles T. Haley Professor of Old Testament at Princeton Theological Seminary and an ordained minister of the Presbyterian Church.

Miller, William R. "Liberation Theology and Homophobia." *American Baptist Quarterly* 8 (1989): 124-139.

Searches for the biblical sources for liberation and justice concerns which have implications for how the church should deal with a range of issues such as homosexuality, abuse of women, and the use of power. Uses Thomas 's concept of a "paradigm shift" to argue that white males need to reevaluate their roles in contemporary social structures. Miller proposes that Liberation Theology provides a framework for such a paradigm shift.

Scroggs, Robin. *The New Testament and Homosexuality: Contextual Background for Contemporary Debate*. Philadelphia: Fortress Press, 1983.

Scroggs describes the prevalent model of homosexuality, namely pederasty, as well as various attitudes toward it, in the Judeo-Greco-Roman world. Against this background a fresh examination of the pertinent biblical texts on the issue is undertaken.

Reviewed by John Boswell in *Journal of Religion* 67 (1987): 365.

Seow, Choon-Leong. "A Heterosexual Perspective." In *Homosexuality and Christian Community*, 14-27. Edited by Choon-Leong Seow. Louisville: Westminister/John Knox Press, 1996.

Looks primarily at the Old Testament texts used most frequently in the debate, but suggests the inclusion of other texts as well, such as texts from the Wisdom literature. One of a series of essays in Part I, "What Do the Scriptures Say?". The other two sections are Part II, "How Do the Scriptures Inform Our Theological Reflection?" and Part III, "How Do We Live Faithfully?". All the contributors are members of the Princeton Theological Faculty.

Seow is the Henry Snyder Gehman Professor of Old Testament Language and Literature and Princeton Theological Seminary and an ordained minister of the Presbyterian Church.

Seow, Choon-Leong, ed. *Homosexuality and Christian Community.* Louisville: Westminister/John Knox Press, 1996.
Essays are divided into three sections: Part I, "What Do the Scriptures Say?"; Part II, "How Do the Scriptures Inform Our Theological Reflection?"; and Part III, "How Do We Live Faithfully?". Contributors, all members of the Princeton Theological Faculty, include A.K.M Adam, Charles L. Bartow, Brian K. Blount, Nancy J. Duff, Thomas W. Gillespie, James F. Kay, Thomas G. Long, Ulrich W. Mauser, Mark McClain-Taylor, Patrick D. Miller, Choon-Leong Seow, Max L. Stackhouse, and Richard E. Whitaker.

Seow is the Henry Synder Gehman Professor of Old Testament Language and Literature and Princeton Theological Seminary and an ordained minister of the Presbyterian Church.

Siker, Jeffrey S. "Homosexual Christians, the Bible, and Gentile Inclusion: Confessions of a Repenting Heterosexist." In *Homosexuality in the Church: Both Sides of the Debate,* 179-194. Edited by Jeffrey S. Siker. Louisville: Westminster/John Knox Press, 1994.

Siker is an ordained Presbyterian minister, and Associate Professor of Theology at Loyola Marymount University in Los Angeles.

_____. "How to Decide? Homosexual Christians, the Bible, and Gentile Inclusion." *Theology Today* 51 (1994): 219-234.

Smith, Abraham. "The New Testament and Homosexuality." *Quarterly Review* 11 (1991): 18-32.

Examines three New Testament texts, 1 Cor 6:9; Rm 1:26-27; and 1 Tm 1:10, in the light of the Greco-Roman cultural milieu and the literary design of each passage.

Smith, Mark D. "Ancient Bisexuality and the Interpretation of Romans 1:26-27. *Journal of the American Academy of Religion* 64 (1996): 223-256.

Smith is Associate Professor of History at Albertson College in Caldwell, Idaho.

Soards, Marion L. *Scripture and Homosexuality: Biblical Authority and The Church Today*. Nashville TN: Cokesbury, 1995.

Stackhouse, Max L. "The Heterosexual Norm." In *Homosexuality and Christian Community*, 133-143. Edited by Choon-Leong Seow. Louisville: Westminister/John Knox Press, 1996.

One of a series of essays in Part III, "How Do We Live Faithfully?". The other two sections are Part I, "What Do the Scriptures Say?" and Part II, "How Do the Scriptures Inform Our Theological Reflection?". All the contributors are members of the Princeton Theological Faculty.

Stackhouse is the Stephen Colwell Professor of Christian Ethics at Princeton Theological Seminary and an ordained minister of the United Methodist Church.

Starr, Richard D. *Speaking the Unspeakable: Homosexuality--A Biblical and Modern Perspective*. Milwaukee: Northwestern Publishing House, 1987.

Starr is a Wisconsin Evangelical Lutheran Synod pastor. Succinctly stated, his position is that "The Christian sees only one cause for homosexuality--sin. It is a sin against nature, society, and most of all, God." (p. 58).

Sweetin, Ellen M. "Called Out of Our Closets: A Lesbian/gay Biblical Ethic of Liberation." M.A. Thesis. Pacific School of Religion. Berkeley, 1986.

Whitaker, Richard E. "Creation and Human Sexuality." In *Homosexuality and Christian Community*, 3-13. Edited by Choon-Leong Seow. Louisville: Westminister/John Knox Press, 1996.

Examines the creation narratives in the first three chapters of Genesis. One of a series of essays in Part I, "What Do the Scriptures Say?". The other two sections are Part II, "How Do the Scriptures Inform Our Theological Reflection?" and Part III, "How Do We Live Faithfully?". All the contributors are members of the Princeton Theological Faculty.

Whitaker is Information Research Specialist and Lecturer in Old Testament at Princeton Theological Seminary and an ordained minister in the United Methodist Church.

White, Leland J. "Biblical Texts and Contemporary Gay People: A Response to Boswell and Boughton." *Irish Theological Quarterly* 59 (1993): 286-301.

Argues that neither Boughton nor Boswell uses "sufficiently elaborated models of culture and cultural variation to address the issue of whether the actions proscribed in the Bible are equivalent in meaning (p. 286)."

See Lynne C. Boughton's "Biblical Texts and Homosexuality: A Response to John Boswell." *Irish Theological Quarterly* 58 (1992): 141-153, as well as Chapter 4, "The Scriptures," of John Boswell's *Christianity, Social Tolerance, and Homosexuality: Gay People in Western Europe from the Beginning of the Christian Era to the Fourteenth Century*, (Chicago: University of Chicago Press, 1980): 91-117 for the treatment discussed in this article, as well as for a listing of other works which deal with Boswell's position.

____. "Does the Bible Speak about Gays or Same-Sex Orientation? A Test Case in Biblical Ethics: Part I." *Biblical Theological Bulletin* (1995): 14-23.

Examines the biblical texts of Genesis 19, Leviticus 18-20, Romans 1:1, 1 Corinthians 6, and 1 Timothy 1 in light of three traditional core values of Mediterranean culture: honor, reproductivity, and holiness. White's thesis is that these texts frame the ethical issue of "homosexuality" in terms of fulfilling traditional cultural roles, and therefore these texts do not address the contemporary issues of same-sex orientation.

Wold, Donald J. *Out of Order: Homosexuality in the Bible and the Ancient Near East*. Grand Rapids: Baker Books, 1997.

Analyzes the biblical passages relating to homosexuality in light of their Near Eastern background, contesting the work of "revisionist interpretation" such as that of John Boswell's *Christianity, Social Tolerance, and Homosexuality*.

312

Wold has a doctorate in biblical and Judaic Studies from the University of California at Berkeley, and has served as an pastor in the evangelical tradition.

See Chapter 4, "The Scriptures," of John Boswell's *Christianity, Social Tolerance, and Homosexuality: Gay People in Western Europe from the Beginning of the Christian Era to the Fourteenth Century*, (Chicago: University of Chicago Press, 1980): 91-117 for the treatment discussed in this book as well as for a listing of other works which deal with Boswell's position.

Wright, David F. "Homosexuality: *The Relevance of the Bible.*" *Evangelical Quarterly* 61 (1989): 291-300.

Challenges the supposed contemporary consensus that biblical passages on homosexuality are irrelevant. Reexamines the early church's use of the both the Old and New Testament relevant passages.

Marriage and/or Divorce

Achtmeier, Elizabeth. *The Committed Marriage*. Philadelphia: Westminster Press, 1978.

Baltensweiler, Heinrich. "Die Ehebruchklauseln bei Matthäus." *Theologische Zeitschrift* 15 (1959): 340-356.

_____. *Die Ehe im Neuen Testament: Exegetische Untersuchungen über Ehe, Ehelosigkeit, und Ehescheidung*. Abhandlugen zur Theologie des Alten und Neuen Testaments 52. Zürich: Zwingli, 1967.

Barilier, R. "Le divorce. Etude biblique et pastorale." *Revue Réformée* 42 (5/1991): 1-45.

Bass, Ardy. "Jesus and Divorce." *The Bible Today* 32 (1994): 359-363.

Beilner, Wolfgang. "Ehescheidung im Neuen Testament." *Theologische-praktische Quartalschrift* 142 (4/1994): 338-342.

Bonsirven, Joseph. *Le Divorce dans le Nouveau Testament.* Paris: Desclée, 1948.

Brooten, B. "Konnten Frauen im alten Judentum die Scheidung betrieben? *Überlegungun zu Mk 10, 11-12 und 1 Cor 7, 10-11.* Evangelische Theologie 42 (1982): 65-69.

Byron, Brian. "1 Cor 7:10-15: A Basis for Future Catholic Discipline on Marriage and Divorce." *Theological Studies* 34 (1973): 429-445.

Cahill, Michael. "The Bible in the Wedding Mass." *The Bible Today* 32 (1994): 353-357.

Collins, Raymond F. *Divorce in the New Testament.* Good News Studies. Collegeville: Liturgical Press/Michael Glazer, 1992.

Focusses on the interpretation in their literary and historical contexts of Jesus' pronouncements on divorce.

After many years teaching New Testament at Louvain, Collins is now Dean of the Catholic University of America.

Cornes, Andrew. *Divorce and Remarriage. Biblical Principles and Pastoral Practice.* Grand Rapids MI: Wm. Eerdmans, 1993.

Crossan, John Dominic. "Divorce and Remarriage in the New Testament." In *The Bond of Marriage*, 1-33. Edited by William W. Bassett. Notre Dame: University of Notre Dame Press, 1968.

Dawes, Gregory W. "'But If You Can Gain Your Freedom' (1 Cor 7:17-29)." *Catholic Biblical Quarterly* 52 (1990): 681-697.

314

Deming, Will. *Paul on Marriage and Celibacy. The Hellenistic Backgrounds of 1 Corinthians 7*. Cambridge (UK): Cambridge University Press, 1995.

Descamps, Albert. "The New Testament Doctrine on Marriage." In *Contemporary Perspectives on Christian Marriage: Propositions and Papers from the International Theological Commission*, 217-273. Edited by Msgr. Richard Malone and John R. Connery, S.J. Chicago: Loyola University Press, 1984.

_____. "Les textes évangéliques sur le mariage." *Revue Theologique de Louvain* 9 (1978): 159-286; e 11 (1980): 5-50.

Donahue, John R., S.J. "Divorce: New Testament Perspectives." *The Month* 14 (1981): 113-120.

Donahue studied under Norman Perrin at the University of Chicago is Professor of Biblical Studies (New Testament) at the Jesuit School of Theology and Graduate Theological Union, Berkeley.

Elliott, J.K. "Paul's Teaching on Marriage in I Corinthians: Some Problems Considered." *New Testament Studies* 19 (1972-1973): 219-225.

Fischer, James A., C.M. "1 Cor 7:8-24--Marriage and Divorce." In *Christian Biblical Ethics: From Biblical Revelation to Contemporary Christian Praxis: Method and Content*, 245-255. New York: Paulist Press, 1984.

Furger, Franz, Hrsg. *Biblische Ethik: Fragen und Antworten*. Freiburg Schweiz: Kanisius Verlag, 1974.

Short booklet, with contributions from Furger, Fredrich Beutter, Eugen Ruckstuhl and Hermann-Josef Venetz. Topics include: Freiheit, Gebote, Verschiedene Wertung biblischer Forderungen, Fordert Jesus die Revolution?, Sklaven, Arme, Ehelosigkeit, Unkeuschheit, Ehebruch, and Onanie.

Furnish, Victor Paul. "Sex: Marriage and Divorce." Chapter 2 in Idem. *The Moral Teaching of Paul: Selected Issues*, 29-51. 2nd ed. Nashville: Abingdon, 1985.

Gatti, Guido. "Matrimonio e famiglia nella Bibbia." Parte Seconda, Capitolo Primo in *Corso di morale*, 165-196. Vol. 3. A cura di Tullo Goffi e Giannino Piana. Brescia: Queriniana, 1984.

Gonzalo Maeso, David. "Puntualizaciones sobre Gn 2, 20-24: formación de la primera mujer y concepto del matrimonio." In *La Etica Bíblica*, 235-244. XXIX Semana Bíblica Española. Madrid: Consejo Superior de Investigaciones Científicas, 1971.

Grelot, Pierre. *Man and Wife in Scripture*. New York: Herder and Herder, 1964.

Hardley, Gary Kaye. *A Scriptural Guide to a Fulfilling Marriage*. State College, PA: Ideals Inc., 1987.

Hart, Thomas M., O.S.B. "Advice on Marriage." *The Bible Today* 32 (1994): 349-352.

Harvey, A.E. [Anthony Ernest]. "Marriage, Sex and the Bible." *Theology* 96 (1993): 364-372; 461-467.

Harvey is Sub-Dean of Westminster, a former theology lecturer at the University of Oxford, and a New Testament scholar.

_____. *Promise or Pretence?: A Christian's Guide to Sexual Morals*. London: SCM Press, 1995.

Discusses the Christian vision of marriage, especially in light of the Biblical injunctions against divorce. Harvey concludes the Jesus did not intend to issue an absolute prohibition against divorce, but rather was challenging people to look at marriage in a new way.

Reviewed by Jule Clague in *The Tablet* 249 (20 May 1995): 639.

Hays, Richard B. "Divorce and Remarriage." Chapter 15 in Idem. *The Moral Vision of the New Testament: Community, Cross, New Creation. A*

316

Contemporary Introduction to New Testament Ethics, 347-378. San Francisco: Harper San Francisco, 1996.

Hays treats divorce and remarriage as a "pragmatic" task (and test) of his proposed approach to New Testament ethics. He proposes three central organizing metaphors from the New Testament, Community, Cross, and New Creation, as a basic methodological approach to utilizing the biblical material in Christian ethics. Hays also names and treats four principal "tasks" of using the Bible in ethics: the descriptive task (what is being said); the synthetic task (how does this or that passage, text, etc., fit within the larger biblical text in a coherent manner); the hermeneutical task of interpreting the biblical texts for ethics, and finally the "pragmatic" task of "living under the Word" (applying the biblical texts to concrete moral issues). Hays treats several other such issues in individual chapters: non-violence, homosexuality, anti-Judaism and ethnic conflict, and abortion.

Hays is professor of New Testament at Duke University Divinity School, and taught for a number of years previously at Yale.

Heth, William A., and Wenham, Gordon J. *Jesus and Divorce: Towards an Evangelical Understanding of New Testament Teaching.* London: Hodder and Stoughton, 1984.

Historical and biblical analysis of the Christian teaching on divorce. The authors argue that the early Church view which allowed divorce but denied the right to remarry has the most to commend it, and therefore a radical shift in evangelical understanding is required.

Hillman, Eugene, C.S.Sp. "Polygamy and the Bible." Chapter 5 in *Polygamy Reconsidered: African Plural Marriage and the Christian Churches*, 139-178. Maryknoll: Orbis Books, 1975.

Hugenberger, Gordon P. *Marriage as a Covenant: A Study of Biblical Law and Ethics Governing Marriage Developed from the Perspective of Malachi.* Supplements to Vetus Testamentum, 52. Leiden and New York: Brill, 1994.

Jackson, Glenna S. "Equality in Marriage." *The Bible Today* 32 (1994): 343-347.

Keener, Craig S. *Paul, Women and Wives: Marriage and Women's Ministry in the Letters of Paul.* Peabody MA: Hendrickson, 1991.

Kysar, Myrna and Robert. *The Asundered: Biblical Teaching on Divorce and Remarriage.* Atlanta: John Knox Press, 1978.

Lardner Carmody, Denise. *Caring for Marriage: Feminist and Biblical Reflections.* New York: Paulist Press, 1985.

LaVerdière, Eugene. "Marriage and Divorce in the Gospel According to Mark." *The Way* 34 (1994): 54-63.

Luck, William F. *Divorce and Remarriage: Recovering the Biblical View.* San Francisco: Harper and Row, 1987.

Reviewed by Richard N. Soulen in *Theology Today* 45 (1989): 263.

MacRae, George W., S.J. "New Testament Perspectives on Marriage and Divorce." In *Divorce and Remarriage in the Catholic Church*, 1-15. Edited by Lawrence G. Wrenn. New York: Newman Press, 1973. Also found in *Ministering to the Divorced Catholic*, 37-50. New York: Paulist Press, 1979.

One of a series of articles on canonical, theological, pastoral, and sociological issues connected with the issues concerning the divorced in the Church.

Martin, Leonard M., C.Ss.R. "Moral Sexual missionária de Paulo: *Subsidios para uma moral do matrimônio no Brasil.*" *Revista Eclesiástica Brasileira* 50 (1990): 515-536.

In Portuguese.

Martin, Thomas M. *The Challenge of Christian Marriage: Marriage in Scripture, History and Contemporary Life.* New York: Paulist Press, 1990.

Historical study which moves from Scripture through the early Church, the Church Fathers, and the medieval and reformation periods. Modern

318

challenges to Christian marriage are addressed, as well as an attempt to spell out a contemporary theology of marriage. Designed as an undergraduate text, includes study questions and recommendations for further reading after each chapter. See especially Chapter 2, "Marriage in the Old Testament," and Chapter 3, "Marriage in the New Testament."

Martin is a professor in the Religious Studies Department of Dayton University.

Molldrem, Mark J. "A Hermeneutic of Pastoral Care and the Law/Gospel Paradigm Applied to the Divorce Texts of Scripture." *Interpretation* 45 (1991): 43-54.

Looks at the primary Scriptural texts through the Law/Gospel dialectic in order to develop a hermeneutic of pastoral care in dealing with the contemporary context on divorce.

Molldrem is the pastor of the First Evangelical Lutheran Church in Beaver Dam, Wisconsin.

Olsen, V. Norskov. *The New Testament Logia on Divorce: A Study of Their Interpretation from Erasmus to Milton.* Beiträge zur Geschichte der biblischen Exegeses, 10. Tübingen: J.C.B. Mohr, 1971.

Includes a detailed discussion of the Church Fathers' and Protestant reformers' treatment of the divorce texts in Scripture.

Phipps, William E. "Is Paul's Attitude toward Sexual Relations Contained in 1 Cor 7:1?" *New Testament Studies* 28 (1982): 125-131.

Rémy, P. "Le rapport à l'Ecriture en morale matrimoniale." *Le Supplément* 161 (1987): 63-72.

Schedl, Cl. "Zur Ehebruchklausel der Bergpredigt in Lichte der neugefundenen Tempelrolle." *Theologisch-praktische Quartelschrift* 130 (1982): 34-49.

Stramare, Tarcisio. *Matteo divorzista? Studio su Mt. 5,3 e 19,9.* Brescia: Paideia, 1986.

Valle, José Luis del, O.S.A. "La Sexualidad. Simbología matrimonial en los escritos proféticos." *Biblia y Fe* 18 (1992): 37-50.

One of several articles under this number's general theme of "La Sexualidad: *Aproximacion Biblica.*"

Vargas-Machuca, A. "Divorcio e indisolubilidad del matrimonio en la Sagrada Escritura." *Estudios Biblicos* 38 (1981): 19-61.

Vawter, Bruce. "The Biblical Theology of Divorce." *Catholic Theological Society of America Proceedings* 22 (1967): 223-243.

Wambacq, B.N. "Mattieu 5, 31-32. Possibilité de divorce ou obligation de rompre une union illégitime." *Nouvelle Revue Théologique* 104 (1982): 154-190.

Weems, Renita J. *Battered Love: Marriage, Sex, and Violence in the Hebrew Prophets.* Minneapolis: Fortress Press, 1995.

Investigates ways in which the Hebrew Prophets' descriptions of divine love, compassion, and commitment to the covenant, as well as the prophetic discourse, rhetoric and sexual metaphors used, became linked to violence against women, such as battery, infidelity, rape and mutilation.

Weems teaches Hebrew Bible at Vanderbilt Divinity School.

Westbrook, Raymond. "Adultery in Ancient Near Eastern Law." *RB* 97 (1990): 542-580.

****

Sin, Forgiveness, Reconciliation, and/or Evil in Scripture

Badini, Giuseppe. "Sin in the Theology of St. Paul." In *Sin: Its Reality and Nature: A Historical Survey*, 79-100. Edited by Pietro Palazzini. Translated by Brendan Devlin. Dublin: Scepter Publishers, 1964.

Buckley, Thomas W. *Seventy Times Seven: Sin, Judgment, and Forgiveness in Matthew*. Zacchaeus Studies. Collegeville: Liturgical Press/ Michael Glazier, 1991.

Examines Matthean notions of sin and judgment and discusses the Gospel's portrayal of Jesus as Savior, in that through this self-offering sin is forgiven, guilt expiated, and humanity renewed in hope.

Burthchaell, James Tunstead, C.S.C. *Philemon's Problem: The Daily Dilemma of the Christian*. Chicago: ACTA [Foundation for Adult Catechetical Teaching Aids], 1973.

Using the *Letter to Philemon* as a touchstone for an approach to contemporary moral issues Burthchaell discusses peace and violence, sex and ritual, prayer and penance--in an attempt to fashion a Christian vision of the world. Written in a popular, rather than academic style.

Carny, Pin'has. "Theodicy in the Book of Quohelet." In *Justice and Righteousness: Biblical Themes and their Influence*, 71-81. Edited by Henning Graf Reventlow and Yair Hoffman. Sheffield: JSOT Press, 1992.

Cooper, Howard. "Sin in Biblical and Rabbinical Thought." *The Month* 254 (September/October 1993): 348-354.

One of a series of articles on various theological aspects of sin.

Craghan, John F. "Sin, Cleansing and Restoration." *The Bible Today* 31 (1993): 68-72.

Focuses on Psalm 51, and is one of several articles in this issue on the theme of "The Bible on Sin."

Crenshaw, James L., ed. *Theodicy in the Old Testament.* Issues in Religion and Theology, 4. Philadelphia: Fortress Press; London: SPCK, 1983.

An introduction plus 8 articles ranging from A.S. Peake's 1905 essay on Job to Crenshaw's own 1975 treatment on the problem of human bondage in Sirach. Other contributors include Walther Eichrodt, Ronald J. Williams, Klaus Koch, Gerhard von Rad, Martin Buber, and Harmut Gese.

Crüsemann, Frank. "Dominion, Guilt, and Reconciliation: The Contribution of the Jacob Narrative in Genesis to Political Ethics." *Semeia,* no. 66 (1995): 67-77.

One of several articles on Old Testament ethics in this issue.

Descamps, Albert, and Gelin, Albert. *Sin in the Bible. New Testament* by Albert Descamps; *Old Testament* by Albert Gelin. Translated by Charles Schaldenbrand. New York: Desclée, 1965.

Originally appeared in French as part of *Theologie du péché.*

Flora, Jerry. "New Testament Perspectives on Evil." *Ashland Theological Journal* 24 (1992): 15-26.

Flora is professor of New Testament at Ashland Theological Seminary.

Fucek, Ivan, S.J. "Il senso e il linguaggio biblico del peccato." Cap. IV in *Il Peccato Oggi: Riflessione teologico-morale,* 103-120. Roma: PUG, 1991.

Fucek is professor of moral theology at the Pontifical Gregorian University in Rome.

Garofalo, Salvatore. "Sin in the Gospels." In *Sin: Its Reality and Nature: A Historical Survey,* 57-77. Edited by Pietro Palazzini. Translated by Brendan Devlin. Dublin: Scepter Publishers, 1964.

322

Gelin, Albert, and Descamps, Albert. *Sin in the Bible. Old Testament* by Albert Gelin; *New Testament* by Albert Descamps. Translated by Charles Schaldenbrand. New York: Desclée, 1965.

Originally appeared in French as part of *Theologie du péché*.

Hoffman, Yair. "The Creativity of Theodicy." In *Justice and Righteousness: Biblical Themes and their Influence*, 117-130. Edited by Henning Graf Reventlow and Yair Hoffman. Sheffield: JSOT Press, 1992.

Humbert, Alphonse, C.Ss.R. "Les péchés de sexualité dans le Nouveau Testament." *Studia Moralia* 8 (1970): 149-183.

John, Jeffrey. "'Authority given to men': The Doctrinal Basis of Ministerial Absolution in the New Testament." In *Confession and Absolution*, 15-39. Edited by Martin Dudley and Geoffrey Rowell. London: SPCK, 1990.

One of eleven essays covering aspects of the Christian tradition, contemporary pastoral practice, and the liturgies of penance.

Kirchhoff, R. *Die Sünde gegen den eigenen Leib. Studien zu "porne" und "porneia" in 1 Kor 6, 12-20 und dem sozio-kulturellen Kontext der paulinischen Adressaten*. Göttingen: Vandenhoeck & Ruprecht, 1994.

Kottackal, Joseph. "The Biblical Understanding of Original Sin." *Bible Bhashyam* 20 (1994): 5-15.

Maly, Eugene H. *Sin: Biblical Perspectives*. Dayton: Pflaum, 1973.

Mariani, Bonaventura. "Ritual Sin in the Old Testament." In *Sin: Its Reality and Nature: A Historical Survey*, 41-56. Edited by Pietro Palazzini. Translated by Brendan Devlin. Dublin: Scepter Publishers, 1964.

McMahon, Michael. "Paralysis of the Heart." *The Bible Today* 31 (1993): 85-88.

Focuses on the cure of the paralytic in Matthew 9:2-8 to show Jesus' attitude toward sin. One of several articles in this issue on the theme of "The Bible on Sin."

Miller, Patrick D., Jr. *Sin and Judgment in the Prophets: A Stylistic and Theological Analysis.* Society of Biblical Literature Monograph Series, 27. Chico CA: Scholars Press, 1982.

Treats the question of the correspondence of sin and judgment in the prophetic writings, concentrating on Hosea, Amos, Micah and Isaiah.

Mueller, Joan. *Why Can't I Forgive you: A Christian Reflection.* Allen TX: Thomas More, 1996.

Mueller reflects upon Jesus' prayers of forgiveness (Lk 23:34) and surrender (Lk 23:46) as they appear in the Gospel of Luke, using the example of a couple whose young on is killed by an unrepentant and unreformed drunk driver. The text is written in a manner readily accessible to undergraduates and adult education classes.

Mullen, Alyce Miller. "A Study of the Relationship of Sin, Distress, and Health in the Old Testament Psalms: As a Basis for a Biblical Theology of Wholeness in Pastoral Ministry. Thesis (doctoral)--Wesley Theological Seminary, 1985.

O'Grady, John F. "Evil and Sin in Mark." *Chicago Studies* 34 (1995): 42-52.

Ravasi, Gianfranco. "All'ombra dell'albero della conoscenza del bene e del male. Note ermeneutiche su Genesi 2-3." *Communio* 118 (luglio-agosto, 1991): 25-35.

One of a series of articles on various aspects of this theme.

Sabugal, S. "El concepto de pecado en el Antiguo Testamento." *Estudios Eclesiásticos* 59 (1984): 459-469.

324

Spadafora, Francesco. "Sin in the Old Testament." In *Sin: Its Reality and Nature: A Historical Survey*, 29-40. Edited by Pietro Palazzini. Translated by Brendan Devlin. Dublin: Scepter Publishers, 1964.

Stuhlmacher, Peter. *Reconciliation, Law and Righteousness: Essays on Biblical Theology*. Philadelphia: Fortress Press, 1986.

Translated from the German.

Stuhlmueller, Carroll, C.P. "The Search for Original Sin." *The Bible Today* 31 (1993): 73-78.

Conducts a "biblical search" on the doctrine of original sin. One of several articles in this issue on the theme of "The Bible on Sin."

Tambasco, Anthony J. "Prophetic Teaching on Sin." *The Bible Today* 31 (1993): 79-84.

Considers especially the prophetic teaching of sin in the aspects of idolatry, externalism and injustice. One of several articles in this issue on the theme of "The Bible on Sin."

Uffenheimer, Benjamin. "Theodicy and Ethics in the Prophecy of Ezekiel." In *Justice and Righteousness: Biblical Themes and their Influence*, 200-227. Edited by Henning Graf Reventlow and Yair Hoffman. Sheffield: JSOT Press, 1992.

Vanoni, Gottfried. "Schalom als zentrale biblische Botschaft." *Theologisch-praktische Quartalschrift* 141 (1993): 3-12.

English digest: "Shalom and the Bible." *Theology Digest* 41 (1994): 171-121.

Shalom means more than peace and its opposite is not merely war, but evil and calamity. Shalom is closely related to biblical righteousness, and is God's gift to humankind. For Christians shalom is also understood as the offering of mutual forgiveness.

Varó, F. "El léxico del pecado en la Epíistola de S. Pablo a los Romanos." *Scripta Theologica* 21 (1989): 99-116.

Vawter, Bruce. "Missing the Mark." In *Introduction to Christian Ethics: A Reader*, 199-205. Edited by Ronald P. Hamel and Kenneth R. Himes, O.F.M. New York: Paulist Press, 1989.

Via, Dan O. *Self-Deception and Wholeness in Paul and Matthew*. Minneapolis: Fortress Press, 1990.

Treats the concepts of sin (self-deception) and salvation (recovery of wholeness), in the context of the anthropology, soteriology and ethics of Paul and Matthew.

Via is Professor of New Testament at The Divinity School of Duke University.

Winninge, Mikael. *Sinners and the Righteous: A Comparative Study of the Psalms of Solomon and Paul's Letters*. Coniectanea Biblica, New Testament Series 26. Stockholm: Almqvist and Wiskell International, 1995.

****

Slavery, Racism, and Apartheid

Bax, Douglas. "The Bible and Apartheid 2." In *Apartheid Is a Heresy*, 112-143. Edited by John W. DeGruchy and Charles Villa-Vicencio. Grand Rapids: William B. Eerdmans, 1983.

See also the article by Willem Vorster on the same theme.

Corcoran, Gerald. "Slavery in the New Testament." *Milltown Studies* 5 (1980): 1-40.

DeGruchy, John W., and Villa-Vicencio, Charles, eds. *Apartheid Is a Heresy*. Grand Rapids: William B. Eerdmans, 1983.

Discusses how the Bible has been used historically to bolster apartheid arguments, and how biblical scholars discount the appropriateness of such argumentation.

Dutch Reformed Church [of South Africa]. *Human Relations and the South African Scene in the Light of Scripture.* Cape Town-Pretoria, 1974.

Official English translation of *Ras, Volk en Naise en Volkereverhoudinge in die lig van die Skrif,* which was accepted by the DRC's General Synod in October, 1974. This document furnishes scriptural support for the South African policy of apartheid. For a good discussion of the problematic nature of this sort of biblical ethical interpretation see Stephen E. Fowl and L. Gregory Jones, *Reading in Communion: Scripture and Ethics in Christian Life* (Grand Rapids: William B. Eerdmans, 1991), especially pp. 96-99.

Eliott, Neil. *Liberating Paul: The Justice of God and the Politics of the Apostle.* Maryknoll: Orbis Press, 1993.

For centuries the apostle Paul has been invoked to justify oppression-whether on behalf of slavery, to enforce unquestioned obedience to the state, to silence women, or to legitimate anti-Semitism. Elliott argues that the struggle to liberate human beings from the power of death and oppression requires "liberating Paul" from the unfortunate consequence of the way he has usually been read, or rather misread, in the churches.

Felder, Cain Hope. *Troubling Biblical Waters: Race, Class, and Family.* Bishop Henry McNeal Turner Studies in North American Black Religion. Maryknoll: Orbis, 1989.

Reviewed by Vincent L. Wimbush in *Theology Today* 46 (1990): 345.

Furger, Franz, Hrsg. *Biblische Ethik: Fragen und Antworten.* Freiburg Schweiz: Kanisius Verlag, 1974.

Short booklet, with contributions from Furger, Fredrich Beutter, Eugen Ruckstuhl and Hermann-Josef Venetz. Topics include: Freiheit, Gebote, Verschiedene Wertung biblischer Forderungen, Fordert Jesus die Revolution?, Sklaven, Arme, Ehelosigkeit, Unkeuschheit, Ehebruch, and Onanie.

Giles, Kevin. "The Biblical Argument for Slavery: Can the Bible Mislead? A Case Study in Hermeneutics." *Evangelical Quarterly*

Giles is the Rector of St. Matthew's Church, Kensington, Adelaide.

Meeks, Wayne A. "The 'Haustafeln' and American Slavery: A Hermeneutical Challenge." Part III, Chapter 1 in *Theology and Ethics in Paul and His Interpreters: Essays in Honor of Victor Paul Furnish*, 232-253. Edited by Eugene H. Lovering, Jr. and Jerry L. Sumney. Nashville: Abingdon Press, 1996.

Munro, Winsome. "Romans 13:1-7; Apartheid's Last Biblical Refuge." *Biblical Theology Bulletin* 20 (1990): 161-168.

Apartheid advocates have often used this Pauline passage as a biblical warrant. This view has been criticized by signers of the 1985-1986 *Kairos Document*, who relativize the passage's applicability by referring to both situational and total biblical context. This approach is critiqued in turn by Munro, who suggests that the passage is part of an overall redaction of Pauline letters connected with the Pastoral Epistles. Munro suggests a hermeneutical method of applying the passage in the sense of identifying a "kindred struggle" among 2nd Century Christians in Asia Minor.

Ms. Munro is a South African who teaches religion at St. Olaf's College in Northfield, MN.

Priest, Josiah. *Bible Defence of Slavery: or, The origin, history, and fortunes of the Negro race, as deduced from history, both sacred and profane, their natural relations, moral, mental and physical, to the other races of mankind, compared and illustrated, their future destiny predicted, etc. To which is added a plan of national colonization adequate to the entire removal of the free Blacks, and all that may hereafter become free, in a manner harnominizing with the peace and well-being of both races, by W.S. Brown.* 6th stereotype ed. Galsgow: W.S. Brown, 1853.

Priest lived from 1788 to 1851.

Smith, Morton. "On Slavery: Biblical Teaching v. Modern Morality." In *Biblical and Secular Ethics: The Conflict*, 69-77. Edited by R. Joseph Hoffman and Gerald A. Larue. Buffalo: Prometheus Press, 1988.

Swartley, Willard M. *Slavery, Sabbath, War and Women: Case Issues in Biblical Interpretation*. Scottdale PA: Herald Press, 1983.

Tumbarello, Giacomo. "La Schiavitù nella Bibbia." *Bibbia e Oriente* 35 (1993): 65-74.

Vorster, Willem. "The Bible and Apartheid 1." In *Apartheid Is a Heresy*, 94-111. Edited by John W. DeGruchy and Charles Villa-Vicencio. Grand Rapids: William B. Eerdmans, 1983.

See also the article by Douglas Bax on the same theme.

****

War, Peace and Non-Violence

**See also Love Command section of the Bibliography*

Atkinson, David. *Peace in Our Time? Some Biblical Groundwork*. Grand Rapids, William Eerdmans, 1985.

Aukerman, Dale. *Darkening Valley: A Biblical Perspective on Nuclear War*. Foreword by Jim Wallis. New York: Seabury Press, 1981.

See the discussion of Aukerman's book in Anthony Tambasco's article, "The Bible and Nuclear War: A Case Study in Methodology for Christian Biblical Ethics," *Biblical Theology Bulletin* 13 (1983): 75-81.

Beck, Robert B. *Nonviolent Story: Narrative Conflict Resolution in the Gospel of Mark*. Maryknoll: Orbis Books, 1996.

Beck argues that Mark portrays Jesus as one who does not avoid conflict, but who enters into it without resorting to violence himself, and which Gospel message therefore challenges our cultural myth of "constructive violence."

Bernbaum, John A. *Perspectives on Peacemaking: Biblical Options on the Nuclear Age*. Ventura CA: Regal Books, 1984.

Brown, Dale W. *Biblical Pacifism: A Peace Church Perspective*. Elgin IL: Brethren Press, 1986.

Burthchaell, James Tunstead, C.S.C. *Philemon's Problem: The Daily Dilemma of the Christian*. Chicago: ACTA [Foundation for Adult Catechetical Teaching Aids], 1973.

Using the *Letter to Philemon* as a touchstone for an approach to contemporary moral issues Burthchaell discusses peace and violence, sex and ritual, prayer and penance--in an attempt to fashion a Christian vision of the world. Written in a popular, rather than academic style.

Cadoux, C.J. *The Early Christian Attitude to War*. London: Headly Bros, 1919. New York: Seabury Press, 1982.

Covers the first three centuries.

Carroll, M. Daniel. "The Prophetic Text and the Literature of Dissent in Latin America: Amos, García Márquez, and Cabrera Infante Dismantle Militarism." *Biblical Interpretation* 4 (1996): 76-100.

Gives a reading of the prophet Amos within the framework of some novels of dissent in Latin America in order to give a perspective on dealing with militarism in Latin America.

Craigie, Peter C. *The Problem of War in the Old Testament*. Grand Rapids: William B. Eerdmans, 1978.

Reviewed by Ronald G. Goetz in *Theology Today* 36 (1980): 598.

Dakin, David Martin. *Peace and Brotherhood in the Old Testament.* London: Bannisdale Press, 1956.

Daly, Robert J., S.J. "New Testament and the Early Church." In *Non-Violence-- Central to Christian Pacifism*, 34-42. Edited by Joseph T. Culliton. New York: Edward Mellen Press, 1982.

Daly is professor of theology at Boston College.

_____. "The New Testament, Pacifism and Non-violence." *American Ecclesiastical Review* 168 (1974): 544-562.

Includes a good overview of the pertinent texts.

Devasahayam, Jebaraj. "Understanding Violence: Learning from the Old Testament." *ATA Journal* 2 (1994): 5-15.

Domeris, William R. "Biblical perspectives on the use of force." *Journal of Theology for Southern Africa* 62 (March 1988): 68-72.

Donahue, John R., S.J. "Who Is My Enemy? The Parable of the Good Samaritan and the Love of Enemies." In *The Love of Enemy and Nonretaliation in the New Testament*, 137-156. Edited by Willard M. Swartley. Louisville: Westminster/John Knox Press, 1992.

Donahue studied under Norman Perrin at the University of Chicago is Professor of Biblical Studies (New Testament) at the Jesuit School of Theology and Graduate Theological Union, Berkeley.

Duchrow, Ulrich, and Liedke, Gerhard. *Shalom: Biblical Perspectives on Creation, Justice and Peace.* Geneva: WCC Publications, 1989.

German original: *Schalom: Der Schöpfung Befreiung, den Menschen Gerechtigkeit, den Völkern Frieden.* Stuttgart: Kreuz Verlag, 1987.

Written in part for the 1990 Seoul WCC Conference on Peace, Justice, and the Integrity of Creation.

Reviewed by Newton B. Fowler, Jr. in *Mid-Stream* 29 (1990): 442-444.

Espinel, J.L. "Nuevo Testamento y pacifismo." *Razón y Fe* 219 (1989): 67-79.

Ford, Josephine Massyngbaerde. *My Enemy is My Guest: Jesus and Violence in Luke*. Maryknoll: Orbis Books, 1984.

Froehlich, Herbert. "Biblical Witnesses to Nonviolent Liberation." *Theology Digest* 41 (1994): 113-116.

> *English digest of:* "Biblische Zeugnisse gewaltloser Befreiung." *Ordensnachrichten* 32 (5/1993): 13-18.

> Explores examples from both Testaments to indicate that the way of God and Christ does not employ violence. Christians, therefore, may have to suffer violence at times so as not to replace old injustice with new.

Furger, Franz, Hrsg. *Biblische Ethik: Fragen und Antworten*. Freiburg Schweiz: Kanisius Verlag, 1974.

> Short booklet, with contributions from Furger, Fredrich Beutter, Eugen Ruckstuhl and Hermann-Josef Venetz. Topics include: Freiheit, Gebote, Verschiedene Wertung biblischer Forderungen, Fordert Jesus die Revolution?, Sklaven, Arme, Ehelosigkeit, Unkeuschheit, Ehebruch, and Onanie.

Helgeland, John, Daly, Robert J., and Burns, J. Patout. *Christians and the Military: The Early Experience*. Philadelphia: Fortress Press, 1985.

> See especially Ch. 2, "The New Testament Background," pp. 10-20.

Hendrickx, Hermann. *Peace Anyone? Biblical Reflections on Peace and Violence*. Chicago: Claretian Publications, 1986.

____. *A Time for Peace: Reflections on the Meaning of Peace and Violence in the Bible*. London: SPCK, 1988.

Hobbs, T.R. *A Time for War: A Study of Warfare in the Old Testament.* Old Testament Studies, 3. Collegeville: The Liturgical Press/Michael Glazier Books, 1989.

> Besides discussion of the Old Testament material, Hobbs includes sections devoted to "New Testament Insights." Brief bibliography is also included, pp. 234-242.

> Reviewed by Scott Morschauser in *Theology Today* 48 (1992): 154.

> Hobbs is Professor of Old Testament Interpretation at McMaster Divinity College in Hamilton, Ontario.

Horsley, Richard A. "Ethics and Exegesis: "Love Your Enemies" and the Doctrine of Non-Violence." *Journal of the American Academy of Religion* 54 (1986): 3-31.

_____. *Jesus and the Spiral of Violence: Popular Resistence in Roman Palestine.* San Francisco: Harper & Row, 1987.

> Briefly discussed by Lisa Sowle Cahill in her article "The New Testament and Ethics: Communities of Social Change," *Interpretation* 44 (1990): 383-395.

Kang, Sa-Moon. *Divine War in the Old Testament and in the Ancient Near East.* Beihefte zur Zeitschrift für die alttestamentliche Wissenschaft, 177. Berlin & New York: Walter de Gruyer, 1989.

Kirk, Andrew. "A Biblical View of the Nuclear State." In *Decide for Peace: Evangelicals and the Bomb,* 46-59. Compiled by Evangelical Peacemakers; edited by Dana Mills-Powell. Basingstoke, Hants, UK, 1986.

Klassen, William. *Love Your Enemies: The Way to Peace.* Philadelphia: Fortress Press, 1984.

> Includes treatment of Jewish and Hellenistic thought as well as the New Testament.

Lambrecht, Jan, S.J.   "Is Active Nonviolent Resistance Jesus' Third Way?:   An Answer to Walter Wink." *Louvain Studies* 19 (1994): 350-351.

Lambrecht is a New Testament exegete.

Linskens, J. "A Pacifist Interpretation of Peace in the Sermon on the Mount?" *Concilium* 164 (1983): 16-25.

Lohfink, Norbert, S.J.   "`Holy War' and `Ban' in the Bible." *Theology Digest* 38 (1991): 109-114.

Violence is the central human sin, and this creates a difficult theological problem in evaluating the Old Testaments concepts of the Holy War and the Ban (consecration to destruction). Lohfink argues that this "holy war" ethos might be understood as only an intermediate (i.e., not permanent) phase in Israel's life, and the God's People must ultimately renounce all forms of violence as Jesus offered God's Lordship without violence.

Lohfink is professor of Old Testament Exegesis at Sankt Georgen in Frankfurt-am-Main.

Marchadour, Alain. "Justice et paix dans la Bible." *La Vie Spirituelle* 72 (1992): 293-306.

Mauser, Ulrich. *The Gospel of Peace: A Scriptural Message for Today's World.* Louisville: Westminster/John Knox Press, 1992.

Primarily an examination of the urgency for working for peace, using relevant passages from the Gospels, Acts, and Paul, Mauser argues that the core of both Jesus' message and actions indicates that Jesus is essentially the peacemaker.

McSorley, Richard, S.J. *The New Testament Basis of Peacemaking.* 3rd ed. Scottdale PA: Herald Press, 1985.

Gives an overview of the pertinent texts. Could serve well as a text for parish-study groups.

Murray, Robert. *The Cosmic Covenant: Biblical Themes of Justice, Peace and the Integrity of Creation.* Heythrop Monographs, 7. London: Sheed and Ward, 1992.

Reviewed by John W. Rogerson in *The Heythrop Journal* 34 (1993): 184-185.

Niditch, Susan. *War in the Hebrew Bible: A Study in the Ethics of Violence.* New York: Oxford University Press, 1993.

Using approaches from anthropology, comparative literature, and feminist studies, the author considers a number of war ideologies present in the Hebrew Bible.

Pawlikowski, John T., and Senior, Donald, eds. *Biblical and Theological Reflections on the Challenge of Peace.* Wilmington: Michael Glazier, 1984.

Quesnell, Quentin. "Hermeneutical Prolegomena to a Pastoral Letter." In *Peace in a Nuclear Age: The Bishops' Pastoral Letter in Perspective*, 3-19. Edited by Charles J. Reid, Jr. Washington, D.C.: Catholic University of America Press, 1986.

Rad, Gerhard von. *Holy War in Ancient Israel.* Translated and edited by Marva J. Dawn and John H. Yoder. Grand Rapids: William B. Eerdmans, 1990.

Schnackenburg, Rudolf. "Die Seligpreisung der Friedenstifter (Mt 5,9) im matthäischem Kontext." *Biblische Zeitschrift* 104 (1982): 161-178.

Schottroff, Luise. "Non-Violence and the Love of One's Enemies." In *Essays on the Love Commandment*, 9-39. Philadelphia: Fortress Press, 1978.

Argues that true love of enemies might involve actions which confront and change the "enemy."

Schottroff is Professor of New Testament at the University of Kassel, Germany.

Schulte, Hannelis. "The End of the Omride Dynasty: Social-Ethical Observations on the Subject of Power and Violence." *Semeia*, no. 66 (1995): 133-48.

One of several articles on Old Testament ethics in this issue.

Sider, Ronald J., und Taylor, Richard K. *Abkehr von Götzen. Biblische Hoffnung als Wegweiser aus dem atomaren Wahnsinn.* Neukirchen-Vluyn: Aussaat Verlag, 1984.

Translation from English.

Sleeper, C. Freeman. *The Bible and the Moral Life.* Louisville: Westminster/John Knox Press, 1992.

Looks at how various churches use the Bible to address contemporary ethical issues, particularly nuclear war and abortion, and also considers the issue of biblical authority in terms of four major styles of moral reflection, i.e., law, prophecy, apocalypse, and wisdom. The book is designed for adult study groups and contains practical exercises.

Sleeper is Professor of Religion at Roanoke College in Salem, Virginia.

Swartley, Willard M. *Slavery, Sabbath, War and Women: Case Issues in Biblical Interpretation.* Scottdale PA: Herald Press, 1983.

____, ed. *The Love of Enemy and Nonretaliation in the New Testament.* Louisville: Westminster/John Knox Press, 1992.

Reviewed by David Gill, S.J. in *Horizons* 20 (1993): 346-347.

Swift, Louis J. "Search the Scriptures: Patristic Exegesis and the Ius Belli." In *Peace in a Nuclear Age: The Bishops' Pastoral Letter in Perspective*, 48-68. Edited by Charles J. Reid, Jr. Washington, D.C.: Catholic University of America Press, 1986.

Tambasco, Anthony J. "The Bible and Nuclear War: A Case Study in Methodology for Christian Biblical Ethics." *Biblical Theology Bulletin* 13 (1983): 75-81.

336

Abstract: The article summarizes a methodological study of a task force of the Catholic Biblical Association on the relationship of the Bible to Christian ethics and brings this to bear on Dale Aukerman's study of the Bible on nuclear war, *Darkening Valley: A Biblical Perspective on Nuclear War,* (New York: Seabury Press, 1981). The author shows that biblical interpretation is influenced by presuppositions, that the Bible functions well for ethics on the level of "story", and that "normativity" of the Bible can mean many different things. The article then commends Aukerman's use of Bible as story but criticizes the limited images that he derives from the story and suggests enlarging the prior judgments brought to the biblical text.

_____, ed. *Blessed Are the Peacemakers: Biblical Perspectives on Peace and Its Social Foundations.* New York: Paulist Press, 1989.

Essays from a task force of the Catholic Biblical Association on the use of Scripture in ethics, and especially on application to issues of world peace.

Vanoni, Gottfried. "Shalom and the Bible." *Theology Digest* 41 (1994): 171-121.

English digest of: "Schalom als zentrale biblische Botschaft." *Theologisch-praktische Quartalschrift* 141 (1993): 3-12.

Shalom means more than peace and its opposite is not merely war, but evil and calamity. Shalom is closely related to biblical righteousness, and is God's gift to humankind. For Christians shalom is also understood as the offering of mutual forgiveness.

Venter, A.F. "Biblical Ethics and Christian Response to Violence." *Theologia Evangelica* 24 (2, 1991): 25-39.

Searches for a biblical ethical response to the township violence in South Africa.

Williams, James G. *The Bible, Violence, and the Sacred: Liberation from the Myth of Sanctioned Violence.* San Francisco: HarperSanFrancisco, 1991.

Discusses the "scapegoat" theory of René Girard and then applies this the Bible and compares the biblical revelation to American culture.

Williams teaches Scripture at Syracuse University.

Wink, Walter. "Beyond Just War and Pacifism: Jesus' Nonviolent Way." *Review and Expositor* 89 (1992): 197-214.

Argues for non-violence and though not non-resistance to evil. Bases his arguments largely on an exegesis of Mt 5:38-42. See also Jan Lambrecht's "Is Active Nonviolent Resistance Jesus' Third Way?: An Answer to Walter Wink." *Louvain Studies* 19 (1994): 350-351.

Winn, Albert Curry. *Ain't Gonna Study War No More: Biblical Ambiguity and the Abolition of War*. Louisville: Westminster/John Knox Press, 1993.

Investigation and discussion of the biblical passages on both war and the abolition of war in both the Hebrew Scriptures and the New Testament.

Yoder, Perry B., and Willard M. Swartley, eds. *The Meaning of Peace: Biblical Studies*. Louisville, KY: Westminster/John Knox Press, 1992.

Yoder, Perry B. *Shalom: The Bible's Word for Salvation, Justice, and Peace*. Newton KA: Faith and Life Press, 1990.

Uses the concept of *shalom* in both Old and New Testament in application to themes of justice, freedom, liberation, law, salvation and atonement.

Zerbe, Gordon M. *Non-Retaliation in Early Jewish and New Testament Texts: Ethical Themes in Social Contexts*. Journal for the Study of the Pseudepigrapha Supplement Series, no. 13. Sheffield, England: JSOT Press, 1993.

Dr. Zerbe shows that the non-retaliatory ethics of the NT stand solidly in line with Jewish tradition except that the NT texts tend to ground their appeal in the example of Jesus and to extend the responses of love and blessing to persecutors of the elect community, a stance in some tension with the notion of deferring vengeance to God.

****

PRE-1962 AND/OR HISTORICAL WORKS ON SCRIPTURE AND ETHICS

N.B. Virtually all the works listed below also appear in their respective "thematic" sections, such as Pauline ethics, Sermon on the Mount, Marriage, etc. The only exception to this would be the works below which deal specifically and solely with Scriptural ethics in an historical context.

General or Miscellaneous Works

Baird, William. "The Fate of Paul in Nineteenth-Century Liberalism: Ritschl and Harnack." Part III, Chapter 2 in *Theology and Ethics in Paul and His Interpreters: Essays in Honor of Victor Paul Furnish*, 254-274. Ed. Eugene H. Lovering, Jr. and Jerry L. Sumney. Nashville: Abingdon Press, 1996.

Baltensweiler, Heinrich. "Die Ehebruchklauseln bei Matthäus." *Theologische Zeitschrift* 15 (1959): 340-356.

Bonsirven, Joseph. *Le Divorce dans le Nouveau Testament*. Paris: Desclée, 1948.

Briggs, Charles A. (Charles Augustus), 1841-1913. *The Ethical Teaching of Jesus*. New York: Scribner's, 1904; Chicago: American Theological Library Association, (ATLA monograph preservation program), ATLA fiche, 1985.

Briggs lived from 1841-1913.

Burton-Christie, Douglas. *The Word in the Desert: Scripture and the Quest for Holiness in Early Christian Monasticism*. Oxford: Oxford University Press, 1992.

Burton-Christie teaches at Loyola Marymount University in Los Angeles, California.

Dailey, Timothy J. "The Use of Scripture in Normative Christian Ethics: The Limit Case of Homosexuality as Viewed in the Contemporary Debate (1955-1984)." Ph.D. Dissertation, Marquette University, 1985.

Delhaye, Philippe. "Le recours à l'Ancien Testament dans l'étude de la théologie morale." *Ephemerides Theologicae Lovanienses* 31 (1955): 637-657.

_____. "Le recours à l'Ecriture Sainte dans l'enseignement de la théologie morale." *Bulletin des Facultes Catholiques de Lyon* 77 (1955): 5-19; 78 (1956): 5-25.

Dewar, Lindsay. *An Outline of New Testament Ethics.* Philadelphia: The Westminster Press, 1949.

Gardner, E. Clinton. *Biblical Faith and Social Ethics.* New York: Harper & Row, 1960.

Gelin, Albert, and Descamps, Albert. *Sin in the Bible.* Translated by Charles Schaldenbrand. New York: Desclée, 1965.

Originally appeared in French as part of *Theologie du péché*.

Hamel, Edouard, S.J. "L'Ecriture âme de la Théologie." *Gregorianum* 52 (1971): 511-535.

In English: "Scripture, the Soul of Moral Theology?" In *Readings in Moral Theology No. 4: The Use of Scripture in Moral Theology,* 105-132. Edited by Charles E. Curran and Richard A. McCormick, S.J. New York: Paulist Press, 1984.

Unpacks the metaphors of "soul" and "nourishment" used by Vatican II to indicate possible roles and applications of Scripture to moral theology. Concludes with a brief look at Pauline morality to illustrate the relationship between a moral theology rooted in both the faith kerygma and human reason. The text was given as a lecture at the University of Sydney (Australia), and follows upon another study published in *Fondamenti biblici della teologia morale* (Brescia: Paideia, 1973.)

Hamel was professor of moral theology at the Pontifical Gregorian University until 1986.

_____. "Ecriture et théologie morale. Un bilan (1940-1980)." *Studia Moralia* 20 (1982): 177-193.

Cette étude indique les principales étapes du renouveau de la morale par l'Ecriture, entre les années 1940-1980. Une première partie montre comment on est passé du biblicisme des années 1940 à l'attitude plus critique des années 1970-1980. Quelles furent les orientations données par le Magistère sur la question? Pourquoi les Protestants ont connu une crise de la référence biblique en morale? Ces jalons d'histoire sont suivis de quelques réflexions d'ordre méthodologique. Pourquoi et comment retourner à l'Ecriture en morale? Comment l'Eglise primitive a relu ou interprété les textes normatifs de l'Ancien et du Nouveau Testament?

_____. "Scripture and Moral Theology: 1940-1980." *Theology Digest* 36 (1989): 203-207.

A digested form of Hamel's original French article published as "Ecriture et théologie morale. Un bilan (1940-1980)," in *Studia Moralia* 20 (1982): 177-193.

Hamel distinguishes three stages of moral renewal in the Roman Catholic Church since 1940: 1) addition of brief scriptural introductions to moral tracts; 2) "renewal" of moral theology in the light of charity and the imitation of Christ; and 3) moralists joining forces with exegetes in using Scripture as a decisive force in theology. Meanwhile in the Protestant community since 1940 Hamel discerns an inverse movement, from Biblical "infallibility" to a divided Protestant view with some holding that now there is "too much" Bible in moral theology.

Hoskyns, Edwyn Clement, Sir, 1884-1937. *Crucifixion-resurrection: the pattern of the theology and ethics of the New Testament / Edwyn Clement Hoskyns & Francis Noel Davey* ; edited with a biographical introduction by Gordon S. Wakefield. London: SPCK, 1981.

Kimpel, Benjamin Franklin. *Moral Principles in the Bible: A Study of the Contribution of the Bible to Moral Philosophy.* New York: Philosophical Library, 1956.

MacArthur, Kathleen W. *The Bible and Human Rights.* Rev. ed. New York: A Woman's Press Publication, 1949.

342

Murray, John. *Principles of Conduct: Aspects of Biblical Ethics.* Grand Rapids: Eerdmans, 1957.

Niebuhr, H. Richard. *The Kingdom of God in America.* New York, Evanston, and London: Harper and Row, 1937.

_____. *The Meaning of Revelation.* New York: Macmillan, 1941 and 1960.

Priest, Josiah. *Bible Defence of Slavery: or, The origin, history, and fortunes of the Negro race, as deduced from history, both sacred and profane, their natural relations, moral, mental and physical, to the other races of mankind, compared and illustrated, their future destiny predicted, etc. To which is added a plan of national colonization adequate to the entire removal of the free Blacks, and all that may hereafter become free, in a manner harnominizing with the peace and well-being of both races, by W.S. Brown.* 6th stereotype ed. Glasgow: W.S. Brown, 1853.

Priest lived from 1788 to 1851.

Robinson, N.H.G. "How the Bible Speaks to Conscience." In *Conscience: Theological and Psychological Perspectives,* 72-78. Edited by C. Ellis Nelson. New York: Newman Press [Paulist], 1973.

Also found in Robinson's own book, *Christ and Conscience,* 171-178. London: James Nisbet, 1956.

Robinson develops the thesis that conscience is the area where the individual experiences the Spirit of God, and that the Bible is the means by which God addresses the human person today. This address is not so much a narrative as a confrontation with conscience which results in confession, repentance, restitution and change. Uses the story of David and Nathan, plus makes some remarks about Jesus' use of parables.

Vaughan, Kenelm. *The Divine Armory of Holy Scripture.* New Revised Edition edited by Newton Thompson. St. Louis and London: B. Herder Book Co., 1943.

Classic example of proof-texting technique. The work is divided into six sections: 1) God; 2) Our Last End; 3) The Theological and Cardinal Virtues;

4) The Word of God; 5) Sin, Justification, Merit; and 6) The Four Last Things.

New Testament Works

Alexander, Archibald Browning Drysdale. *The Ethics of St. Paul.* Glasgow: Maclehose and Sons, 1910.

Andrews, Mary Edith. *The Ethical Teaching of Paul: A Study in Origin.* Chapel Hill: The University of North Carolina Press, 1934.

Badini, Giuseppe. "Sin in the Theology of St. Paul." In *Sin: Its Reality and Nature: A Historical Survey,* 79-100. Edited by Pietro Palazzini. Translated by Brendan Devlin. Dublin: Scepter Publishers, 1964.

Baker, Eric W. *The Neglected Factor--The Ethical Element in the Gospel.* New York: Abingdon Press, 1963.

The 1963 Cato Lecture.

Briggs, Charles A. *The Ethical Teaching of Jesus.* New York: Scribner's, 1904.

Briggs lived from 1841-1913; this work is preserved in the ATLA monograph preservation program; ATLA fiche 1985-0450. Chicago: American Theological Library Association, 1985.

Burch, Ernest Ward. *The Ethical Teaching of the Gospels.* New York and Cincinnati: Abingdon Press, 1925.

Cave, Sydney. *The Christian Way: A Study of New Testament Ethics in Relation to Present Problems.* London: Nisbet, 1949.

Dewar, L. *An Outline of New Testament Ethics*. London, 1949.

Dodd, C.H. *Gospel and Law: The Relation of Faith and Ethics in Early Christianity*. Cambridge: Cambridge University Press, 1951.

Enslin, Morton Scott. *The Ethics of Paul*. New York: Harper & Brothers, 1930.

Flew, R. Newton. *Jesus and His Way: A Study of the Ethics of the New Testament*. London: Epworth Press, 1963.

An expansion of the 1948 Cato Lecture, and published after Flew's death in 1962.

Garofalo, Salvatore. "Sin in the Gospels." In *Sin: Its Reality and Nature: A Historical Survey*, 57-77. Edited by Pietro Palazzini. Translated by Brendan Devlin. Dublin: Scepter Publishers, 1964.

Grant, F.C. "The Impractibility of the Gospel Ethics." In *Aux sources de la tradition chrétienne*, 86-94. Edited by Oscar Cullman. Paris: Delachaux et Niestle, 1950.

Hoskyns, Edwyn Clement, and Davey, Francis Noel. *Crucifizxion--Resurrection: The Pattern of the Theology and Ethics of the New Testament*. Edited, with a biographical introduction by Gordon S. Wakefield. London: SPCK, 1983.

Hoskyns lived from 1884-1937.

Jeremias, Joachim. *The Sermon on the Mount*. Facet Books Biblical Series, no. 2. Translated by Norman Perrin. Philadelphia: Fortress Press, 1963.

German original: *Die Bergpredigt*. Calwer Hefte, no. 27. Stuttgart: Calwer Verlag, 1959.

French translation: *Paroles de Jésus: La Sermon sur la montagne, le Notre-Père dans l'exégèse actuelle*. Lectio Divina, 38. Traduction de Dom Marie Mailhé, O.S.B. Paris: Editions du Cerf, 1963.

Jeremias outlines three traditional approaches to the ethical material of the Sermon: perfectionist code, impossible ideal, or interim ethic. He sees certain values in each, but notes they share a common failing in viewing the Sermon as Law rather than Gospel, in other words, an indicative depiction of incipient life in the Kingdom of God, which presupposes as its condition of possibility the experience of conversion.

Knox, John. *The Ethics of Jesus in the Teaching of the Church: Its Authority and Relevance*. Nashville: Abingdon Press, 1961.

Lillie, William. *Studies in New Testament Ethics*. Edinburgh: Oliver and Boyd, 1961; Philadelphia: Westminster, 1963.

Manson, T.W. *Ethics and the Gospel*. New York: Scribner's, 1960.

An unrevised version of the Ayer Lectures given at Colgate-Rochester Divinity School and published posthumously.

Marshall, L.H. *The Challenge of New Testament Ethics*. London: Macmillan, 1947.

Moule, C.F.D. "The New Testament and Moral Decisions." In *Expository Times* vol. 74 Edinburgh: T. & T. Clark, 1962-1963.

Pierce, C[laude]. A[nthony]. *Conscience in the New Testament: A Study of Syneidesis in the New Testament; in the light of its sources, and with particular reference to St. Paul: with some observations regarding its pastoral relevance today*. Studies in Biblical Theology, 15. London: SCM Press, 1955.

Priess, Theodore. "Life in Christ and Social Ethics in the Epistle to Philemon." In *Life in Christ*, 32-42. London: SCM, 1954.

Scott, Charles Archibald Anderson. *New Testament Ethics, An Introduction*. The Hulsean Lectures, 1929. Cambridge: University Press, 1929.

Scott, E. F. (Ernest Findlay). *The Ethical Teaching of Jesus*. New York: Macmillan, 1924, 1936.

Scott lived from 1868 to 1954.

Segalla, Giuseppe "`New Testament ethics': a survey (1933--1976)." *Theology Digest* 27 (1979): 3-9.

Segalla is professor of New Testament Exegesis at the Theological Faculty of Milan.

Spicq, Ceslas, O.P. *The Trinity and Our Moral Life according to St. Paul*. Westminster MD: The Newman Press, 1963.

French original: *Vie morale et Trinité Sainte selon Saint Paul*. Lectio Divina, 19. Paris: Editions du Cerf, 1957.

Tinsley, E.J. *The Imitation of God in Christ: An Essay on the Biblical Basis of Christian Spirituality*. London, 1960.

Wilder, Amos N. "The Basis of Christian Ethics in the New Testament." *Journal of Religious Thought* 15 (1958): 137-146.

____. *Eschatology and Ethics in the Teaching of Jesus*. New York: Harper, 1939, 1950.

Old Testament Works

Crenshaw, James L., ed. *Theodicy in the Old Testament*. Issues in Religion and Theology, 4. Philadelphia: Fortress Press; London: SPCK, 1983.

An introduction plus 8 articles ranging from A.S. Peake's 1905 essay on Job to Crenshaw's own 1975 treatment on the problem of human bondage in Sirach. Other contributors include Walther Eichrodt, Ronald J. Williams, Klaus Koch, Gerhard von Rad, Martin Buber, and Harmut Gese.

Dakin, David Martin. *Peace and Brotherhood in the Old Testament.* London: Bannisdale Press, 1956.

Davidson, R. "Some Aspects of the Old Testament Contribution to the Pattern of Christian Ethics." *Scottish Journal of Theology* 12 (1959): 373-387.

Eichrodt, Walter [Walther]. "The Law and the Gospel: The Meaning of the Ten Commandments in Israel and for Us." *Interpretation* 11 (1957): 23-40.

Fletcher, V. "The Shape of Old Testament Ethics." *Scottish Journal of Theology* 24 (1959): 47-73.

Gehman, H.S. "Natural Law and the Old Testament." In *Biblical Studies in Memory of H.C. Alleman,* 109-122. Edited by J.M. Myers, et. al. New York: Augustin, 1960.

Gemser, B. "The Importance of the Motive Clause in Old Testament Law." *Supplements to Vetus Testamentum* 1 (1953): 50-66.

Greene, W. B. "The Ethics of the Old Testament." *Princeton Theological Review* 27 (1929): 153-193; 313-366.

Hammershaimb, E. "On the Ethics of the Old Testament Prophets." *Supplements to Vetus Testamentum* 7 (1959): 75-101.

Johnson, L. "Old Testament Morality." *Catholic Biblical Quarterly* 20 (1958): 19-25.

Mariani, Bonaventura. "Ritual Sin in the Old Testament." In *Sin: Its Reality and Nature: A Historical Survey,* 41-56. Edited by Pietro Palazzini. Translated by Brendan Devlin. Dublin: Scepter Publishers, 1964.

Muilenburg, James. *The Way of Israel: Biblical Faith and Ethics.* New York: Harper, 1961.

North, Robert, S.J. "The Biblical Jubilee and Social Reform." *Scripture* 4 (1951): 3232-335.

North is Professor Emeritus at the Pontifical Biblical Institute in Rome.

Spadafora, Francesco. "Sin in the Old Testament." In *Sin: Its Reality and Nature: A Historical Survey*, 29-40. Edited by Pietro Palazzini. Translated by Brendan Devlin. Dublin: Scepter Publishers, 1964.

Thompson, Ernest Trice. *The Sermon on the Mount and Its Meaning for Today.*

Reviewed by Irvin W. Batdorf in *Theology Today* 4 (1948): 288.

Thompson lived from 1894 to 1985.

****
****

INDEX OF NAMES

354

362

STUDIES IN RELIGION AND SOCIETY